THE VISION REVISITED

CAROLYN C. ROBINSON

THE VISION REVISITED

A History of

Meredith College

1971–1998

MEREDITH
COLLEGE

THE MEREDITH COLLEGE PRESS

Published by

THE MEREDITH COLLEGE PRESS

3800 Hillsborough Street

Raleigh, North Carolina 27607-5298

Design and production by

RUNNING FEET BOOKS

Morrisville, North Carolina

∞ The paper used in this publication meets the minimum
requirements of the American National Standard for
Information Sciences—Permanence of Paper for Printed
Library Materials, ANSI Z39.48-1984.

The photographs on the following pages were reprinted
courtesy of Steve Wilson: 81, 152, 190, 245, 292. All other
photographs are from the Meredith Archives.

ISBN: 1-879635-01-1

LC NUMBER: 98-89707

10 9 8 7 6 5 4 3 2 1

FIRST EDITION

The College's most valuable history can be found in the minds and hearts of all who have passed through her doors.

—SARAH ELIZABETH VERNON WATTS, '35

CONTENTS

ACKNOWLEDGMENTS

THROUGHOUT THIS WORK, I have feigned embarrassment at the number of pages allotted to Meredith's last twenty-seven years—only slightly fewer than historian Mary Lynch Johnson allowed for her more than a century-long record from the 1835 Baptist State Convention, when the idea of a female seminary was conceived, through 1972, when *A History of Meredith College*, Second Edition, was published. On the other hand, I have sincerely rejoiced in Meredith's competence and confidence as the College prepares to face a new millennium. It takes chapter and verse to account for survival—indeed the prosperity—of "the fittest" in an era of demise for many women's colleges.

It also takes people who believe that the telling is worth the doing. I am profoundly grateful to President Weems and Vice President Spooner, who invited me to write this portion of Meredith's biography, to vice president and dean of the College emeritus, Allen Burris, who checked for correctness of research interpretation, and to Suzanne Britt, who critically read each chapter as it groaned through the DeskJet printer. I also appreciate the senior management team's resistance to editing.

Martha Harrell and Sharon Woodlief have been particularly helpful, as have the staffs of the Carlyle Campbell Library and of the Office of Marketing and Communications. From the library, Ted Waller has encouraged me even as I invaded the sanctity of the college archives, for which he is responsible; and from the Office of Marketing and Communications, director Jeannie Morelock and graphic design manager Trisha Gwaltney have demonstrated great care in arranging for the production of this book. The willingness of the trustee chairman, administrators, academic department heads, and directors of administrative divisions to submit to formal interviews and of some trustees, faculty, staff, students, and alumnae to converse informally has added the personal dimension that is so typical of the college they represent.

My only regret is that Meredith's family is too large to mention each member by name; the constraint has been genuinely painful.

C.C.R.

PROLOGUE

ASK MEREDITH WOMEN for college memories. Recent graduates will speak of friendships, of favorite professors, and, in this age of speedy transportation and speedier communications, of going places and doing things. But among those whose student days spanned one of the college generations between 1942 and 1986, many will recall with genuine pleasure the aroma of bread baking across Hillsborough Street from the campus. When the Wonder Bakery, successor to the old Royal Baking Company, stopped baking in the eighties to become a quick stop for buyers of day-old bread, it lost its power to penetrate the senses of the college community. Progress, or some other encroachment on the culture, had prompted the relocation of its ovens, their heady, yeasty fragrances now spreading nostalgia across someone else's front lawn. But for almost half a century, Meredith women had breathed deeply of the leaven that permeated the whole of their college experiences.

There's an analogy here. It begins with a parable of Jesus as retold by Matthew and Luke:

> Another parable spake he unto them; The kingdom of heaven is like unto leaven, which a woman took, and hid in three measures of meal, till the whole was leavened.[1]

The message gathers momentum as the disciples are called also to be salt and light in their society, and it continues through the ages as people respond through their churches and institutions to the promptings of their own spirituality. The late George Buttrick, a twentieth-century theologian, Presbyterian minister, and seminary professor, wrote of leaven as "a *silent agency*"—"[s]hrewd ears would be required to detect leaven busy at its task"; as an *"invisible and inward"* process—it "works by *contagion*, until the whole is leavened."[2]

CONSIDER MEREDITH IN the context of the parable and of the last years of the twentieth century. In 1971, when Mary Lynch Johnson's *A History of Meredith College*, Second Edition, left the book bindery and made its way into the hands of grateful readers and researchers, the nation was undergoing self-analysis following the assassinations of civil rights leader Martin Luther King, Jr., and of presidential hopeful Robert F. Kennedy in 1968. We were adjusting to a new power—that of the youth culture—which seemed to be manifest in the 300,000 seekers of "peace and music" at the three-day Woodstock Festival in upstate New York in 1969. It was the same exhilarating year of Neil Armstrong's walk on the moon. We found ourselves in an ongoing controversy—then known as Women's Liberation, later the Feminist Movement—which, after five years, was settling in as a permanent philosophy. We were immersed in the Vietnam War—already eight years old—the country's collective mind sometimes protesting against, sometimes supporting, the fighting forces in Asia, the Hawks and Doves at home.

Those tumultuous days ushered in the seventies—a time of students' contagious restlessness and their financial supporters' shaken faith. Eastern cults, like the "Moonies" and the Hare Krishnas, stripped youthful seekers of their convictions and reindoctrinated them to new sets of beliefs, and, from those tenacious groups, parents sometimes "kidnapped" their own children for deprogramming. In the throes of that culture, Meredith's President E. Bruce Heilman resigned and John E. Weems succeeded him as the sixth president of the eighty-year-old college.

Distracted by the planning and arranging of September inaugural festivities surrounding the new president, Meredith people might have taken little note of a politically motivated break-in at Washington's Watergate Hotel in August 1972. In fact, Americans were at first far more preoccupied with President Nixon's heralded visit to China than with the invasion of the Democratic National Committee's headquarters by a few Republican underlings. Later, however, the event and all its consequences consumed us for months on end, until, in 1974, the House Judiciary Committee voted Articles of Impeachment, and Richard M. Nixon resigned the presidency of the United States.

Despite the nation's rapt attention to events in Washington, Meredith conducted its affairs as it always had—in the tension of change. In 1972, it launched a progressive continuing education agenda of enrichment opportunities for both women and men and a re-entry program for women. Thus it became a true pioneer in the now-popular movement of adult education. The program's impact could be measured a quarter century later by Meredith students, 21–25 percent of whom were above the age of twenty-three.

But the nation could never measure the impact of the Vietnam War. In 1973, a peace treaty was announced to a relieved world. Simultaneously, a battle of emotion and determination raged in state legislatures across the land as proponents and opponents of the Equal Rights Amendment raised their voices every way but in unison, and a stormy decade later, the ERA died for want of ratification; however, the Women's Movement had gained a foothold strong enough to witness, in 1972, African-American Shirley Chisholm's seeking the Democratic Party's presidential nomination; in 1981, Sandra Day O'Connor's becoming the first woman appointed to the United States Supreme Court; in 1983, astronaut Sally Ride's traveling in space; and, in 1984, Geraldine Ferraro's eagerly accepting the Democratic Party's nomination for vice president of the United States.

The thought of women's aspirations to such high places was almost foreign to the nation, as had been the idea of women's education to some North Carolina Baptists in the mid-to-late 1800's. But in the decade of those bold political initiatives, Meredith trustees were perceived as not at all radical in electing the first female—Sandra Thomas—to a vice presidency. And discarding some of the social shackles of a bygone era, the College ceased its *in loco parentis* role but held firm to some of its social policies. The Honor Code remained an integral part of student life.

In the United States, national honor was reborn in the celebration of the nation's Bicentennial in 1976. And early in its third century, America was, at least briefly, the focal point of nations as eyes turned toward Camp David, the Maryland presidential retreat, where President Carter encouraged long-time adversaries, President Sadat of Egypt and Premier Begin of Israel, to sign a "Framework for Peace." The new hope for the Middle East was dashed in 1979, however, by Iran's capture of American hostages and by a near meltdown of the nuclear plant at Three Mile Island, New York. The nuclear disaster somehow reminded us of the menacing Cold War being waged between our nation and its allies and the Soviet Union and the Communist Bloc. But a glimmer of hope would again break through in 1985 when Russian President Chernenko's death paved the way for his successor, Mikhail Gorbachev, and President Ronald Reagan to agree to negotiations on nuclear arms control. By 1989, the Cold War would end, and, by 1992, so would the Soviet Union.

Meanwhile, Meredith saw a need for post-baccalaureate work in areas not available to working women at nearby universities. And, as in many cases, past predicted future: In 1984, the College re-established graduate studies, a Baptist Female University feature that had lain dormant for most of a century. Two years later, federal laws on sex discrimination would call into question the legality of graduate work for women only. But once the dust settled, Meredith's singular commitment to women remained intact.

The dust of society's unprecedented perplexities never seemed to settle, however: The national deficit climbed into the trillions of dollars; a rising crime rate and increased drug use alarmed citizens and law enforcers alike; and AIDS, a new and deadly disease, baffled the medical profession and thousands of suffering patients. On opposite sides of the globe, China's brutality toward the young demonstrators in Beijing's Tienanmen Square sickened human-rights advocates—as did apartheid in South Africa—while the emancipation of Eastern Europe, signaled by the fall of the Berlin Wall in 1989, was cause for worldwide rejoicing.

Occurrences at Meredith might have dimmed in comparison, but on the campus of a small college, all events seem global. While the world hardly noticed, some Baptists and their institutions stood in distress—or sat helplessly by—as ultra-conservative members of the denomination planned and executed a takeover of the Southern Baptist Convention and many of its agencies. Educational institutions lost academic freedom and, in some cases, accreditation, as their boards of trustees were packed with extremists. Southeastern Baptist Theological Seminary in neighboring Wake Forest was one of the first to succumb. Amid strong opposition from some leaders of the Baptist State Convention of North Carolina—one of the few remaining moderate arms of the denomination—the alert administration and Board of Trustees of the College found a way to amend Meredith's charter, thereby fashioning its own "declaration of independence." The resolution adopted on February 22, 1991, stated the board's intention to elect its own members—a privilege heretofore assumed by the convention—and "to further the purposes of the institution as they are stated in its charter." The action was a fitting reward for Meredith's century of educating women, for its unwavering determination in the light of myriad cultural changes, for its confident leap into its second century. So the banner of academic freedom waved aloft as the College approached its centennial observance, beginning February 27, 1991, and continuing for an entire year. In 1997, the trustees would distance Meredith further from the Baptist State Convention of North Carolina—so far, in fact, that the College would lose its monetary support from the organization of its founding. But in taking a step away from the Southern Baptist Convention of the nineties, Meredith took a step toward its true heritage of "freedom from sectarian influence."[3]

And now in the latter years of the twentieth century and the early years of Meredith's second century, the College has taken a quantum leap into the Information Age. Nineteen ninety-five was known as the "Year of the Internet."[4] The *World Almanac and Book of Facts 1997* estimated that "more than 30 million computer users populated this electronic global village [of one hundred countries] by late 1996 and that some 8 to 10 million had access to the World Wide Web."[5]

But with all the instant electronic communications, society's struggles continued. In America's corner of the global village, we have contended with political gridlock in Washington; the effectiveness—or lack thereof—of elementary and secondary education; grade inflation in higher education; the judicial system; health insurance; homelessness; child abuse; terrorism; poverty; gun control; racial tension; and the morality of people in high places. We have heard cries of corruption fall on law enforcement agencies and on prisons that are populated with what many perceive to be an inordinate number of poor, young, black males. We have watched radicals pelt the airwaves with militia propaganda aimed at government conspiracies. Such anti-government theories apparently triggered the tragic bombing in 1995 of an Oklahoma City Federal building, in which 168 workers and children died. In 1997–98, still more children lost their lives as middle- and high-school students used guns to settle their grievances on the school grounds.

And, in the throes of *this* culture, President Weems has announced his plans for retirement. It is important to note that, in 1998, Meredith was one of only eighty-plus women's colleges remaining in the United States. In the late nineties, Raleigh neighbors Peace and St. Mary's chose to re-define themselves, Peace changing from junior to senior college status, and St. Mary's dropping its two-year college curriculum altogether while retaining its high school program. Many of the 300 women's colleges existing in the sixties have closed their doors, and others have staked their futures on co-education.

At Meredith, more than 50 percent of all alumnae have graduated in the last quarter century and have taken or are taking their places in society. As students, most were of traditional age and status, some older women; some Honors Scholars; some Teaching Fellows; some graduate degree seekers. They selected from new majors, degrees, and programs; they learned—and learned from—state-of-the-art technology in new or refurbished buildings; they meditated in campus gardens and worshiped in Jones Chapel; they demonstrated that "Meredith is the maturing of a woman";[6] and they sat in classrooms of the teacher/role models then occupying the earthly spheres vacated by their legendary predecessors who have graduated from this life.

AND A MEREDITH alumna savors again the aroma of bread baking across Hillsborough Street as she returns to one of Buttrick's questions: "How far the leaven has penetrated who can tell?" and to his answer: "The process will continue until the whole is leavened."[7]

I

A TIME OF TRANSITION

1971

RALPH WALDO EMERSON'S essay on "History" asserts, "All history becomes subjective; in other words there is properly no history; only biography." This volume, then, is the continuing biography of a college grown to adulthood. Its essence is the lives of a great many people—inhabitants of a century of change, climbers to the edge of an era of technological wonders, interpreters of Meredith's vision of educating women for their times.

The written biography began with Mary Lynch Johnson's *A History of Meredith College*, which introduced the College through the men and women who conceived it, nurtured it past its infancy, and guided it through its first sixty-five years. Published in 1956, the history was revised and reissued in 1972 to add events of the next sixteen years.* The second edition was too near publication to include the period of transition in which the fifth president of Meredith resigned and the sixth assumed office.

In the foreword, Dr. Johnson wrote of the resignation of President E. Bruce Heilman: "The swiftly moving, significant events of [his] admin-

---

*Other Meredith histories include *An Oral History of Meredith College Alumnae*, catalogued in 1989 and compiled by Jean Batten Cooper, '54, as the thesis for her Master's Degree in Liberal Studies at Wake Forest University; and *Images: a Centennial Journey*, a pictorial history of the College, written by Suzanne Britt, instructor of English, and published by the Meredith Press in 1991.

Historian Mary Lynch Johnson autographs for eager readers
A History of Meredith College, *Second Edition.*

istration required a long and important new chapter. As this section was virtually completed before he accepted the presidency of the University of Richmond . . . , no mention is made of that great loss to Meredith."[1]

Constraints of the publishing schedule also made it impossible for the historian to record more than a reference to the naming of a new president: "John Edgar Weems, vice-president for finance and administration at Middle Tennessee State University, was elected President of Meredith College on October 14, 1971. When he assumes office on January 1, 1972, a new chapter will begin in 'the ever unfolding text' of Meredith's history."[2] Before turning the page to the "new chapter"—the Weems administration—this history will better serve its readers and the college whose life it records to review the end of the Heilman years.

Bruce Heilman accepted the presidency of the University of Richmond at 2:00 P.M. on March 26, 1971. The official announcement reached Meredith an hour later in a special convocation, when Shearon Harris, vice chairman of the Board of Trustees, read a statement from Dr. Heilman:

Today a decision which has come about over a period of some three months is being culminated. I regret that I cannot personally transmit the details to you, but find it necessary to be on the campus of the University of Richmond, where . . . I am to be elected President of that institution, effective September 1. . . .

I came to Meredith because I saw a grand opportunity. I have been committed to spending my life here if that proved appropriate. . . .

Actually, I have not finished my task and will continue to provide the best leadership I know during the next five months. While you may not look to me for long-range decisions, we can together consolidate and fulfill and move to action plans already made and decisions already reached.[3]

One of the "decisions already reached" affected Leslie Syron, department chairman for sociology, one of the first two scholars to participate in the recently funded sabbatical leave program.* Dr. Syron later wrote, "Who at Meredith . . . can forget the snow and sleet that upstaged both Bruce Heilman's resignation and my departure for London? Cliff Cameron's plane could not land, so a substitute announced [Heilman's] resignation; but my plane took off for the first stage of a longed-for sabbatical."[4] It was late for snow, but old-time Raleighites could remember wintry bites of past springs. And although C.C. Cameron, chairman of the Board of Trustees, could not reach Raleigh from Charlotte, Harris, a resident of the capital city, relayed the breaking news.

Heilman returned from his short stay in Richmond long before Syron ended her study at the University of London. He attended to unfinished tasks with his usual exuberance and, by way of the *Alumnae Magazine*, reflected on his years at the College:

Meredith is . . . a great institution. Her people, including those hundreds who have been her students over the years, are an outstanding example of the best to be assimilated into a society which needs their kind[s]. The campus looks even more beautiful as I think about leaving it, the facilities measure up in an even more impressive fashion as I compare them with institutions of like kind. The community in which it lives is unparalleled. The spirit which exudes from within and without is unlike any I have witnessed anywhere.

---

*According to historian Mary Lynch Johnson, the trustees had adopted "a system of sabbatical leaves" in Dr. Campbell's administration but had not funded it until 1970. Under the new system, William Ledford, chairman of the Department of Foreign Languages, had traveled in Spain during the first semester (MLJ, *History*, 335–336).

Expectation runs high. Financial circumstances are perhaps the best they have ever been. Enrollment is at its peak. The administration and faculty are able to fulfill the commitments of planning already completed, and trustee leadership is the best.

I know now better than I could have known when I was looking to the future as a part of Meredith, that I believe my own propaganda.[5]

In the same magazine, alumna and trustee Laura Weatherspoon Harrill, '27, majored on some of the president's specific accomplishments: continuation of high academic standards; increases in faculty compensation by 52 percent; sabbaticals; an increase in the number of faculty with doctoral degrees; and an expanded student body, whose numbers rose by 44 percent "with no significant change in quality by the usual measures."[6]

Almost immediately following Heilman's resignation, the presidential selection committee of trustees set out to find his successor. L.M. Massey chaired the committee of Shearon Harris; Elizabeth James Dotterer, '30, of Sanford; Nelson Strawbridge and W.J. Broadwell of Durham; Seby Jones of Raleigh; and C.C. Cameron of Charlotte. Also, consultants to the selection committee represented other segments of the Meredith family. Academic department chairmen Sarah Lemmon, history; Roger Crook, religion; and David Lynch, music, served with Sally Horner, assistant professor of chemistry, for the faculty. Craven Allen Burris, dean of the College; Joe Baker, business manager and treasurer; John T. Kanipe, Jr., executive director of development; and Mary Bland Josey, director of admissions, served for the administration. Edith Stephenson Simpson, '48, past president of the Alumnae Association, was liaison for the alumnae and Gail Knieriem, president of the Student Government Association, for the student body. Dr. Lemmon chaired the committee of consultants.

As President Heilman's moving date approached, the executive committee of the Board of Trustees designated Dean Burris as acting president, granting him the full powers of the presidency. Almost a quarter century later, Burris, who had come to Meredith in 1969, remembered his dual role as a "mammoth task," saying he should have appointed an acting dean. But, as freshman Margaret Farmer observed, "This . . . was a time in which the students became more familiar with the dean and more appreciative of his humor and good leadership. Anyone who had to search the whole of Johnson Hall to find Dr. Burris was certainly made aware of the complexity of his position."[7] In fact, Meredith students soon solved, for themselves at least, the puzzle of where, when, and how to locate him: "When he was upstairs, he was the president, and when he was downstairs, he was the dean!"[8]

The president's move upstairs occurred during the 1970 renovation of the administration building. Since Meredith's relocation in 1926 from downtown Raleigh to its present campus several miles to the west, the library had occupied the second and third floors of Johnson Hall, and the president had administered college policies from the first floor, east wing; however, the library's exodus in 1969 to a new facility, named in honor of Carlyle Campbell, had permitted the practical expansion of offices downstairs in Johnson for the dean, the registrar, and the business manager, as well as the creation of a spacious upstairs suite for the president. And with the sometimes-irreverent irony of youth, students immediately observed the president's having positioned his offices off the rotunda's second-level balcony and directly below the inscribed words of Jesus: "I am the way, the truth, and the life."

Meanwhile, Dean Burris encountered additional changes in the way and the truth of *his* life. After the executive committee had named him acting president, the trustees also drafted a proposal to amend the by-laws, changing Burris's permanent title from dean to vice president and dean of the College; Baker's from business manager and treasurer to vice president for business and finance; and Kanipe's from director of development to vice president for institutional advancement. The amendments, introducing the title of "vice president," would clearly define the organization of and the responsibilities within the administration. As the College had grown in size and scope, directors had served under directors, possibly confusing outsiders—and insiders—who had little or no knowledge of the job descriptions and flow charts. At its semi-annual meeting on September 24, the full board approved the actions of the executive committee.

The trustees made another significant decision that day. At the suggestion of the administration and faculty, W.H. Westphal, chairman of the instructional programs committee, discussed the "growing importance of women" in business and industry. His committee had come to believe, he

Bryan Rotunda, following the renovation of Johnson Hall in 1970.

said, that Meredith needed "to move toward a B.S. degree," allowing "more flexibility to . . . graduates in the areas of science, mathematics, and home economics."[9] On Westphal's motion, the trustees authorized implementation of the Bachelor of Science degree" by the regular due process . . . at the most advantageous time,"[10] thereby resurrecting an option that had been buried for thirty-three years. The College had granted the B.S. from 1914–26 to students in such specialized subjects as home economics and general science; from 1931–33 to prospective teachers seeking certificates in elementary education; and from 1932–38 to music majors.

Following the productive meeting, the trustees joined faculty, staff, students, and guests on the east campus to put another house in order—that of the recently completed E. Bruce Heilman Residence Hall. While under construction, the building had been called "New South," but when seniors occupied it in October 1969, they dubbed it the "Heilman Hilton." On that September day in 1971, however, Meredith gave the residence an official name and dedicated it in honor of the fifth president of the College. Although former President Heilman had assumed his duties in Richmond only three weeks earlier, he and Mrs. Heilman, with their five children, returned for the ceremonies.

IN ITS EIGHTIETH charter year, the College braced itself for an onslaught of societal changes in "the real world"—as students everywhere deemed all existence beyond campus confines. But Meredith seemed to be in good hands under its acting president, its astute trustees, its experienced and dedicated faculty, administration, and staff. Financial support had made possible the construction of not only one residence hall but of two. Enrollment was up. Bright promises seemed to beckon the College into the future as the community reveled in the commencement just past, when Meredith awarded degrees to its largest class of 220 seniors; when Suzanne Reynolds became the first graduate to earn a 4.0 average on all academic work; when Gwyndolyn Matthews Hilliard made history as the first African-American to receive a degree at Meredith; and when the senior class gave a precedent-setting initial gift of $7,000 to endow a visiting lectureship in honor of Lillian Parker Wallace, professor of history, 1921–62.* Beyond year-end ceremonies in May, eleven high school students enrolled in the inaugural Summer Study/College Credit for High School Students, and seven of those young women applied for admission in August of 1972.

The season of firsts continued to the end of the semester as seniors Marjorie Moore Council, Ann Victoria Googe, Renee Elks, Sara Joyce Munden, and Marjorie JoAnne Weaver basked in the glory of not only completing their requirements for graduation but also for being the first Meredith students to receive certification by the Council on Social Work Education. The recently approved constituent membership in the council distinguished Meredith as the only private college in North Carolina to merit that accreditation. In fact, at the time, Meredith and Baylor University were the only Southern Baptist institutions with CSWE-approved programs.

But as euphoria soared on the campus, gloom settled over higher education in general. In the first place, Americans were in the doldrums because of a sluggish economy. Also, they smarted under the previous year's violence on the nation's campuses. A faint glimmer of light was appearing, however, according to a 1970 entry in the *Encyclopedia of American Facts and Dates*:

---

*Dr. Wallace died sixteen days after the Class of 1971 established the endowment in her honor.

The unrest that had disturbed colleges throughout the country in 1970 was largely dissipated and there were no occurrences of the violence that had so shocked the nation, such as at Kent State University in Ohio [when the Ohio National Guard killed four students in a Vietnam War protest]. Many major problems still confronted educational institutions. The National Science Foundation reported that federal aid to colleges and universities was the lowest since 1966, with education also being caught in government budgetary considerations.[11]

While Meredith received no federal funds, except for financial assistance to students, nor was it particularly vulnerable to "government budgetary considerations," it was certainly aware of the nation's economic problems. And while the College experienced no violence or uncontrolled protests among its student population, it was attentive to trends.

The *Alumnae Magazine* departed from tradition to run in the June edition an insert from Editorial Projects for Education, Inc., titled "Are Americans Losing Faith in Their Colleges?" The article suggested an almost-unprecedented reluctance on the parts of individuals, businesses, and governments to fund the nation's colleges and universities. Student behavior, including a flagrant disregard for "traditional values," and the inability of authorities constructively to channel the new activism allegedly undermined the public trust. The magazine material predicted dire consequences for "the smaller and less affluent colleges."[12] This report followed an earlier study by the Carnegie and Ford Foundations titled *The New Depression in Higher Education*, which showed Meredith "as one of 12 out of 41 institutions considered not in financial trouble, or at least not in jeopardy of failing to do acceptably that which she is seeking to do."[13]

While Meredith was "not in trouble" in those days of soaring inflation, the faculty — temporarily, at least — felt the economic pinch in its collective pocketbook. Members of that body heard unwelcome news at their September meeting from business manager Joe Baker, who declared that "salary checks to be distributed on September 24 will reflect no raises for those who began work under a new contract after August 15, 1971 . . . ."[14] To comply with President Nixon's "New Economic Policy," and as part of a nationwide effort to reduce inflation and unemployment, the College was required to freeze wages for ninety days, effective August

15. Baker assured the faculty, however, that he would find "some legal way to grant the raises contracted for . . . ."[15] He found the way through attrition and allowable small cost-of-living increases.

In addition to the economic concerns of his colleagues and to the innate dynamics of academe, Dr. Burris faced the clamor of a student body eager for independence. Student demands were doubtless inspired, in part, by the June 30 passage of the 26th Amendment to the Constitution of the United States, which lowered the voting age from twenty-one to eighteen years. Meredith women had returned for the fall semester with self-determining hours on their minds. The year-old student life committee of the Student Government Association had proposed that the closing times of 11:00 P.M. on Monday through Thursday nights, midnight on Fridays, an hour later on Saturdays, and 11:30 on Sundays be replaced with hours that students, with their parents' permission, set for themselves. The committee's lines of responsibility resembled those of Congress to the President of the United States: Changes in regulations must survive the committee, the student body, and, finally, the president's veto pen before becoming the law of the campus.

The *Twig* promoted self-limiting hours early in the fall term when Susan Van Wageningen concluded an editorial with the question, "Is Meredith a baby-sitting agency or an institution of higher learning?"[16] On the same page, an editorial cartoon depicted a well-dressed, serious, young woman, who balanced in her hands the issue of self-limiting hours against that of responsibility, each matter registering equal weight. In contrast, a later edition carried a caricature of the acting president, apparently by the same unidentified student artist, showing Burris measuring the proposed rule change against his rejection, with rejection far outweighing the student proposal. Not until the spring semester, after the new president's arrival, were self-limiting hours adopted, and then only on an experimental basis for seniors living in "North" dormitory. A year later, the policy became law campuswide.

On-campus concerns were not the exclusive thrust of the *Twig*, either by news item or editorial. Issues such as the Vietnam War; inflation; a residue of nationwide student unrest on the one hand, apathy on the other; and the fledgling movement known as "women's lib" invited analyses of philosophies, traditions, and authority. Behind the scenes, however, the *Twig* staff found difficult and time-consuming the week-to-week grind of publishing a paper. Early in the semester, editor Van Wageningen penned "A Cry for Help," in which she chastised students for leaving the publishing of *their* newspaper to the "efforts of three or four students," and in which she complained of "a heavy heart, tired eyes, sore fingers from typing, and a compounded migraine headache."[17]

If apathy prevailed in the newspaper business, energy abounded in other matters. For example, Cornhuskin', the twenty-six-year-old autumn festival, prompted fierce competition between classes. And the faculty joined the fray. Each class adopted a theme, developed it, and paraded it before their peers. Coveted awards for original songs, tall tales, hog-calling, corn-shucking, and apple-bobbing were steppingstones to the big prize of Cornhuskin' itself. At its beginning in 1945, Cornhuskin' was a simple distraction from the routine of campus life, but by 1971 it consumed students for weeks prior to its occurrence. Reporter Anne Wall commented on the competition under the *Twig*'s headline of "Juniors take Pumpkin[;] Sophomores place second":

> The emotions of Meredith students are mixed; Juniors are elated over a victory; Seniors are elated over being close to 'getting out'; Sophomores want to know why the Freshmen didn't play by the rules; and the Freshmen would still like to know what the rules are. The Juniors and Freshmen tied in script. The Juniors cut no one; the Freshmen cut Sophomores; the Sophomores cut women; the Seniors cut Meredith tradition and the faculty cut themselves. It was, to say the least, a cutting experience. . . .[18]

An editorial in the same issue questioned the spirit of the tradition: "Must the students rely on constant criticism of existing conditions to provide a theme? . . . When the theme is developed at the expense of unduly criticizing conditions *or* even individuals, the whole concept of Cornhuskin' is distorted."[19] The *Twig* both refuted and confirmed "distortions" in future versions of the competition. In 1972, Cornhuskin' was touted by editorialists Eleanor Hill and Janice Sams as having been "much more in line with the general 'fun' concept than some have been in years past . . . where the scripts and costumes have bordered on sheer repulsiveness."[20] Two years later, a letter to the editor from student Meredith McGill denounced the tradition for causing "division and ill feelings." She offered, "Please, let's keep Cornhusking [sic], but let's keep it in its place."[21]

Another major event each autumn was the semi-annual Meredith Playhouse production. While the College produced plays in both the fall and spring, it had not until 1971 offered a musical. The play was *The Sound of Music*. Margaret Farmer wrote,

> Behind the polished and delightful production seen by a tremendous audience were hours of work unparalleled by any previous Playhouse presentation. In the hopes of having at least ten children try out, Mrs. Linda Bamford [instructor of speech and theater, 1970–75], placed in the paper an advertisement which brought the response of seventy-five children competing for seven parts.[22]

Religion professor Bernard Cochran played Captain Georg Von Trapp. Students in the cast included Susan Tew as Maria; Nancy Crews as Liesl; Patsy Johnson as Mother Abbess; Ann Goodson as Baroness Elsa Schraeder; and Lissy Wall, Jeanie Alford, and Elizabeth Triplett as Sisters Berthe, Margaretta, and Sophia, respectively.

The "cast" of the *Alumnae Magazine,* published quarterly, changed dramatically that fall when Norma Rose, longtime professor of English and chairman of the department, resigned as editor, a post she had occupied since the magazine's inception in 1946. The winter issue carried the name of Carolyn Covington Robinson, '50, as successor to Dr. Rose. Then director of alumnae affairs, Mrs. Robinson was Meredith's first director of publications and had been a member of the magazine staff since 1968.

As magazine editor, Mrs. Robinson shouldered a few additional responsibilities—few indeed compared to those of Jane Greene, '29, assistant librarian for twenty-six years, who had agreed to undertake for one year supervision of the Carlyle Campbell Library's entire operation. Miss Greene seemed to be the obvious choice to succeed the retiring Hazel Baity, '26, head librarian since 1940. Greene was one of a larger-than-usual number of new administrative staff directors who filled vacancies in 1971: Paul Holcomb, J.D., succeeded Charles Patterson as director of estate planning; Gene Phillips, B.D., followed Charles Parker as campus minister; Jean Teague, A.B., became director of student activities; and Marie Capel, M.Ed., created the guidance and placement service. Not exclusively Meredith's staff member, but with an office on the campus, M. Austin Connors, Ed.D., became director of Cooperating Raleigh Colleges, the consortium of Meredith, Peace, St. Augustine's, and St. Mary's

Colleges and North Carolina State and Shaw Universities, which had been coordinated from its inception in 1967 by John A. Yarbrough.

THE DYNAMICS OF change drive colleges and universities. But sometimes life-altering ideas subtly point institutions in new directions over time while simpler and more tangible developments seem immediately to energize the community. Such was the case with creative uses of the year-old Weatherspoon physical education building, which housed Meredith's first indoor pool. In the fall semester, a new group of synchronized swimmers performed its premiere, *Once Over Lightly*, attracting an audience of more than two-hundred people, including Herbert Weatherspoon, whose generosity, with that of his family, made the new building possible. Fran Vandiver, instructor in physical education, organized and directed the show. The swim team later named itself "Aqua Angels" and became a regular among Meredith's various performing groups.

In every academic year, there seemed to be almost as many groups— some organized, some not—on the campus as there were individuals. All composed the college community. Carlyle Campbell, fourth president of Meredith, said, community is "at the heart of civilization, social history; civilization began when someone said 'let's' [and] 'I' became 'we.' "[23] And when a member of the community excelled, the "I" was applauded by the "we." Such was the case when Carol Grant, a freshman in 1971, received a national March of Dimes Award in Atlanta on October 8 for her "tireless efforts" in educating the public about birth defects.[24] Not only had she chaired the state's Teen Action Program (TAP) in 1970, but the following year, she was also elected Young Adult Chairman for the North Carolina chapter. She had fought a losing battle to end freak shows at the State Fair in 1968 but was successful in inspiring the State Legislature in 1969 to pass a bill "prohibiting the exhibition of children under the age of 18 [who have] birth defects."[25] Born with phocomelia (shortened arms), Grant also wore braces on her legs. Following her graduation in 1975, she earned a master's degree as well as a doctorate in rehabilitation counseling at East Carolina and Southern Illinois Universities, respectively. Late in Jimmy Carter's term as president of the United States, he appointed her to the national Architectural and Transportation Barriers Compliance Board, and she was in line to chair the board when Carter lost his bid for reelection to Ronald Reagan.

Although Meredith had previously accepted physically challenged students, it enrolled Carol Grant as the Federal and State Governments were demanding reasonable access to buildings and other facilities. Joe Baker reported the College's having modified a bath, changed one room, and built some ramps for her. "From that point on, within another year or two, we had to have ramps and access routes . . . and elevators for buildings of three or more floors."[26]

UNDER THE PRESS of responsibilities, Dr. Burris might have imagined his term as acting president was longer, but he wore the mantle of chief administrator only from September through December. On October 14, 1971, two months after Burris's appointment, L.M. Massey, chairman of the presidential selection committee, called a special meeting of the board to present the committee's top prospect. By way of the candidate's resume, Dr. Massey introduced the vice president for finance and administration at Middle Tennessee State University, recommending "the election of John E. Weems as the sixth president of Meredith to take effect on January 1, 1972."[27]* Dr. Weems was elected by unanimous vote.

Chairman C.C. Cameron announced the news to reporters: "We feel fortunate in securing a man of Dr. Weems's experience and expertise in the field of higher education who can continue to lead Meredith toward academic excellence, financial stability and service."[28] Weems, who was also present for the announcement, said, "I am very impressed with the tradition of academic excellence at Meredith, and I am particularly impressed with the high calibre of students here and the obvious dedication of the faculty."[29]

On the following day, Friday, October 15, the college community met the new president in convocation. On stage with him to receive a welcoming ovation were his wife, Frankie Gooch Weems; their daughter, Nancy, 10; and their sons, John Mark, 17, and David, 12.

---

*Although the college catalogue has, from 1972, listed Craven Allen Burris as president between Drs. Heilman and Weems, minutes of the Board of Trustees indicate that John Edgar Weems was elected by the trustees as the sixth president and was so introduced at his inauguration, both by the chairman of the Board and by the printed inaugural program.

2

A NEW CHAPTER

1972

CARLYLE CAMPBELL, PRESIDENT of the College from 1939–66, offered timeless insights into the evolution of institutions like Meredith. On Founders' Day of 1966, the year of his retirement, he said,

> When we consider such institutions as Meredith in historical perspective, we are likely to have two distinct, immediately conflicting, reactions: first, of the immense changes in circumstance and procedure, so obvious and so pervasive as to create a feeling of sharp contrast between the past and present; then, on deeper reflection, a recognition of an underlying consistency and integrity of purpose which make these transformations secondary to the conviction that both past and present are but successive chapters in an ever-unfolding text.

In 1972, the text unfolded, and a new chapter began.

John Edgar Weems was thirty-nine when he was elected president of Meredith College. A native of Nashville, Tennessee, he chose George Peabody College in his hometown for his undergraduate as well as his graduate education. Upon receiving the Bachelor of Science degree in 1953, with majors in economics, business administration, and education, he was one of seven young men selected by Proctor and Gamble to participate in the company's executive training program. But after two years, he returned to Peabody, earning the Master of Arts degree in administration of public education and business education before joining the faculty of Atlantic Christian (now Barton) College in Wilson, North Carolina. Later he moved into administration as director of admissions and placement, soon adding the duties of student personnel services to his workload. In 1959, he accepted the position of dean of admissions and records at Kentucky Wesleyan and, in 1961, carried the same title to Middle Tennessee State. There he implemented a system of computer registration that was adopted as the model for Tennessee's entire state-supported system of higher education.

Again in his home state, he resumed work toward a doctorate in administration of higher education, his dissertation dealing "primarily with institutional research designed for making sound administrative decisions in higher education."[1] Peabody awarded him the Doctor of Education degree in 1965. Meanwhile, promotions at Middle Tennessee State accorded him a deanship and then a vice-presidency. At the time the trustees tapped him for the Meredith presidency, Dr. Weems was responsible for all areas of Middle Tennessee State's administration except for the faculty and student personnel divisions.

When the Weems family moved to Raleigh, they and Meredith were not strangers. Between his introduction in October and his arrival in January, the president-elect had several times met with students and other members of the community. But once he made the permanent move, his calendar was filled. One of his early commitments was to deliver the January commencement address back at Middle Tennessee State. And he was frequently on the speakers' circuit for Meredith groups that were vying for opportunities to make his acquaintance. He received a cordial welcome. In fact, when he addressed the Durham–Hillsborough Alumnae Chapter, Mayor Fred Cates of Hillsborough announced that the town council had named Weems honorary mayor.

Over the course of the next several months, the College more or less dictated the president's schedule. Early in the year, he joined the executive committee of the Board of Trustees in a meeting called to accept a challenge gift of $150,000 from trustee C.C. Barefoot and Mrs. Barefoot, and to recommend to the full board that "New North," the twin dormitory to Heilman, be named Barefoot Residence Hall.

Also in January, the Lectures in Religion series featured Elton Trueblood on one of his several visits to the campus. A Quaker, philosopher, and author, Dr. Trueblood was "probably the best known American writer in religion."[2] His work dealt primarily with the philosophy of religion; and as he developed his topics at Meredith—"The Future of the Christian Faith" and "The Development of an Honest Belief"—he applied his philosophy to the culture of the period.

The annual January Religious Emphasis Week was "always a spiritually significant experience in the school year."[3] The 1972 version was promoted on the front page of the *Twig* under the bylines of students Judy Yates and Dianne Reavis: "In an age of cold reason saturated with flaring emotions, riot, and unrest, one may not feel that it is so great to be alive. But we of REW (Religious Emphasis Week) have chosen to celebrate the hopeful aspects of life."[4] Ed Christman, guest theologian and chaplain at Wake Forest University, advanced the theme of "What a Great Day to be Alive!"

It would not have been far-fetched to adapt the theme of that Religious Emphasis Week to the annual Founders' Day observances, as celebration was usually the mode. At his first Founders' Day on February 25, Weems presided over a morning convocation observing Meredith's eighty-first charter year and featuring an address by Henry Hall Wilson, president of the Chicago Board of Trade. In a ceremony emulating a portion of the first Founders' Day in 1909—the year in which Baptist Female University became Meredith College—a coterie of people traveled to old City Cemetery downtown to place flowers on the grave of Thomas Meredith, the founder whose name the College adopted. Celebrations continued through an evening banquet honoring C.C. and Kilty Barefoot for having given "the second largest gift from . . . individuals to the Meredith Advancement Program."[5] With the Barefoots, both for dinner and for the afternoon dedication of Barefoot Residence Hall, were their five daughters, two of whom—Barbara Barefoot Smith and Beverly Barefoot Ceglia—are alumnae of the College.

The importance of Meredith's seventh residence hall would be measured by the number of its occupants. Already full, Barefoot Hall had brought resident enrollment to 1,102 that year. Mary Bland Josey, who was alert to numbers as they applied to the economy, had projected the need for an incoming freshman class of 340–365. But actual enrollment exceeded expectations. She reported,

As of May 15, 1972, it looks as if the freshman class, including day students, will be about 370–375 in number. With 1,125 former and new resident students having paid advance deposits . . . , plans have been made to use the eighteen spaces on the second floor of the infirmary for resident students, and a waiting list for new students has been started.[6]

A full house was also expected for the highly anticipated three-day symposium on "Urban Life and the Political Process," a March event that promised as keynote speaker the Honorable Shirley Chisholm, representative from the Twelfth Congressional District in New York. Congresswoman Chisholm, having aspired to higher political achievement, had declared her candidacy for the Democratic presidential nomination, the first African-American woman to seek the highest elective office in the land. Following the symposium, at which the candidate spoke to more than 1,300 people, the *Twig* trumpeted, "A fast-talking Shirley Chisholm breezed into North Carolina Monday. . . ."[7] An overnight guest in the Mae Grimmer House, Chisholm invited the alumnae office staff to join her for early-morning conversation and coffee. Her white male secretary issued the invitation and brewed the coffee. In those days, few male secretaries could be found in Meredith's neighborhood; and the idea of a white male's serving a black female was a phenomenon. It still is. Although Chisholm would lose her party's nomination, she would gain advocacy for her cause to end racial and gender bias.

The thirtieth annual Alumnae Seminar preceded the symposium by four days. Co-sponsored by the Alumnae Association and the Department of Psychology, the one-day event featured Martha S. Grafton, dean emeritus and acting president of Mary Baldwin College. Mrs. Grafton's address, "Women's Lib: a Second Look," was among the early speeches at Meredith to focus on the women's movement of the seventies. Crediting the then-current crusade to Betty Friedan's nine-year-old fiery treatise, *The Feminine Mystique*, Grafton taught a history lesson:

Women's Liberation, a movement which can be considered almost as old as humanity . . . ranks along with war, civil rights, law and violence, and ecology as one of the prime concerns of the decade. . . . If today's feminist movement came out of the civil rights movement, as many think, the first drive was closely associated with abolition of slavery and [with] temperance.[8]

Gender was not a concern at the student-faculty basketball game in March, but competition was fierce. The students won 34–32, despite the eighteen points scored by religion professor Bernard Cochran. Ellen Bullington, a reporter for the *Twig*, wrote, "The faculty had a slight height and a considerable weight advantage, plus their star, Dr. Cochran. Dean Burris showed great ability with his fantastic drop shots, and well-placed lay-ups. He also demonstrated a talent for giving the ball to the wrong team. . . ."[9]

The focus shifted from student-*faculty* relations to student-*family* relations when Wayne E. Oates, professor of psychology at Southern Baptist Theological Seminary, addressed the subject at a Meredith Christian Association (MCA) forum and again when mothers, fathers, siblings, and other kin came visiting for Parents' Weekend. The recently formed Parents' Association convened its second annual meeting on a Saturday, but the top attraction of the day was the crowning of Springs Queen, Nancy Crews, and the presentation of her court.*

Meanwhile, back at the president's residence, the Weemses spared no efforts to open their home to guests, both the curious and the altruistic. President Weems reported,

> This house has been tested and put to use. In a brief three-month period more than three thousand people have been invited into our home for entertainment in one way or another. These occasions have ranged from casual dinners for other couples, to formal dinners for twelve, to seated dinners for the entire faculty, to a large buffet for the total senior class, to receptions for five hundred.[10]

The first president's residence on the campus, the Massey House was named in honor of trustee Luther M. Massey and his wife, Vivian Dawson Massey, who contributed the initial funding toward its construction. Ground was broken on Founders' Day 1971, and the spacious and elegantly appointed residence was waiting when its first occupants, the

---

*The Celebration of Spring replaced the forty-five-year tradition of May Day in 1971, and a spring dance concert, first staged in 1975, replaced the traditional May Day and Springs Court dances.

Weems family, arrived to claim it as their home. Dedication of the house was scheduled for President Weems's inauguration day. Special guests would include Dr. and Mrs. Massey; their daughter, alumna Carolyn Massey Kitahata, '51; and the many donors of rooms, furnishings, and landscaping.

But months before the inauguration, the College bustled with year-end activities. Surprised students welcomed a dinner-hour distraction in early May when United States presidential hopeful Senator Terry Sanford dropped by the dining hall to campaign for the Democratic Party's nomination. The *Twig* singled out his response to one of the burning issues of the day: "Sanford favors immediate withdrawal of troops [from Vietnam] while supplying the necessary economic aid for rebuilding of the devastated country. . . ."[11]

Sanford's visit closed the books on politics, at least until after commencement. But the College opened its new *History of Meredith College, Second Edition*, by Mary Lynch Johnson as alumnae made their annual pilgrimages back to the campus for Alumnae Day. Eager readers crowded the Massey House to claim copies of the revised history for themselves and to honor the author at an autograph tea. At the same time, guests toured the new residence and met the Weemses at home.

Coming "home" herself, Nancy Blair Viccellio, '35, addressed the alumnae at their annual meeting. In fact, much of commencement weekend honored alumnae, who played second fiddle only to the seniors. Dr. Johnson was in the spotlight both as author of the history and as honoree of the Class of 1972, whose gift to the College was the establishment of the Mary Lynch Johnson Library Enrichment Endowment. With a contribution of $2,000 and a commitment from its members to designate future gifts to the endowment principal, the class specified that "Annual earnings . . . will be used for acquisition of learning resources, with preference being given to needed periodicals."[12]

Mary Yarbrough, retiring chairman of the Department of Chemistry, also received multiple honors. She and Charles Tucker, assistant professor of sociology, were named Outstanding Christian Educators, an annual award created by Greensboro's First Baptist Church and later funded by the Parents' Association. Dr. Mary, as she was affectionately known to generations of students, and Mabel Claire Hoggard Maddrey each received an Alumna Award. Yarbrough was again recognized in commencement exercises when President Weems announced receipt of a bequest toward an endowment to establish the Mary E. Yarbrough Chair of Chemistry. The letter of intent, dated April 12, 1970, and addressed to "President, Meredith College," contained moving personal words:

> I am not acquainted with you nor you with me, and you will never know me as you will not receive this letter until after my death. My daughter, Helen Davie Bedon, was a graduate of Meredith as a chemistry major in 1945 and went on to receive her Ph.D. degree in this field and to teach chemistry. She loved the college and also Miss Yarbrough dearly. . . . [My daughter] died in 1966.[13]

Also on Class Day, the Saturday preceding commencement, the College dedicated the Margaret Bright Gallery of Class Dolls. Located on the third level of Johnson Hall's Bryan Rotunda, the gallery displays as many dolls as there have been graduating classes, beginning with 1902. Each doll, dressed by the class it represents, reflects the culture of its time. A gallery visitor finds the sedate young woman of the early 1900s and the flapper of the '20s; the flower child of the '60s and the feminist of the '70s; the casual woman of the '80s and the career woman of the '90s. Dorothy Loftin Goodwin, '47, who inherited Miss Bright's responsibility for and care of the collection, reminded *Alumnae Magazine* readers that Miss Bright, the first caretaker of the dolls, died in June 1969, "after having attended every commencement, beginning in 1903, when she had enrolled as a freshman at Baptist Female University. . . ."[14]

While the College would remember Class Day for celebrations, honors, and dedications, it would remember graduation day, in part, for the rain that doused the best of plans. The ceremony, set for Elva Bryan McIver Amphitheater, was quickly shifted to Jones Auditorium, a situation that necessitated a tight squeeze for all. Possibly more than one person in Jones that day recalled the previous year's commencement exercises in Weatherspoon Gymnasium, when folding chairs supplemented the bleachers' seating capacity of 670, and a malfunctioning electrical system—some said it was body heat—triggered the fire alarm. Although, after a moment of uneasiness, the audience reacted calmly, the 1971 graduation event was the first and last scheduled for the gym.

Threat of fire was rarer than threat of flood, but the fact remained that commencement crowds had outgrown the seating capacity of Jones Auditorium. In both years, however, the seniors were as thoroughly graduated as if they and their families had been more comfortably accommodated. In 1972, the 213 candidates for the Bachelor of Arts degree and the 13 for the Bachelor of Music heard the Reverend J. Dewey Hobbs, minister at the First Baptist Church of Marion, North Carolina, preach the baccalaureate sermon in the morning and the Honorable Naomi E. Morris, judge of the North Carolina Court of Appeals, deliver the commencement address in the afternoon. At the end of the day then, and even before his inauguration, President Weems had survived an entire semester at Meredith.

SUMMER IS THE shortest distance between two terms. But after every commencement, the College experiences a few interminably long and bleakly silent days of closure before preparations for another semester begin. Once the inundation starts, the campus is awash with reminders of the brevity of the season: summer school; special interest camps for young people; workshops for older people; the refurbishing of a dormitory; or the modernizing of a classroom building.

In the summer of 1972, the new Cate Center attracted much of the attention. In the heat of a southern July, the student store, lovingly known as the Bee Hive, moved—lock, stock, and textbook—from its old, frame, termite-infested quarters to its sleek, new home across the campus. The center would also house other student-related facilities, but not until construction was more nearly complete, possibly in October. When the trustees met in September, President Weems urged them to tour the building. "It's like a visit to the 21st century," he boasted.[15]

Space was a precious commodity. When movers exited the Bee Hive with the last boxes of No. 2 yellow pencils and blue, spiral-bound notebooks, the art department, with "print-making supplies, ceramics, and power tools (*implementa electrica*)," entered the forty-six-year-old relic, "formerly the rear section of the auditorium, circa 1926–1949."[16] The home economics department also claimed a portion of the old "temporary" building's stockroom for refinishing furniture.

While the campus hummed with summer activities, some Meredith people were thousands of miles away. For example, William Ledford, chairman, and Katalin Galligan and Helen Daniell of the foreign language department conducted special studies in Spain and France. Dr. Ledford's group centered its work in Madrid, while students of Drs. Galligan and Daniell studied in Paris and Nice. These forerunners of the Meredith Abroad program allowed students to earn special studies credits.

Other summer events were unrelated to the College except that they occurred there. Some visitors participated in Project Help; some in the Southern Baptist Convention-sponsored Journeyman Program; some in football, basketball, cheerleading, and majorette clinics; some in a Family Life Education conference; and some in a Latter Day Saints retreat. Summer-school students and equitation enthusiasts swelled the overall seasonal population to 3,000.

Meanwhile, another college catalogue went to press; textbook orders congested the book store; the housing staff paired freshman roommates; prospective teachers came for interviews; long-time faculty revised courses; the dining hall served three meals a day; a mammoth new computer—Meredith's first—was lifted by crane to Johnson Hall's third floor; the inauguration committee met frequently; and the College honored the Baptist State Convention staff and Raleigh's Baptist pastors and their families at a fourth annual picnic. And plans took shape for Meredith's pioneer program in continuing education. Dean Burris cited the self-study of 1968 as having originated the idea for the program. The study, he said, showed "a great deal of vision as to where Meredith ought to go to meet the needs of women in modern society."[17]

A PIONEER IS one who conquers a frontier. The definition applies not only to the College and its new program but also to Anne Clarke Dahle, '54, the first coordinator of continuing education. After several years of teaching, of working as a computer programmer, and of rearing her children, Dahle earned a master's degree in mathematics at North Carolina State University. "In the process," she said, "I was really struggling with how hard it is for women who have been out [of school] to find a place to get back, how to do it, what to do."[18] Through her career in continuing education, as coordinator and later as director of the successful re-entry program, that early experience seemed to have translated into a calling. Through the next twenty-two years, her passion would be to guide other women in their searches for "a place to get back, how to do it, what to do."

Dahle began her work in the fall, and, by spring, continuing education offered three enrichment courses: one in religion and one in art, taught by department chairmen Roger Crook and Leonard White, respectively, and one—a study in historic preservation titled "Saving Yesterday for Tomorrow"—developed by Emyl Jenkins of Raleigh. Two decades later, Dahle would recall that "We had a number of newcomers to Raleigh sign up for [the latter]. They are now leaders in historic societies; I see their names [in print] from time to time."[19]

The continuing education program was already functioning when the faculty convened for an August workshop to hear Robert E. Stoltz, director of the regional office of the College Entrance Examination Board (CEEB), predict problems soon to face higher education. One factor that Stoltz introduced was a sure decline in the national birth rate; therefore, he said, colleges must "consider new [applicant] pools—especially adult and part-time students."[20] Meredith, the pioneer, had already blazed the trail. That first year, the College put in place a new option for admission of high school graduates who were over twenty-three years of age. Waiving regular requirements, it would accept the women as degree candidates, but only after satisfactory completion of fifteen hours of work. Two women enrolled under the plan. One of the two, Eugenia Sealey Cross, graduated; whereas, in the two decades from 1976–96, 857 re-entry women earned undergraduate degrees under the plan.

In a sense, every member of the college community is a pioneer, consistently reshaping the institution. In 1972, the College reflected on the influence of former English department chairman Julia Hamlet Harris, who had retired in 1952 and died in 1965. Dr. Harris had left the greater part of her estate to Meredith. A terse entry in the minutes of the executive committee of the Board of Trustees for August read, "It was announced that the Merit Scholarships of Meredith College would be continued and the names of the Merit Scholars would be changed to Julia Hamlet Harris Scholars to honor a long-time faculty member . . . who has endowed these scholarships through a bequest from her estate."[21] The *Twig* offered further details: Harris "bequeathed the College her estate of $135,000 with the request that the gift be used for scholarships for promising and deserving students."[22] During the process of renaming the scholarships, Eleanor Edwards Williams, '37, a former student of Dr. Harris's, looked at and beyond the generous bequest: "In leaving her monetary estate to Meredith College," Williams wrote, "Dr. Harris added a powerful postscript to her generous giving of herself as scholar, teacher, and friend. Naming the Honor Scholarships in her memory was like giving a proper title to an heroic poem." Williams recalled another image of her former teacher: "She taught culture by presence. . . . Her entrance into a room somehow made the ceilings taller."[23] The Class of 1950 would further honor Harris's memory by its gift in 1975 of a portrait of the long-time English professor. The painting by artist Hallie Siddell of Raleigh stands on an easel in the Harris Rare Books Room of the Carlyle Campbell Library.

THE COMINGS AND goings of the scholars who teach are among the dynamics of academe. While the two new department chairmen appointed in 1972 had joined the faculty in the sixties, they were accepting new responsibilities, new challenges. Clara R. Bunn, assistant professor of biology, assumed the role of acting chairman of her department in January 1973, while John Yarbrough, who had held the post since 1943, was on sabbatical leave. A member of the faculty since 1969, Dr. Bunn earned the A.B. in chemistry at Meredith and the M.S. and the Ph.D. in biology at North Carolina State. The trustees would name her permanent chairman in March 1973.

Sally M. Horner, assistant professor and new chairman of the Department of Chemistry, taught at Meredith for the 1965–66 term and returned in 1967. She succeeded Mary Yarbrough, who retired after thirty-four years. At the time of her appointment, Dr. Horner was on sabbatical leave for research in X-ray crystallography at Duke. She began her undergraduate work at Meredith, but both her B.S. and Ph.D. degrees came from the University of North Carolina at Chapel Hill. Horner's predecessor, "Dr. Mary," would continue to teach.

As surely as academic people come and go, academic programs evolve. The 1972–73 catalogue offered for the first time an arrangement with American University in Washington, D.C., for Meredith students to participate in a Washington Semester, "which introduces students from all over the nation to a first-hand study of American politics." The same catalogue listed Special Studies—Community Internship—for the first time. (Additional options, such as Independent Study, Directed Independent Study, Honors Thesis, and Group Study have appeared in subsequent course listings.) And Dean Burris reported that future catalogues would likely offer business and economics courses to "prepare Meredith students for higher management positions in industry."[24]

In that era, the predicted impact of the computer on future generations of teachers, students, and programs was probably more theory than fact. Meredith's foray into computer technology was in the form of IBM data processing, primarily for use in the business office but a boon also to the offices of institutional advancement, the registrar, and the president.

Little, if any, argument arose as to the usefulness of computers, the renaming of scholarships, the appointment of new department heads, or the creativity of some academic offerings, but much debate erupted in the August faculty meeting over a motion to allow student membership on the Academic Council.* The pros clamored for democracy, while the cons decried a confusion of responsibilities and raised the recurring question: If instructors were ineligible for membership, why should students be eligible? After two postponements, the faculty cast ballots in December, defeating the proposal by a vote of 33–28.

Voting was a hot topic that fall. The pending presidential election, pitting incumbent Republican Richard Nixon against Democratic Senator George McGovern, produced campus polls showing that seventy-five percent of faculty responders supported McGovern for his stance on the Vietnam War, honesty in government, the economy, and the environment.[25] As for students, the numbers were uncertain, except to the extent that "A relatively higher proportion of underclassmen support President Nixon than upperclassmen," as reported in the *Twig*.[26]

Freshman Kathy Hall voted in Wake County that year, although her parents lived in Edgecombe County. Eager to cast her first ballot after the voting age was lowered to eighteen, she, like many students nationwide, took seriously the opportunity. In October 1971, she tried to register to vote in a Raleigh precinct, but the registrar refused her application on the grounds of residency requirements. Hall appealed to the Wake County Board of Elections and again was rebuffed. Undaunted, she carried the matter to Superior Court, where Judge Coy Brewer heard her case *de novo*, but not before she had opened a bank account in Raleigh and

---

*At the time, the Academic Council comprised departmental chairmen but later developed a policy whereby members could not succeed themselves in successive three-year terms. (Conversation with Dean Burris, February 8, 1994).

changed her address on her driver's license and college records from her parents' home in Tarboro to Stringfield Hall, Meredith College. When Judge Brewer ruled in her favor, the Board of Elections appealed to the Supreme Court of North Carolina, arguing that Hall was in Raleigh only to attend Meredith; that she went home for holidays; that her parents paid her tuition; that her grades went to them; that she had personal property, including her dog, in Tarboro; and that her church membership was in her hometown. But the Supreme Court of North Carolina ruled in her favor. Its proceedings for March 15, 1972 read,

> After certification for initial appellate review, the Supreme Court, Sharp, J., held that finding that student had abandoned her former domicile and had acquired new one in place where she was attending college supported judgment that she was entitled to vote in such place.[27]

More of Justice Sharp's opinion is on record:

> Whether a particular student is entitled to register and vote in the town where he or she is attending college must be determined by the application of the rules stated herein to the specific facts of that individual's case. Decision here relates directly to the plaintiff only. This is in no sense a class action.[28]

Hall admitted to full knowledge of the use of absentee ballots, but she chose the more challenging route to the voting booth. While she did not "fix" the problem for all college students, she set an example of working within the system.

On a much broader scale, the Vietnam War seemed to be the rallying point behind political unrest. But history notes that the conflict divided the country in off years as well as in election years. Apparently, it was the major cause of student rebellion, and one of the epidemics of that rebellion was the use of mind-altering drugs. In 1971 the trustees had reaffirmed a previous policy: "Meredith College students shall not possess or use drugs illegally on or off campus. Any known violation shall result in suspension or expulsion."[29] In 1972, Dean Marie Mason issued the results of a survey of students in area colleges. At Meredith, 670 responses out of 1,000 students surveyed revealed that one percent had used drugs, presumably marijuana, on the campus and 13 percent outside the college confines. Dr. Mason interpreted the percentages as "extremely low as compared to other campuses in the city."[30] The alleged violators were unknown.

While drug use seemed to be escalating everywhere, other symptoms of youthful unrest began a slow but steady decline. Sophomore Janice Sams participated in a protest demonstration at the State Capitol in April and compared student attitudes of the day with those of the recent past: "Gone was the violence (perhaps as a result of Kent State); gone was the blatant intolerance to speakers; and gone was the real urge to chant obscene slogans." Instead, she wrote, "there were pleas for students to register to vote and to exercise that privilege. There were pleas for united petitions from universities and colleges in response to the war, and pleas for these institutions not to support the 'war companies' who manufactured 'dead bodies.'"[31]

Conveying the gentler demeanor of students nationwide, Meredith women seemed to reflect "a more relaxed attitude than in previous years," according to a discussion among the trustees. "There is no indication that they are less concerned about the problems of the world than they have been before, but their general attitude concerning the methods of bringing about change appears to be different."[32] Change did not occur by osmosis; conscious efforts aided and abetted the evolution. For example, the Student Government Association sponsored a leadership workshop aimed at "decreasing campus 'unrest' and increasing campus interest and cooperation."[33] And a desire for harmony spurred black students to seek a united voice in campus life, resulting in a new club called "Black Student Unity." Dispelling speculation that the new sisterhood would isolate the sixteen African-Americans on campus, the organizers stipulated that "white students would be eligible for admission later."[34] The small but active minority population sought a cultural awareness that would chip away at racial bias.

Interestingly enough, this period was one of students' growing concern for the wider community. Meredith women had traditionally offered their time and talents in service projects but, by 1971, the College saw the need systematically to match students' interests to the community's requirements. Leslie Syron, chairman of the service-oriented sociology department, accepted the challenge of coordinating service activities, publishing in 1972 Meredith's first *Directory of Volunteer Opportunities*. The pamphlet listed twelve agencies and, in some cases, several areas within an agency in which students volunteered.

One special community project did not precisely fit the categories identified in the directory; rather, it called for a cooperative venture between Oakwood, a Raleigh neighborhood in transition, and the College. The old Victorian homes in Oakwood, which had surrounded Meredith's original campus, were being refurbished by homeowners abandoning the suburbs. Challenged by the neighborhood's new residents and the Oakwood Garden Club, Sarah Lemmon envisioned a project and developed a proposal uniquely suited to Oakwood and to the history and sociology departments. She and her counterpart in sociology, Dr. Syron, believed that if the old neighborhood knew and understood its history, it would be better armed "to battle the destructive forces of inner city decay that often follows urbanization."[35] So some of Meredith's history and sociology majors would amass data on "the origins of the Oakwood neighborhood, its growth and development, its original inhabitants, and the identification and description of the area"[36] for a study on "Value Development in Transitional Oakwood." The proposal caught the imagination of the North Carolina Committee for Continuing Education in the Humanities, and the organization funded the project. Dr. Lemmon said, "It is hoped that a humanistic approach to the phenomenon of urbanization may ease the tensions of change."[37]

As the College strengthened ties with the community, it also reaffirmed its association with North Carolina Baptists—descendants of those who had founded the institution almost a century earlier—through a program of competitive scholarships for Baptist young women. The admissions office developed the idea, and the director defined it as an arrangement whereby a need-based, renewable award of $100–$1,000 per year would be available to one entering freshman from each of the ten Baptist associational regions in North Carolina.

The relationship between the College and its community seemed to perpetuate a mutual confidence. Similarly, a step-by-step relaxing of campus regulations implied a deepening faith in the wisdom of the Meredith student. For example, she could at last choose whether to attend Wednesday worship services. And she was required to be present for only one convocation each week.

That generation was also the first in a long time to read the *Twig* as a weekly rather than a bi-weekly publication. The initial issue of the fall term announced the change. The staff of the four-page paper kept up the pace, as promised, perhaps recalling with a touch of envy a special eight-page edition compiled the previous spring by a Western Civilization class. An editorial in the March 30 issue had read,

> As members of Dr. Parramore's Western Civilization class, we have been poked, shoved, and driven in desperation to the realization of the importance of being well-informed. This issue of THE TWIG is the result of our efforts to help you know a little more about your college, your state, and your country. . . . THE TWIG desperately needs your active participation to become the true voice of Meredith. This issue is an attempt at catching your attention, at providing you the opportunity to take a stand.[38]

Thomas C. Parramore, professor of history, who came to Meredith a decade earlier, was perhaps the most outspoken faculty member—publicly, at least—against student apathy and for student responsibility.

While it tried subtly to teach responsibility, the College also determined to practice it. Fiscal accountability was not the least of its concerns. President Weems told the trustees that the Association of American Colleges "predicts that 48 percent of the nation's private, accredited four-year colleges and universities will exhaust their liquid assets over the next decade." He added,

> So immense has the problem become, in fact, that some fund raising officials recently came forth with the assessment that nonprofits need upward of $50 billion by 1975 just to stave off disaster.
>
> Nonprofits are cannibalizing their endowments, not to build grand and glorious edifices nor to fill the first violinist's chair, but simply to keep running on a day-to-day basis.[39]

But Meredith postponed the financial doomsday as foretold by the prophets until some unnamed tomorrow. President Weems warned, however, that the College would "require $144,000 additional each year to maintain [its] present . . . expenditure level."[40] His statement followed Vice President Baker's optimistic report to the faculty that Meredith had experienced an exceptional year, the restricted endowment and investments totaling approximately $1.8 million.[41]

Vice President Kanipe looked ahead to Phase 2 of the Meredith Advancement Program (MAP), which would add to the endowment coffers. Phase I, he said, specified a goal of $5,000,000 for capital funds, and more than $4,200,000 had already been committed.[42]

INAUGURAL FESTIVITIES BEGAN on September 21, a cool, rainy Thursday. Dinner in Belk Hall preceded an adaptation of television's popular *This is Your Life* to the life of the new president. The John Weems Show, hosted by Mary Jean Burton and written by Gloria Smith and Karen McLean, all juniors, ran the gamut from hilarious to sentimental. But David Lynch, chairman of the music department, restored a measure of formality and ended inauguration eve with a recital on the Cooper Organ in Jones Auditorium.

Thursday's wet weather caused some consternation for the inauguration committee, chaired by Dr. Lemmon. The ceremonies were set for the Elva Bryan McIver Amphitheater because no indoor facility on the campus could accommodate the "family," much less friends; expected representatives from one-hundred colleges and universities; and guests from twenty learned societies, educational entities, and professional organizations. But Friday—Meredith College Day in Raleigh— as proclaimed by Mayor Thomas W. Bradshaw, Jr., was warmed by a bright sun that mercifully and quickly dried the amphitheater's brick seats and grass footrests in time for the ceremony. Early arrivals, then, could listen comfortably to the forty-five-minute preludial concert by the Triangle Symphony.

Dignitaries in dazzling academic regalia processed at eleven o'clock. The presidential party included three representatives from the Baptist State Convention: T. Robert Mullinax, executive secretary; W. Perry Crouch, general secretary-treasurer; and Thomas M. Freeman, president. Other members of the party were Luther M. Massey, trustee and chairman of the presidential search committee; Mary Lynch Johnson, college historian; Mayor Bradshaw; Ben C. Fisher, executive secretary, Education Commission of the Southern Baptist Convention; Seby B. Jones, chairman of the Board of Associates; Faye Arnold Broyhill, trustee; C. Allen Burris, vice president and dean of the College; Alyce Epley Walker, president of the Alumnae Association; Carolyn Carter, president of the Student Government Association; O.L. Sherrill, executive secretary of the General Baptist Convention; John M. Lewis, pastor of Raleigh's First

*The inaugural procession on September 22, 1972, is led by
marshal Gwen Noble, '73, President John E. Weems, O. L. Sherrill,
executive secretary of the General Baptist Convention; and
C. Cliff Cameron, chair of the Board of Trustees.*

Baptist Church; C.C. Cameron, chairman of the Board of Trustees; and
the presidents of the institutions composing Cooperating Raleigh Colleges. Ms. Carter; Mrs. Walker, Mrs. Broyhill; Drs. Burris, Freeman, and
Fisher; and Messrs. Jones and Bradshaw brought greetings from their respective organizations, and, under the title, "A Goodly Heritage," Dr.
Johnson reviewed the administrations of the previous presidents. Before
introducing Dr. Weems, Mr. Cameron recognized Drs. Campbell and
Heilman, the fourth and fifth presidents, respectively. The rites of investi-
ture included Dr. Massey's presentation to Dr. Weems of the Presidential
Medallion, a case silver replica of the college seal encircled by a "filigree
of oak twigs with leaves and acorns, and . . . suspended from a ribbon of
maroon and white, the college colors."[43]
President Weems titled his inaugural address "Upheld by the Affec-

tions of a Great People," borrowing a phrase from M.L. Kesler, trustee of the College from 1896–1927, who had also insisted that the institution's survival depended not only on money but also on "great and loving hearts." This characterization, said the president, "was never more true than in the eight years between the chartering and the opening date of the Baptist Female University." But, he added, "there has never been a dearth of great people to help Meredith blossom throughout her history. . . . Many have contributed a lifetime of service; others have shared the ideals in a monetary way."[44]

Weems read from Miguel de Cervantes' *Don Quixote*, reminding the audience's visionaries that they might see something of themselves in the heroic fictional character, and recalling that *Man of La Mancha*, the popular musical adaptation of Cervantes' classic, challenged the idealist "to dream the impossible dream."

Reflecting on the evolution of the liberal arts, Weems compared the practicality of curricula of the earliest colleges to the rigidity of more recent interpretations, separating the arts and humanities from more specialized curricula. Although "only in recent years have the two concepts begun to amalgamate," he said,[45] Meredith's dreamers of impossible dreams have *always* insisted upon providing "the finest educational experience available."[46]

By implication in his address and by proclamation in later remarks, Weems defined himself as a futurist. In the context of that designation of himself and, therefore, of his administration, he said on inauguration day,

Are we truly grasping for an unreachable star? I think not. But it will take the same courage, tenacity, and devotion which has long been exhibited here to attain the noble quest. We have set our sights to be the very best in women's education. . . . For me this quest is the challenge to provide a truly modern liberal arts education. . . . To keep a college abreast of developments and conversant with the frontiers of knowledge is a noble quest within itself.[47]

3

WOMEN AND

WOMEN'S COLLEGES

1973–1975

"MEREDITH IS THE maturing of a woman." The statement comes from President Weems's inaugural address and expresses a philosophy that rings true in every era of Meredith's history. Twenty years past the inauguration, writer Suzanne Britt, an instructor in the English department, suggested that women mature, in part, by the difficulties of their choices. In her pictorial history, *Images: A Centennial Journey*, published in Meredith's one-hundredth charter year, Ms. Britt said that the period in which a woman chooses a college is "a crisis of decision—the landmark year between random, careless youth and thoughtful, conscious maturity."[1] From each side of two decades, Dr. Weems and Ms. Britt have spoken to the maturing of thinking minds and liberating spirits.

In the years following President Weems's inauguration, the maturing of women—indeed, the maturing of women's colleges—was redefined. Almost every aspect of society had changed, including the perception of educated women. Gone were the concepts of learning for the sheer joy of it and of learning for its own sake, and present was the radical new notion that women must learn for *their* own sakes—not merely to please parents, husbands, children, and watchful communities nor to qualify for a certain social circle in life after college.

Society had come to expect more of women and of women's colleges. In 1974, the *Wall Street Journal* published an article, "Making a Case for

Women's Colleges," citing Elizabeth Tidball's study of entries in *Who's Who in American Women*. Discovering that most of the 1,500 women of achievement whom she researched were alumnae of women's colleges, Tidball concluded that "female coed college graduates are less than half as likely to be 'career successful' than are graduates of women's colleges."[2] Nevertheless, some of the prestigious colleges for women—Vassar, Sarah Lawrence, Skidmore, for example—had already surrendered to the national trend of coeducation while others held tenaciously to their founding purposes. In 1972, Mt. Holyoke made a conscious decision to reaffirm its "for women only" status; Mills College would follow in 1990. Bryn Mawr, Smith, Wellesley, Hollins, Randolph-Macon, Salem, and Meredith, among others, unceremoniously went about the business of educating women.

Meredith's single-sex status had not been publicly questioned at this juncture. In fact, the College was so focused on emerging opportunities for women that coeducation was a moot issue. President Weems had already appointed a brainstorming committee to devise ways of encouraging students "to compete for the new kinds of careers opening for women."[3] The community was not surprised, then, when he addressed the 1973 North Carolina Legislature—the only male to do so—as a proponent of the Equal Rights Amendment; when, in 1974, Meredith appointed its first female vice president; nor when the College implemented in 1975 a program designed to raise the sights of its women students.

The proposed Equal Rights Amendment to the Constitution was simple and familiar: "Equality of rights under the law shall not be denied or abridged by the United States or any State on account of sex."[4] After passing both houses of Congress, it went to the states for ratification. When it came to the floor of the Senate of North Carolina, President Weems was there. In his address, he harkened back to Meredith's beginnings:

> The struggle to establish Meredith College indicates that North Carolinians in the 1830's faced the same issues being presented today concerning the Equal Rights Amendment. It took almost 60 years from the time our school was proposed before it was agreed that a college [for women] should be founded. Educational opportunities were not readily available to women and basically the same arguments were used to suggest that women did not need academic

training and were, in reality, better off without it. Meredith College has spent 74 years proving to the State of North Carolina and the nation that women have great contributions to make.[5]

Of rights and responsibilities he said,

> History will show that granting of rights is progressive. Double and false standards inevitably erode the confidence of the governed. In my opinion, we have a distinct moral responsibility to give all of our citizens equal protection under the law. It is an old, illogical and irrational idea that someone can be protected by abridging [her] rights . . . . [W]omen deserve total justice, equal protection, equal opportunity, and equal responsibility. . . .[6]

Weems later admitted to greater enthusiasm for the support of Senator Charles B. Deane, Jr., who sponsored the legislation, than for the amendment itself.[7] Both Senator Deane and President Weems were wary of extremists who spoke for and against the ERA and credited those lobbyists with the vote against ratification in North Carolina.

The mood of Meredith students toward the amendment was difficult to measure. The editorial position of their newspaper was pro ERA; however, as one would expect, letters to the editor argued for both sides. A similar clamor echoed through the nation, but elected officials had the final say, and ratification failed.

The College had some amending to do, as well. But compared to the nation's tumultuous journey through the channels of the Equal Rights Amendment, Meredith's voyage toward changing its rules of government was smooth indeed. An amendment to Article V of the bylaws added a vice president for student development and described the administrator's responsibilities: coordination and direction of "the offices of Admissions, Campus Minister, Counseling, Dean of Students (includes Student Government, Student Activities, and Student Housing), Financial Aid, Placement and Career Planning, Student Health Services, and other activities relating to these offices."[8] A selection committee conducted the search. By memorandum dated May 12, 1974, Clara Bunn, chair, conveyed the committee's opinions: the new vice president should be a woman with a Ph.D. degree, the terminal degree "preferable but not necessary"; a fresh face from outside the Meredith community—"for a new outlook"; a person trained in student personnel services—but "qualifications and experience outweigh this factor"; an administrator experienced in "dealing with faculty and students directly." She should also be "self-confident," "dynamic," "enthusiastic and discriminating."[9] In the hope that such a person existed, the College advertised the position in the *Chronicle of Higher Education*, encouraging women to apply and touting Meredith's location as "one of the most stimulating academic atmospheres in the nation." The search was intense but brief: Sandra Carol Thomas accepted the postition by letter dated August 16 and began her duties on September 2, although the appointment was not official until the full Board of Trustees elected her at its semi-annual meeting on September 27.

Bill Norton, director of information services, titled his statewide news release "Meredith Names Vice President for Student Development." While the *Twig* ran essentially the same story, its front-page headline for September 12 evoked excitement: "Meredith appoints first woman V.P." In the same issue, Genie Rogers directed a portion of her editorial to Dr. Thomas: "You have set one precedent already, and, who knows, perhaps one day someone will follow you to the never-before-achieved accomplishment of becoming Meredith College's first woman president."

Thomas had already resigned as dean of Lindenwood College in St. Charles, Missouri, to finish her dissertation for the Ph.D. While her graduate studies included work at Harvard and at the University of Colorado, she completed her doctorate in higher education and college and university administration at St. Louis University and her master's in college and student personnel administration at Indiana University. She had earned her undergraduate degree in English and Spanish in her native state at the University of Texas in Austin.

Her then-recent attendance at a Latin American conference on the changing world of women contributed to her manuscript, "Women and Politics: Ways to Broaden the Political Participation of Women in the Americas," which won first place in a competition sponsored by the Inter-American Commission for Women. As a result, Thomas was honored by and invited to address the general assembly of the Commission—a branch of the Organization of American States—in Washington, D.C. Later, in her first address to Meredith students, she challenged them to "educate themselves for responsibility . . . in international, national, local, and college affairs," and to "be involved in legislation which affects women and women's needs. . . ."[10]

Eager to provide suitable office space for their new colleague, administrators confiscated one end of the blue parlor. A remnant of the days when the words "social grace" were spoken as one, the tastefully appointed parlor stretched along one side of Johnson Hall's west wing. As expected, a minor controversy arose over the dismantling of that hallowed hall, the rose parlor on the opposite side having fallen to progress some years before. Through Editor Rogers, the *Twig* supported the change: "Dr. Thomas is fresh, eager, and excited about helping Meredith students. Considering this, we should welcome her to an office where she is close to us."[11]

Momentum was on the side of progress in ways other than an increasing need for office space. For example, both Vice President Thomas and President Weems supported the idea of improving students' perceptions of themselves and of improving society's perception of women. The president's sense of urgency escalated when he sat in Belk Dining Hall with a student who said she aspired to be a legal secretary. Why, he wondered aloud, would she not want to be a lawyer? Her surprising skepticism about herself moved him to appoint an ad hoc committee on raising the sights of women. The title itself reflected Weems's position, as expressed in his ERA address to the General Assembly and in a February 1973 interview with students Mary Owens and Barrie Walton: "Women need to expect to be a part of the economy and . . . aspire to . . . top management position[s]," he said.[12]

Women's issues sprang up in the consciousness of whoever allowed them to take root. Weems, nevertheless, reported to the faculty in 1974 that both liberal arts and women's colleges were facing "some uncertain times," although, he added, "We are at full capacity with a full-time equated enrollment of approximately 1300 students, making Meredith the largest private women's college in the South."[13] He credited Meredith's reputation and the work of the admissions office rather than the women's movement for that status.

Uses of titles and names loaded women's arsenals with ammunition for the struggle against a culture that was slow to change. The College was sometimes the target. Phyllis Trible, '54, wrote,

It strikes me as odd that Meredith should continue to refer to female heads of departments as chair*men*; that masculine pronouns should continue to be used as generic terms, especially at a women's college; and that alumnae should be identified by the names of their husbands. . . .

At Meredith, I was taught to distinguish between the masculine alumnus/i and the feminine alumna/ae. Would that our consciousness about the Latin language transfer to our consciousness about the English language . . . .[14]

Jane Cromley Curtis, '71, also protested:

I'd like to have my name back, please. . . . I was very disappointed to notice that all my mail from Meredith came addressed to Mrs. [husband's name]. . . . If such formidable agencies as the Social Security Administration and the . . . Department of Highway and Motor Vehicles can acknowledge me . . . as Jane Cromley Curtis, maybe my very own college can do that, too.[15]

Then came an opposing view from Elizabeth Garner McKinney, '42:

I read the letter . . . from the alumna who wanted "her name back" on her mail from Meredith. If that is her wish, then her request should be granted; but please don't address my mail as Ms. Elizabeth Garner McKinney. . . .

I like my name the way it is, and the title by which I am addressed has nothing to do with my rights as a person.[16]

From social expressions, such as gender-specific language, to visiting speakers, such as Wilma Scott Heide, president of the National Organization for Women; from academic innovations, such as a B.S. degree in business administration, to national or global observances, such as International Women's Year, Meredith wended its way, sometimes gingerly, sometimes boldly, through the women's movement and other cultural developments of the early- to mid-seventies.

At a student government-sponsored convocation in 1974, Heide spoke on "Sexism is a Disease and Feminism is the Cure," declaring that "sex stereotyping is as detrimental to men as it is to women."[17] World-renowned anthropologist Margaret Mead addressed a Meredith audience that year on the topic of "Where Today's Students Fit In." With some disappointment, President Weems recalled her lecture and others by eminent speakers of the times, saying, "We bring people in for their knowledge and want them to share their research, findings, and insights into the world, and we get a raising the sights of women speech."[18]

Meanwhile, the Bachelor of Science degree program was finalized. After a thirty-five-year hiatus, the degree was again offered in 1973—in chemistry, home economics, and mathematics, with biology and business administration being added the following year.

And a new English course, Stereotypes of Women in Modern Fiction, created excitement for continuing education students who said, "[We] no longer are just treading water; [we] are moving ahead with the current."[19] As swiftly as the current raced in the seventies, women activists might have paddled through the rapids still more vigorously following the release of a 1973 *Newsweek* and Associated Press survey of college publications editors showing that women's rights placed only fourth in a survey of "the five issues of most concern" on college campuses. First among the issues was the Vietnam War; second, the environment; third, racism; and fifth, drug addiction.[20]

No such polling data for Meredith women are available; however, records of students' opinions are plentiful. For example, the *Twig* suggested that the national energy crisis was among the top concerns of Meredith women. Lessons from the news media taught that the dilemma of the early seventies was due, in large part, to the nation's having continuously used more oil than it produced but also to OPEC's (Organization of Petroleum Exporting Countries) having dramatically raised the price of oil, causing shortages and adding serious problems to an already inflated economy. Long lines of gas-thirsty cars and frustrated drivers were common sights at service stations along Hillsborough Street. In homes all over the city, people lowered their thermostats. Meredith's dual heating system solved few problems, although it used natural gas and oil interchangeably. In 1973, the gas company warned that no gas would be available to the College after November 16, and the oil company allocated only 168,000 gallons of its precious fuel for the year, signaling a potential shortage of 40–50 thousand gallons. The crisis left the College with no alternative but to cut two days from the December exam schedule, add a week to Christmas vacation, and increase spring break by two days. Students could make up their class work at a later time.

The crisis, which affected all sources of energy, continued into 1974. Students became conservationists. They hailed the administration's decision to douse exterior display lights; they fumed at lights burning in empty classrooms; and while they appreciated the dramatic display of the new fountain between the giant magnolias at Johnson Hall's front door, they also calculated the energy expended by its twenty multicolored lights and ten water height stages. A letter to the *Twig*, signed by juniors Woody Dicus, Cookie Guthrie, Meg Pruette, and Elaine Williams dubbed the fountain "our contribution to the energy crisis."[21] But problem solving is rarely simple. In that case, maintenance of the valves and pumps required minimal use, so the administration announced that the water and light display would be continued but on a limited basis. The twenty-foot circular fountain, which eventually could be flaunted in all its glory—and in good conscience—was named for and dedicated to Henry M. and Blanche Shaw of Raleigh on September 27, 1974.

The *Twig* both agitated and mollified the community's new-found obsession with extravagance. Editor Genie Rogers vented her frustration: "I was appalled to enter the library last Friday and find that on a perfectly gorgeous day both the heater and the fans were running. . . ."[22] Four editions later, Meredith McGill defended the library, explaining that the lights alone provided one-fourth of the building's heat, even on a cold day. She also answered queries about the heating and cooling of residence halls, reporting that Stringfield, Vann, Brewer, and Faircloth, the original dormitories, were equipped with sensors, "which control the temperature in areas instead of individual rooms."[23] About that time, Joe Baker threatened to employ a full-time thermostat adjuster.

Students did not exhaust their fervor in the energy crisis; they exerted an abundance of it in questioning the ongoing compulsory attendance policy at convocation. Their complaints disparaged not only the policy but also the programs—mediocre at best, they said—and poor faculty attendance. President Weems appointed five faculty members and five students to lead a discussion of the matter at the December 1973 faculty meeting and later to make recommendations. By the following April, the ad hoc committee submitted a resolution which the faculty was ready to adopt and the students wanted to hear: The attendance requirement would be dropped and the schedule changed from weekly to monthly convocations. The resolution also called for a standing convocation committee and funds to underwrite its work.

If students hungered for interesting programs at convocations and other events, some speakers doubtless helped to satisfy those appetites. In March 1974, United States Senator John Tunney, Democrat of California, kicked off a four-day symposium on "The Press, the President, and the People." The topic was timely, given an intense interest in the burgeoning Watergate scandal. In successive sessions, North Carolina's Attorney General Robert Morgan; State Senator Hamilton Horton from Forsyth County; Henry Hall Wilson, former White House aide; Britt Hume, an associate of syndicated columnist Jack Anderson; and *Raleigh Times* editor, A.C. Snow, lit up the stage of Jones Auditorium with such topics as "The Press and Mr. Nixon: the Case for the Defense" and "Responsibility of the Press to the Office Holder."

In less than six months, Richard Nixon resigned as president of the United States. As he sank in the quagmire of his administration's desperate attempt to bury its misdeeds, he took high-ranking officials with him. The debacle that mesmerized the nation through months of intrigue and despair ended with Senate hearings, bringing to light the culpability of the president and his conspirators. Participants on both sides of the law—many who might otherwise have become footnotes in history—achieved celebrity status. Some spoke at Meredith. For example, Jill Wine Vogler of the Watergate Special Prosecution Force delivered the 1974 commencement address; six months later, Egil Krogh, Jr., Nixon's undersecretary of transportation and the first of the Watergate coverup team to be sentenced for his involvement, addressed a convocation audience on the topic of "Prison: the Great Equalizer."

Uninvolved in Watergate but one of the year's more controversial speakers, Sidney Abbott was relegated to an evening engagement, even though the SGA had proposed that she address a Monday morning convocation audience. But at the time of the proposal, the required attendance policy was still in effect; therefore, the student government representatives compromised, agreeing to an evening event where attendance was voluntary. The booking of Abbott, a lesbian and author of *Sappho Was a Right-On Woman,* led to some consternation by students who opposed an avowed lesbian's having a campus forum, and, according to

President Weems, the whole affair challenged the 1966 speaker policy as set forth by the Board of Trustees to "insure orderly practices in keeping with the academic freedom and excellence maintained at Meredith College."[24] Banning the engagement, however, would call into question the policy's "academic freedom" clause.

No cloud of contention hovered over the campus when Shana Alexander addressed a convocation audience in December 1975, but perhaps some apprehension rained down when she suggested to the *News and Observer* that "the written word is becoming extinct."[25] A regular on CBS television's highly rated *Sixty Minutes*, Alexander was the first woman on the writing staff of *Life* Magazine and the first female editor of *McCall's*.

Lectures, concerts, drama, and art exhibitions, usually open to the public, have contributed to the scholarship—and the entertainment—of the Meredith family and the Raleigh community since the early 1900s. Annual events such as Religious Emphasis Week, Black Emphasis Week, Founders' Day, and commencement, as well as one-time occasions such as symposia and workshops, have also left a legacy of interesting speakers—some well-known, some not—who imparted substantive thoughts and compelling words. Established lectureships, however, were relatively new. The Distinguished Faculty Lectures, introduced in 1964, continued, and, in 1973, Meredith announced its inaugural Staley Distinguished Christian Scholar Lecture. Eric Charles Rust, professor of Christian philosophy at Southern Baptist Theological Seminary, spoke on "Christian Thought in a Naturalistic Era." Two years later, the lectureship became the first such series to be endowed. The Thomas F. Staley Foundation was the benefactor.

The lecturers' stage and the listeners' arena converged on a direct path to the classroom and wherever else learning took place—in the basement of Poteat Residence Hall, for instance. Lyn Aubrecht, assistant professor of psychology, created an animal laboratory there, where would-be experimental psychologists gained knowledge in the concepts of their science. At first, eight rats occupied the premises, but the rodent family soon grew to a dynasty of twelve—Billie, Laverne, Waldo, Maggie, Bo, Delve, Niki, Josephine, Tammi, Hermann, Chew, "and their sister." The *Twig* took note of their "special suite," featuring "air-conditioning, piped-in music, breakfast in bed, and maid service . . . ."[26] Dr. Aubrecht eventually displaced the animal experiments with technology.

Ideas born in laboratories, classrooms, and meeting rooms often served as springboards for new programs, as in 1973, when the Academic Council determined that a senior might earn a second but different baccalaureate degree by meeting certain requirements, including at least thirty additional hours in residence. And, while new programs were conceived, old ones were often reconsidered. Through all the years and in great numbers, Meredith women had become teachers, and many of them still prepared for that profession. Although career choices were less predictable in 1975, teacher education was very much a part of the plan when the curriculum committee proposed the awarding of continuing education units for non-credit enrichment courses in order "to have a standard of reporting educational efforts from one institution to another."[27] The State Department of Public Instruction gave the proposal a boost by its willingness to accept CEUs as a basis of credit for teacher recertification. Meredith's stellar teacher education program had recently received reaccreditation.

Also in 1975, Meredith, the only private college in North Carolina so recognized, received full accreditation by the Council on Social Work Education. The long struggle was over. The College had been granted constituent membership in 1969, which was continued on a year-to-year basis. Although the council had placed Meredith on probation for the 1973 spring term, it encouraged the College to reapply after implementing planned improvements. And a September letter from Leslie Syron to President Weems conveyed the good news that the program had indeed been approved for another year. Dr. Syron pointed with pride to two graduates of the Class of 1973 who placed at the second-semester level as they started their master's program in the Graduate School of Social Work at the University of North Carolina: "When a 'new baby' program is regarded as equivalent to the first semester of graduate school work, I think you can beam with pleasure!" she said.[28]

Syron, herself, "beamed with pleasure" when she reported the possibility of Meredith's becoming the "first college in North Carolina . . . to launch a Human Services Program."[29] Human services, wrote Suzanne Reynolds in the *Alumnae Magazine*, would encourage students "who want to work with people" to set their career goals.[30] A departmental brochure clearly explained the theory behind the program: "Think how art, music, psychology, or sociology could be used in a career in rehabilitation," it proffered.[31] The primary component of the curriculum would be an internship in the student's chosen field, preparation for which would include development of attitude, skills, and knowledge. On the subject of "working with people," Reynolds quoted Dean Burris: "Meredith College has always been committed to encouraging its students to be humanitarians. The number of our alumnae who through their vocations and avocations have performed services which enhance the quality of life witness to this commitment."[32] Implementation of the program, to be directed by sociology instructor Eugene Sumner, was scheduled for the fall semester of 1974.

About the same time, the history department inaugurated its Capital City Semester, a block course in which Meredith women with students from other colleges immersed themselves in state government. They saw politics in action, participated in seminars, heard speakers from several branches of government, volunteered their services, and wrote research papers. After the first semester, Dean Burris reported that the pilot project "did not attract as many students from other colleges as we had hoped, but it was very successful for our own students."[33] The course survived, and a year later the department inaugurated a new major in political studies.

In those years, Meredith's role on the stage of academe underwent intense scrutiny. The script was reread and often rewritten as new offerings diversified the curriculum; as career emphases threatened—in the minds of purists—the liberal arts tradition; as Scholastic Aptitude Test scores dropped nationally while grades at Meredith rose dramatically; as tenure for faculty could not be counted on as an automatic reward for length of service; and as Meredith weighed its mission of educating women in the context of the Triangle's burgeoning population.

The administration vowed to make endowed professorships a top priority, aiming for at least one such professorship in every academic department. A grant for educational enrichment from the William R. Kenan, Jr., Charitable Trust significantly boosted that hope, and, in May 1975, the College named its first distinguished visiting professor: Arthur Poister joined the music faculty for the 1975–76 school year. While he had retired from Syracuse University eight years earlier, he had held similar professorships in as many colleges, universities, and conservatories as he had accumulated years of retirement. "Dr. Poister," said department chairman, David Lynch, "is probably the most influential organ teacher in the United States."[34] Having studied under Poister, Lynch spoke from experience. The pupil's admiration of the teacher was further evidenced by Lynch's covert trip to Syracuse University to help dismantle and ship to Raleigh Poister's old teaching organ. The visiting professor's discovery of it in his Meredith studio was a happy surprise.

Dr. Poister's appointment, which continued for a second year, was made possible by the Kenan grant. Both the grant and the appointment attested to and enhanced Meredith's academic reputation. Other evidences of that repute had preceded and would follow the first visiting professor. For example, two national honorary societies/fraternities—Pi Kappa Lambda, music, and Phi Alpha Theta, history—chartered chapters at the College in 1973 and 1975, respectively. Only one year later, Meredith's Phi Omicron Chapter of Phi Alpha Theta was named the best chapter in Division I colleges, the competition including more then one-hundred colleges. At the same time, the faculty reflected a 10 percent rise in the number of doctorates—to about 50 percent. Eighty percent of all department heads could claim that distinction.

Meredith continued its quest for outstanding visiting professors, and it was no less diligent in its search for permanent teaching scholars. The College appointed new chairmen of three academic departments in two years. Ione Kemp Knight, '43, was named acting chairman of the Department of English for the fall semester of 1973 while Norma Rose was on sabbatical leave. With Mary Lynch Johnson and Dr. Rose, Dr. Knight was one of "the Big Three," a student-coined epithet that carried through Dr. Johnson's retirement. Knight had headed the English department at Shorter College before returning to Meredith, her alma mater. She earned the master's degree at the University of Pennsylvania and the Ph.D. at the University of North Carolina at Chapel Hill before engaging in post-doctoral research at the University of London, the British Museum, and Oxford University.

William Bradley Turpin came in 1973 to chair the psychology department; however, he remained for only one year, having been replaced in 1974 by R. John Huber from Skidmore College. Dr. Huber, 33, was not only the youngest department chairman but also the first Roman Catholic on the faculty. After twenty years, he would reminisce about his own and Meredith's heritage, calling his tenure "a good fit." He said, "When I was in Providence, Rhode Island, I saw the first Baptist church that was built in the United States, and when I went in and looked at it, I felt a kinship. I . . . felt I was a part of the system and serving that system. A notion of stewardship comes to mind. . . . "[35] Dr. Huber earned the B.A. degree at Kent State University, the M.A. at the University of Vermont, and the Ph.D. at the University of New Hampshire.

Also in 1973, Joseph Browde left Columbia College for Meredith to chair the education department. Dr. Browde earned the B.A. degree at Rutgers University and the M.A. and Ed.D. at Syracuse. While he held a B.D. from Eastern Baptist Theological Seminary, he could be heard occasionally in the pulpit of Raleigh's First Presbyterian Church—and could usually be seen in the choir.

While departments greeted new chairmen, the Carlyle Campbell Library rallied around its new acting head, when Jane Deese retired and Michael Dodge became her successor. About the same time, the library welcomed a 300 percent increase in funds for acquisitions, the growth in income including a grant from the Arthur Vining Davis Foundation for library endowment.

IN 1974, ONE might have thought it premature to look ahead as far as 1990 to student population worries, but a thirty-year decline in enrollment at private colleges signaled difficulties ahead. The decline had not yet affected the College; in fact, in 1973–74, Meredith had enjoyed its largest student body to date, and indications were that enrollment in 1974–75 would surpass that peak. But Weems expressed concern at the small number of commuters: "Within a 20-mile radius of our campus are approximately 600,000 people. Projections . . . suggest that this area will contain 1.2 million by 1990. We would be smart to see this as a pool of potential applicants. . . . It will be necessary for us to expand our efforts in the direction of community students."[36] He pointed to possibilities: "We view the continuing education program as the launching pad for many adult students who will ultimately seek a degree at Meredith. The success of this program could contribute handsomely to our stability."[37] Already Mrs. Dahle was reporting that several non-traditional-age students, who had entered on a non-credit basis, had changed their status and were seeking credit. And the admissions office expanded its efforts, increasing the number of commuter applicants by 100 percent in the next two years.

As analyses continued, the summer school schedule changed in 1974 from one five-week term to three three-week sessions, each class meeting three hours daily. The new calendar would accommodate public school teachers as well as Meredith students who might wish to attend additional summer sessions elsewhere.

A summer's study in England was an exciting new venture in 1974. The idea went on trial as two faculty members and twenty-two students accomplished a semester's work in London that summer. Roger Crook, chairman of the Department of Religion, had been named director of Meredith in Europe at the beginning of the spring semester, and he, his wife, and one of his six sons spent the summer in England, as did Sally Page of the English department. Dr. Page taught English drama, and Dr. Crook taught the history of Christianity in England. They were joined by Peter Feek, an English educator, who offered a class in the ancient history of the country. Then the three professors collaborated on a course that introduced contemporary England, supplementing class work with tours to historical sites. The 1975 version of Meredith Abroad (the program's new name) saw the number of students increase by five and the faculty members by one. The College thus entered a time when every Meredith student would have "the opportunity to spend one semester in Europe, being taught by our own faculty members, . . . to provide a full semester's credit with little, if any, more cost than a semester on our campus in Raleigh."[38]

Possibilities for Meredith Abroad seemed to reach as far as one could see; however, the College sometimes cast a wary eye toward trends that occasionally crept unnoticed into the scheme of things. In November 1973, Dean Burris mentioned to the Academic Council that "grading standards and practices" might need attention.[39] And early in the spring term of 1974, Eleanor Hill used her editorial privilege to denounce in the *Twig* the unusually high number of students on the dean's list for the previous semester, her critical piece warning against Meredith's becoming an "insignificant diploma mill. . . ."[40] But Mary Bland Josey assured the faculty that the College had held steadily to the number of students in the top quarter of their high school graduating classes; however, she reported that Scholastic Aptitude Test scores had decreased nationally over the previous decade. President Weems echoed Josey's observation, recalling the nationwide drop in the verbal portion of the SAT from its original norm of 500 to its then-current average of 448. He quickly quoted statistics for Meredith: with an average of 487, he said, the College was thirty-nine points above the national verbal mean score that year.[41] Josey also commented that first-year grade averages at Meredith had climbed from 2.20 in 1963 to 2.63 in 1972. Dr. Lemmon pointed to the curriculum revision in 1969 for a partial explanation: "Now instead of the freshmen being required to take certain subjects," she said, "they are allowed choices enabling them to gravitate toward the area in which they feel most confident."[42] The dialogue continued. In a letter to the editor, Josey answered some of the *Twig's* allegations:

> In drawing inferences from the proportion of students on the Dean's List and of freshmen with B averages or higher (33 percent of the year's freshman class), all of us need to . . . view these facts in proper context. In 1969 there were changes in the academic program which included more flexibility in course choices for the freshman year than existed in the past.
>
> Though the *Twig* and I share the same concern about the length of the Dean's List, we need to recognize there are legitimate philosophies about grading that differ from ours. As long as we have sound instruction, none of us need quibble too much over grade point averages. . . . Do students enter Meredith expecting a more challenging program than they find? . . .[43]

Also by way of the *Twig*, Frank Grubbs, professor of history, joined the conversation:

> I am somewhat concerned that our students will read your editorials and believe that things are going down at Meredith. This is not the case. Returning alumnae are constantly amazed at the progress which Meredith has made since they graduated. Let us not create a "gasoline panic" when calling for better programs. I think that your point is well taken: you wish to make a good college better.[44]

A second editorial apologized for having omitted a reference in Josey's letter to an article in the *News and Observer*, which reported that colleges nationwide were noting a rise in students' grades.

THE COLLEGE WAS small enough to adapt its academic offerings and practices to its students' needs yet large enough to offer a varied selection. But still the winds of specialization swirled more briskly than some liberal arts traditionalists thought safe. Dean Burris pointed to the earliest catalogues of Baptist Female University which "made no distinction between liberal arts and vocation."[45] And President Weems said, "Women are becoming more determined to use their college training in economically productive ways. . . . Our versatility in this area is . . . one of the major reasons for immediate past successes."[46]

By 1973, Marie Capel, the assistant dean of students for vocational guidance, carried a new title: director of placement and vocational guidance. From its genesis in 1971 as liaison between students and the job market or graduate school, the office had grown in those two years to include vocational guidance and testing. In Ms. Capel's first year at Meredith, she organized a Graduate School Day, in which eleven schools participated and—a first for Meredith—she administered the Graduate Record Exam on the campus. During the spring semester, recruiters interviewed more than two-hundred student job applicants.

Also in 1973, Meredith received a federal grant to study the feasibility of a venture into cooperative education. Mary Yarbrough, former chairman of the chemistry department, was campus adviser. In 1974, after a year of discussing possibilities and gathering convincing information, the College gave the new program its blessing. A student with at least fifty-eight hours of college credit could alternate a semester of study with a period of full-time, career-related employment and earn academic credit for it. While the program's opportunities were not immediately seized upon by large numbers of students, other facets of career planning—seminars, job fairs, career days, day-to-day guidance—became increasingly popular. In 1974, representatives of school systems, graduate schools, and businesses interviewed more than 500 Meredith students. The office expanded its program of career development, and its new name—Office of Career Services and Cooperative Education—reflected the change. It also moved from Johnson Hall to Cate Center, a mecca for some of the student services not categorized as strictly academic.

Attesting to the College's commitment to provide vocational guidance and pre-professional direction for its students, attorney Paul Holcomb, director of estate planning, assumed the role of adviser to pre-law students, and Clara Bunn, chairman of the biology department, to pre-med students. In addition to law, medicine, and social work courses, pre-professional studies were established over the ensuing years in such areas as dentistry, veterinary science, theology, library science, special education, journalism, and others. For the first time in 1974, through Cooperating Raleigh Colleges, Meredith women could participate in North Carolina State's year-old Reserve Officer Training Corps (ROTC). Subsequent college catalogues stipulated that an Army or an Air Force commission was possible under the program.

"REAL WORLD" MATTERS were often weighed heavily on the grounds of both cultural and academic considerations. The voting booth's accessibility to the student was one such issue. The student life committee submitted to the Academic Council a resolution strongly urging the suspension of classes on election day, November 6, 1973, but the council's vote nullified the resolution. An editorial in the *Twig*, implying that teachers often scheduled tests on election day to make time to cast their own votes, deplored the decision: "Students who cut classes to go home and vote would not be allowed to take make-up tests; therefore, Meredith students are [subtly] being prevented from voting."[47] The editorial writer apparently had not received word of Dr. Lemmon's motion in Administrative-Academic Council to amend the schedule for 1974 so as to offer no classes on election day and to compensate for the lost class time by deleting a day from autumn recess. Two years later, the subject returned to the Administrative-Academic Council in the form of a resolution calling for suspension of classes for election primaries, as well. Dr. Thomas moved, Dr. Burris seconded, adoption of the resolution, but the discussion that followed produced a majority vote of "nay." In the same meeting, the Council voted to suspend classes for three hours on Meredith's first Play Day since 1966.

On February 24, 1973, the trustees held their own election. Clara Carswell of Charlotte and United States freshman Senator Jesse Helms of Raleigh were tapped to fill two- and three-year unexpired terms, respectively. Mrs. Carswell was present and, after the unanimous vote, took her seat on the board. Senator Helms had sent regrets. Mrs. Carswell's potential effectiveness on the body was not questioned by the community; however, Helms's election was an enigma to many. The archetypal southern conservative's representing one of the moderate southern states was considered by some to be unusual in itself; that he would be making policy for a college identified as progressive seemed an anomaly to his critics. Faculty and staff hesitated to react negatively in public, but *Twig* editor, Janice Sams, was fearless:

> "Guilt by association" can be extremely detrimental to an institution of higher learning, particularly one which strives academically to mold free and responsible women into involved citizens. . . .
>
> The unanimous election of Senator Jesse Helms to the Board of Trustees will probably not destroy [Meredith's] image, but I do not think his selection can be made without some question or comment. As an editorialist with WRAL-TV in Raleigh, Senator Helms often employed an attitude which seems entirely too contradictory to the very principles by which Meredith College stands.[48]

Sams cited Helms's position as a proponent of the Speaker Ban Law; his attacks on Martin Luther King in particular and the Civil Rights Movement in general; his opposition to Medicare and other social issues. As it turned out, Helms attended no meetings of the Board in his three-year term, allowing those fearing his influence to breathe a collective sigh of relief.

Another trustee election made history at the 1975 Baptist State Convention in Asheville when Lucile Oliver of Pinelevel became the first female non-alumna to gain a seat on the Board.

CONCERNS OF AND *for* students were as much in the Meredith tradition as were the seriousness of academics and the hilarity of Cornhuskin'. But as the cultural landscape shifted, so did the vantage points for change. The early- to mid-seventies found Meredith still feeling its way toward meeting the needs of minority students. In February 1973, Black Voices in Unity—organized in 1972 as Black Student Unity—sponsored its first annual Black Awareness Week. Through oratory, art, music, film, and live drama, the week indeed stirred an awareness of black culture and was described by the *Raleigh Times* as "an attempt to give white students a new insight into what it means to be black. It also was designed to help increase black self-awareness among the black students."[49] The emphasis helped editor Sams of the *Twig* appreciate "what we . . . must continually strive for if we are ever to relate as human beings to each other."[50] Soon afterwards, BVU called for "better circumstances" at the College.[51] Its charges of individual harrassment and humiliation were particularly serious. The organization also asserted that black women were not elected to leadership positions nor inducted into Silver Shield; that minorities were not represented in the admissions office; that few minority professors taught few minority studies; and that Meredith offered no counseling for black students. Sadly, some of BVU's concerns—particularly those relating to individual behavior—might have lingered to some degree at Meredith, as they did in many communities of mixed races and differing cultures. But they and other accusations have been addressed over the years. In 1994, Dean Burris said, "Generally speaking, for the last twenty-five years, we've been committed to trying to attract black faculty, and we've attracted some good ones. We have hired a good many Black Americans—and other races, for that matter—but it has not been an easy road." If they were really good, he said, "they would get offers at higher salaries than Meredith could pay; otherwise, they would leave for the same reasons that white teachers leave"—because they were working toward advanced degrees, because they didn't fit in here, or because they weren't competent.[52] As to whether the student body should reflect society, to the degree that it is possible for a single-sex college to do so, Burris said, "I don't think the student body has to reflect. It is self-selecting. I hope people who come from a culture that's a little different feel welcome here, whether they're African-Americans or South Asians."[53]

The *Twig*'s first edition of the 1973–74 term introduced "Joyce Martin's Black Perspective," a column that assured minority students a voice through the newspaper. Late in that college generation, Deborah Matthews, '77, served on the Judicial Board of the Student Government Association and as president of the day students. In 1977–78, Joyce Montgomery, '78, chaired the Judicial Board, was named to *Who's Who in American Colleges and Universities,* and was tapped into Silver Shield. Both Matthews and Montgomery were African-Americans, as was Yvette Brown, 1989–90 president of the SGA and, as a freshman, was president of her class. And, in 1989, the Office of Admissions employed Vanessa Goodman, '88, who had been elected president of her senior class, as a recruitment assistant for minorities; in 1993, Ms. Goodman was named assistant director of admissions.

BVU also requested professional counseling, as had some individual students. The SGA's legislative board and student life committee proposed the creation of such a position; the administration approved; and Elizabeth Wilson, the first full-time college counselor, joined the dean of students' staff in the fall of 1973.

Students' concerns covered a wide range of issues, some as narrow as others were broad, many involving rules for campus living and regulations governing the community. Some of their issues continued into the nineties. For example, open house, which would include male visitation in the residence halls, was an ongoing topic for discussion. In the fall term of 1973, the legislative board of the SGA considered a bill that would allow a three-hour "open house" on Sunday afternoons. In 1974, however, the trustees upheld the president's veto.

At the same time, the student life committee called for revision of the drug policy, deleting the words "mandatory suspension or expulsion" for known violations. The committee preferred the penalty of probation, inasmuch as it provided some opportunity of "helping a fellow student with her [drug] problem, rather than multiplying her woes with swift punitive action."[54]

The intensity of such discussions was eased by what seemed to be comic relief, such as an SGA report in the *Twig*: "Dr. Weems has now approved the hair roller policy. . . . Rollers can now be worn everynight [sic] in the cafeteria and during Saturday and Sunday breakfast. Rollers can also be worn in the library on Saturday afternoons."[55]

The "lighter side" could also apply to some of the entertainment that students booked for themselves. The Bathtub Ring, a campus singing group, could usually count on a "gig" for a traditional event or two. Founded in 1968 by Betty King, Ayn Sullivan, and Peggy Timmerman, all members of the Class of 1970, the group had first performed during Rush Week at a Phi luau. The *Student Handbook* reads, "Their blend of rebellion against and honoring of Meredith traditions has made them a perennial favorite at Cornhuskin' and other campus events."[56] In the late nineties, the Bathtub Ring was still alive and well as underclass women had replaced—by audition, of course—graduating seniors. But for some occasions, students went far afield to find their crowd-pleasers. Such was the case in 1974 when creative juniors transformed the usually formal junior-senior into a party of jeans-clad classmates, seniors, and their dates. While spaghetti was the only entree on the menu, the real main course was an after-dinner concert by the world-renowned Serendipity Singers. And, taking advantage of the football season at neighboring universities, students, with the help of Dean Joyce White, planned mixers with West Point cadets for the Friday nights before the UNC-Army game in October and the Duke-Army game in November. The *Twig* reviewed the October invasion: "Dancing rarely lagged as the band, 'Faded Blue,' played excellent music."[57] The gym provided the dance floor; the hut offered a coffee house for conversation; and the new Cate Center attracted the pool players.

Cate Center opened in the 1972–73 school year and was dedicated on Founders' Day, 1974. It provided space for student activities on the second floor and the post office, book store, and Kresge Auditorium on the first. The center was named in honor of Kemp Shields Cate of Chapel Hill, whose great niece, Frances Cate, was a sophomore at the time, and whose niece, Jane Cate Fowler, had graduated in 1953. The retired escheats officer at the University of North Carolina had given Meredith more than $400,000, the College's largest single gift to date. Cate's contribution was supplemented by grants from the Z. Smith Reynolds and Kresge Foundations.

As Cate Center became functional, trustees targeted other areas for change. They determined in September 1973 to construct a new riding ring, "properly designed and large enough to accommodate horse shows."[58] The new show ring was dedicated on Founders' Day, 1976, in memory of Zeno Martin, business manager and treasurer, 1943–53, who was primarily responsible for bringing equitation to Meredith, and in honor of Lorna Bell Broughton, '16. In April, Mrs. Broughton's brother, Victor Bell, co-sponsored the arena's first major event, a show attracting more than two hundred participants.

Another structure had already taken shape in the minds of administrators and trustees and, later, on the drawing boards of architect Carter Williams. In February 1973, Claude Williams, vice chairman of the trustees' buildings and grounds committee, recommended that the College build a fine arts building to ease the crowding of the music and art facilities. With the stipulation that approximately one-third of the needed funds would be in hand before the first brick was laid, the board voted "aye" to the recommendation. Since 1949, the music department had thrived in

The 1974 show, Applause, *receives acclaim, as does Jones Auditorium, then recently renovated to serve as a theater.*

and outgrown its space in Jones Auditorium and Music Building; the art department claimed foster homes all over the campus, but Joyner Hall was its headquarters. The trustees also instructed the College to air-condition and refurbish Jones Hall—its auditorium for music and drama productions, its classrooms and practice areas for the teaching of art and drama. On completion, the renovations received rave reviews. Of the auditorium, drama critic Bill Morrison wrote in the *News and Observer,* "It's a most handsome theater, comfortable and acoustically sound, with the show [*Applause*] soaring easily to the upper reaches of the balcony. . . . "[59]

As committees and individuals pondered the proper location for the new building—ultimately being designed only for music—they suffered through eleven months of indecision. Until they knew where to build, they could not know when to start. By January 1974, the decision seemed conclusive. Some trustees pictured the structure between the Mae Grimmer Alumnae House and Joyner Hall, but students, faculty, and alumnae voiced opposition. In addition, the master plan showed a yet-to-be-built chapel on that very spot. Eight months later, the building sat—in the mind's eye and only briefly—between Cate Center and the Weatherspoon Building. Finally, in September, the trustees decided to house the music department close to its roots, its new home to be constructed next to Jones Hall and overlooking the lake and amphitheater.

The location was generally agreed upon by the trustees, even if it meant the dismantling of the old log hut nearby. Built in 1942 for meetings and social occasions, the hut had become, of late, a coffee house. The cozy friendliness of roaring blazes in its two mammoth stone fireplaces had alleviated many a case of homesickness in students who, because of the times and the social regulations, had been limited by having few places to go and fewer ways to get there. Both they and the faculty— particularly the long-timers—disparaged destruction of the hut but were assured the trustees would consider a new version of the old cabin at a later date. In fact, said Joe Baker, they considered moving the hut to a different location until the lowest bid came in at $35,000.

As construction of the music building began, the President's Dining Room, which would accommodate up to sixty people, was almost ready for use. In the lower regions of Belk Hall, the handsome but windowless dining area was carved out of the forty-five-year-old dark and eerie passageway familiarly known as the tunnel. While less than ideal, especially for claustrophobic diners, the President's Dining Room was rarely empty at the dinner hour, its popularity extending beyond the College to the community.

Plans for the President's Dining Room, Cate Center, and the music building were carefully laid before the launching in 1968 of the Meredith College Advancement Program (MCAP), the most ambitious to date of all Meredith's fund-raising drives. The goal of MCAP was $5 million in five years, the money to finance five new buildings, renovations of older structures, and miscellaneous college needs. On Founders' Day in 1973, the year that Meredith's gift income exceeded $1 million for the first time, MCAP chairman, Shearon Harris, announced that commitments had exceeded the goal by $93,000. Indeed, five new buildings—the Weatherspoon Physical Education and Recreation Building; the Massey House; Heilman and Barefoot Residence Halls; and Cate College and Continuing Education Center—attested to the success of the drive.

The financial picture was good in 1973, and the administration intended to keep it that way. Despite inflation—"the greatest financial problem facing our college in these uncertain times," said Weems[60]—guardians of the purse strings made every effort to hold tuition and fees to affordable levels, particularly in light of the fact that, in 1974, 20–22 percent of the students received financial aid. In 1973, the $2,600 cost for a year at Meredith was considerably lower than private education's national average of $3,241. Opponents of below-average student charges argued that the faculty and staff, therefore, could not be paid on the level of institutions of like kind. The College compensated, at least to some degree, with benefits and privileges. But some of the remuneration for services rendered was dictated by Federal law. For example, Vice President Baker announced in April 1974 that the new Wage and Hour Law would affect some pay scales and that on May 1, the effective date of the bill, "all Meredith employees would be paid at least $2 per hour."[61] His annual report contained even better news: "Effective July 1, 1974 every employee at Meredith will be eligible for the same fringe benefits regardless of position."[62]

In 1975, the State of North Carolina slightly brightened the economic futures of its private colleges and their in-state students, earmarking $200 per student for each school's financial aid account and a tuition grant of $100 per semester for each undergraduate North Carolinian.

President Weems, the futurist, insisted early that Meredith develop a substantial endowment. In his fourth year, he could point with pardonable pride to the growing financial base and to his administration's endowment goal of $30,000,000. At the time, approximately $3 million had been added to the coffers.

The president also predicted the importance of computer technology to institutions like Meredith. In three years, the College advanced from a data-processing system of limited use to a computer terminal connected to the Triangle Universities Computer Center. "One of the major uses of the computer will be information retrieval," said Weems. "It is my philosophy that the best decisions can be made by those people with the most accurate information. . . ."[63] Congruent with his statement was his decision that Meredith's trustees would be "the most informed board in the country."[64] And primarily for their information but also for myriad other uses, he initiated two publications: first, in the earlier years, the

President's Notebook series, and later, Strategic Planning Documents, both of which emanated from his office at the rate of several each year.

Video technology also made its debut in 1973–74. A studio camera using black-and-white film, a video-cassette player, and a television receiver were the first components of the eventual impressive store of technical equipment to swell the holdings of the Carlyle Campbell Library.

Library holdings have always been a measure of academic effectiveness. But no yardstick, thermometer, scale, or vessel could gauge the energy expended by a college like Meredith for the general well-being of its students, whether they wanted it or not. Concern for students' safety had increased over the years as the need for it had multiplied. The rounds of one nightwatchman— sufficient security for most of the previous years— was perceived as more apropos of the Victorian era than of the restless society of the seventies. The student population, as well as the number of campus facilities, had grown, and students came and went during later hours. As of 1972, nighttime security guards complemented the daytime force. In 1974, Mr. Baker reported that they would receive police training in the use of firearms and academic training from Wake Technical Institute. Daniel G. Shattuck was named the first chief of security in 1972; when he retired in 1996, his successor, Michael Hoke, inherited a force of fifteen women and men who wore badges but carried no guns.

AS THE COLLEGE was concerned for its students, alumnae were concerned for their college. Among President Weems's early observations was that Meredith alumnae "must be the most fiercely loyal in the world. . . ."[65] And Dean Burris remembered his first impressions of Meredith in 1969: "I was young and green and used to other settings; I had never before seen alumnae[/alumni] like the alumnae here."[66] Their material gifts were one measure of their devotion. Inspired by new development on the west campus, Laura Weatherspoon Harrill, '27, a participant in the Weatherspoon family's gift of the physical education building, assumed her own personal project of soliciting funds for the purchase of oak trees to be planted near Cate Center and the Weatherspoon Building. The slogan of her direct mail campaign to alumnae was "Go MOD with me in '73," MOD being the acronym for Meredith Oak Donor. Through her landscape gardener's discerning eye, Mrs. Harrill envisioned an avenue of oaks extending from the Mae Grimmer Alumnae House to the Massey

House. Her project resulted in the planting of ninety trees, including a grove of twenty at Cate Center. The grove—each tree of a variety different from the others—was Lucile Withers Ferrell's gift in honor of her Class of 1907.

While Harrill beautified the landscape, Sarah Elizabeth Vernon Watts, '34, refurbished the Harris Rare Books Room in the Carlyle Campbell Library for a historical collection. Not only did she furnish the room, but she also undertook the job of collecting items of historical significance. Portraits of Thomas Meredith and his wife, Georgia Sears Meredith, dominate the wall space over a display case of treasures such as President Richard Vann's Bible from the cornerstone of old Faircloth Hall on the original campus; Lillian Parker Wallace's Phi Beta Kappa key; President Carlyle Campbell's watch; the original words and music to "You're the Queen of Our Hearts," by Mary O'Kelly Peacock, '26; and the Gold Medallion, the Governor's Award for Achievement in Literature, which was presented to Bernice Kelly Harris, '13, the first novelist to be published by the University of North Carolina Press. In the Harris Room, books and original art work abound, and individual and class scrapbooks combine to write their own biography of the College. Occupying shelf space with museum pieces are contemporary file boxes, one for each class, "cunningly made to look like beautiful books bound in maroon"[67] and gilt-stamped with the college seal. Inside each file are appropriate memorabilia—programs, snapshots, and the like—from the class represented. The boxes were a gift of William M. Watts and his corporation, Mid-State Paper Box Company.

Throughout Meredith's history, alumnae have given money, personal treasures, time, leadership, and talents. They have also given of themselves to their society and, therefore, to their College. In 1975, Susan Jackson Mellette, '42, associate professor of internal medicine at the Medical College of Virginia, received the Virginia Cancer Society's highest award for her outstanding contributions to cancer control, and Betty Duckworth, '68, was named manager for female affirmative action for the southern region of the Xerox Corporation; in 1974, Anne Bryan, '71, was elected president of the Meredith College Alumnae Association, the youngest woman in many years to hold that office; in 1973, Elizabeth Davis Reid, '46, filled a seat on the Raleigh City Council, and Casey McDaniel, '73, became a special agent with the State Bureau of Investigation, proving that even very young women were capturing jobs previously reserved for men.

ON OCTOBER 1, 1972, Oliver L. Stringfield, M.D., son of Oliver Larkin Stringfield, early fund raiser for BFU, wrote President Weems a letter:

> You said you were surprised by Meredith girls at first "because they come on so strong." Do you know why? Anyone who has been on the campus for any length of time will get that unconscious feeling of well being by noting the uplifted faces of the girls and their "doing their own thing." There is an invisible CANOPY hovering over the campus supplyed [sic] and governed by the Almighty which supplys [sic] the fuel for this spirit. There you have it.[68]

Meredith liked to think that if students "came on strong," they exemplified the benefits of a woman's college environment. In any case, they contributed greatly to spirit and to academic reputation. In the 1973 North Carolina Student Legislature, the Best Small College Legislation Award went to the Meredith delegation that sponsored a bill "for protection of information or sources received and used by a newsperson."[69] That same spring, Cathy Murff won a Phi Beta Kappa Award for her paper titled "North Bloodworth Street: the Effects of Economic Progress," which was judged "the best historical research done by a student in Wake County in the past year."[70] And Debbie Edge received the same award in 1975 for "William Boylan: Adopted Son of Wake County." The list grew to include Julie Jones for "Whigs in the North Carolina Revolutionary Period"; Mazie Fleetwood for "North Carolina Supreme Court Justices of the Nineteenth Century"; and the fifth history major in seven years so recognized, Nancy Martin for her paper on the Pearsal Plan. And the near "monopoly" continued into the eighties when Phyllis Wurst, '84, again captured the prize, and Silda Wall, '80, won the State Historical Society's Hugh Lefler Award for her paper titled "Josephus Daniels: Personal Injector in Political Policy."

In 1974, another talented student, sophomore Beth Leavel, worked magic through her original choreography for *Applause*, the fall playhouse production. Ms. Leavel had studied dance before entering Meredith, but her love for the stage was sparked by drama coach Linda Bamford's having realized her potential in choreography, and by her previous year's role

as Rabbit in the College's production of *Winnie-the-Pooh*.[71] In his review
for the *News and Observer*, Bill Morrison wrote that *Applause* was "con-
vincingly danced—with several droll touches along the way from chore-
ographer Beth Leavel. . . . " He also hinted of things to come: "The show
had a Broadway sheen. . . ."[72] Even before the rave review, Leavel con-
fessed to the *Twig* that she dreamed of working on Broadway. The cast
thought she was well on the way, and indeed she was. In her first major
role there, she sang, danced, and acted her way into the character of
Annie Reilly—"Anytime Annie"—in the multi-year run of *42nd Street*.

For Beth Leavel, Broadway was the road to success; for Meredith,
Hillsborough Street was still the road to everywhere in town. The College and the city never developed the "town versus gown" rivalry of
some academic communities. To the contrary, history records numerous
instances of happy cooperation. On the memorable occasion of July 4,
1973, Meredith welcomed 8,000 revelers who rocked the campus at the
city's "first Independence Day celebration in years. . . ."[73] Memories of
the event lingered, at least in the mind of columnist A.C. Snow, who
wrote in the gloom of the following February, "The Meredith ducks . . .
made news last July 4 when, during [director] Ira Wood's 'Richard, the
Third' at Meredith's pond, they drowned out the actors' lines with their
quacking."[74]

WHEN SENIOR CLASS president, Jo Ann Williford, unveiled the 1975 class
doll, she described the doll's apparel: skirt, tank top, sheer shirt, tie scarf,
clogs, and an International Women's Year pin. That summer, the *Alumnae Magazine* pictured Vice President Sandra Thomas presenting an identical pin to India's Prime Minister Indira Gandhi at Mrs. Gandhi's New
Delhi home. (Thomas had represented the World Education Fellowship
in India in December 1974.)

International Women's Year, 1975, evolved from a 1972 resolution of
the United Nations General Assembly. President Gerald Ford ordered its
observance in the United States, and Meredith celebrated it for a week
but observed it all year. To begin the campus celebration, Betty Friedan,
founder of the National Organization for Women (NOW) and the National Political Caucus, addressed a college and community audience on
October 6. Her topic was "The Women's Movement: Where Are We
Now and Where Are We Going?" During the celebration, Lisa Sergio,

who had spoken in 1972 at a United Nations Workshop, appeared for a return engagement. Sergio was the first woman radio commentator in Europe and, for many years, a newscaster and opera and concert broadcaster in the United States.

Vice President Thomas, an official delegate of the U.N.'s World Education Fellowship to the International Women's Year World Conference in Mexico City, June 19–July 4, reflected on the year's significance:

> International Women's Year . . . is a call to action for the recognition of the achievements, the potential, and the status and conditions of women throughout the world, with the vision that it will bring advancement for women in every country, and that it will introduce an era when governments give high priority to the goal of women's equality, ergo, the betterment of the condition of all people.[75]

KNOWLEDGE REPRODUCES ITSELF in understanding. How students and alumnae use it as leavening is the College's primary contribution to society. It stands to reason, then, that if Meredith is the maturing of a woman, it is also a participant in the maturing of a society—locally, nationally, and globally.

4

"TREASURE IN

EARTHEN VESSELS"

1976–1980

IN 1976, ALLEN Burris defined the Christian college as "the church ministering to society's needs in higher education."[1] The church college, he
said, "acknowledges its Christian pre-supposition and places its Christian
bias at the heart of what it is about. But, like a hospital whose first duty
is to heal, a college's first duty is to educate."[2] Burris's thoughts on the
Christian college composed the lead article for the first edition of *Meredith*, successor to the *Alumnae Magazine*.

Because of the College's religious heritage, its community spoke easily
of its spiritual dimensions; however, such speech was often foreign to society in general, particularly outside the Bible Belt. But even before the
premier edition of the new magazine found its way to mailboxes around
the country, a smattering of religious language crept into national conversations and raised questions, if not eyebrows, on the six o'clock news.
This was the period of Jimmy Carter's rise to national political power. A
Southern Baptist, governor of Georgia, and candidate for president of the
United States, Carter spoke the idiom of a southern churchman, though
much of the nation had never learned the language. An editorial writer in
the *Christian Century* said,

> The arrival of a "born again" Southern Baptist layman on the na-
> tional political scene . . . pushed [journalists] into the unfamiliar ter-

ritory of subjective religious feelings, and away from more familiar and objective issue decisions as they were influenced by religion. When Jimmy Carter began talking of his "born again" experience in the North Carolina primary in April 1976, reporters latched on to the familiar labels of "conservative" and "fundamentalist" to describe the candidate's religious views. Gradually, it became journalistic shorthand to identify Mr. Carter's "religious" supporters as evangelicals, a term which suggested to many readers a group of rigid, deeply committed Christians who have taken strong stands on political and religious issues.[3]

Partly because of such labels, people like Jimmy Carter and colleges like Meredith were—and are—sometimes misunderstood. Burris's magazine article, however, clearly articulated Meredith's philosophy, comparing the dual nature of the church college to that of the human creatures found in the first two chapters of Genesis: "they are made in the image of God and they are made of the dust of the earth." In like manner, he said, "the church college, as a human institution, . . . partakes of [the] attributes of power and responsibility with all the limitations of earthliness. In this context, we have no excuse for inaction and no basis for pride in our own power and virtue."[4]

Certainly the College was not guilty of inaction in the mid- to late-seventies; however, some distractions were pardonable in 1976 as voters prepared to cast their ballots for the first elected president since Watergate and as the nation observed, often with spine-tingling, emotion-packed fervor, its Bicentennial Year. Meredith went early to the bicentennial party. For Parents' Weekend in 1975, students fashioned a Liberty Tree by hanging signs and effigies from the limbs of a small red maple between Johnson and Joyner Halls. Through the *Twig*, history Professor Frank Grubbs reached beyond his classroom to teach the meaning of the tree:

> The Liberty Tree was used during the Revolution Period as a focal point for Colonial dissent against the British in Boston and other towns. The Boston Tree was the most famous and was cut down twice by the British. The Meredith tree will be decorated [similarly] to the first Boston tree and all items on the Meredith tree will be copied after the original. . . . As far as we know, Meredith is the only College in North Carolina planning such a restoration.[5]

Students decorate a liberty tree in commemoration of
America's Bicentennial in 1976.

And as far as anyone knew, Meredith was the only college "flying" a
19 x 12-foot flag patterned after specifications set forth by the first Continental Congress in 1777. Home economics major Mary Lou Journigan,
'75, hand-sewed the flag in a special studies history course. Frequently on
loan for bicentennial observances, the flag came home only occasionally
and, because of its size, was draped from one of the upper levels of Bryan
Rotunda rather than flown in the literal sense. Among Meredith's indirect
contributions to the celebrations were the several alumnae who accepted
leadership roles in their cities and counties; for example, Julia Bryan, '73,
served Meredith's larger community as executive director of the Wake
County American Revolution Bicentennial Commission. As the bicentennial wound down, Bryan returned to Meredith as assistant director of
development.

For the bicentennial convocation on February 2, 1976, Alvin Poussaint, associate professor of psychiatry at Harvard Medical School, spoke
on "The Rise and Fall of the Civil Rights Movement." Dr. Poussaint was
also a psychiatrist at Massachusetts General Hospital, a member of
PUSH (People United to Save Humanity), treasurer of the Black Academy

of Arts and Letters, author, and student of black and white relations in the United States.

Bicentennial observances ushered in 1976, and the presidential election ushered it out. Meredith people chose political sides and supported their candidates—either Jimmy Carter, the Democratic Party's nominee, or Gerald Ford, winner over Ronald Reagan for the Republican Party's nomination. The fall's first edition of the *Twig* showcased politics, running cleverly biased pieces under even more cleverly constructed titles, such as Phyllis Burnett's "Will America recall Ford?"[6] America would readily re-elect the incumbent if sophomore Carol Lancaster had her say. An active student partisan, Lancaster worked in an official capacity to organize a campaign stop at Meredith for Jack Ford, son of the incumbent. At the Heck Memorial Fountain in the courtyard, Ford delivered a speech on behalf of his father and of vice presidential candidate, Robert Dole. The *News and Observer* for October 9 reported, "President Ford's 24-year-old son Jack promised a Republican victory in North Carolina in November to the cheers of some 1,500 women at Meredith College here Friday."[7] Lancaster had been a youth coordinator for Ronald Reagan in the North Carolina presidential primary and one of twenty "Reaganettes" at the Republican National Convention. Kim Farlow, a *Twig* reporter, called her "a 5'1" package of political dynamite."[8]

At least two Meredith students witnessed the January 20, 1977, inauguration of Jimmy Carter, the thirty-ninth president of the United States. Deciding on inauguration eve to make the trip, juniors Vicki Jayne and Ginger Gay left Meredith within the hour and arrived in Washington, D.C. at 3:00 A.M. Jayne told the *Twig* that, from their perch atop a CBS News trailer, the pair enjoyed an unobstructed view of Carter and his running mate, Walter Mondale, taking their oaths of office.[9]

SIMULTANEOUS WITH EARLY political rhetoric and bicentennial observances, Meredith inaugurated its Raising the Sights of Women program. In 1975, the College had received a grant of $75,000 from the Andrew W. Mellon Foundation to underwrite RSW for three years, beginning in August. Director Sarah Lemmon, who had chaired the committee and been instrumental in fashioning the proposal, said RSW was not to offer students "a whole smorgasbord of careers but to help them strengthen their psychological tools so they [would] know what to do."[10] Toward that end, Meredith would sponsor symposia and panels; artists-in-residence; student exchanges; and other enrichment possibilities. Workshops for training faculty and student leaders would underscore the importance of the program across the curriculum.

A year after the first grant had arrived, Lemmon accompanied President Weems and Vice President Kanipe to New York City to appeal to the Rockefeller Foundation for additional funding. A foundation staff member dashed the hopes of the delegation with her terse statement: "I don't think you can raise the sights of Southern women."[11] That opinion notwithstanding, a different—and enthusiastic—foundation official called several months later with happier news: "I have just been reading your proposal, and I don't know of anything else like it anywhere in the country. . . . We want to give you $25,000," she said, "but you have to show us what you will do with it."[12]

The committee did a great deal with the Rockefeller grant and others. In addition to ongoing symposia, such as assertive decision-making and a Life Directions Seminar for freshmen, Raising the Sights of Women provided countless opportunities for students to participate in off-campus events. One of the hallmarks of the program was demonstrated by four students who attended a 1977 International Women's Year observance in Houston, Texas. On their return to the campus, they demonstrated in every way available the advantages of their opportunities. The same held true for gymnastics team members who enrolled in a week-long clinic in Florida and for the Outing Club who went camping and skiing in Colorado. Under the RSW umbrella, other students participated in programs, such as the North Carolina Student Legislature and the United Nations Seminar at Harvard where, in a mock U.N. session, Meredith women vicariously became the delegates from Sweden.

In RSW's first year, freshmen suggested a spring festival of creativity, bringing to the campus for two days Heather Ross Miller, Suzanne Newton, Sylvia Wilkinson, and Patricia H. Howell— writers who read and discussed their work. The festival also sponsored a musical treat as Alice Parker, composer, conductor, and arranger for the Robert Shaw Chorale, conducted her original choral work, *Journey: Pilgrims and Strangers*, benefiting from student vocalists and an orchestra from North Carolina State. At voice instructor Jane Watkins Sullivan's suggestion, the College commissioned Parker to compose another work just for Meredith. The commissioned cantata, *Commentaries,* was based on the poems of Emily Dickinson and performed not only by Meredith's Chorale, Chorus, and Renaissance Singers but also by the Brenau College Women's Concert Choir, the Mississippi University for Women Concert Choir, and the North Carolina Little Symphony. The 1978 premier performance of *Commentaries* was the cornerstone of a four-day choral festival at the College. The festival was reminiscent of a similar event at Loyola University in New Orleans in 1977, where the Chorale was one of ten ensembles and the only all-female choir invited to participate.

Students chose Women in Sports as the theme for the second semester of Raising the Sights of Women, inviting to the campus Janet Guthrie, the first woman to drive a race car in the Indianapolis 500. The physicist-turned-sportswoman captured the attention of the *News and Observer*: "A bachelor's degree in physics may have helped in her mechanical pursuits, but she denies she is unique. 'All that talk about women not being competent in math is brainwashing,' she said. 'Music is an intricate a subject as math, and women have traditionally and easily mastered that.' "[13]

Maggie Odell, *Twig* editor, wrote of her hope that the theme would arouse new diligence in bringing women's athletics to Meredith. Her editorial reminded readers that "It hasn't been long since Billie Jean King opened the question with her defeat of Bobby Riggs, the most celebrated male chauvinist pig in America. . . ."[14] The editor alluded to the heralded tennis match of 1973, which brought victory to the female tennis star and energized the women's movement. Odell would have been a freshman that year; perhaps she had participated in, or at least witnessed, reaction to the match. The *News and Observer* had reported the celebration:

> Some 300 students at all-female Meredith College here celebrated Mrs. King's victory over Riggs by trying to stage a "jockey raid" on N.C. State University.
>
> The students massed on Hillsborough Street in front of Meredith and asked for a police escort down the street to predominantly male N.C. State.
>
> But the policemen talked them into heading back to Meredith where they held a joyous celebration.[15]

The cutline for a photograph in the story read, "Meredith students chant 'Bobby Riggs is 55 and we are No. 1.' "[16]

Raising the Sights of Women offered something for everybody. One of its popular presentations, a symposium titled *What Future for My Generation?* intrigued its Meredith audience. Beginning with the showing of *2001: A Space Odyssey*, the four-day symposium ended with the closing of a time capsule to remain sealed for fifty years. When the capsule is opened in 2028, its contents will indicate "lifestyles, interests, and purposes of society in general and Meredith in particular, 1978 version."[17] Its "myriad articles" are "as Meredith as a 1978 *Twig* and as universal as a Big Mac wrapper."[18]

Some years later, in a conversation with head librarian Jonathan Lindsey, Dr. Lemmon reflected on Raising the Sights of Women. Particularly pleased with the active roles of students in the plans and procedures, she said, "It was in the practice of doing [that] one of the objectives . . . [was met]. . . . There was a great deal going on during those three years, and I think the campus resources, both intellectual and tangible/physical, were greatly increased during that time."[19]

ONE OF THE major considerations of the seventies was curriculum reform. While the changes were adopted in the late seventies, the ideas were generated as early as 1974. For fifty years or more, the College had combined a student's credit hours and quality point ratio to determine her classification. In 1975, however, the instruction committee and Academic Council succeeded in their efforts to eliminate the QPR component in such considerations, classifying students with 1–25 hours of credit as freshmen; with 26–59 hours as sophomores; with 60–89 hours as juniors; and with 90 or more hours as seniors. The change came in the midst of intense study by a Task Force on Curriculum Reform, chaired by Sally Horner of the chemistry department. That summer, a study committee of Drs. Burris, Horner, Lemmon, and L. Frazier participated in a two-week, UNC-sponsored Institute for Undergraduate Curriculum Reform at Appalachian State University and later submitted its proposal to the task force for study. After a year's consideration, the task force recommended to Academic Council that the general education categories—Humanities and the Fine Arts; Natural Sciences and Mathematics; and Social Sciences—be changed to Human Values; Society; the Natural Universe; the Human Body; Language; and the new category "Life Directions." The council, however, voted to retain the old categories, with the addition of Health and Physical Education. It also expressed a philosophy:

> Meredith College is committed to the education of the whole person. Therefore, basic requirements for all students are designed to encourage the full development of all of the capacities for human knowledge—sensing, feeling, and thinking. Courses in the arts, sciences, and humanities are required of all students as essential to a liberal education that is dramatically related to traditional knowledge, values, and insights and to the demands of a changing age. These courses are divided into four categories which expose the student to a broad distribution of human knowledge and to different modes of learning about herself and her world.[20]

In unveiling the new general education program, the Academic Council offered the following statement, which has since been printed in each edition of the college catalogue:

> Each student should examine human values and begin the lifelong process of developing her own beliefs about the meaning of existence in relation to herself, to others, and to God. She should encounter the great creative achievements of mankind and discover those values which are for her most essential to a rich, full, and significant life. She should understand herself in society and develop her knowledge about the human community, both in local, national, and world expressions and in its past and present forms. She should have an informed concept of herself as a part of the natural universe, and she should develop skills in the processes of scientific reasoning and mathematics. She should know her own body and should develop skills consistent with her physique, natural abilities, and interests. She should develop an analytical and practical mastery of language as the primary medium through which we learn and share our knowledge.
>
> Toward these ends each student who receives the B.A. or B.S. degree must fulfill the requirements.[21]

The task force, said Burris, "affirmed concern for vocation and vocational education . . . and gave rise to career planning and cooperative education."[22] As the general changes took effect, individual departments busily fashioned new and improved programs, or they revised old ones. In his 1976–77 annual report, Dean Burris matched departments and descriptive terms: art, "complete rethinking"; business, "major significantly strengthened"; elementary education, "reworked"; foreign language, "significant changes next year"; music, "revised curriculum for all majors;" sociology, "anticipates study and revision;" equitation, "program has improved markedly this year."[23]

For relevancy in a rapidly changing culture, curriculum revision was commonplace. Since Dr. Huber had become chairman of the psychology department in 1974, he had steered the focus away from the philosophical and toward the scientific, declaring that his predecessors had "put together a psychology major with spit and bailing wire."[24] Now, he said, the department's two priorities were to put a "solid curriculum" in place and to get students involved: "In the first year, we had student representatives come on board and attend department meetings, and since that time they have had input. I like to think we're a little bit ahead of our time on that. We applied that first year and got the psychology honorary [Psi Chi]."[25] In just two years, the department, in cooperation with North Carolina State, hosted the 1976 Carolinas Psychology Conference. The event, attracting several hundred students from the Carolinas and neighboring states, was the first of the annual conferences for undergraduates in the area. It grew out of a philosophy of "trying to provide opportunities for women to become the very best scientists possible."[26]

In some instances, revised curricula brought new faces to the fore, and vice versa. In 1977, alumna Rebecca Murray became chairman of the Department of Education. Murray received her A.B. at Meredith in 1958, her M.Ed. at the University of North Carolina at Chapel Hill, and her Ed.D. at Duke. She left Columbia College in South Carolina to return to Meredith, where she immersed herself in campus activities. Her students usually saw her as an encourager; the College in general saw her as a lover of the classroom, of Meredith history, and of the stage on which she acted in many a presentation of the Meredith Playhouse and, later, of Meredith Performs. But policy makers and planners from entities as diverse as Meredith and City Hall sometimes felt the sting of Dr. Murray, the gadfly, as she questioned motives and actions.

John Holt had moved from acting to permanent chairman of the Department of Foreign Languages in 1976. He had recently completed his

Ph.D. degree at Harvard, after having earned his A.M. there and his A.B. at the University of Virginia. Ann Kurtz succeeded him in 1979. Dr. Kurtz's extensive teaching experiences abroad included her then-most-recent tenure at Damavand College in Iran, a country very much in the news at the time of her appointment. She had earned her A.B. at Wellesley and her A.M. and Ph.D. at the University of Maryland.

In other instances, reorganization dictated personnel changes. As the continuing education program grew sufficiently to warrant additional administrators, Sarah Lemmon, history department chairman since 1962, was named the first dean of continuing education and special programs in 1977. Frank Grubbs, already a member of the history department, succeeded Dr. Lemmon. Dr. Grubbs completed his work for the A.B. at Lynchburg College and for the A.M. and Ph.D. at the University of Virginia. Both he and his future wife, Carolyn Barrington, '60, had joined the department in 1963, and their ensuing courtship delighted starry-eyed students, as had the romance of L.E.M. Freeman, religion, and Katherine Parker, home economics, five decades earlier. Historian Mary Lynch Johnson recorded the Grubbs's marriage in 1965 as "the first between faculty members" since the Freemans wed in 1916.[27]

Another reorganization occurred when Sally Horner, chemistry department chairman, joined the administration as the first director of institutional research in 1978. Reginald B. Shiflett, who replaced Dr. Horner, earned the B.S. degree in chemical engineering as well as the Ph.D. in chemistry at the University of Virginia. Before coming to Meredith, Shiflett was chairman of the division of natural sciences at Campbellsville College, a Baptist institution in Kentucky.

In 1980, as dean of students, Dorothy J. Sizemore became the newest member of the student development staff, and, by virtue of her office, a member of the faculty. Charles Davis resigned his chairmanship of the mathematics department to join the administration as assistant dean and registrar. Replacing him was Ed Wheeler, "a young scholar and teacher with deep roots in Baptist colleges."[28] Dr. Wheeler, who had taught at Northern Kentucky University for seven years, was an alumnus of Samford for his A.B. and of the University of Virginia for his Ph.D.

Having just completed his doctorate at the University of Utah in 1980, Eugene M. Sumner assumed the chairmanship of the Department of Sociology and Social Work as Leslie Syron asked to be relieved of her administrative duties. Sumner joined the faculty in 1973 after holding several pastorates and an administrative post with the Free Will Baptist Children's Home in Middlesex. He is a graduate of Mt. Olive Junior College and of Atlantic Christian College. He earned the M.Div. degree at Southeastern Baptist Theological Seminary and the M.S.W. at the University of North Carolina at Chapel Hill.

IN THE MID-SEVENTIES, predictions of a dearth of college-age students dominated planning sessions and even some casual conversations. In 1976, President Weems said,

> There is no growth indicated for private higher education in North Carolina in the next five years. . . . because of a decline in high school graduates. Demographic material . . . indicates that there is an out-migration flow from the State of North Carolina. Most private colleges within the state have depended upon recruitment activities in other states to maintain their enrollments. As a result enrollments in private institutions now exceed fifty percent in out-of-state students. National figures suggest that this availability of students also will decline rapidly in the 1980's.[29]

Such predictions would not have seemed to bode well for Meredith in light of the fact that 83 percent of its students were North Carolinians, but the College continued to enjoy year after year of record-breaking enrollment. In fact, the *Twig* called attention to a housing shortage in the fall of 1978: "Due to the increase in resident students this year . . . three and four girls are sharing single rooms because of overcrowded conditions."[30] The spring term of 1979 was no different: Forty-nine new students enrolled, bringing the resident population to 1,104, the highest ever recorded for a second semester. And that number would be thirty-four fewer than enrollment for the second semester in 1980. Dean White had shed some light on the overcrowding when she reported a 1977 retention rate of 85.5 percent, as compared to the national average of 67 percent for women's colleges. To ease the dilemma, Dr. Thomas recommended in April 1979 that as many as twenty seniors, preferably those graduating in mid-term, be allowed to live off-campus; however, no students accepted the invitation, either that year or the next. In September 1980, ninety-six prospective freshmen opted for a residence-hall waiting list, hoping that attrition would finally admit them to the college of their choice.

Overcrowding was a solvable problem, markedly preferable to the opposite extreme. Other predicaments thrust upon the College, to its bewilderment, also required creative and sometimes painful solutions. For example, another energy crisis struck in the winter of 1977, as Raleigh suffered its coldest temperatures since 1918. The maintenance staff quickly insulated exposed pipes and installed new radiator controls in the original residence halls, "making it possible for the first time to regulate heat in each room."[31] But Mr. Baker took additional steps toward conservation. Some were drastic: Hot water temperature was lowered, and all thermostats were set at 65 degrees; heat in Johnson Hall and the classroom buildings was turned off from Friday to Sunday nights, making the weekend use of specified buildings almost non-existent. While Baker's practices might have seemed harsh, he was, after all, responsible for balancing a budget against six fuel oil price increases that winter. And in the warmer days of April, campus residents and workers, who had shivered in January, February, and March, understood that Meredith's having saved about twenty-five gallons of oil every hour was necessary to surviving the winter with any warmth at all.

The high cost of energy was indicative of the economy of the period. Inflation was a nemesis of the one-term presidency of Jimmy Carter. College fund raiser Royster Hedgepeth, new vice president for institutional advancement, understood economic pressure as it applied to educational institutions. In his first year, he wrote, "The bulk of college spending occurs in those areas where inflation has been most severe—areas ranging from salaries to energy costs. In some cases, the rate of increase in operating costs has approached 20 per cent a year for the past five years." He cited startling statistics of the years 1973–1978: "the cost of oil has increased 298 per cent and the cost of electricity 98 per cent. . . ." Dr. Hedgepeth warned that if tuition climbed at the rate of expenses, Meredith would price itself out of the market. Inflation, he said, was one of three factors "reshaping the face of higher education in America."[32] The other two pressures, he said, were the shortage of students and changes in attitudes toward higher education, from the standpoints of both students and supporters.

Snow blankets the campus in the winter of 1996.

Into 1978, Weems continued the flow of information regarding a declining student-age market. For example, he said, in North Carolina in 1980, "there would be 74,000 high school graduates, and . . . in 1990 there would be only 56,000. . . ."[33] How those statistics would affect Meredith depended, to a degree, on how the College defined itself, Hedgepeth said. "America's colleges and universities cannot be all things to all people. They must define whom they serve, where their money will be spent, and how they will present themselves. . . . Terms such as *market analysis, product management,* and *cost effectiveness* will be an integral part of the college's new definition." He added, "In the process of definition, there is an inherent conflict between the need to change and the need to remain the same."[34]

Royster C. Hedgepeth joined the administration June 1, 1977, succeeding John T. Kanipe, who had accepted the presidency of Southern Seminary Junior College. Hedgepeth reached Meredith by way of Hampden–Sydney, one of the then-few remaining private colleges for men—perhaps the only one—where he was associate director of institutional development. The thirty-two-year-old had earned the B.A. at Wake Forest, the master's at the University of Florida, and the Ph.D. at Cornell. The first new vice president since Sandra Thomas's election in 1974, Hedgepeth arrived as Thomas prepared for a year's leave of absence, the College's having honored her request to fill a gubernatorial appointment as executive director of the new office of citizen affairs for the State of North Carolina.

In one of Hedgepeth's early sessions with trustees, he reported that Madaline Elliott Buchanan, '28, wanted to give money to Meredith for her class project to raise $50,000 toward a chapel fund. Minutes of the meeting read, "In discussing this matter, it was deemed necessary first to determine whether or not Meredith wishes to accept money for the construction of a chapel. . . . Following discussion [it was moved and seconded] that Meredith accept funds for the purpose of building a chapel and that it be included in the long-range priorities."[35] Long-range priorities, according to Hedgepeth, depended upon raising in the next few years more than $17 million for buildings, faculty and program development, and scholarships. In September 1979, when the Board of Trustees approved the fund-raising effort, they also adopted its name—the Visions Program—and its goal of $20 million. The goal was divided into two parts: $6 million for faculty development and capital outlay and $14 million for the general endowment. A month before the board formally inaugurated the Visions Program, the executive committee learned that Sarah Cook Rawley, '29, and her husband, D.A. Rawley, had given Meredith stock in a family-owned newspaper, the sale of which, Hedgepeth said, would mean approximately $628,000 in unrestricted money for the College. Rarely were gifts of that size unrestricted.

Only months into the Visions Program, Vice President Hedgepeth resigned. As of January 14, 1980, he was succeeded by Jerry E. McGee, a graduate of East Carolina University, who had earned his M.A. from Appalachian State and his Ed.D. from Nova University. Dr. McGee came from a five-year stint at Gardner-Webb, also a Baptist college, where he had served as assistant to the president. On football Saturdays, he donned a striped shirt and was spotted on television screens as an official in the Atlantic Coast Conference of the National Collegiate Athletic Association. But on Monday through Friday—and some weekends—McGee coordinated the ambitious fund-raising effort, to be divided into two four-year phases, beginning in March 1980 and concluding in June

1988. The College anticipated raising approximately $10,000,000 in each phase.

THE LIST OF top priorities grew shorter on completion of the Harriet Mardre Wainwright Music Building. Dedicated on February 25, 1977, it was named to honor the memory of an alumna whose generous bequest had inspired an additional magnanimous gift from her husband, Irving H. Wainwright of Richmond, Virginia. The building's Clara Carswell Concert Hall, itself dedicated just a month earlier on January 21, 1977, was the site for the ceremonies. As new as it was, the 175-seat Carswell Hall had already been acclaimed as an answer to a community need, and rave reviews accompanied almost every mention of its acoustical capabilities. In addition to Carswell Hall, the Harriet Mardre Wainwright Music Building housed twenty-two teaching studios, eight practice rooms, three classrooms, and a music library. At the time of the dedication, 130 of the 1,500 degree candidates were music mjors. Among the first guests of Wainwright were alumnae who returned on March 19 for "A Day of Music at Meredith," theme for the annual Alumnae Seminar.

Mr. Wainwright said he admired Meredith's "sound management, growth with progress, and compassion for those being served." He also said that he and Mrs. Wainwright had been aware "of the plight of independent colleges in times of accelerating inflation."[36] Some foundations and corporations were also knowledgable of the struggles in private higher education, the Kresge Foundation, for example, having been generous in the past, was helpful again with a contribution toward the music building. On the reverse side of the check from the foundation, Stanley S. Kresge had handwritten this statement: "In the name and for the sake of Jesus Christ."

Dedication of Wainwright Music Building was an event of Founders' Day, 1977. That celebrated day, like its predecessors, was memorable for its own style of ceremonies and observances of heritage. The longtime practice of placing flowers on Thomas Meredith's grave had shifted from the literal to the metaphorical in 1976, thanks to alumna Sarah Elizabeth Vernon Watts and her family. The Wattses provided a small garden near Jones Auditorium, mounting there a plaque, on which is quoted a simple poem by Richard T. Vann, president of the College from 1900–1915:

THOMAS MEREDITH
(1795–1850)
While others slept below, he climbed the height.
He stood alone, with vision strained afar.
And, peering long into the lingering night,
He saw the morning star.

At that place, the wreath-laying ceremony has continued, and, from time
to time, a member of the college family reports inquiries as to whether the
tiny garden is Thomas Meredith's actual grave site. College archives do
not record a motive for the Watts's gift, but friends of Mrs. Watts might
surmise that her interest was in rescuing the tradition before it fell to the
inevitable fate of mental and physical inaccessibility caused by the intimidating traffic, both human and vehicular, around the City Cemetery in
downtown Raleigh, where Thomas Meredith's grave remains.

Under the assumption that the College was continually being founded,
the trustees added a new tradition to the annual Founders' Day observance by remembering an early founder and recognizing a contemporary
counterpart. In 1976, the first year of the practice, Oliver Larkin Stringfield and C.C. Cameron were selected for the honors. Stringfield, "the man
destined to bring success to the new venture in education," was elected a
trustee in 1892 and employed as a fund raiser for Baptist Female University in 1893.[37] Cameron, elected a trustee in 1960, had chaired the board
in 1969 and 1971–1974. A volunteer fund raiser for the College, he was
founder of one of the largest mortgage banking firms in the nation.

Oliver Larkin Stringfield died in 1930, but his family and Meredith re-
tained close ties. The previous chapter quotes his son Oliver Linwood
Stringfield's conviction that "there is an invisible canopy hovering over
the campus."[38] Time and again, the son's adage was repeated. Certainly,
tangible progress seemed evidence enough that the protective canopy was
in place. On a campus valued at $22 million, landscaping, building, and
remodeling excited donors and recipients alike. Such was the case when
trustee J.C. Faw; his wife, Patsy; and their children, Diane, a Meredith junior, and Jimmy, saw an opportunity to beautify the courtyard behind the
new Harriet Mardre Wainwright Music Building with a garden of aza-
leas, rhododendron, and evergreens. The Faw Garden was dedicated during Parents' Weekend activities, April 16, 1977.

Meanwhile, members of the Class of 1928, led by Mabel Claire Hoggard Maddrey and Mary Rodwell Smith of Raleigh, planned a fiftieth anniversary gift far surpassing other class gifts, both in amount and scope. The initial installment, in excess of $50,000, sparked the drive to build the long-awaited chapel. An on-campus place of worship had not reached the top of the list of needs—nor even the list of heartfelt wishes, as far as the administration and trustees were concerned—until the Class of 1928 placed it there; however, records indicate that architects for half a century "took the hopes of a place of worship to the drawing boards, and every master plan from the beginning shows a chapel facing the front drive."[39] But since relocating from downtown to the edge of the city, the College had some catching up to do, as far as construction was concerned. The last of the temporary buildings had been replaced as recently as the late sixties and early seventies. Also, students were encouraged to worship in the local churches rather than to isolate themselves from the townspeople. In fact, Meredith and most of Raleigh's larger churches provided Sunday bus service until the number of students with their own cars rendered chartered transportation unnecessary. But when President Weems announced the drive to raise funds for a chapel, he expressed pleasure at the interest of alumnae: "Their efforts greatly stimulate the fund drive that will provide a focal point for worship on the campus and affirm our heritage in Christian higher education."[40]

Soon, a chapel planning committee sat in the midst of constituent groups and individuals who mentally designed the chapel in their own images, so to speak. In 1981, the editor of *Meredith* wrote of the committee's apparent struggles: "The words and thoughts [have] seemed to come easily. The building has not. In fact, it may be safe to say that no other structure on the campus has elicited so much interest and so many deeply felt and openly expressed opinions."[41] When chairman Marion Lark reported for the chapel planning committee, he said,

> The committee began to see that if the chapel is to be a building that will thoughtfully reflect our Christian heritage, it was necessary to give attention . . . to theological understanding and symbolism rather than architectural design. In other words, we came to the conclusion that it is more appropriate to build a place of worship from the "inside out" than from the "outside in."[42]

Larry Williams, campus minister, also served on the committee. To him, "building a chapel is like 'parenting.' Both tasks take a lot of skill, a lot of patience, and a lot of love."[43]

When the executive committee of the Board of Trustees met in September 1980, they considered the proposed locations, one between the Mae Grimmer Alumnae House and Joyner Hall and the other on the drive in front of the alumnae house. Architects Carter and Turner Williams, as well as twelve of the fourteen voting members of the buildings and grounds committee, recommended the latter site. At the same meeting, trustee and president of the Alumnae Association, Mary Virginia Warren Poe, '48, moved that the executive committee "authorize the architect . . . to proceed with designing a chapel in the traditional style of architecture, with a steeple, designed basically for worship, of moderate proportions but of great beauty and highest quality."[44] The motion carried.

First estimated at $500,000, the cost was revised upward to approximately $1,058,000. But the very prospect of a chapel inspired alumna Martha Salisbury Smoot, '33, to see that an organ was installed there in memory of her mother, Mary Estelle Johnson Salisbury, one of the "Immortal Ten" members of the first class of 1902. Mrs. Smoot's efforts added $62,000 to the fund. Until the chapel was built, Wednesday worship services were held in Jones Auditorium or, occasionally, in Bryan Rotunda, while more intimate devotions were offered in various nooks and crannies.

Jones Auditorium and the proposed chapel combined would not have accommodated some audiences, including commencement crowds; therefore, Meredith was dependent upon the Elva Bryan McIver Amphitheater for such occasions. Often, the College reserved North Carolina State's William Neal Reynolds Coliseum or Raleigh's Memorial Auditorium as alternative sites in the event of bad weather. The weather was fine on the evening of September 18, 1978, for the inaugural Lillian Parker Wallace Lecture by Great Britain's former prime minister, the Right Honourable Sir Harold Wilson. An audience of about 2,000 heard the nation's long-time ally speak on "The Transatlantic Connection from Winston Churchill to Today," in which he told of his relationships with American presidents from Truman through Ford. The four-term prime minister had retired from office in 1976. On this, his first visit to the United States in four years, he warmly greeted members of his audience at a courtyard reception following the evening lecture.

The number of Raleighites attending open-to-the-public occasions seemed to increase from year to year. A more impressive phenomenon, however, was the number of people—a predicted 25,000 in 1975–76—using the campus for their own agendas. The calendar already showed a summer schedule of thirty-four events, from the state games of the Special Olympics to the North Carolina Congress of the PTA; from the statewide Festival of Magic to the national convention of the American Dairy Science Association. Only a year later, Joe Baker reported that 52,000 visitors had discovered the inviting campus, and, in 1979–80, the guest list numbered about 75,000.

A footnote to the summer of 1977 elaborated on members and guests of the National Men's Garden Club Association who suffered food poisoning from a meal served on a summer day in Belk Dining Hall. Of the 750 people who ate lunch there, 200 became ill, and the Health Department determined that chicken salad, refrigerated the night before in a deep container, had not cooled thoroughly and therefore caused the illness. A physician and member of the garden club wrote in the organization's newsletter,

> No one had any idea that in the center of that deboned, chopped chicken being removed from the refrigerator lay the now chilled Staphylococcus germs that had remained warm long enough the previous evening to produce its debilitating and sometimes terrifying toxin. . . . Some 13–14 ambulance units and crews answered our distress call. . . . The hospitals all turned out as though an atomic bomb had hit.[45]

Ironically, as the luncheon progressed that day, the Health Department routinely inspected the kitchen, awarding it an above-average grade of 95. And as distressing as the illness was, it would have been more disturbing had poor sanitation caused the problem.

But from the college menu—then and always—one could find more nourishing entrees to the campus than simply the open doors to facilities. For example, in the spirit of friendly cooperation between the College and the community, Meredith and the Junior League of Raleigh cosponsored a forum on eleven Monday nights in the fall of 1976, exploring such topics as the interaction of state and national governments; religion, morality, and human rights; crises in the cities; and the future of the community and the quality of life. The first speaker for the series was Saul Mendlovitz, president of the Institute for World Order and professor of law at Rutgers University, and the final speaker was Barbara Hubbard, president of the Committee for the Future in Washington, D.C., and author of *The Hunger of Eve*. The interim participants, except for a return engagement of Lisa Sergio, were from among North Carolina's civic leaders and educators.

By invitation, Meredith hosted in 1978 the fiftieth anniversary celebration of the Inter-American Commission of Women of the Organization of American States. The OAS comprised twenty-six member nations, and the commission expected a delegate from each. The organization chose Meredith because of "its high academic standards and leadership development of its students."[46] Speakers included His Excellency Jorge Luis Zelaya, assistant secretary general of the OAS; Her Excellency Maria Eugenia Oyarzum, ambassador to Chile; the Hon. Gabriela Touchard Lopez, president of CIM; and the Hon. Carmen Delgado Votaru, principle U.S. delegate to CIM.

PAGE (Parents for the Advancement of Gifted Education), a program founded in 1978 for gifted and talented children, was also a cooperative effort. Meredith provided not only the facilities but also the first director and several faculty and student volunteers to lead classes, such as computer technology and astronomy in the sciences, and music appreciation and drama in the arts. The *Twig* professed the faith that PAGE was "the only program of its kind in the state of North Carolina and only one of a few in the entire nation."[47] Lyn Aubrecht, professor of psychology, was PAGE's first director; he reported in 1996, eighteen years after PAGE's creation, that the program still thrived.

If statistics for Cooperating Raleigh Colleges were reliable indications of Meredith's general appeal, they were also bases for truth in Weems's belief that high expectations are "hallmarks of a superior college."[48] In the mid-seventies, more than half the exchanges between the six colleges and universities of CRC involved Meredith. More specifically, for 1976–77, the consortium reported that 109 Meredith students were enrolled in courses at North Carolina State, and 284 State students took courses at Meredith. Enrollment in courses at State was one of five options for

Meredith's undergraduates. Other possibilities included Shaw University and Peace, St. Mary's, and St. Augustine's Colleges.

But students could also select from their own campus programs that had been inaccessible to earlier college generations. Meredith Abroad, for example, enjoyed increasing popularity. At first glance, the possibilities seemed most beneficial to students; however, the faculty also vied for the annual teaching positions, faculty development and international travel having become almost synonymous terms. Also, the College expanded its travel opportunities for alumnae. In 1977, Roger Crook, chairman of the religion department, traded his three-year-old "subtitle," of director of Meredith in Europe for that of coordinator of international studies, his responsibilities to include "planning, promoting, and directing programs directly or indirectly related to study abroad" but not be limited to the semester abroad program in London.[49] In an interview with Julia Bryan, Crook provided some background information: Shera Jackson, '69, Raleigh's 1973 Community Ambassador to West Germany, returned to her job as admissions counselor after a summer in Herford and environs, enthusiastically describing the old castles on the Rhine that Meredith could buy for "a song." That winter, Crook and Joe Baker looked into possibilities. They found that any one of the old castles would have provided facilities and ambiance for a Meredith campus in Europe; however, estimates for costs of repairs and remodeling soon dispelled the dream. "Our alternative was to see about using existing institutions which could accommodate our students when the facilities would otherwise be unoccupied," Crook said, and he found such a residence hall at the University of London. "We are convinced," he added, "that an international thrust is imperative. . . . To be well educated, we think, a student needs a cosmopolitan approach. We feel that living abroad, for even a short time, and studying in another culture enriches education in a way that text book work simply cannot." Our program is unique, he said. It costs the same as a semester at Meredith, "and it is always geared this way so that it is possible for any student who can take a semester at Meredith to take this program."[50] In 1979, the Meredith entourage spent the initial two weeks in Scotland before moving from St. Andrews to Durham, England, and finally settling at Whitelands College near Wimbledon for the rest of the stay.

Vice President Thomas also believed in introducing Meredith people to cultures different from their own. During spring break in 1976, she took a group of twenty students for a week's study in Mexico. The next year's exploration was a bit more elaborate as she led forty-seven people, including students and faculty members, to Peru for "cross cultural learning" in a "global classroom."[51] The classroom expanded to include a jungle expedition into the rain forest region; side trips to Cuzco and Machu Piccu; a Peruvian fiesta; and exchanges of ideas on cultural issues. And, for a concert in the salon of the Entre Nous Society, Meredith pianist Thomas Hardison played universally recognized works as well as the premier performance of "Lines," a composition by his faculty colleague Peter Klausmeyer. As for the appreciative audience, which included the cultural attache of the American embassy in Peru, Thomas—referred to by her group as "Safari Sandra"—reported "hearty applause and a standing ovation" for Hardison's performance.[52] The vice president continued leading educational tours throughout her years at Meredith. At Christmas, 1979, faculty, students, and other friends followed her to Cuba, an excellent place, she said, "to study . . . the concept of revolution and also to experience third world development."[53]

If *Meredith*, the college magazine, were wired for sound, the 1979 winter edition would have blared forth spring and summer travel plans. Page 26 alone was a drum roll in print for "the second annual Meredith in Britain for Alumnae and Friends," to be coordinated by Dr. and Mrs. Crook; for a "nine-day travel odyssey through the best of Spain," to be led by Sandra Thomas; for six weeks of study at the University of Perugia, Italy, with two weeks of travel, offered by Bluma K. Greenburg of the art department; and for a tour of Egypt, Jordan, and the Holy Land, to be led by John and Frankie Weems. The same page pointed toward 1980, when the College would host a European tour to include the *Passion Play* at Oberammergau.

While young women from Meredith studied abroad, some high school students extended their intellectual reaches in summer programs on the campus. In 1973, thirteen students enrolled in the new Summer Study for High School Students; in 1974, fourteen participated. At that point, the admissions committee recommended to the Academic Council that Meredith open some courses to area young women who were high school senior scholars, enabling them to earn early college credits. Later catalogues described an evolution: "High school senior girls in the local area who are ready to undertake college-level study may enroll as special students in courses at Meredith. A student approved for participation in the Senior Scholars Program may attend classes for college credit in the summer prior to her senior year or in either or both semesters of her senior year."[54] Also geared to high school students was merit weekend, an annual event for national Merit semifinalists and other select gifted students from the Carolinas and Virginia. The 1976 version explored the avantgarde topic of "Human Engineering: Hope or Thrust of the Future?" Faculty panelists Lyn Aubrecht, psychology; Betty Webb, English; George Hoffman, biology; and Allen Page and Roger Crook, religion, were charged with developing the theme as well as with helping the young women deal with complex ethical questions.

As the College led students to confront the complexities of their culture, it also enticed them to explore their own educational and economic interests. Both cooperative and continuing education rapidly won converts. Starting with one student in one job in 1973–74, cooperative education mushroomed to thirty-seven placements in 1976–77. Marie Capel boasted of a student's placement in Sears Roebuck's first ever co-op position; the same was true, she said, of the Washington, D.C., office of the National Labor Relations Board. In 1976, at the request of the City of Raleigh and with a grant of $1,900 to underwrite the effort, Capel and Shirley Ihnen, special projects coordinator, completed a study of cooperative education in the four senior colleges and universities in the capital city and recommended municipal job classifications that could translate into cooperative education positions.

Career preparation had indeed found a place at Meredith. Dean Burris said, "In our efforts to find common ground for the twin concerns for the liberal arts and vocational education, the College attempted to make some progress toward meeting the growing desire for careers by the students."[55] Career Day in 1977 must have reflected the desired progress. Occupational Outlook, '77, (OO77) attracted to the campus one-hundred representatives from business, government, service jobs, and graduate schools. Students exuded enthusiasm. Kathy Keith was one of the nation's sophomores selected by Mobil Oil for its "Explore the Business World" program. Keith spent four days discovering business in the "real world" of New York City with students from colleges and universities from around the nation, including Duke and William and Mary from the neighborhood. After the exploration, Keith reimbursed her host company by acquainting her peers with opportunities in business.

In 1979, the Woodrow Wilson Foundation appointed Meredith—one of the fifty colleges in the nation—to its Visiting Fellows Program. Through the three-year program, which would fund a Fellow each semester, students would associate with outstanding career people "with liberal arts backgrounds who have succeeded in one or more fields of endeavor, not necessarily the traditional ones."[56] In November, Meredith welcomed Max and Esther Krebs of the United States Foreign Service, as the first Fellows on campus. And, perfectly fitting the specification of "not necessarily the traditional. . . ," Johanna Dunn, who held a doctorate in art history but was a vice president of the New York Futures Exchange, was one of five Fellows who came later. The *Twig* reported that Becky Batson Shaw, '69, a staff member at the foundation, was instrumental in Meredith's appointment to the program. When the specified three years expired, the Parents' Association voted to underwrite the visiting fellows for another three, with head librarian, Jonathan Lindsey, succeeding Sarah Lemmon as coordinator.

Continuing education, meanwhile, captured the imaginations of and offered possibilities to countless women past the traditional college-student age. If they could not come to Meredith for classes, Meredith sometimes took classes to them. Such was the case for thirteen employees of Rex Hospital, who completed Helen Jones's English course on their own campus, scheduling their classes around shift changes. But back at the College, increasing numbers of students returned to pursue their interrupted or postponed educations. The staff increased, and its headquarters expanded. When Sarah Lemmon became dean of continuing education and special programs on July 1, 1977, Anne Dahle assumed responsibilities as director of counseling and the credit program; and Rosalie Gates, an assistant professor in the history department, became director of enrichment. The "special programs" segment of Lemmon's title included Raising the Sights of Women; cooperative education; and some summer and miscellaneous programs. With her appointment came continuing education's move into a modular unit behind Belk Dining Hall.

Dean Lemmon sought to expand the types of programs offered by continuing education. Agreeing that a paralegal course was right for Meredith, the trustees approved it as a post-baccalaureate offering in February

1979. Dean Lemmon said, "To the best of our knowledge, this is the only post-baccalaureate legal assistants program between Philadelphia and Atlanta. . . . We believe we are meeting a definite need for career women interested in law but not interested in attending law school at this time."[57] Meredith offered the first "edition" in the summer of 1980, limiting the enrollment to thirty women, twenty-seven of whom completed the program. By late September, twelve were working under their new certification. Lemmon reported "an auspicious beginning," thanks to the board of advisers, the faculty, the library's "good collection through purchase and gifts from friends in the legal community," and to alumna Emily Johnson, '75, who returned to promote the concept and direct the annual summer studies.[58] Johnson held the J.D. degree from the University of North Carolina at Chapel Hill.

The College had long delighted in the progress of continuing education. Women in the re-entry program developed a kinship of sorts, at first meeting informally as the Koffee Klatch but changing their name in 1979 to WINGS (Women in New Goal Settings) and becoming the collective voice of adult students. In fact, WINGS evolved into a major organization that merited a vote in the Student Government Association. The organization's purpose was "to provide information, fellowship, support, and leadership opportunity for all students at Meredith; to serve as a liaison between the WINGS student and the on-campus community; and to voice WINGS student concerns through representation on the SGA Executive Committee."[59]

For WINGS in particular and for continuing education in general, Virginia Norton was one of the trailblazers, not as faculty or staff, as many of the pioneers were, but as student. A senior in 1977–78, a grandmother, and, at 61, the oldest degree candidate of the period, Norton exemplified the appreciation and enthusiasm that many re-entry students declared. If Meredith was good for Mrs. Norton, Mrs. Norton was also good for Meredith. After enrolling in 1973, she participated in campus life to the fullest, serving as president of the non-resident students' organization, winning the outstanding day student award, and being tapped into Silver Shield. The *News and Observer* named her Tar Heel of the Week, citing the subject's own epithet for herself: "Generation Gap Jumper."[60] Of her hunger for learning, Norton said, "I am often hesitant to leave campus to go home, being fearful that some lecture or concert or play may take place without me."[61] Of her joy in discovering "this smorgasbord of delights," as she called the academic menu, she said, "For the literary enthusiasts who always wanted to read with understanding the love poetry of Robert Browning or Milton's *Paradise Lost*; or for southern women who wanted to understand Faulkner's interpretation of woman's role during the Civil War, there are experts in every field to lead the way."[62] Reflecting on cultural traditions and new-found choices for women like herself, she asked a rhetorical question: "Who knows what painter's pictures have been drowned in dish pans of the past?"[63]

While women like Norton were ecstatic over choices, the Carlyle Campbell Library touted its own "smorgasbord of delights." In 1976, the library joyfully received financial support from the W.K. Kellogg Foundation for Meredith's membership in the Southeastern Library Network, for a computer terminal that would link the College to the network, and for training the staff to use the terminal. The grant having arrived in librarian Michael Dodge's final year at Meredith, his successor, Jonathan Lindsey, elaborated on the benefits of SOLINET: "This system unites Meredith's library with many other libraries over the country and helps facilitate the location of volumes and the securing of cards for the card catalogue."[64]

The Carlyle Campbell Library agressively increased its use of technology, but in the eyes of at least one student, one of the library's new electronic devices was "an outrageous atrocity . . . committed against the integrity of the Meredith College students."[65] The *Twig* had reported the recently installed security system in an innocuous statement on page 2 of the August 30, 1978, issue: "Located in each item in the library is a metal strip which must be desensitized before that particular item may be removed. . . ."[66] This meant that all library patrons exited through a sensor that would sound an alarm if one attempted to smuggle out an article. Three *Twig*s later, a guest editorial writer lambasted the installation of the electronic security system, calling it "literally appalling" and "the gradual destruction of our Honor Code." She added,

> Although in reality the idea may be well founded, in that there was
> a degree of theft prevailing in the library, the installation of such an
> instrument, however, is a virtual slap in the face to the students who
> abide by the Honor Code.

It is sheer hypocrisy to claim that we have a working Honor Code and simultaneously install a machine that questions the honesty of students, faculty, and friends of the College. . . .[67]

The writer abhorred the fact that the student life committee and the Silver Shield had no time to educate students to the problems before the sensoring device was put into effect. Twenty years later, people who traveled in and out of the library accepted the system as a matter of course, accustomed as they were to similar commentaries on their society. In the last quarter of the twentieth century, an unconscionable greed spawned theft; and metal detectors, burglar alarms, and hidden cameras searched out offenders in airports, department stores, convenience marts, banks, office buildings, private homes, automobiles, and the Carlyle Campbell Library at Meredith College.

But despite the theft detector, the library acquired new Friends. Alumna Sarah Elizabeth Vernon Watts, who had already instigated several projects, such as the Thomas Meredith memorial in 1976 and the library's historical collection in 1973, led a movement to re-establish Friends of the Library, the original and then-defunct version having been formed in 1941. Such a group, thought Mrs. Watts, would not only create interest in and provide resources for the library but would also bring writers and other associates of books and ideas to the campus. L.A. Peacock, professor emeritus of English and dean of the College, 1948–69, served as the organization's first president. The board set membership fees at $5.00 for a contributing member; $10.00 for an associate member; $25.00 for a sustaining member; and $100.00 for a life member. In the first four months of its infancy, Friends of the Carlyle Campbell Library welcomed 180 charter members, almost one-fourth of whom were life members. Carolyn Andrews Wallace, '40, director of the Southern Historical Collection in UNC's Louis R. Wilson Library, spoke at the first meeting on May 5, 1977. She suggested that the Friends group's greatest good would be monetary support for the library. "With the number of students increasing from nine hundred in 1966 to thirteen hundred in 1976," she said, "it is no wonder that the growth in the library, gratifying as it has been, has not kept pace with that of the student body."[68] She reminded her listeners that, according to the standards of the Association of College and Research Libraries, Meredith was about 6,000 volumes short. But Dr. Wallace was optimistic, as had been Julia Hamlet Harris in her message to the first Friends of the Library group in 1948: "You may do anything from building a wing on the old library to furnishing it with duplicate copies of More's *Utopia*."[69]

The organization scheduled two meetings a year: a membership dinner in the spring and a book-author luncheon in the fall. The inaugural luncheon on October 26, 1977, was an auspicious occasion, featuring Tarheel novelists Reynolds Price and Frances Gray Patton, with Walter Spearman of the University of North Carolina as moderator.

Trustees learned of the new organization at their September 25 meeting, the day on which the Board of Associates established an endowment to supplement faculty salaries. FAME (Faculty Applied Meredith Endowment) was the brainchild of Laura Weatherspoon Harrill, '27, who chaired the ten-year-old Board of Associates in its only fund-raising project to that time. Assistant Professor George Hoffman, returning after a year's absence to teach for one more semester in the biology department, received the first FAME grant in 1978. While Dr. Hoffman's stipend helped pay his salary, later grants definitively fit the awards category. The family of Pauline Davis Perry, '38, honored her by establishing two cash awards in the endowment to replace the Outstanding Teacher Awards initiated by the First Baptist Church of Greensboro and later funded by the Parents' Association. The Perry awards honored excellence in teaching and outstanding research, publication, or artistic achievement, and, at the inaugural Dinner With Our Friends in April 1980, the first honors went to Jay D. Massey, chairman of the health, physical education, and recreation department, for teaching, and to Thomas C. Parramore, associate professor of history, for research and publishing. On the same occasion, President Weems announced the Board of Associates' establishment of two Laura Harrill Awards for faculty adjudged by the president to be deserving of merit for campus involvement, academics, and commitment. Mrs. Harrill was present at the dinner and was as surprised at the establishment of the awards in her name as were Olive Taylor and Joe Maron at receiving them. Mrs. Taylor was an instructor of mathematics and Mr. Maron an assistant professor of art. Dinner With Our Friends also recognized retirees and those members of the faculty and staff who had given twenty-five years of service to the College.

Such annual occasions extended the long list of time-honored practices by a college already abounding in tradition and traditions. In the seventies, the word "tradition" did not always inspire reverence in a student-age population bent on breaking the mold, defying "the system." But the young women at Meredith protected their own traditional events with tenacity. Cornhuskin', for example, always evoked protective passion. In 1978, some students and faculty dared to suggest changing the celebration from Thursday to Friday night. The *Twig* interpreted an emphatically negative reaction: "[S]tudents complain over placing Cornhuskin' on a weekend night because it will interfere with their social plans; yet when Cornhuskin' interferes with Thursday classes, the students complain about the classes interfering with their celebration of the fall festival."[70] Before writer Kristie Beattie signed off, she punctuated her editorial with a bit of sarcasm: "Granted, a solid education is not the first priority of every woman here, but because Meredith is here for the purpose of providing an education, academics *must* be given priority."[71] Subsequent activity calendars suggest that the wheels of change turned slowly; Cornhuskin' remained a Thursday evening phenomenon until 1995 when, on its fiftieth anniversary, it was rescheduled for Friday.

The faculty's quadrennial performance of Lewis Carroll's *Alice in Wonderland* was another of the traditions lovingly embraced, despite its time- and energy-consuming preparations. The first showing of *Alice* lit up the stage on March 15, 1924; the fourteenth version in 1976 was as well received as any previous one could have been. The first performance featured Carolyn Mercer, '22, instructor in French, as "an irresistible Alice, round-faced and wide-eyed,"[72] and the fourteenth introduced Vice President Sandra Thomas in the starring role—"a natural choice for Alice with her softspoken voice and fair complexion."[73] The 1976 production also introduced Dr. Huber of the psychology department as the new White Rabbit, a role played from 1924–1968 by the late Lillian Parker Wallace. As the student body expanded, so did the number of performances of each version of *Alice*. In 1996, the show attracted a full house for dress rehearsal and a standing-room-only audience for its two scheduled performances.

The Philaretian and Astrotekton Societies traced their tradition all the way back to the first year of Baptist Female University. Until 1920, the two literary societies, organized as Club A and Club B, met every Saturday night for the purpose of "inspiring each other with a love for literature and with a desire to promote the higher principles of self government and self control."[74] For students, society by assignment in the early years gave way to freedom of choice as Rush Week became one of the most competitive of all activities, each society vying for the largest number of recruits. The societies had dropped the word "Literary" from their names in 1950, their constituents professing the love of deeds over the love of words. In the seventies, they had become service clubs, the Astros adopting the Shelley Child Development Center for physically and mentally handicapped children and the Phis committing their efforts to the local Cerebral Palsy Center. But the Human Services program was then the clearing house for service projects, and there seemed to be slight *raison d'etre* for either society. In 1976, project leaders Ruth Cralle, Astro, and Menda Sue Godfrey, Phi, saw "very few dedicated members in either society. . . ." In fact, they questioned "whether Billy Astro and Milton the Bear would ever arise from their present lethargy."[75] But traditions died hard, and the service clubs continued to the end of the decade and beyond, each with its own activities, and each with its own form of rush.

The societies' apparent malaise might have been symptomatic of the times. In 1972, Janice Sams, editor of the *Twig*, mentioned in the *Alumnae Magazine* "the formal killing of 'Apathy' in early January."[76] But from later reports, such as those relating to the two societies, apathy appeared to be alive and well in 1977, and the *Twig* published a cartoon by senior Beth Wicker. The two young women pictured were in conversation. One asked, "What's 'apathy,' Julie?" Julie replied, "Gosh, I don't know. Who cares?"[77]

Two entities which had never been apathetic in their relationship were Meredith and its founding organization, the Baptist State Convention. In 1979–80, the 1,115,124 North Carolina Baptists contributed through the Cooperative Program $498,768.17 to the College.[78] The generosity of the state convention was not predicated on constant accord, although the bond was strong and usually cordial. Occasionally, murmurs emanated from one side or the other—or both. In 1976, for example, trustee Shearon Harris spoke of "a matter of concern" that the convention might limit the number of trustees from any single church to serve on Baptist boards. Mr. Harris's view was that such a move "would probably deny the institutions of the state some extremely able leadership. . . ."[79] The following year, President Weems confided to the trustees his belief that "a change in the attitude and tone of the convention was apparent in the relation of the colleges to the church and to the Convention. . . . [and] that it might be necessary for colleges to begin justifying to the Convention the need for support."[80] Still another hint of concern entered the minutes of the executive committee for November 1980: A week after Weems had attended the annual meeting of the Baptist State Convention, he said "there appeared to be a conservative trend within the Convention, but that there was no indication of growth among the ultra-conservative groups."[81]

Labels, such as "conservative," "moderate," and "liberal," had no bearing on an interesting exchange between Meredith and the Convention in 1980. That summer, Cecil Ray, the convention's executive secretary, queried President Weems and trustee chairman, Seby Jones, as to the possibility of Meredith's selling four acres of its prime real estate for a new Baptist building. The trustees, however, expressed reluctance "to sell any of the land now owned by Meredith College because of the possibility of future expansion."[82] At their November executive committee meeting, they heard from their buildings and grounds committee additional reasons not to sell:

1. The property in question is the wooded corner of Wade Avenue and Faircloth Street. If a building is constructed on that site, along with the proper parking spaces, the grove of trees would have to be taken down and Meredith would lose the screen which now exists between the College and the shopping center.
2. Over the years the Convention probably will need more property for expansion, and the only land available for expansion would be additional property from the Meredith campus.
3. This area would lend itself to only limited parking.[83]

The vote was 12–2 against selling.

While the relationship between the state convention and the College remained solid, the Southern Baptist Convention, through some of its leaders, was beginning to rankle. In his first term as president of the huge body of Southern Baptists, Bailey C. Smith was widely quoted in major newspapers, including the *News and Observer,* as having said "God Almighty does not hear the prayer of a Jew."[84] On the day following the newspaper reports, the faculty unanimously passed and mailed the following statement to President Smith:

We, the faculty of Meredith College, are proud of our Baptist heritage and affirm the strength which we gain through the roots of this heritage.

A part of this heritage is the freedom of open inquiry and the freedom of individual conscience. It is, however, a political reality that the voice of one who has been elected president of the Southern Baptist Convention may be popularly understood to be representative of all Southern Baptists and Southern Baptist institutions. It is in light of this reality that we note the recent statement of Bailey C. Smith, President of the Southern Baptist Convention, ". . . God Almighty does not hear the prayer of a Jew."

While we recognize Mr. Smith's right to his views, we do not accept this as our view. Standing within the Judeo-Christian tradition, we affirm that God is the God of all people and that God alone is judge.[85]

In its semi-annual meeting of September 26, 1980, the Board of Trustees voted unanimously to support the faculty's statement.

AS THE CULTURE changed, so did the problems and concerns of students and Meredith's ways of addressing them. Vice President Thomas reported to the trustees in January 1977 that the college counselor as well as the campus minister were dealing with students who, "particularly this year," had home problems.[86] No statistics are available as to the number of students whose parents were among the 1,083,000 divorce cases in the United States in 1976,[87] but the counselor's section of the *Annual Report of the President 1976–1977* elaborated on the encroaching pattern: "It became apparent during the year that many students were experiencing problems related to the separation or divorce of their parents. In an effort to meet some of the needs of these students, the counselor and campus minister attempted to provide a group situation in which the students could express and deal with their feelings and concerns. . . ."[88]

The Federal Government also expressed concern for students in the mid- to late-seventies, through an Internal Revenue Service mandate disallowing discrimination. In compliance, in a January 1976 meeting, the executive committee of the Board of Trustees issued a statement declaring that "Meredith College does not discriminate against applicants and stu-

dents on the basis of race, color, national or ethnic origin" and a directive
"that such a statement be included in all brochures and catalogues dealing with student admissions programs and scholarships." Furthermore,
vowed the trustees, "Meredith College has a racially nondiscriminatory
policy as to employment of faculty and staff . . . [and] does not discriminate against applicants for employment on the basis of race, color, and
national or ethnic origin."[89] Bill Norton, who oversaw publications, was
adamant that the policy statement be included in all printed material pub-
licizing the College. He had to be; noncompliance would have meant loss
of Meredith's status as a charitable institution. The 1977 catalogue carried the first nondiscriminatory policy statement, which would be virtually unchanged in the nineties, except for additions, as shown below,
dealing with handicap and age:

> Meredith College admits women students of any age, race, creed,
> national and ethnic origin to all the rights, privileges, programs,
> and activities generally accorded or made available to students at
> the College. It does not discriminate on the basis of age, race, creed,
> national and ethnic origin in administration of its educational poli-
> cies, admissions policies, scholarship and loan programs, and ath-
> letic and other school-administered programs. Furthermore, it does
> not discriminate in admission or access to its programs and activi-
> ties on the basis of handicap as defined by Section 504 of the Reha-
> bilitation Act of 1973. The vice president for business and finance
> at Meredith coordinates the College's nondiscriminatory policy on
> the basis of handicap.

INTERCOLLEGIATE ATHLETICS SEEMED to take on new life in the seventies.
Perhaps the momentum was inspired by the success of Meredith's first
full-semester golf team in 1976, its having placed sixth in the Duke invi-
tational competition; or the first winning seasons of both the tennis and
volleyball teams. Already in place were basketball, gymnastics, and swim
teams. If sports enthusiasts of 1976 could have peered into 1980, they
would have witnessed the golf team's winning the NCAIAW state championship and the tennis team's taking the conference title.

The teams were known as the Meredith Angels. From the earliest days
of the College, "Angel" was a frequently used epithet for a student; and
"Angel Farm" had been the home of the Angels since the campus moved

from downtown Raleigh to the Tucker farm in 1926. Finally, in 1980, the executive committee of the Student Government Association led the College to adopt the angel as the school's official mascot, and the student body selected senior Teresa Parker Hamby's stylized drawing as the official representation of the Meredith Angel.

"Why angels?" asked Caroline Vaught McCall, '64, in a 1989 college publication. Mrs. McCall, editor of *Meredith Writes Home*, a newsletter for parents of students, answered the question for her readers:

> In the early years of the College, a "brother-sister" relationship developed between Wake Forest College (then located in the town of Wake Forest, only 17 miles from Raleigh) and the new Baptist Female University (Meredith College). Though Meredith exerted strict social rules, the young women were allowed to share concerts, lectures, etc. with their "brother" college. In 1903 the editor of the Wake Forest newspaper wrote, "There is a ladder extending from the Baptist school in Raleigh to Wake Forest, and angels come and go."[90]

McCall also found that the campus water tank, circa 1926–63, frequently bore the words "Angel Farm" in letters large enough for all of West Raleigh to read. The daring display of questionable art was usually attributed to Wake Forest or North Carolina State students, who were reckless enough to climb the tank and clever enough to elude the nightwatchman's flashlight, to say nothing of his ire. And in the eighties, parents proudly displayed their bumper stickers and oversized pins declaring, "My daughter's a Meredith Angel." While critics decried the angel image as that of a "Baptist girls' school" rather than of a progressive woman's college, the Meredith Angels were as socially sophisticated as their counterparts—the Lady Deacons of Wake Forest, for example—and as athletically aggressive in Division III of the National Collegiate Athletic Association (NCAA) as the Lady Tarheels of Division I.

None of the Angels played in the Olympic Games; however, it would be safe to say that they joined other athletes and sports enthusiasts throughout the nation in stunned disappointment when President Jimmy Carter requested of the United States Olympic Committee a vote "against participation in the [1980] Moscow Summer Olympics" in Russia, and the committee adhered to his request. Carter's decision was among the "punitive measures against the USSR . . . in retaliation for the Soviet invasion of Afghanistan."[91]

With no athletic scholarships to offer, Meredith was rarely featured on the sports page of the daily paper; however, the College made news elsewhere as it graduated from the provincial image of many of the women's colleges of the era into higher degrees of sophistication for its students through travel and other opportunities for understanding their world. Early in 1978, senior Cindy Truelove flew to Ghana to attend a conference sponsored by the United Nations Trade and Development Conference and the IBM Foundation for Global Equality. In the meantime, her classmate Vicki Jayne planned a second trip to Washington, D.C., in as many years. As editor of the *Twig*, Jayne was invited to a White House news briefing, at which she could question President Carter, whose inaugural ceremonies she had attended a year earlier.

President Carter's administration was beset by problems, two of which were the steaming inflation rate at home and the simmering hostage crisis abroad. When the Ayatollah Khomeini wrested control of Iran in 1979 from Shah Pahlavi, who was in New York for medical treatment, the dissident forces captured the United States Embassy in Teheran and held fifty-two Americans hostage for 444 days—until after Ronald Reagan had soundly defeated Jimmy Carter in the 1980 presidential election and had been inaugurated as fortieth president of the United States.* Meanwhile, the nation's people became increasingly hostile toward the Ayatollah and his regime. Inspired by the popular song, "Tie a Yellow Ribbon 'Round the Old Oak Tree," Americans everywhere displayed yellow ribbons as a show of support for the hostages, and, in March 1980, the SGA sponsored a ceremony in which students so adorned one-hundred campus oaks.

In addition to Ann Kurtz, new member of the foreign languages department, who had just arrived from Iran, Meredith also claimed personal ties to the territory through Helen Turlington, former assistant professor of sociology, and her husband, Henry Turlington, a former trustee. In 1977, the Turlingtons had left their respective posts to serve as missionaries in Iran, and, for a time in 1979, their well-being was uncertain.

---

*The Charter Centennial issue of the student newspaper for February 27, 1991, reported that, in a 1980 mock election, 46 percent of the Meredith students voting had cast ballots for Reagan and 38 percent for Carter.

But finally the good news of their safety reached the campus, and *Meredith* reported that "Helen and Henry Turlington . . . were the last Southern Baptist missionaries to leave the country, according to the *Biblical Recorder*. . . ."[92] On their return home, Mrs. Turlington rejoined the faculty.

WITH ALUMNAE NUMBERING in the thousands, and with all its constituencies growing, Meredith constantly dealt with death in the college family. In that context, the years 1976–80 were, in many ways, some of the saddest. The historical account of an era cannot note all rites of passage; but neither can it fail to acknowledge the loss of some of the very young women, whose tragic deaths so deeply affected their peers in the residence halls and classrooms, or the older, wiser, legendary women and men, whose influence had already shaped the College forever. Ellen Amanda Rumley, a senior, died October 3, 1976; Linda Morgan and Susan Gencarelli, both juniors, died in 1978. All three students were killed in automobile accidents. And students Lynn Knott and Martha Nell Tucker died in 1976, both of natural causes. Carlyle Campbell, Meredith's fourth president, who served for twenty-seven years, died on July 27, 1977. Louise Lanham, associate professor of English, 1935–54, died April 1, 1976; Ralph McLain, professor of religion and chairman of the department for thirty-two years, died August 27, 1977, only three months after he retired; L.E.M. Freeman, professor of religion and head of the department, 1910–49, died January 21, 1979; and Ellen Brewer, professor of home economics, 1922–1966, died September 19, 1979. The deaths of trustees—both current and former—included Kemp S. Cate, July 23, 1976; Robert W. Kicklighter, October 19, 1978; Bland B. Pruitt, February 12, 1980; Henry M. Shaw, June 15, 1980; and Shearon Harris, Vice Chairman of the Board, August 28, 1980. Harry Dunston, cook, and Louise Booker, member of the housekeeping staff, each having served Meredith for forty-one years, died in May 1980 and July 17, 1980, respectively; and Mary Davis, in her fourth year as resident adviser, died August 28, 1976.

In memory of Ellen Rumley, and with the financial help of her parents, the seniors in 1977 specified their class gift as a gazebo, which was later built near the lake and the Elva Bryan McIver Amphitheater. And in their daughter's honor, Sarah Katherine Furches Rumley, '43, and Leon Rumley established the Ellen Amanda Rumley Memorial Scholarship Endowment. Classmates and friends of Lynn Knott bought and hung in the Fireside Room of Cate Center a seascape by Lynn's favorite artist, Austin Johnson.

Because Dr. Campbell's death occurred between semesters, Meredith chose the first convocation of the new academic year to remember him. Norma Rose, '36, spoke for the faculty; Zelma Green Williams, '61, for the alumnae; Edith Stephenson Simpson, '48, for the trustees; and John E. Weems for the administration.

The *News and Observer* also paid tribute to President Campbell:

Campbell was a man of great civility, scholarship and religious conviction. And despite his distinguished bearing, he was a completely unpretentious man—open, approachable and genuinely caring for others. During his 29 years as head of the Baptist liberal arts college on Hillsborough Street, he imparted those ideals of knowledge and insight that give meaning and purpose to the lives of thousands of the school's alumnae.[93]

While Shearon Harris's service on the Board spanned only ten years, it was of such significance that his fellow trustees had voted in April, before his death in August, to "look with favor" upon constructing a new building for the math and business departments and naming it in Mr. Harris's honor.[94]

To reflect on these "saints"—students, faculty, staff, and trustees alike—is to revisit the meaning of "treasure in earthen vessels." In his 1976 *Meredith* article under the same title, Dean Burris said, "Every Christian is a minister, called to mediate between God and other people, called to do the work of the world. This assumption is at the heart of curriculum planning, faculty selection, and instruction in a Christian college."[95]

5

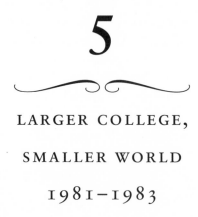

LARGER COLLEGE,

SMALLER WORLD

1981–1983

ON HER RETURN from a summer seminar in India, Susan Gilbert, assistant professor of English, said,

> I think it is right remarkable that Meredith, which was once a traditional—a very provincial—college, has a faculty of real world travelers. . . .
>
> We have in our minds now a picture of the Indian women and children, and somehow we have to help the young women at Meredith include in their life experiences a concern for those people. At eighteen or twenty, students can't be blamed for having their imaginations focused more narrowly on their own lives. Surely in these times they're worried about jobs. Will they be prosperous? Will they be secure? Our experiences in India must make us, their teachers, more secure in helping them gain perspective on their enormous wealth—to help them see it, be comfortable with it, be generous, and to find ways of being happy in being generous.[1]

Dr. Gilbert was one of fourteen professors from Raleigh who participated in the 1982 Meredith-sponsored seminar, which was funded by a Fulbright-Hayes grant from the U.S. Office of Education. She kept company in India with colleagues Dorothy Preston, mathematics; Ann Kurtz and William Ledford, foreign languages; Evelyn Simmons, economics;

and nine faculty members from the Cooperating Raleigh Colleges consortium. Mrs. Simmons directed the group's search to determine how science and technology had affected India. She said the seminar "was designed for us to gain insight into Indian problems and prospects and culture; to return to the Raleigh community and infuse others—students, faculty, and the community at large—with some of these ideas that would create a better understanding between the United States and India."[2]

Gilbert recalled a highlight of the trip: "I don't know how many of us had been received by a head of state before, but we—only our group—were in Mrs. Gandhi's residence for an hour around the conference table on Saturday morning."[3] Indira Gandhi had met in 1974 with Vice President Sandra Thomas, representative of the World Education Fellowship, and in 1976 with history professor Rosalie Gates, participant in a two-month seminar in India. Dr. Kurtz's meeting with Mrs. Gandhi was her second opportunity for an audience with a head of state, she having met with the Shah of Iran in 1978.

In April 1983, K.R. Narayanan, India's ambasador to the United States, enriched the India-Meredith exchange when he addressed the subject of U.S.–Indian Relations in a public lecture on the campus. In smaller groups, he spoke informally about Gandhi, about the progress of his country as an industrial power, and about issues common to the United States and India. Narayanan noted that "no bilateral differences exist between the two nations, just differences in their approach to the rest of the world."[4]

While his colleagues traveled in India, Lyn Aubrecht, associate professor of psychology, used a sabbatical leave to travel the world of politics in Washington, D.C., where he was on the staff of Congressman Austin J. Murphy of Pennsylvania, chairman of the House Subcommittee on Select Education. Dr. Aubrecht accepted his appointment as Congressional Science Fellow of the American Psychological Association because of his advocacy for programs for gifted children. Whatever he contributed to Representative Murphy's efforts toward such programs, he also found himself immersed in "the sale of AWACS planes to Saudi, Arabia; the Clean Air Act; the 'Apple Computer Bill'; Student Financial Aid; and . . . [research on] the MX missile."[5]

AIR TRAVEL AND instant communication decreased the size of the world. And programs that attracted students to Meredith increased the size of the College. In the early days of the 1981 fall term, three applicants for admission vied for every available space. Mr. Baker had already urged the trustees to act on alleviating a continuing "critical housing shortage" by transforming the fourth floor of Barefoot Residence Hall from attic to living quarters.[6] But the renovations were not enough. By 1983, a modular housing unit provided rooms for twenty-three more students, increasing the residence possibilities on the campus to about 1,245.

An ideal student population, said the administration, would be approximately 1,600, including residents and commuters. In the 1982–83 term, enrollment declined at twenty-one of the thirty private senior colleges in North Carolina, and even with its residence halls overflowing, Meredith felt the pressure of the shrinking student-age population. In the fall of 1982, admissions counselors were on the road almost constantly. And to four Open Days during the year, they invited high school seniors and their parents to see for themselves the college routine and to absorb the campus ambiance. High school juniors were not ignored; Meredith gave them and their parents full attention as they conferred with both faculty and admissions people during an annual Visitation Day. These recruitment efforts were in addition to the Summer Scholars program, through which rising high school seniors took college-level courses; and to Acteens Day, when members of the Baptist organization for teenage girls flooded the campus. And just to be sure it had covered all bases, during Christmas break in 1983, when prospective students would likely be free to watch television, Meredith aired its first television commercial on the local ABC and CBS affiliates.

The Class of 1983 had unwittingly posed a problem by graduating 353 seniors, approximately thirty-five more than usual, leaving the admissions staff with thirty-five additional spaces to fill. The housing policy was clear: A student *under* the age of 23 lived either on the campus or with her husband or a close relative, but in unusual circumstances, a senior might receive special permission to live off campus; however, a student *over* the age of 23 was not "eligible for campus housing," unless she reached that age while a resident.[7]

In 1981–82, half the commuting students and ten percent of the student population were over twenty-three years of age. Also during that term, twenty-five international students made their impact on the campus. More students and more programs necessitated additional faculty and staff. "Additional" faculty did not necessarily imply "new" faculty. For example, Betty Webb, '67, was a new department head but a seven-year veteran of the English department. As a Danforth Scholar, she had spent the previous three years pursuing the Ph.D. at the University of North Carolina in Chapel Hill. The Irish literature specialist was named chairman of her department in 1981, succeeding Norma Rose, who continued to teach. Having been a student of Dr. Rose's, Dr. Webb was reticent to acknowledge a new "pecking order." But one of her directives was that the department shed its reputation of formality, beginning with the use of first names in extra-classroom situations. She admits to having had difficulty speaking the first name of her professor "tripplingly on the tongue," as Hamlet admonished his players to "speak the speech,"[8] but Webb was taken aback when the former chairman issued her own instructions: "Betty," said Rose, "if you want to be less formal, you're going to have to stop answering 'yes ma'am' to everything I say."[9]

In its informal mode, the department honored Donald Samson, its one male member, at a wedding shower on St. Valentine's day in 1982. The *Twig* zealously, and with tongue in cheek, covered the event: "The groom was lovely in his red flannel shirt and black garter, which was worn fetchingly around his upper arm." Gifts from his colleagues included "a multitude of kitchen gadgets" and a pottery casserole dish.[10] At the shower, Dr. Rose reportedly won the prize for knowing the greatest number of married couples in British literature. (She captured the edge by naming all six wives of Henry VIII.)

The Departments of Art and Education also came under new leadership in 1982. Craig Greene, a member of the faculty since 1977, was appointed chairman of the art department and Daniel Todd of the education department. Dr. Greene studied at Mars Hill College for the A.B.; at the University of North Carolina in Greensboro for the M.F.A.; and at North Carolina State University for the Ed.D. During his tenure of almost two decades, he would be highly effective in bringing the then-scattered art department under one roof. Dr. Todd, on the other hand, remained only briefly as chairman of the education department, but in the second year of his stay at Meredith, his department became one of three to offer graduate work. In addition to his three years at Meredith, his service to higher education included Pembroke State, North Carolina State, the University of North Carolina at Charlotte, East Carolina University, and

Appalachian State. He had earned the bachelor's and master's degrees at East Carolina and the Ph.D. at the University of North Carolina in Chapel Hill.

About 70 percent of the faculty held doctorates. Of the administration's emphasis on credentials, Dean Burris said, "I wouldn't say that every good teacher who has, say, a master's degree will become a better teacher by getting a doctorate, but I think that, in most cases, it's true. . . . We're in the business of education, and if we assume that formal education doesn't improve one, we're pretty hard to defend."[11] While teachers with terminal degrees were available in most disciplines, there was "still considerable difficulty in finding doctorates in business," he said.[12]

Finding enough money in their pockets was also difficult, according to the faculty. Although salaries had increased about ten percent in 1981–82, inflation was high, and the teaching staff voiced concern that neither their purses nor their services—meritorious or otherwise—were rewarded in "real dollars." But sometimes tenure was more desirable than money. In 1982, thirty-one of the seventy-eight full-time faculty enjoyed that assurance. Those who taught in the smaller departments seemed to be more at risk than others because the governing policy expressly stated that no academic department could be completely tenured. The trustees discussed suspending those rules in unusual circumstances but discarded the idea in favor of authorizing multi-year contracts for up to five years. Joe Maron, assistant professor of art, was the first recipient of such a contract.

TO CREATE A fifth vice-presidency, the trustees again amended the by-laws, naming Joe Baker to the new administrative post of vice president for administrative affairs. Baker, who had served for seventeen years as vice president for business and finance, thereby assumed the role of official representative of the president and liaison to North Carolina Baptists. On October 1, 1983, Charles E. Taylor, with a B.S. and M.B.A. from East Carolina University, joined the administration in the post vacated by Baker. At the time of his appointment, Taylor was business manager of Vance-Granville Community College in Henderson, North Carolina. At Meredith, he would be responsible for financial services, information services, the office of campus activities, the college store, central services and printing, environmental services, maintenance and housekeeping, food services, light and sound, the post office, security, the stables, and the switchboard. But as the decade of the eighties unfolded, perhaps the employment of a full-time painter and a full-time plumber was more indicative of the College's expansion than was the naming of a fifth vice president.

Contracts with architects and builders, as well as with administrators, faculty members, and staff people, signaled a growing institution. "Historic" was Joe Baker's word for the fact that both the chapel and the business building were on the drawing boards in 1981. Not since 1926 had two buildings been under construction simultaneously, he said. The business building was dedicated on August 30, 1982, and the chapel twenty-five days later on September 24, 1982. When the contractor applied for a building permit for the Harris Business Building, he was surprised to learn that, in 1973, the city had zoned some of the land in Meredith's immediate neighborhood as "agricultural productive," including "a large portion of the western part of the . . . campus which at that time was outside the city limits."[13] Then when Raleigh annexed the College property, it failed to rezone the acreage as "office and institutional." A tongue-in-cheek *Meredith* news item, titled "Right Needle, Wrong Haystack," wondered "if the city fathers take Meredith's nickname, the Angel [*Farm*] more seriously than the College does." A three-week waiting period and a speedy hearing met the requirements for rezoning, and, finally, the Harris Building was underway. "And one more row has been hoed at the Angel Farm," said the magazine.[14]

The 24,000-square-foot structure would house the Departments of Business and Economics and of Mathematics. As recorded in the previous chapter, the building, which faces the Carlyle Campbell Library and is adjacent to Joyner Hall, was named in honor of the late Shearon Harris, a Meredith trustee and the former president, chief executive officer, and chairman of the board of Carolina Power and Light Company. Harris had also been a director of the North Carolina Foundation of Church Related Colleges and parliamentarian of the Baptist State Convention. Present at the dedication on August 30, 1982, were Mrs. Harris and her daughters, Jenny Harris Wallace and Sarah Harris, who presented a portrait of Harris for the new building. Fred Tolson was the architect and Davidson and Jones the builder.

One of the intriguing features of the Harris Building was its purple walls. The *Twig* sought the reaction of Dr. Wheeler, chairman of the mathematics department and one of Harris's tenants. He said, "I thoroughly enjoy the color scheme. . . . Besides the aesthetic considerations, I've noted that confronting a student by a purple wall at 8:00 A.M. markedly increases her alertness in class."[15] But one of the most talked-about topics in general was the accelerated interest in business and math. When Lois Frazier, chairman of the Department of Business and Economics, said, "Business is a viable, changing, dynamic field,"[16] one needed only to look at statistics for proof. About the time she made the statement, her department had attracted approximately 200 majors. In fact, in the previous spring, Dr. Frazier had reported that 1,226 Meredith students were taking some kind of course in business.

The firm of F. Carter Williams designed the chapel, and, again, general contractor Davidson and Jones built it. Even before its dedication, the building was named in honor of Christina and Seby Jones, both of whom were generous contributors to the College. The honor also recognized Mr. Jones's advocacy for Meredith as a trustee. He was president of Davidson and Jones.

Somehow, every stage of construction of the chapel was of intense interest to people who were already intensely interested in Meredith, and to some who were merely acquaintances. St. Mary's, the neighboring Episcopal junior college for women, was a case in point. The school's chaplain, Starke Dillard, hand-delivered to the College a gift of $100 from the students and faculty of St. Mary's, "with the hope," reported the *Twig*, "that Meredith's chapel becomes as dear to our campus as St. Mary's chapel has been to them."[17] Early in 1982, a horde of "sidewalk superintendents" crowded the front drive as a huge, yellow crane gingerly lifted the cross-topped steeple to the roof, but none of the onlookers seemed prepared for the emotion of the moments.

The work of two chapel committees might have contributed to the personal interest displayed in the construction. The programming committee, chaired by Marion Lark, pastor of the First Baptist Church of Henderson, North Carolina, was dubbed the "Inside-Out" Committee, and the buildings and grounds committee of the Board of Trustees, chaired by Claude Williams, was known as the "Outside-In" Committee. The former group entertained ideas from Meredith constituents; visited other campuses in an effort to understand all the ways a chapel could benefit the College; and studied archival documents as bases for their recom-

On a very early spring day in 1982, the steeple is put in place, and a cross is hoisted to the pinnacle of the Seby and Christina Jones Chapel.

mendations. For example, they applied to their thinking Thomas Meredith's historic phrase, "on strictly religious principles," from his 1838 Baptist State Convention resolution to establish a female seminary. In addition to the historical and the religious components, the committee considered the functional and the aesthetic—"'a strong presence' but not an overpowering one," they determined.[18]

The 13,000-square-foot chapel sanctuary seats about four hundred people. The building also houses the offices of the campus minister. A small meditation chapel, made possible by a bequest from Ellen Brewer, is adorned with a batik—also a gift of the Class of 1928—by artist Pat Stumpf. And the batik was not the final gift to the chapel from the class; in 1988, it donated—to hang over the fireplace in the common room— a Paul Mennis oil painting of the original campus.

The architects wisely included a bride's room in the plans; in January 1983, Mr. Baker reported that the three-month-old chapel had been the site of sixteen weddings and that eighteen more were penned in on the college calendar. Over the next decade, the number of weddings in the chapel would very nearly equal the number of weekends in the same time period. Marie Mason, coordinator of campus activities, said that by the end of the summer of 1993, the weekends were already booked for 1994, although the fees had increased from $75–$100 for people with Meredith connections and from $200–$300 for others.

President Weems spoke of the building as a "special gift to the greater community." He also saw it as a "special witness" and as "the gentle reminder of our religious heritage."[19] In the dedicatory address on September 24, 1982, Duke McCall, president of the Baptist World Alliance and chancellor of Southern Baptist Theological Seminary, said,

> I thank God that we . . . can be reminded by this chapel that at the very heart of the human search for knowledge and truth is set this symbol of the redemptive act of God in Christ Jesus to remind us that "If you continue in my word (my message), then you are my disciples indeed; and *you shall* (not *you may*) know the truth and the truth shall set you free."
>
> May every benediction here be but a sign that the worship is ended and the service has begun.[20]

Dedication of the Estelle Johnson Salisbury Organ on Sunday, April 10, 1983, completed the chapel sanctuary. W. David Lynch played a recital to a standing-room-only crowd. Custom-built by the Andover Organ Company of Lawrence, Massachusetts, the ornate instrument of 1,394 pipes was the only mechanical action organ in the family of the seven North Carolina Baptist colleges. It resembled an eighteenth-century model; in fact, said Dr. Lynch, "There are organs like this built in the 17th century in Europe that still play."[21] While Martha Salisbury Smoot initiated the largest gift toward the $150,000 instrument, the DuPont Foundation contributed $50,000. And, as a special golden wedding anniversary gift to each other, Mabel Claire Hoggard Maddrey, '28, and her husband, Gordon Maddrey, furnished a carillon of Flemish bells. Since its installation by the Maas-Rowe Carillon Company of Escondido, California, it has chimed the hours from 7:00 A.M. until midnight. At noon and at 5:00 P.M., it plays a concert—often of familiar hymns—for Meredith and its neighbors.

The chapel faced a beautified front drive. In a valiant stand against age and weather, the few gnarled old cherry trees, circa 1926, that still lined the avenue from Hillsborough Street to Johnson Hall had been rejuvenated by a host of younger trees. Through a letter to the *Twig*, Donald Samson of the English department had planted the idea of students' requesting cherry trees for Valentine's Day gifts in 1980. In 1981, he again promoted his cause: "I think . . . you would rather receive a cherry tree, which will cost $20 for a four to five foot tree and last for twenty years or more, than an $80 dozen of roses which would wilt in four days."[22] The idea took root. In April of the same year, Samson wrote another letter: "In the last two years, fifty Japanese cherry trees have been planted along the drive in front of Johnson Hall for all of us at Meredith to enjoy."[23]

More cherry trees, more people, more cars were undeniable evidences of growth. In the past decade, Vice President Baker said in 1982, the student body had grown to about 1,600 young women. "And where to park [students'] cars is only one of the situations we face."[24] He named other challenges: an abundance of governmental red tape; a gross payroll of $352,668.42; a greatly expanded food service; and the privatization of some services, such as the cleaning of classrooms and offices. Ten years ago, he said, the operating budget was just over $3 million; in 1982 it was more than $9 million. Tuition and room and board had almost doubled from $2,500 to $4,400. But the good news that the endowment had increased to about $10 million from only $2 million brought a sense of freedom from fear of the proverbial rainy day.[25]

As fees climbed, some of the people who charged them as well as some who paid them asked why. Others wondered why charges were not higher, inasmuch as Meredith's costs remained far lower than those of most of the private colleges in the state. President Weems explained: "Meredith is less likely to face competition [for students] from private schools than from public schools [where the tuition is lower], and this has a very strong effect on the amount of tuition that Meredith is able to charge."[26]

THE COLLEGE GREW not only in numbers of people and facilities but also in the interpretation of its mission. Continuing education continued blazing trails. In 1982, the post-baccalaureate Cultural Resources Management Program awarded its first certificate to Jane Williamson Teague, '54, executive director of Raleigh's ArtsPlosure. And, in 1983, the Legal Assistants Program—one of only three on the east coast—earned the approval of the American Bar Association.

For several years, adult students had composed approximately 12 percent of the student body; in 1983 alone, forty of them progressed from the re-entry level to degree-seeking status. Recruiting was often a word-of-mouth phenomenon, but advertising also helped. In October of that year, the program's new director, Dr. Ironside, announced An Evening at Meredith for women over twenty-three. If the idea of personally introducing the College to prospective students had worked for high school women, it should be helpful for older ones as well. Ellen Ironside was named associate dean for continuing education in 1983. An undergraduate philosophy major at Wells, the New Yorker earned a master's degree in music from Columbia. "When I began to think about what I might do when I grew up, I found I wanted to know more about adults' development,"[27] she said, and, on moving to Chapel Hill with her family, she enrolled at the university in a doctoral program in adult education, and "Meredith's continuing education program was waiting not too far beyond her dissertation."[28]

A long-time advocate for continuing education for former students, the office of alumnae affairs had introduced in 1981–82 its Meredith-on-the-Road seminars, to be offered wherever an organization of alumnae deemed suitable. In the first year, Jon Lindsey taught a short course in resource information to alumnae in Richmond and Anson Counties, North

Carolina, and Rebecca Murray offered Children's Literature Revisited to a group in Red Springs. In the 1982–83 term, the Alumnae Re-entry Club (ARC) was organized to function much like a traditional alumnae chapter. One of its first projects was to establish the Anne C. Dahle Scholarship for adult students. By 1996, the scholarship's principal had climbed to $47,000.

Dahle cited some of the changes in the continuing education program since 1971: "registration by mail, evening classes, transfer credit for nursing school programs, official transcript evaluation for pre-admission advising, contract majors, credit for extra-institutional situations. . . ."[29] Her best experiences, she said, involved students: "More than one who has come in timid and frightened has developed self-confidence, self-understanding, as well as academic knowledge, and has gone out with a better ability to cope with her environment."[30] Especially, she remembered Lillie Lawson-Jones, who graduated in 1982 after only five regular semesters and three summers:

> Lillie Lawson-Jones dropped out of high school in the tenth grade because of disagreement with her mother. She worked in a variety of jobs, including driving a taxi in a large northern city. Later she moved south to live near her grandparents. When she was just past thirty, a series of unfortunate incidents led to her imprisonment. Her term was for eighteen to twenty years. She tells me that on her first day in the correctional center for women that she made a vow to take advantage of every opportunity that would improve her situation. . . .
>
> She had completed the high school equivalency (GED) prior to her incarceration and had made acceptable scores. She took the Scholastic Aptitude Test in prison and again scored satisfactorily. By the time she could apply for study release, she had applied to Meredith and had conferred with me about her courses for the first semester.
>
> This was a new experience for both of us. She had to learn college procedure, and I had to learn prison procedure. . . . She may have been the first study release person to attend a small liberal arts college where the student is expected to participate in a total program, not just attend classes. . . . Faculty members and students

happily provided transportation. . . . Prison officials were understanding and helpful. . . .

For Lillie, learning was an exciting experience. She made no effort
to avoid difficult courses and met each challenge with enthusiasm.[31]

When Lawson-Jones applied for parole, she knew it would be granted
only after she had found a job and a place to live. A retired member of the
college staff rented her a room, and she landed a job with flexible hours.
Dahle continued,

Again Lillie had to work through a new experience—freedom. . . .
When she entered college, her goal was to become a social worker.
. . . Lillie is in her second year of a graduate program in social work
at the University of North Carolina in Chapel Hill. . . . It is not
often that an academic adviser is able to watch such progress.
Working with Lillie Lawson-Jones has been that most rewarding
experience of my last five years. Probably of my entire career.[32]

As exceptional people in exceptional times lift careers beyond day-to-
day routine, a vision revisited can inspire a college to step boldly past the
ordinary. Meredith climbed above the status quo in February 1983 with
the re-establishment of graduate studies. Offering the master's degree was
not a spur-of-the-moment decision, the 1978–80 self-study having raised
the possibilities. Clara Bunn chaired an ad hoc committee on graduate
studies, its members including Allen Page, religion; Lyn Aubrecht, psychology; Gene Sumner, sociology and social work; Jon Lindsey, library;
Susan Gilbert, English; and Allen Burris, *ex officio*. Of their work, Page
said, "If there is a stone unturned, it is because we didn't find the stone."[33]
The committee's recommendation was short and to the point:

The offering of post baccalaureate studies is consistent with Meredith College's mission, purpose, and history of providing outstanding educational opportunities to women. Therefore, we recommend
that the college proceed to establish a process by which specific
graduate programs can be considered and implemented.[34]

The offering of graduate studies was consistent with Meredith's mission
in 1983, as it had been in 1902. Although the College had awarded only
three such degrees in the ten years between 1902 and 1911, it had indeed,

in those early years, granted the master's degree.[35] The Academic Council endorsed the recommendation, and the faculty amended it to read, "that the college proceed to establish a process by which specific graduate programs *and other post-baccalaureate programs* can be considered. . . .[36] By unanimous vote, the Board of Trustees authorized graduate studies in business administration, education, and music on February 25, 1983. News of the giant step was accompanied by a statement of rationale from each chairman of the three departments involved. Lois Frazier of the business department said, "Until Campbell University initiated a satelllite master's program in business at Peace College in Raleigh, the nearest MBA possibilities were at the University of North Carolina in Chapel Hill and at Duke."[37] Daniel Todd, education, quoted statistics: "There are 3,159 women teaching in the public schools of seven area counties to which Meredith is accessible; of those teachers, 2,200 do not have graduate certification, there is no elementary education master's degree in Raleigh, and Meredith is already the certifying agent for elementary education students at North Carolina State University."[38] And David Lynch, music and the performing arts, said, "Not only are no such programs available in our geographic area, there are only a few comparable ones in the entire Southeast."[39] In fact, the committee had discovered that, in Meredith's neighborhood, only East Carolina and the University of North Carolina at Greensboro offered master's degrees in music performance. Meredith would offer one in performance and one in pedagogy.

"Meredith must not limit its future by defining itself too narrowly," said President Weems as he encouraged the establishment of graduate studies.[40] And Dean Burris added, "Of the thirty women's colleges in the nation with graduate programs, Meredith will be one of two offering graduate programs exclusively for women. . . ,"[41] the second being Simmons College in Boston. As plans were made and procedures outlined, dual responsibilities became apparent: Meredith must continue to scrutinize its mission in the light of educating women for their times, and, to survive the approaching lean years of available college-age students, it must maintain a steady enrollment. In the practicality of the second area of concern, plans called for classes to be scheduled "for the convenience of the working adult woman"; for the instruction to come from the regular faculty "plus some outside appointments for special expertise"; and for a six-year time limit to be set for completing the master's degree.[42] The first year's enrollment more than doubled expectations. By August 1983, forty-eight students had applied to begin the MBA, and forty were expected to enroll; matriculation of all thirty applicants in education was anticipated; and, of the eight music department applicants, four or five were near certainties. A month later, at the September 1983 meeting of the Board of Trustees, the president reported that ninety students had actually enrolled. Establishment of the program was partially underwritten by a portion of a million-dollar bequest that came to the College from the estate of Minnie Huffman Reddish formerly of Morganton, North Carolina. Dr. Bunn accepted the post as first director of graduate studies.

With all the indications of success in the new graduate studies, the core of the academic program remained at the undergraduate level. Given the number of graduate students seeking the MBA, it was not surprising that undergraduates also had been declaring majors designed to groom them for careers in business and the professions. Both the Departments of Business and Home Economics, for example, boomed with popularity. In 1981 and 1982 respectively, each of those departments installed charter members of national honor societies: in business, the Gamma Rho Delta Chapter of Delta Mu Delta, and, in home economics, the Delta Omicron Chapter of Kappa Omicron Phi. In 1982–83, home economics initiated concentrations in child development and family relations; clothing and fashion merchandising; consumer resource management; foods and nutrition; interior design and housing; as well as general home economics. The American Dietetic Association approved the department's program in dietetics. In the same year and at the invitation of Duke University, the biology department, under its new name of biology and health sciences, offered its senior majors the opportunity to spend their final year at Duke in medical technology and to graduate from Meredith with a degree in that specialty. Curricular changes dictated a new name not only for the biology department but for the math department, as well: in 1982, it became the Department of Mathematical Sciences. Even the Department of English opened its door to specialization when, in 1983, it began offering for juniors and seniors a concentration in professional communications.

In that year, for the first time, the number of students receiving the Bachelor of Science degree exceeded the number earning the Bachelor of Arts degree. Those and other statistics began to tell a story. For example, the number of graduates who became teachers dropped from 22.4 percent in 1979 to 12.5 percent in 1982; but the number who went into business and industry climbed from 41.9 to 51.0 percent.[43] With some frequency, questions arose about vocational education in a liberal arts college. Dean Burris commented on the subject in *Meredith*:

> The theme I've pounded on is that we try to plan and provide an education which takes into account all the needs of our students on the proposition that a liberal arts education . . . is not only not incompatible with vocational education but is essential to it, and vice versa. . . .
>
> Meredith has always included concern for work. We've always trained working women. And, in the last ten years, we've tried to make that more explicit, both in our propaganda and in the programs we've supported and pushed.[44]

IN HIS ANNUAL message for 1983, President Weems recounted the three phases of his administration: Phase one, the securing of Meredith, 1972–76, was "devoted primarily to securing funds and devising a financial plan that ultimately would make Meredith one of the most financially secure private institutions in our region." Phase two, the unfolding of Meredith, 1977–1981, "prov[ed] to ourselves and the community at large that Meredith could provide many new needed services." In Phase three, academic reshaping, 1982–83, the College sought to "devise a program that would prepare the . . . student for living in the 21st century."[45]

Records of the twelve years of the then-current administration attest to the pattern, but they also show each phase overlapping the others. For example, the securing of Meredith in the seventies gained momentum in the eighties. In fact, in 1983, the projected eight years needed to complete the $20 million Visions program were adjusted to six. Dr. McGee spread the good news that every group of supporters had increased its level of giving. He told of the *Chronicle of Higher Education*'s report that Meredith ranked "among the top colleges and universities in the country in the largest gifts received during 1983."[46] It was one of the years in which the Alumnae Association placed among the finalists for the United States Steel Award for annual giving, the 37.2 percent of contributing alumnae placing Meredith in the top 15 percent of all colleges in the nation. The faculty were also generous. Sarah Lemmon's gift of her residence in 1982 serves as a case in point: The home, across Faircloth Street from the campus, filled Meredith's need for a guest house, as Dr. Lemmon knew it would.

IN PHASE TWO, the College attempted to distance itself from any perceived provincial image. The first paragraphs of this chapter indicate that the "unfolding" of Meredith continued beyond the five years assigned to it. It was a time when the world seemed to be everybody's responsibility. Affairs of nations and their people intruded by television upon the nesting places of those who had eyes to see and ears to hear. Occasionally, listeners heard the term "global village."

Airplanes transported travelers to farflung places in a few hours, including the students in Meredith Abroad. Those who participated in 1981 recalled the excitement of England's royal wedding. Senior Jill Kibler remembered July 29 as "The day we all looked forward to and which made our trip complete. . . ." She told of the "few brave souls [who] camped out along the wedding route [to see] Prince Charles, Lady Diana, and other members of the Royal Family firsthand."[47] Melody West, '83, spent the following summer in the same territory. She wrote,

> The students who went to Britain . . . saw the Royal Family, met Sylvester Stallone, saw Elizabeth Taylor, witnessed the horror of IRA bombings, walked on Hadrian's Wall, camped out at the hospital where Prince William was born, saw the Rolling Stones, met a guard at Windsor Castle, and heard a certain professor sing in an Irish pub.
>
> They also attended an embassy party in Paris, visited Shakespeare's birthplace, walked on mosaic floors made by the Romans, walked in the footsteps of Chaucer's pilgrims, and saw the Crown Jewels.[48]

A HISTORY OF the College has been, is, and will be greatly enriched by its neighborhood of educational institutions, state government, the Research Triangle Park (RTP), business and services, the arts, and by people from around the nation and, indeed, from around the global village. As a growing Meredith provided services, an also-growing community returned the favors. After almost two decades at Meredith, Dr. Shiflett of the chemistry department reflected on his move to Raleigh—a wise one, he said, for a chemistry professor. "For something very specialized that we want our students to see and have some experience with, we can go over to N.C. State or to some of the companies in the Triangle and get exposure that would be much more difficult for students at an isolated college."[49]

Conductor Gerhardt Zimmermann conducts the North Carolina Symphony in its annual Labor Day concert by the Meredith lake.

On a list of Meredith's characteristics, one would never find the word "isolated." In 1981, Bob Wharton joined the faculty because he saw Raleigh "as a theater town and [was] bent on Meredith's being as strong in community theater as some of the long-established playhouses, such as Theater in the Park and the Raleigh Little Theater."[50] In addition to teaching, Wharton directed Meredith Performs, an "ambitious new approach to theater on the campus."[51] In his second year, he persuaded a local television station to produce a professional ad as a public service announcement. The spot aired frequently during the ticket-buying season, and the results were impressive, as were the performances of Rodgers and Hammerstein's *The King and I*, Charles Dickens's *Nicholas Nickelby*, and other presentations, including concerts by the choral and dance groups. Mr. Wharton was right; Raleigh was a theater town, and reviews for Meredith Performs often compared favorably with those of the more professional playhouses in the city.

And what would any college give to see the handsome new North Carolina Museum of Art relocate from downtown to the school's own neighborhood in 1983? Or what would any college give to host the North Carolina Symphony's Labor Day concert, heard by thousands of music lovers, by the campus lake every September? (Admission: free!) The first such event was held on Sunday, September 5, 1982, and the annual concert has continued through 1998. Music has contributed significantly to the College's reputation. In fact, the music department once ran an advertisement in a symphony concert program that read "Where there's Meredith, there's music." [52] In turn, the symphony has been and is an arts treasure for the College, as is the Raleigh Symphony, and the National Opera Company. And the North Carolina Museum of Art, relocated to Meredith's neighborhood in 1983.

Almost as joyous as hearing a symphony or visiting a gallery is finding the very course one seeks at a Cooperating Raleigh College. By 1982, junior Kellie Farlow had taken three courses at North Carolina State. She wrote about her experiences in a guest editorial for the *Twig*:

> My NCSU registration card entitles me to . . . (1) use of the library, (2) intercollegiate athletic events, (3) use of the University Student Center, (4) membership in Friends of the College, (5) use of university infirmary, (6) use of Student Supply Store, and (7) other university facilities, services, and programs.
>
> It just seems a shame to me not to take advantage of one of the best universities in the country . . . when we are one mile down the road. . . . [53]

In the eyes of Meredith people, North Carolina State University has long been "one of the best" in many ways. Statistics are unavailable as to how many Meredith women and State men have met in college and married later, but a 1983 photograph in a college magazine depicted a different kind of love affair between the two schools. The picture showed what appeared to be hundreds of Meredith students lining a beltline overpass, cheering wildly as a bus transporting the 1983 N.C. State basketball team rolled down the highway below. On their way to the airport and Albuquerque, New Mexico, for the NCAA finals, the team's players could not have missed seeing a huge banner that Meredith students had draped over the bridge. It read, "Bring it back, Pack." The Wolfpack indeed brought it all back, N.C. State's having won the national basketball championship that year.

The consortium of Cooperating Raleigh Colleges was among Meredith's many resources. It received a Title II-A Higher Education Act grant
for 1981–82, which, with a gift to Meredith from the Jessie Ball DuPont
Religious, Charitable, and Educational Fund, helped provide "the complete run" of *Music Index*. The acquisition, housed at Meredith, was "the
primary research tool for a strong music department . . . [and] not otherwise available in any academic institution in Wake County."[54]

Local people in business and government and in the denomination also
brought high levels of expertise to the campus. For example, North Carolina insurance commissioner John Ingram taught the capital city class a
lesson in the responsibilities of his office. About the same time, state treasurer Harlan Boyles and municipal funds analyst John Barnes instructed
residents of first Heilman on the whys and wherefores of inflation. And,
in a speech sponsored by student government, R.G. Puckett, editor of the
Biblical Recorder, identified some organizations—such as the Moral Majority—and some people—such as Jerry Falwell, Bill Bright, and Jim
Bakker—as "ringleaders in the attempt to legislate morality."[55]

In March 1982, Jay T. Mullins, director of the Shearon Harris Visitors'
Center of Carolina Power and Light Company, spoke in convocation on
nuclear energy. He said he expected the nuclear power plant, then under
construction about twenty miles from the College, to be on line in 1985
with one unit and in 1989 with the second.[56] The first unit, he said, would
supply electricity for 400,000 people, although Wake County's population at the time stood at only 300,000. In close time proximity, the business policy class heard David Rendal, vice president of Northern Tele-
com, speak on international marketing. And, in 1983, Delta Mu Delta,
the honor society for business administration, brought to the campus
Jane Bergman, marketing and research specialist for WRAL-TV, for a discussion on Career Paths in Marketing. Government also made its many
contributions. Meredith hosted a 1982 winter seminar for the North Carolina Federation of College Democrats, drawing on local leaders—Jane
Patterson, secretary of administration; Chris Scott, secretary-treasurer of
the state AFL-CIO; and Judge Willis Whichard of the Court of Appeals—
as speakers.

TOWNSPEOPLE ALSO GAVE the College high marks for including them in
events of mutual interest. When Ross Millhiser, vice chairman of the

Board of Philip Morris in New York, visited in April 1982, the planners invited thirty-five local business leaders to lunch. Perhaps neither the guests nor the business students who heard him could have imagined the extent of the disfavor that would be heaped upon the giant tobacco companies in the mid-nineties. Mr. Millhiser came to discuss topics other than problems associated with smoking, however; he came to praise liberal arts colleges: "I never knew a time when we needed the Meredith Colleges of our land more," he said. . . . "I think I could more readily entrust the destiny of Philip Morris to a scholar of Greek philosophy who employs modern science to deepen his understanding than to a genius of sophisticated technology to whom Greek philosophy is Greek."[57]

Mr. Millhiser was one of an interesting variety of speakers. Among other notables in 1982 were Gwendolyn Brooks, poet laureate of Illinois and the first black woman to receive a Pulitzer Prize; Alexander Julian, an award-winning designer of men's fashions; and Chris Sizemore, who had suffered through a multiple-personalities disorder, and whose story became public through the film titled *The Three Faces of Eve*. But each academic year offered its own rewards. In 1981, for example, just one two-day symposium on "Toward Conscious Conscience" had stirred such interest that classes were suspended at three o'clock Monday afternoon until eight o'clock Wednesday morning. The purpose was "to explore definitions of conscience. . . ; to raise levels of awareness about the roles of conscience for the individual and in culture; and to provide a variety of forums through which the Meredith community can grapple with the outcomes of conscience as a conscious benefit of personal interaction and decision making."[58] Virginia Carter, vice president of Tandem Productions; Frank Wood, professor of neuro-psychology at Bowman Gray; Hedda Sharapun, associate producer of *Mr. Rogers' Neighborhood*, and Carll Tucker, editor of *Saturday Review*, addressed the topics.

IN THE THIRD phase of the administration's emphases, the College addressed academic reshaping, but one modification was not initiated by Meredith. In the 1981–82 term, the Council on Social Work Education directed that the College replace its certification program with a degree program, offering a major in social work.[59] The change appeared for the first time in the 1982–83 catalogue. And a year later, totally at Meredith's prerogative, computer science made *its* debut as a major. The

1981–82 catalogue had also carried a new entry that drew attention more to location than to subject matter: "Through an arrangement with Marymount College in New York City, students may visit the college for one semester. The program provides many opportunities for study in the Manhattan area."

To a greater degree than ever before, technology became the tool of choice, both for teaching and for learning. Ignited by the gift of a teaching computer from the Data General Corporation, the "computer explosion on campus"[60] yielded a fall-out of a fully equipped laboratory in the new Harris Building and some computers in other buildings. Music students were among the first to learn the value of technology in their studies, but all freshmen learned word processing in English 111. In 1983, Dean Burris said, "The regular course in the introduction to computing is growing faster than we can get teachers to teach it. And, the new major is thriving."[61] As early as 1981, Meredith added an office of computer services—or information services, as it was later called—although some computer technicians had been employed earlier. Mr. Taylor, who oversaw such operations, said in 1983 that the office "supports some 1600 computer programs, 2000 procedures to run these programs and 150 million bytes of data storage."[62]

While Meredith lived in the new world of technology, it returned to the Middle Ages for a time in September 1983. Beginning with convocation on Monday and continuing through a courtyard fair on Friday, a week-long medieval festival recreated the ambiance of the period. The festival was a "week of music, lectures, films, drama, art, games, feasting, simulated combat, heresy, worship, sheep milking, medieval science, troubadors, knights, monks, nuns, tradesmen, shepherds, kings, queens, and fools."[63] Duke University lent the College a display of ancient manuscripts; the coastal town of Manteo's brass rubbing shoppe lent expertise in its craft; and the religion department lent its talents to write and perform a heresy trial. Guest speakers; musicians; and, at times, a costumed faculty, contributed to the mood.

THE LARGER MEREDITH became, the greater were its concerns for security. From time to time, the College suffered the indignities of mischief, threats, even vandalism. In October 1981, for example, a bomb threat disrupted a Meredith Performs production of *Once Upon a Mattress* in Jones Auditorium. After the security staff and the Raleigh police saw to the evacuation of the building, searched thoroughly, and found nothing, the play continued. Even more surprising were the several episodes of arson in the early evening of Tuesday, February 16, 1982. In the first and most destructive incident, the arsonist set fire to a wastebasket in a third-floor restroom in Johnson Hall, completely destroying the room and costing the insurance company $32,000. That same evening, six additional blazes were extinguished quickly, but the trauma of fear and uncertainty made for a long evening. On the following Sunday morning, a smoke alarm on the fourth floor of Vann Residence Hall alerted students to a hot iron left on a stack of clothes in the laundry room. And a week after the initial scare, someone set fire to a sign-out card in Vann. Bill Norton, director of information services and official college spokesperson, became a regular on the six o'clock news as reporters interrogated him on the status of the investigation. Concerned parents also wanted answers. The College assured the public of increased security; of Raleigh police investigations; of a "community watch" by an SGA-appointed student task force; of additional smoke detectors in all buildings. And the North Carolina Arson Awareness Council offered a $10,000 reward for incriminatory evidence.

With the sign-out card burning, the harassment stopped, but detectives continued their work. Surprisingly, they found that the largest blaze was not the first after all, earlier ones having been discovered but dismissed as accidental. All in all, twelve fires were set between January 24 and February 23. The arsonist, thought to be a student, was not identified.

Threats to and destruction of property were signs of the times—but not the only signs. As women, in particular, heard the gospel of thinness preached by fitness experts and makers of perfume and clothing, some enthusiasts threatened their own bodies with eating disorders. In 1983, Dr. Thomas was solicitous of the six to eight students suspected of anorexia nervosa. While it was a small number, she said, it "represents a sizeable increase over the number of cases at any previous time."[64] Her staff attended counseling workshops and designated places at which students could find help with such disorders and with other kinds of mental, emotional, and social problems.

Students needed academic help, as well. The English department found it necessary to offer a non-credit course to prepare students for English 111. Louise Taylor, associate professor in the department, reported that "forty students identified as likely to have difficulty were sent a letter telling them about the course and that thirty-two of them enrolled in the voluntary course."[65]

THE DEGREE OF importance attached by students to their interests was usually discernible through the *Twig*. In the fall of 1981, for example, women's issues still elicited response, as ERA supporters made their rounds seeking ratification for the amendment, which would fail in 1982. Of another issue that concerned women, Melody West, a junior, wrote,

> At the November 6 SGA meeting, the Meredith College student body decided to add its name to a petition urging Raleigh newspapers not to print the names of rape victims.
>
> It is uncertain how influential this petition will be, but at least the Raleigh papers will be aware of the concern in the area over printing these victims' names.[66]

And an editorial writer called for Duke University, where former President Nixon earned his law degree, to reconsider its refusal to house the Richard M. Nixon Library:

> Duke University has been made an offer to build a library to house Nixon's 6,000 hours of tapes and 36 million pages of archives from the White House. Duke University Administration and Faculty have made a stand that they do not want to commemorate Nixon by building a shrine to honor him.
>
> Although some concern is understandable and justified in this situation, over concern seems to be somewhat unfounded. The Nixon Library would be a great asset to the triangle area. The Library would draw national attention to this area. Because Watergate has only occurred once in the history of the United States . . . this library would stand as a historical monument to attract many historians and political scientists to the area. . . .[67]

THE ADMINISTRATION'S FOURTH phase, beginning in 1983, saw Meredith as "the New Leader." And, in that capacity, said Weems, it is important that "our accomplishments are viewed by other institutions as attainable."[68] This historical record documents some of the ways by which Meredith emerged as a new leader. When the president coined the phrase, however, he probably gave little, if any, thought as to how the College would lead in the denominational struggles of the seventies and eighties. The situation was reminiscent of remarks by Edward Hughes Pruden, senior minister at the First Baptist Church in Washington, D.C., during the presidencies of Roosevelt, Truman, Eisenhower, Kennedy, Johnson, and Nixon, all of whom he knew. (President Truman had attended his church.) While he was pastor-in-residence at Meredith, 1970–79, Dr. Pruden wrote for the *Alumnae Magazine* an article titled "From a Pulpit in Washington": "Washington Baptists sometimes say that they are Northern Baptists with a southern accent and Southern Baptists with a northern exposure. They hope that some day this spirit may be shared throughout the country, and the War Between the States be laid to rest."[69] Little could he have known then of the civil war to be fought in the eighties and nineties between Baptist inerrantists and moderates. Trouble was brewing in the Southern Baptist Convention, and battle lines were being drawn. The *Christian Century* warned,

> The biblical-inerrancy dispute that is currently upsetting the Southern Baptist Convention is the most dangerous controversy the denomination has ever faced, according to Walter Shurden, professor of church history and dean of the school of theology at Southern Baptist Theological Seminary in Louisville.
>
> "The unique thing," said Shurden, "and the most dangerous thing, is that we now have for the first time . . . a highly organized, apparently well-funded, partisan political party going not only for the minds of the Southern Baptist people but for the machinery of the Southern Baptist Convention." He charged that "the Southern Baptist inerrantists are a part of both the new religious and political right wing," and that they have been promoting a "fundamentalist ecumenism" and a "new non-denominationalism" by cooperating more with other biblical-inerrancy advocates than with other Southern Baptists.[70]

When *Biblical Recorder* editor R.G. Puckett spoke to the Student Government Association that same year, he accused the "New Right" of trying to accomplish politically what they couldn't achieve spiritually.[71] It was the beginning of unprecedented changes for Baptists and, therefore, for Meredith. But at the time, North Carolina Baptists had designated more Cooperative Program dollars to Meredith than ever before. While they had contributed $498,768.17 in 1980, as reported in Chapter 4, they had designated $704,000 for Meredith in 1981, attesting to a continuing pleasant relationship—so far—with each entity proud of and cooperative with the other.

GIVEN THE CULTURE of the new decade, Meredith students, like most Americans, expressed opinions about the thousands of men and women marching on Washington to oppose the draft registration and on Chicago to support the Equal Rights Amendment. They discussed the grain embargo that President Carter imposed upon the Soviet Union for its action against Afghanistan. They wept for joy when, in 1981, Iran released the Americans whom it had held hostage for 444 days. Meredith freshmen sponsored a religious service celebrating the event. Juniors Ann Stringfield, Debbie Huchinson, Georganne Narron, and Marie Hiott drove to Washington to see the drama unfold. Stringfield reported, "I recognized a few of the hostages. Elizabeth Ann Swift waved a flag at us. Others gave victory signs, waved, shouted, or simply smiled. Two hostages were practically hanging out the windows [of the bus]. We yelled. We waved. We laughed. We cried. . . . "[72] On the campus, students ceremoniously removed the yellow ribbons, which had adorned the trunks of one-hundred campus oaks since the hostage crisis began.

Students then, as students always have, tempered their academic work with other interests— sports, for example. That the golf team played in the 1981 AIAW Division III national tournament was hardly an everyday occurrence, however. The golfers not only made history by taking second place in the tourney, but they were also members of Meredith's first athletic team to receive a bid to compete for a national championship. The invitation to play in Sioux City, Iowa, followed the team's winning the state title and finishing second only to Wake Forest in the regionals. In Sioux City, additional honors went to rising sophomore Luann Johnson, who finished fifth individually and was named All-American. Not to be overshadowed, an inspired tennis team captured the state title in 1982.

And students enjoyed an innate capacity for refreshing frivolity. One of the *Twig*'s lead stories in 1982 reported on two Meredith groups, the No No's and the 90 Percent Angels, who placed in the top five of an air band contest sponsored by WQDR, a local radio station. The paper explained, "The term 'air band' applies to a band which mimes with silent, homemade instruments to the recording of actual performers."[73] Jan Drach, lead singer for the No No's, sang into a hair brush. The 90 Percent Angels—with lead singer Carole Stebbins; keyboard (ironing board) player Randi Jones; guitarist (tennis racquet) Karen Mills; and drummer (barrels and stools) Nancy Byrns—appeared on WRAL-TV's eleven o'clock news.

However proficient the airband "musicians," or even the golfers and tennis players, academics always came first. A student studying in the Carlyle Campbell Library had "a date with Carlyle."[74] (In fact, Lou Rosser, English, would report in 1997 that one of her re-entry students spent so many hours of her pregnancy in the library that she named her new son "Carlyle.") In 1982, students apparently had many such dates if the unusually large number of seniors named to *Who's Who Among Students in American Colleges and Universities* indicated intellectual prowess. Members of a campus nominating committee submitted the names of thirty-one of their peers on the basis of "decidedly above average academic standing, community service, leadership ability and future potential."[75] The honor attracted particular attention in 1982 because only one-third of that number had made the list in 1981. Phyllis Wurst, one of the seniors named to *Who's Who,* captured the Lillian Parker Wallace Phi Beta Kappa Award for "the best historical research paper in Wake County,"[76] a feat that was becoming almost routine for Meredith, as recorded in Chapter 3.

Soon thereafter, the *Twig* reported a contest of a different ilk: the first annual freshman-sophomore mathematics competition. Sophomore Beth Madren and freshman Cheryl Bailey pulled away from the fourteen other contestants to win first and second places, respectively. The news story implied admiration for the contestants, who had "tested their analytical skills and acumen against the treacherous shoals of the . . . competition."[77]

The math students' academic victories and the Meredith Chorale's instant celebrity boded well for diversity. In November 1982, the chorale performed in Reynolds Coliseum with renowned singer Barry Manilow—and at his invitation. The forty-voice group sang backup for Manilow's encores "I Write the Songs" and "One Voice."

SO MEREDITH, THE larger college, knew and became known in a smaller world. As Suzanne Britt wrote in 1991,

> We do not live in a vacuum, despite youthful convictions that only the here-and-now matters, only the immediately useful seems appropriate to learning. Meredith College has understood and demonstrated this fundamental conviction about education. It is what the tired professor says to the querulous student after a classroom lecture. When the student asks the age-old question, "Will this *count?*" the professor answers, with all the energy she can muster, "*Everything* counts." And the gap between what we know and what we can do, in this world or the next, mercifully narrows.[78]

6

MORNING'S ENERGY

1984–1985

WAS IT "MORNING in America"? Long after President Ronald Reagan's 1984 election to a second term, political analysts continued to remind the electorate of a perceived "morning again" sensibility of his presidency. The same analysts searched for historical precedents that would explain the nation's new-found political leanings of the eighties. Americans had not made "a simple shift to conservatism," wrote Bill Boyarsky, a Reagan biographer. "The change was subtle and contradictory. . . ." But however the turn to the right was precipitated, he said, it was "in a way that benefited Reagan."[1] And Michael Schaller, author of *Reckoning with Reagan, America and Its President in the 1980s*, observed a phenomenon: "College students liked talk of renewal from America's oldest serving president. On campuses where a few years before undergraduates had pelted Lyndon Johnson and Richard Nixon, 20-year-olds screamed 'U.S.A.! U.S.A.!' in response to Reagan's oratory. He tapped a popular yearning to restore a sense of community, real or imagined, lost over the previous two decades."[2]

Even among Reagan supporters, few took the eighties as an unqualified step forward because of the increasing emphasis on material success, image, and corporate greed—sometimes at the expense of compassion, kindness, open-mindedness, and generosity. But, in a sense, the mid-eighties brought morning to the College. For the nation, "morning" meant restoration; for the College, it meant exploration. Morning meant academic renewal; optimum enrollment, even in a declining student market; new and refurbished campus facilities; an established place in the Information Age; and financial security. The College was alive with morning's energy.

A lively concept sprang into being in May 1983, when the admissions committee recommended "that the College develop some identifiable program to enrich the educational opportunities for superior students."[3] Actually, a challenge for superior students had been part of the academic conversation for some time, but the ensuing ad hoc committee attacked its assignment with such vigor that chairman Bernard Cochran was ready in September to recommend that Meredith establish an honors program. He offered the committee's rationale:

> The Honors Program at Meredith is envisioned as an intellectually stimulating and innovative educational experience which will serve to attract and retain the superior student. While in the best sense all academic instruction at Meredith is viewed as "stimulating and attractive," a special, identifiable "Honors" track will allow the especially gifted student to develop academically to her fullest potential. . . .[4]

The program would admit honors students, on scholarship, to each entering class until, after four years, approximately seventy young women would claim that status. Through her honors colloquia and her senior-year honors thesis, each scholar would be exposed "to a thorough examination of a broad spectrum of human knowledge."[5] She would be expected to maintain at least a 3.0 grade point average in all her work, and, at graduation, would be designated an Honors Scholar graduate. In 1984, when Meredith enrolled its first twenty-one honors students— more than the projected fifteen to twenty—the prognosticators upped their predicted total number from seventy to eighty by 1988.

As the College finalized plans for its first class of honors students, it also established its first endowed professorial chair. Even before Dr. Johnson's death in 1984, the determination was clear: the professorship would be designated the Mary Lynch Johnson Chair of English. In fact, the Brown Foundation had already promised to underwrite $100,000 of the endowment as soon as Meredith raised $400,000. Johnson died on July

17, and, on July 20, the college community gathered in Jones Chapel to pay tribute to the legendary teacher, whose commitment to Christian education at Meredith spanned 65 years. The college magazine reported,

> Dr. Johnson entered the academy division of Meredith (then Baptist Female University) when she was a sixth-grade student. From that time until she taught "The Poems of Milton" in the fall of 1982 she was connected with Meredith as student, professor, and college historian. She graduated in 1917, returned to teach in 1918, and was made chairman of the department of English in 1952. She remained in that post until her retirement in 1969 but continued to teach to full classrooms through the division of continuing education. . . .[6]

In 1984, the department in which Dr. Johnson had served for so long led the College to introduce Writing Across the Curriculum, a program through which every academic department would endeavor to improve the writing skills of its students. Also, the English department, along with art, economics, history, Latin American studies, psychology, religion, and sociology, participated in a new, team-taught, interdisciplinary course titled "Woman's Odyssey." Funded by a grant from the Duke University–University of North Carolina Women's Studies Center, the course began in the spring of 1985 to help students "integrate the connections" among "education, selfhood, career, and family, and . . . address the problems confronting women in many aspects of life in the modern world," said Peggy Starkey, assistant professor of religion and coordinator of Woman's Odyssey.[7]

Meanwhile, other departments in the arts and humanities planned innovations of their own. For example, the cooperative efforts of the Department of Foreign Languages and of the student development division, which was responsible not only for housing but also for promoting cultural awareness among all students, created a Spanish hall in one of the dormitories. By April 1985, eighteen students had applied to live on the hall, where they would concentrate on Spanish language and customs.

And more and more students were "speaking the language" of dance. In 1984–85, the health and P.E. department, as it was familiarly known, changed its name to the Department of Health, Physical Education, and *Dance*, attesting to the importance of dance in the curriculum.

THE YEAR CHALLENGED planning committees to observe in new ways some of the old traditions. The Founders' Day convocation, for example, opened the fall term, whereas its customary late February date was usually a harbinger of spring. And the moving of the Baccalaureate service to the chapel after a thirty-five-year observance in Jones Auditorium "gave a new flavor to this very special time of worship for the Class of 1985," according to the Rev. Sam Carothers, campus minister.[8] A significant aspect of the occasion was that an alumna, the Rev. Margaret Hess, '78, preached the first Baccalaureate sermon in the new chapel.

In that same year, Meredith again availed itself of Dr. Lemmon's talents, to say nothing of her dedication, by appointing her acting head* of the department of education for the spring semester, until Mary Johnson, associate professor of education and a four-year veteran of the department, assumed the permanent role the following fall. Dr. Johnson earned both her bachelor's and master's degrees at Western Carolina University and her Ed.D. at Duke. She had come to Meredith in 1980 but was lured away, except for her continuous teaching in the graduate school, by the Wake County School System in 1984. A consistent advocate for public school teachers, Johnson later said, "There is a national crisis in education, and it is not all education's fault. I think it deals with some of the cultural changes . . . and the expectation that schools are supposed to do everything for everybody."[9] While she had become well-acquainted with Meredith, Johnson's colleague Ronald Bird, who assumed headship of the Department of Business and Economics at the same time, was new to the College. He was still "new" when he left after only one year.

As participants called attention to progress in the arts, humanities, and business, advocates for math and science did not sit idly by. The mathematics department took center stage in 1984, when one of its students excelled in a North American mathematical competition. Several official documents recorded the event, but the *Twig* couched the news in the student vernacular:

Early on the morning of Saturday, December 1, 1984, while most Meredith students were still dreaming about the Christmas dance

---

*The designation "head" replaced the title "chairman" in 1983.

that evening, six [others] joined 2,144 students from 350 colleges and universities in Canada and the U.S. in the William Lowell Putnam Mathematical Competition. . . .

[Sophomore] Laura Litchfield placed among the first quarter of the contestants nationally. . . .[10]

Dean Burris reported that Litchfield placed "very high in the scale along with . . . students from the University of North Carolina at Chapel Hill, North Carolina State University, Duke and Davidson."[11] Meredith's academic reputation continued in good company its merited place.

In the good company of the Bowman Gray School of Medicine of Wake Forest University, Meredith established a Physician Assistant Training Program, which would require a student to major in health science at Meredith, with 101 semester hours at the College and 1,000 hours of clinical experience, and to complete the program at Bowman Gray. And in collaboration with Duke, the College announced a new offering in medical technology. The 1984–85 catalogue described it as involving "three years at Meredith and one full calendar year at Duke University Medical Center. This program prepares students to enter the field as medical technologists with the Bachelor of Arts degree. . . ." In later years, the catalogue added a statement to the effect that "Career opportunities in hospitals, laboratories, research, public health facilities, and educational institutions are widely available."[12] But if catalogue perusers thought a program in medical technology was too specialized, or even that it was new, they might have been surprised to find the following statement in the 1899–1900 bulletin of Baptist Female University:

> Young women who propose entering the profession of medicine, and who do not feel able to take a four years' course, should give, at least, a year or two to the study of those branches which form the basis of a medical education. To meet the needs of this class, a two years' Medical Preparatory Course is offered.[13]

If Meredith was concerned about the whole person, as it claimed to be, then it promoted physical fitness. In 1984–85 the College added weightlifting to its training programs. To what degree weightlifting prepared the athletes of 1985 is unclear, but the volleyball team boasted of a 9–0 record, "even after playing Francis Marion, a division II school," crowed the *Twig*. The newspaper took its bragging rights seriously: "As the Angels walked into the gym their hearts sank when they watched this [Francis Marion] team, who looked like the U.S. Olympic team, warm up."[14]

While the College never made claim to fielding a team in the Olympics, it played its own Superbowl. A new intramural sports program stirred competitive spirits, and students organized twenty-six teams of flag football alone. The teams would compete in September and play for the Superbowl III championship on the 25th. Intramural soccer and volleyball followed.

A CURSORY GLANCE at Meredith from the inside out rightly reveals a college, which, within the framework of its mission, shapes its academic program to the needs of women and their times. On the other hand, a picture of the College from the outside in never mirrors the soul of the institution. From that vantage point, one sees a community very much like a small city—buildings, roads, parking lots, landscaping, population. In fact, in 1984, Vice President Taylor likened the everyday services offered by Meredith to those of a city: "utilities, security, housing, food," and retail.[15] But the onlooker could not always discern the transformations taking place within the "city limits."

The freshman class in 1985 was the largest class to date. Its 405 members had been selected from 879 applicants from fifteen states and three foreign countries. They represented more than 150 high schools. Among the freshmen were four National Merit semifinalists, several National Merit commended students, and a National Achievement commended student. Fifteen scored high enough on advanced placement tests to qualify for sixty-seven hours of advanced standing. The profile of the class also revealed that five members received Meredith College Academic Scholarships, twelve won Julia Hamlet Harris Scholarships, and seven qualified for Music Scholarships. Twenty students were invited to participate in the honors program.

As students changed the "city," the "city" also changed them. *How* they were to be changed led the institution periodically to revisit the vision of its founders. This chapter has recorded some of the resources used for the academic transformations of undergraduate degree candidates, but graduate studies figured more and more prominently in the then-present and future plans. As the College scrutinized the graduate curriculum, it approved a second master's degree for the Department of Music: as of November 1984, a graduate student could earn a master's not only in performance and pedagogy but also in music education. In a graduate a program that required two years of course work, students in any one of the disciplines could take up to six calendar years to complete a degree. Approximately 180 graduate students had enrolled, and a 1985 profile showed that they represented "more than fifty companies, many schools and public school systems, and several churches in the Research Triangle area."[16] Twenty-four percent of them were Meredith graduates; 38 percent came from seventeen other North Carolina institutions; and another 38 percent represented thirty-nine colleges and universities from outside North Carolina and one from a foreign country.[17]

Unlike the graduate program, continuing education's enrichment program had been around for a long time, constituting a body of students who were not, by definition, degree seekers. Of enrichment, Dr. Ironside said,

[E]ducational value and service to the community are the primary criteria which direct our programming. . . . We believe it is important for Meredith to offer a quality comprehensive, non-credit program with content appropriate to the higher education setting. Thus, we see the Enrichment Program as a kind of "standing invitation" to the lifelong learners in our community, a "showcase," and a place where people may discover something about Meredith, and perhaps about themselves.[18]

Statistics for each spring semester from 1980–85 showed that the number of enrichment seekers accepting Meredith's "standing invitation" had grown year by year, except for 1984 when the numbers dropped significantly but temporarily. In the spring of 1980, enrollment in the program was 525; in 1985, it was 1,651.

Despite the rosy enrollment picture at every level, the facts remained that a buyers' market was expected greatly to influence the aspirations of Meredith and other colleges and universities over the next few years. President Weems reported to the trustees in February 1985 that many of the thirty-eight private colleges in North Carolina were losing students and that some might have to close because of their losses. On an optimistic note, he said that "Duke, Davidson and Wake Forest are strong institutions and following them Meredith and Guilford represent the strongest of the rest."[19]

Although cheered by enrollment numbers, the College nevertheless saw a gloomy forecast in the traditional-age student market and sought new venues for preaching the good news of Meredith. In fact, the admissions staff appointed Alumnae Admissions Representatives (AARs) in Florida, Georgia, New Jersey, South Carolina, Virginia, and Kentucky as liaisons to young women prospects in their respective areas.

Meanwhile, students remained comfortable in their college routines, even as they aspired to reshape their parts of the world. In an election year, one of their challenges was to make the changes they wanted by the votes they cast. Politicians courted Meredith students. In their bid for the same United States Senate seat, both former Democratic Governor James Hunt and incumbent Republican Senator Jesse Helms, held their statewide youth rallies at the College. Hunt infused a breath of fresh air into his teetering campaign, sending—at her own request—Bonnie Franklin, star of television's popular situation comedy *One Day at a Time*, to speak for the candidate in Jones Auditorium. Later, clad in a Meredith sweatshirt, she answered questions and signed autographs, perhaps overhearing some Helms supporters, who were quite vocal in protesting the occasion's political focus.

Apparently gaining momentum from the energy of an election year, both student Democrats and Republicans made news in 1985. The *Twig* reported first on the Democrats:

> Since about 1982 the Meredith Democrats have been unseen or unheard of. . . . Last year changed this. With a little help and enthusiasm from Becky Auman [junior] and Dr. Allen Page [professor of religion] Meredith was back on the Democratic map. . . . Last March, in Winston-Salem, at the North Carolina College Democrats' Convention, Meredith was recognized for its hard work and became the first recipient of the Best Small Club Award.[20]

Two weeks later, the paper touted the Republicans:

> Just like the National Republican Party, Meredith's College Republican Club is growing and we hope you will become a part of it.

Last year at the National Convention Meredith won most out-standing College Republican Club for a woman's college on a national level.[21]

While the *Twig* probably never reached federal and state lawmakers and, therefore, had little chance of significantly influencing them, its editors expressed their sentiments anyway. For example, co-editor Beth Blankenship disliked having to "buckle up" in her car: "The seatbelt law has passed in North Carolina, and there's really nothing I can do about it. . . . I feel that this law has taken away one of my fundamental freedoms of choice. . . ."[22] In 1985, the two editors took opposing stands on one of the "laws" of the campus. Soon after installation of the telephone system, switchboard operators were instructed to avoid giving students' private numbers to outsiders. Co-editor Cynthia Church was incredulous:"Oh, please, what next?" she wrote. "Now, the outside world can't get into us because they can't get our number."[23] In the same issue, co-editor Beth Blankenship expressed her relief : "Have your number put in the phone book if you want it to be public knowledge. As for me, I'll take my privacy any day."[24]

From the use of telephones to the care of college property, the growing campus "city" sometimes found it necessary to mimic the bureaucracies of its "real world" counterparts. Beginning in the 1984–85 term, Meredith assessed a damage deposit fee of $50.00 from each resident student, all or part of which she would reclaim upon graduation or withdrawal, depending upon the condition of her room or whether a lost key had necessitated new locks.

But the academic community usually discussed topics infinitely farther reaching than whether to limit the distribution of telephone numbers or to refund a damage deposit. One who inspired more substantive discussion was Alex Haley, author of *Roots*, who attracted more than 800 people to a morning convocation during "the strongest and most well attended" Black Emphasis Week in three years.[25] Later in the spring, several African-American students attended in Atlanta a seminar on Black Students on White Campuses. Returning with enthusiasm and workable ideas, the students were able to influence some attitudes toward change.

As students underwent various metamorphoses in their college experiences, they were able to move beyond their natural habitats toward changing someone else's world. In that context, the Meredith Christian Association excelled in leadership. In 1984, the campus minister, Sam Carothers, reported "an exciting year for Meredith in the area of student missions."[26] One student, he said, spent six months in Togo, West Africa, operating a Baptist Student Center on a university campus; another opted to become an intern at the Raleigh Food Bank; still others would, in the near future, be ministering in Germany and Argentina.

For other types of work, twenty-one students chose co-ops, either the full-time alternating program (a semester in class and a semester at work), in which five were enrolled, or the parallel part-time program (part-time work, part-time school), which, with sixteen students participating, constituted "the largest enrollment during a regular semester in the history of Meredith's program."[27]

SOMETIMES, A YOUNG woman's private world changed almost too radically for coping. Through the help of her friends, a resourceful student handled her own crisis and helped others struggle through theirs:

> After learning of my parents' separation last semester, my entire world rocked and tossed in utter disarray, leaving me feeling quite betrayed and alone. However, my friends, with their strong hearts and endless compassion, have helped me work through the situation. Their support is proving invaluable to my dealing with the situation and my coming through on top of things. As more and more students on this campus and other college campuses are directly affected by the epidemic of separation and divorce, this type of support is needed.[28]

Those statements in the March 18, 1985, *Twig* led to the formation of a support group for students in similar circumstances. By the time the April 1 issue went to press, six young women had joined.

But most common bonds fostered happier circumstances than those created by broken relationships. The Meredith ring, for example, has been a "tie that binds" since 1954, according to Dru Morgan Hinsley, '52, who, at her retirement in 1996, had managed the Meredith Supply Store for almost as long as she had been an alumna. Carolyn Carter, '73, elaborated to members of the Class of 1997 just after they had received their rings in their junior year: "This ring which is a symbol of everything precious that Meredith stands for binds you in a tangible way to the Sisterhood which now numbers over 12,000. My observation is that more people wear their Meredith rings than any other college or university that I am aware of."[29] And Annette Gregory, reporting on the ring tradition in the *Twig*, wrote, "Meredith was the first college to adopt the dinner ring style."[30] The ring, with its oval onyx stone, into which is etched the slightly off-center college seal, is a creation primarily of Ann Lovell, '54. An oak leaf engraved on the band and flanking the stone further distinguishes the ring as Meredith's. A ring on the finger of a student or an alumna possibly introduces more strangers than one can imagine. In 1995, a student wrote,

> This summer I was approached in two unusual places because an alumna spotted my ring.
>
> One was on the shore of Emerald Isle, North Carolina and the other was in a store in Soho, New York. . . .
>
> All that matters is that we could relate to each other and feel the bond of sisterhood that this college creates.[31]

In 1984, Emily Pool Aumiller, '50, also proved the point in her letter to the editor of *Meredith*, although her Southern accent initiated the conversation:

> Recently my husband and I stopped for an early Saturday supper at a trendy restaurant on Highway 17 in Ramsey, New Jersey, where attractive young college people serve potato skins and fried veggies and variations on a theme by Hamburger. When our waitress, a cheerful and beautiful brunette, brought our bill, she asked me, "Are you from the South?"
>
> "Yes, I'm from the Carolinas. . . ."
>
> "I went to college down South," she said.
>
> Naturally I asked where, and when she said Meredith, we were both incredulous. Then she added, "I should have noticed your ring. They don't let me wear mine here. It might fall in the soup."
>
> Anyhow, the brief encounter between Karen Smith of Allendale, New Jersey, '83 biology major, and Emily Pool Aumiller, '50 English major, warmed our hearts.[32]

A primary tie that binds the campus "city" is the faculty. Literature through all the ages has extolled educators. Amos Bronson Alcott wrote in 1840 from an interesting viewpoint: "The true teacher defends his pupils against his own personal influence. He inspires self-trust. He guides their eyes from himself to the spirit that quickens him. He will have no disciple."[33] The late Ralph McLain of Meredith's religion department expressed the same idea but from a student's viewpoint: "A good student never stays attached to the limitations of her teachers."[34] In 1988, when Meredith was ranked fifteenth among the nation's small comprehensive colleges, President Weems credited the faculty: "I am pleased that they are being recognized for their hard work and high standards," he said.[35] Historian Mary Lynch Johnson quoted from President Bruce Heilman's inaugural address: "[F]aculty members are at the heart of the academic enterprise, and the end result depends on their quality."[36]

As a body, these scholars covet academic freedom as one of their "unalienable rights [of] life, liberty, and the pursuit of happiness."[37] The faculty often raises its collective voice in support of *a* cause that ultimately boils down to *the* cause of academic freedom, even if the vocal reaction causes strained relationships. Such was the case in 1985 when, by resolution, the faculty supported its colleague Clyde Edgerton in his perceived struggle with academic freedom at Campbell University, a sister institution of North Carolina Baptists. Mr. Edgerton's first novel, *Raney*, had satirized conservative Baptists but had been well received by critics and the general public. Its publication would have been less threatening had it not appeared when Campbell's president, Norman Wiggins, was also president of the Baptist State Convention. The Meredith faculty's resolution voiced support for Mr. Edgerton; in reaction, the executive committee of Meredith's trustees, also by resolution, expressed regret that Campbell might have been offended. As far as public records show, the matter ended there, and Clyde Edgerton has continued his writing—and his irony—through several novels since.

IN 1984, A new building gave the chemistry department a rebirth of sorts, beginning with the announcement of a gift of approximately $100,000 toward a chemistry research center. With the gift came the condition that the center be named in honor of Mary Yarbrough. Plans moved swiftly. Groundbreaking was on the Alumnae Day agenda for May 12, and the honoree herself turned a spade or two of dirt. On May 10, 1985, one year after the groundbreaking and six months after Dr. Yarbrough's death, the Mary E. Yarbrough Research Center, adjacent to Hunter Hall, was dedicated. Joe Baker said the facility represented "a significant step forward," adding, "For the first time in the history of Meredith College there is a facility on campus totally dedicated to research. This building contains two labs, one climatically controlled, two offices, and a greenhouse [that] will add substantially to the science programs at Meredith. . . . This is truly a fitting monument to the progressive leadership of Dr. Mary Yarbrough."[38] The legendary professor of chemistry and physics, 1928–72, died following a stroke on November 14, 1984, and a service in Jones Chapel honored her memory. A member of Meredith's Class of 1926, Yarbrough was the first woman to earn a graduate degree from North Carolina State University. The *Raleigh Times* paid tribute to her: "Her lamp stayed steady, lighting for younger women the path to career achievement. She held that lamp ahead of them, but never so far ahead that they would despair of following."[39]

Mary Yarbrough was an alumna *extraordinaire*—one of many. Meredith was and is fortunate in the high degree of loyalty of its former students. For their careers, their communities, and their college, many of them have held lamps, carried torches, lit pathways—each in her own fashion. Alumna Roxie Collie Laybourne, '32, started a career in taxidermy after earning a master's degree at George Washington University. But, according to an article in a 1982 *Smithsonian* magazine, she became an "ornithologist and research associate in the Smithsonian's Division of Birds . . . [and] a part-time zoologist with the Division of Law Enforcement of the FWS (Fish and Wildlife Service)." Mrs. Laybourne was so accomplished in ornithology that two subspecies of birds were named in her honor. In fact, said writer Mike Lipske, she was "this country's absolute last word on the identification of feathers."[40] The distinction has led aircraft engineers and archaeologists alike to rely on her expertise.

Laura Weatherspoon Harrill, '27, almost made a career of lending to Meredith her generous heart and her eye for beauty. In 1984, after her successful oak-planting campaign a decade earlier, she identified another spot on the campus that needed attention and wrote to certain alumnae asking for support:

When I found that at least as much—if not more—traffic passes through the east gate [as] the south entrance on Hillsborough Street, and that so many people traveling on Interstate 40 see the east campus, I thought, "What a commentary Meredith could make by replacing the existing entrance with a gate and a fence as attractive as the other campus landmarks." So I made my decision to ask for permission to appeal to the alumnae for funds, knowing that I would underwrite any difference in amount raised and amount spent.[41]

Harrill's idea became tangible over the summer, and, on September 28, a new gate was dedicated in honor of and named for the late Elva Wall Davis, '10. Mrs. Davis's daughter, Nan Davis Van Every, '43, was the major financial underwriter. The wrought-iron gate, centered with an oversized "M" for "Meredith," is affixed to lantern-topped stone columns, which are similar to those ushering in the long front drive at Hillsborough Street.

If visitors who attended the dedication rites toured the campus, they likely saw an interesting new sculpture on the Faw Garden side of Jones Auditorium. The commissioned work, *A Joyful Noise,* sculpted at the College by artist Dorothy Gillespie, was a collection of colorful aluminum strips affixed to the outer wall of Jones. Sara Hodgkins, secretary of North Carolina's Department of Cultural Resources, commented, "It looks like she tossed ribbons up on the wall."[42] At the dedication on January 23, 1984, critics used words such as "excitement" and "energy" to describe the sculpture. According to Blue Greenberg, art instructor at Meredith and art critic for the *Durham Morning Herald*, Gillespie was "a major force in the women's art movement."[43] The artist counted the Guggenheim Museum among the collectors of her work.

The sculptor was one of the "extra dimensions" made possible by the Kenan grant, which had also brought other distinguished guests to the campus for varying lengths of time: Betty Adcock, poet; Ann Vorus, director of the Raleigh School of Ballet; Edouard Morot Sir, professor emeritus of French at the University of North Carolina; Julian Stanley, professor of psychology at Johns Hopkins University; Peggy Kirk Bell, golf professional; Leon Megginson, research professor of management at the University of Alabama; George Watson, senior lecturer in English at the University of Aberdeen, Scotland; and Elizabeth Kennan, president of Mt. Holyoke College.

Dorothy Gillespie's week on the campus was credited, at least in part, with rekindling interest in a new art building, and, in September, the trustees declared the need for such a facility. The big question was whether it should be a separate building or a wing added to Jones-Wainwright. Before the problem was resolved, Fred Tolson was named architect, and, by February 1985, he unveiled his preliminary plan: The two-story art building would stand alone between Cate Center and the Weatherspoon Gymnasium. With a million-dollar price tag to work toward, the trustees declared that funds would be pledged or in hand before the foundation was laid.

Vice President Baker predicted the building's worth to both art and women artists: "It will make possible the establishment of a Center for Women in the Visual Arts. The fact that Meredith is committed to the education, enrichment, and career development of women, plus the close proximity of the campus to the North Carolina Museum of Art, makes Meredith the ideal home for such a program."[44] Among the attributes of such a center, said Baker, would be the role it would play in providing a possible graduate program in art.

Whether Meredith needed the art center was never a question. But disappointment permeated the trustees, the administration, and the art faculty when builder Davidson and Jones estimated that construction costs would almost double the projected amount. And whether the architect would return to the drawing board depended upon the trustees' answers to some of the same questions they had posed a year earlier: Should they authorize construction of a smaller facility near Wainwright and Jones? Should they persist in their preference for the west-campus location but reduce the size of the building? Should they adhere to the plans for the larger center but build it in phases? Department head Craig Greene was adamant that all art programs be under one roof. As the year ended, another question arose as to whether contributors toward a building of a certain size and type would welcome significant changes. The *Twig* quoted an anonymous trustee as having speculated that Meredith "would have to give contributors the opportunity to revoke their donations."[45] The struggles would continue through completion of the building.

Further enhancing the reputation of the art department—scattered across the campus as it was—Dr. Greene announced in February 1985 that renowned artist Ben Long would soon be setting up his easel on third floor of Johnson Hall to paint the official portraits of former Governor James B. Hunt and of President Weems. In North Carolina, the name "Ben Long" evoked images of the artist's frescoes in the little mountain Episcopal churches of West Jefferson and Glendale Springs, North Carolina.

While the art department claimed its share of the College's attention, the daily routine of academe never suffered from a dearth of guardianship—nor from a shortage of humor. On February 22, 1985, the same day that Dean Burris announced to the trustees that "approximately 50 percent of the faculty is tenured,"[46] Rhonda Zingraff recorded the minutes of the faculty affairs committee's meeting on tenure recommendations: "Following weeks of hard thinking, the committee members distinguished themselves at this meeting with a refreshing blend of cerebral and kinetic accomplishments: heads were in gear and hands were in the air!"[47] Another honest reaction is also on record for all time: Charles Davis, registrar and secretary of the Academic Council, was seldom given to hyperbole, but cancellation of the February 1983 meeting of the council somewhat altered his demeanor. The minutes read, "There was only one item of business that the proposer agreed could wait until the March meeting. There was heard around the campus a great rejoicing!"[48]

Dr. Davis, formerly a professor of mathematics, sought to keep the registrar's files "manageable" by facetiously prodding the admissions office to enroll students with surnames of rarely seen initials, such as "I" or "U" or "Q." On February 4, 1985, Davis wrote the first memorandum of a facetious exchange:

ADMISSIONS ALERT! Before you complete your admissions process for fall, 1985, I think you should know that we are graduating three (3) out of our five (5) U's in May, 1985. I will do what I can from this end to find at least one of them lacking graduation requirements but should this be impossible, I think you should be prepared to step into the breach and do your duty.

Sue Kearney, who succeeded Mary Bland Josey as director of admissions at Miss Josey's early retirement in 1984, responded to Davis on May 20:

I wish you to be aware that we did not take lightly your ADMIS-SIONS ALERT. . . . Your concern about our loss of U's in May 1985 came a bit too late for us to do a special SEARCH for students whose last names begin in that letter. We have, however, been able to plug in one hole. We will have at least one freshman enrolling whose last name begins with U. I do hope, as you suggested, that you were able to hold back at least one of the three graduating seniors!

As I know you are often concerned also about the thinness of your I and Q files, you will be happy to know that we have two enrolling freshmen whose last names begin with I and one whose last name begins with Q. . . . I hope you will agree that we have stepped into the breach and done our duty!

Other humorous incidents were probably not laughable at the time they occurred, but their memories doubtless bring a smile; for example, in all seriousness, the senior class spent time, effort, and money "in search of twelve of North Carolina State's finest men"[49] for a 1984 calendar to depict a State student for each month of the year. "The nominations are in," announced the *Twig* in September 1983. "After the pictures are received, the entire Meredith student body will vote on which nominees they feel are calendar material. . . ."[50] The calendars sold for $5.00 each, and profits went for class projects.

The sight of men on the campus—whether in photograph or in person, whether North Carolina State's "finest" or those of other colleges and universities—was as commonplace as the students' push for open house in the residence halls. But in November 1985, a visitor of a different species made the local news: "A 200 pound black bear was captured by the Raleigh police and Wildlife officers Monday morning between 7:30 and 8:30, but not before he took a tour of the Meredith campus and surrounding Raleigh area."[51] The *Twig* reported fully:

"The bear was sighted near the stables between 11:00 and 12:00 A.M. by Meredith security," according to Chief Dan Shattuck, head of security at Meredith. The bear was kept in the general area of the stables and the president's home.

"It is not really known how the bear got to the campus," said Lt. A.D. Bachelor of the Raleigh Police Department. "He could have followed a river. We just don't know, but Wake County is not known for its bears. . . ."

The bear was tranquilized and taken . . . to a better suited environment.[52]

Certainly not intending to prophesy other-worldly visitations, a *Raleigh Times* editorial, published three months before the bear's appearance, commended Meredith for allowing "such extensive use of the campus by outside organizations and individuals."[53] The College set boundaries, however, as to the use of the campus, and perhaps the limitations grew more rigid as suggestions of permanence entered the conversations. Reminiscent of earlier discussions with the Baptist State Convention regarding a building site, the trustees again received an inquiry—this time from a representative of the School of Pastoral Care of the North Carolina Baptist Hospital, who asked about leasing enough land to erect a small building for a regional Life Enrichment Center. Again, the request was denied.

So despite thousands of visitors and unusual requests for the use of its land, the 225 acres remained intact. On at least two occasions during the year, clever displays of student ingenuity beckoned friends and strangers alike to the campus. The first rainbow of helium-filled balloons, under which new students and all other comers passed on the first day of fall orientation, was erected in 1983 and has since become the standard welcome to a new academic term. The second occasion was a quiet, almost ethereal, Christmas display. In early December, the SGA sponsored the placing of luminaries along the front drive, all other campus streets, and in the courtyard. For each white bag containing a candle anchored in sand, students, faculty, or staff paid fifty cents, or bought five bags for $2.00. More than 5,000 luminaries glowed that night as hundreds of townspeople drove slowly through the campus. An impromptu concert emanated from around the Shaw Fountain, where about 300 students gathered spontaneously to sing Christmas carols. The *Raleigh Times* was so taken with the scene that it printed on the following day a photograph measuring the full width of page 1.[54] And the luminaries, with Johnson Hall in the background, provided the cover for the *Biblical Recorder* of December 21.[55] From donations and luminaria sales, the Student Government Association cleared $200, which it donated to the Raleigh Food Bank.

A student lights one of the 5,000 luminaria that beautify the campus at Christmas.

The local media often awarded Meredith good press and positive television coverage. For example, in late 1985, newspapers around the state ran comments of the newly crowned Miss North Carolina, Joni Bennett Parker, '83. In a press conference, she had said that her decision to attend Meredith was "one of the most important in her life."[56] Unabashedly, the College acknowledged such stories as excellent public relations. But, in the desire to aim its message at specific audiences, Meredith also paid its share for radio and television spots, newspaper notices, and magazine ads. In 1985, however, it went beyond its customary practices by contracting with a local outdoor advertising firm for eight billboard locations to promote the graduate program.

Students have always been the College's most effective representatives. However limited their territory, the young women studying abroad have spread the good news of their alma mater. In 1985, the Meredith Chorale added its talent and charm on its first concert tour in Europe, including travels to West Germany, France, Austria, and Switzerland. The thirty-one singers, directed by artist-in-residence James Powers, performed at public sites and several churches. "In Rothenburg," reported the *Twig*, "the chorale arrived at the St. Jakobskirche just as a wedding party emerged. The chorale assembled on the steps and sang 'A Blessing' to the . . . bride and groom."[57]

THIS CHAPTER HAS alluded to Meredith's having installed in 1984 its own telecommunications system, which included a telephone for each residence hall room. A student would no longer pay an annual installation fee but only a $7.50 charge for the use of her phone plus her long distance calls. Vice President Taylor estimated a savings of more than $100,000 per academic year in long-distance service discounts and in the elimination of the per-phone seventy-dollar installation fee. The system was installed by the Heins Telephone Company and partly underwritten by the Parents' Association.

On the subject of technology, Dean Burris made a telling statement about Meredith's advanced standing in the field: "The proposal to require computer experience of every student was studied by the academic computing committee and deemed unnecessary. Use of the computer in so many disciplines, especially freshman English, made a requirement superfluous and burdensome."[58] As President Weems encouraged progress in technology, the year 1985 seemed to be an ideal time to create the position of media specialist and employ John Kincheloe to fill it. Mr. Kincheloe joined the faculty and the Carlyle Campbell Library staff at the beginning of the fall term.

IN 1984–85, MEREDITH'S files contained names and addresses of 10,245 alumnae: Among the 6,467 in North Carolina were 1,903 in Wake County. The remainder lived in forty-eight states and twenty-seven foreign countries. Forty-four percent of the alumnae contributed to the college in 1983–84, giving Meredith a coveted place nationally in the percentage of alumni/ae contributing to their alma maters. Financially, the College was strong and getting stronger. In August 1985, Dr. McGee announced a gift of $400,000 toward the art center, a grant of $250,000 for honors scholarships, and a pledge of $500,000 to endow a professorial chair in the Department of Business and Economics. Because of the first gift, the new building would be named the Gaddy-Hamrick Art Center; the grant for scholarships came from the Jessie Ball Dupont Religious,

Charitable and Educational Fund; and the endowment to establish a chair was pledged by the Board of Associates.

As contributions increased, so did Meredith's ability to assist financially its students. One of the College's aspirations was that no qualified student be turned away for economic reasons. In 1983–84, about 342 young women, or 22 percent of the student body, received some financial assistance, usually in the forms of grants and scholarships, but some as loans and campus employment. And the North Carolina Legislative and Tuition Grants program, which began in 1975–76, had increased to $950 per in-state student. Even some students from middle-income families received help if family size and other conditions warranted it. But John Hiott, director of scholarships and financial assistance, expressed concern for the future. How long, he pondered, would the College be able significantly to assist students in paying for their educations? He cited new directives from the federal government:

> Federal grants will be directed to the low income students. Larger grants, with no increase in the total amount of grant money, mean fewer students from middle income ($15,000–$20,000) families will receive significant grants. Work study funds will be increased and loan funds will continue to be supported. This will force the student to assume a larger share of her educational expenses and commit herself to a long-time debt. The interest rate on Direct Student Loans is proposed to move from 5 to 8 percent.[59]

Hiott regretted the lack of financial assistance for students in other programs. "We do not have any college administered funds for graduate students," he said. "The re-entry students encounter a barrier at the point of establishing their 'budget,' which is the basis of our determination of their 'need.' We need larger resources for these categories as their numbers continue to increase."[60]

EVEN "IN THE morning," Meredith knew about reaching—for more resources for its students, for academic excellence, and for financial security. It seemed also to reach for a renewed sense of self and of purpose. Not only did the mid-eighties predict difficult days to come, but they also seemed to prepare the College to face them.

7

WHO IS MEREDITH?

1986

EVER SINCE 1909, when Baptist Female University became "Meredith," the College has treasured its identity as "a small, liberal arts, Baptist college for women." Perhaps by 1986 it measured its smallness more by student-teacher relationships than by the size of its enrollment or the extent of its acreage. And, with a broad general education core, it held to its liberal arts definition while adding some specialized courses to the curriculum. But of the fact that Meredith was *Baptist-related* and *a college for women*, there was never any doubt—until events of the eighties called on the College ultimately to define itself in those traditional respects.

ON AUGUST 8, 1994, the Raleigh *News and Observer* ran a front-page article titled "A female minister's 30-year path of righteousness." The subject was Addie Davis, Meredith Class of 1942 and "the first woman to be ordained a minister in the Southern Baptist Convention."[1] The story was not only about a woman minister but also about a changing denomination: this incident would foreshadow almost two decades of division among Southern Baptists, and Meredith would sometimes find itself at the center of the controversy.

Ironically, in 1964, the year of Addie Davis's ordination, the same denomination that established Baptist Female University so that women could receive an education equal to that of men, opposed "women taking on supreme clerical authority."[2] In its autonomy as a local congregation, however, Watts Street Baptist Church in Durham ordained Davis anyway. She held pastorates in the American Baptist Convention because, said the *News and Observer*, of the churches in the Southern Baptist Convention, "none needed a pastor so much as to hire a woman."[3] Conditions changed slightly over the years, however, and women—including other Meredith alumnae—have indeed held pastorates in North Carolina and in other southern states. In fact, said the newspaper, "In three decades . . . more than 1,000 women have followed Davis in becoming Southern Baptist ministers."[4] The 1994 story sounded hopeful in many respects, but it also revealed that, in 1984—twenty years after the precedent-setting event at Watts Street Church—Southern Baptists had passed a resolution opposing the ordination of women. Randall Lolley, president of Southeastern Baptist Theological Seminary, had spoken to the issue in a convocation address at the seminary:

> The resolution consists of 86 lines; it has 542 words. Four times, the resolution mentions "ordination." Four times it mentions "ministry." Fifteen times it mentions "women."
>
> Thus, the real agenda in the resolution was neither ministry nor ordination, but WOMEN. Women themselves—all the women in all the churches of this Convention.
>
> And in that hotly controverted resolution, the most debated concept is in the 10th WHEREAS—the woman was last in the creation and "first in the Edenic fall."
>
> Now that phrase makes plain the real issue before Southern Baptist churches today. It is *not* vocation. It is *not* ordination. It is WOMANHOOD![5]

Dr. Lolley cited scriptural references to women and their ministries; to historical facts regarding women in the church during and since biblical times; and to the resolution's language of "last in creation and first in the . . . fall," for which he substituted "last at the cross and first at the tomb." He said,

> So you are a woman. Congratulations! The issue is whether you are a Christian woman. If so, you are already a minister—inevitably, unavoidably. At Bethlehem and at Golgotha, in Joseph's Garden

and in Pentecost's upper room, the Lord Christ Himself has given you your credentials for ministry.[6]

At English professor Betty Webb's suggestion, the Meredith faculty had requested that the president issue a statement of support for Lolley.

Six months later, minutes of the executive committee of the Board of Trustees recorded George McCotter's express concern for the annual convention. McCotter had urged his trustee colleagues to seek the status of messenger from their various churches and to attend the meeting in Dallas, Texas, the following June. "Important decisions which will shape the convention for years to come will be decided there," he had predicted.[7]

In November 1985, the executive committee had again discussed problems which seemed to be impinging upon Baptist institutions and agencies, and again, the minutes sounded an ominous tone: "Baptists must continue to be alert to special interest groups who would seek to control and dominate the convention."[8] But even in their pessimism, the trustees believed somehow in an imminent lift in "the effectiveness and stability of the organization."[9] Over the next several years, however, the number of scriptural literalists calling themselves "inerrantists" would increase, as would the trustees' pessimism, and Meredith would seek a new relationship with North Carolina Baptists.

In September 1986, President Weems published a confidential message to the trustees, the faculty, and the staff. He titled the forty-six-page document *A Matter of Importance*. Early in the publication, he touched the heart of the problem for Meredith:

> Freedom at our college is dependent upon the members of our Board of Trustees. The Meredith trustees have always fostered a climate of free inquiry on our campus. In order for our college to remain free, it is essential that we continue to have board members committed to academic freedom and who reflect their own best judgment, not that of special interest groups.[10]

Weems cited specifics:

> It is assumed that by 1988 all the boards and institutions of the Southern Baptist Convention, with the exception of Southern Seminary, Louisville, Kentucky, will have solid conservative majorities. It is evident that this special interest group has as its objective the

control of all seminaries, boards, state Baptist newspapers, colleges, and as many local Baptist churches as possible.[11]

In the same document, the president pledged to make every effort to keep Meredith free, "regardless of the course of events in the convention."[12] In light of the fact that trustees were elected by the convention, a fundamentalist takeover of boards of trustees was the crippling fear of Baptist institutions. When Meredith's trustees met in September, many voiced the opinion that the College should "plan her own strategy to prevent damaging actions against the school."[13] Elizabeth Barnes, '60, associate professor of theology at Southeastern Seminary, moved that a committee be appointed to "study the critical issues" facing Meredith regarding the convention.[14] Chairman Seby Jones named Charles Barham to chair the committee and appointed Theo Pitt and Luther Brewer to serve with him. At that point, the power of the inerrantists was in the early stages of development, and several years would pass before Meredith and North Carolina's Southern Baptists were sure of their relationship to each other.

BUT WOMEN AND men alike understood the ultimate definition of a woman's college; nevertheless, when Elizabeth Tidball came to the campus on October 21, 1985, to praise women's colleges, she turned Meredith upside down. Possibly the decade's foremost authority on female education, Dr. Tidball initiated with President Weems a discussion of Title IX of the 1972 Educational Amendments Act, which prohibits sex discrimination. Recalling her experience as a trustee of Mount Holyoke and Wellesley, Tidball suspected that, by limiting its graduate programs to women, Meredith was not in compliance with Title IX. Weems immediately launched an investigation. After informing his administration and consulting the college attorney, he asked Senator Jesse Helms for clarification, and he wrote to thirty women's colleges with graduate programs. To the presidents of well-known institutions like Bryn Mawr, Columbia, Converse, Goucher, Hood, Mills, Mundelein, and Queens, he asked the following questions: "Do you allow men to enroll in your graduate programs as degree candidates?" "Is it your understanding that under the sex discrimination section of Title IX men must be admitted to graduate programs?" "If you admit men . . . has it adversely affected your undergraduate program for women?" Of the twenty-eight presidents who responded, all said they admitted men to their graduate programs, and all denied any adverse effects on their undergraduate schools. Eleven of the twenty-eight were sure that Title IX required the admission of men; four did not think so; and the rest did not care because they admitted men for philosophical rather than legal reasons.

Meanwhile, Weems talked with Bernice Sandler, director of the Project on the Status and Education of Women with the Association of American Colleges. Dr. Sandler said, "Title IX exempts private, undergraduate admission, but it does not exempt graduate admission. There are no exceptions for graduate admission if the institution receives any financial aid. . . . So if men apply, it gets very hard to say no to them."[15] Renee Keever, associate director of college relations, elaborated on financial aid: "Although Meredith's federal funding is limited, the college does accept aid for student loans and receives interest subsidies through bond issues sold to the federal government for construction of several campus buildings."[16]

All the above action occurred between Tidball's speech in October and the end of the year. The minutes of the November meeting of the executive committee of the board of trustees read, "The discussion pointed out that the law most likely does not exempt schools for their graduate programs."[17] To examine the matter further, the chairman appointed a committee headed by David Britt and staffed by Charles Barham, Hugh Ashcraft, Laura Weatherspoon Harrill, and Gordon Sinclair. In February, Judge Britt's ad hoc committee had concluded that Meredith must either admit men to the graduate program or do away with the program altogether. To the executive committee of the board Britt recommended "that qualified male applicants be admitted to the graduate program."[18] The motion passed. But when the full board met eighteen days later, Britt called for further study to determine what was best for the College.

Of the February 28 semi-annual meeting of the Board of Trustees, Keever wrote,

Trustees arrived on campus for their regularly scheduled meeting with more than the usual attention. Before their afternoon session began, a determined group of alumnae, faculty, and students gathered in Bryan Rotunda in Johnson Hall and lined the stairway to urge trustees to oppose admitting men into the graduate program or to ask for more time in making their decision. Some wore buttons with slogans such as "Preserve the Purpose" and carried signs that read "Meredith College: where old traditions never die."[19]

Adding color to the story, the *Meredith Herald** reported that Kathleen Folger, a junior, took the minority position, as revealed by the poster she carried: "Meredith College grow or die."[20]

Once the trustees made their way through the demonstrators, up the stairs, and into the conference room, invited guests Mary Lily Duncan Gaddy, '42, president of the Alumnae Association, and Bridgette Parker, president of the Student Government Association, each voiced opposition to the admission of males. President Weems ultimately made several recommendations: that every constituent group in the College discuss the matter and report its views to the executive committee of the board; that a questionnaire be mailed to every alumna; and, on the assumption that the College would retain the graduate school, that a separate administrative structure be formed for it.

The faculty submitted several resolutions of its own, each one echoing the others: that the College retain the graduate school—with male students if necessary—provided the changes would not affect the undergraduate program. While the faculty acted as a body, Paige Leist of the *Meredith Herald* elicited individual comments from the heads of the three graduate departments:

Ron Bird, business and economics: "Federal law is very explicit about making all graduate programs co-educational. Having a few men enroll in the program won't hurt anything. We'd be able to offer a unique service."[21]

Mary Johnson, education: "I can't foresee any changes being made to accommodate males; however, I don't want to see anything jeopardize the single-sex tradition of the undergraduate program."[22]

David Lynch, music: "I'd be very happy to have men in the graduate program." It would be a "happy situation" to have a SATB (soprano, also, tenor, bass) ensemble, he said.[23]

Finally, in a session less intense than some, the executive committee heard a new slant on the controversy at its April 14 meeting. The presi-

---

*Students changed the name of the *Twig* to the *Meredith Herald* in 1986. See Chapter 8.

dent reported findings that private colleges like Meredith had "the right of self-definition. . . . [which] means that each such institution may decide how its student body will be constituted."[24] The minutes of that meeting also read that "Judge Britt shared a written opinion from Ms. Suzanne Reynolds, [Meredith alumna, Class of '71], an attorney and member of the Wake Forest Law School faculty." Reynolds's opinion was not recorded in the minutes; however, the prevailing knowledge—among alumnae who had elicited her legal research— was that she also found Meredith exempt. Reynolds was one alumna of many who responded to the situation. Those who returned the survey voted 1,786 to 969 for limiting graduate degree candidates to women only.

The saga continued. In May, the executive committee of the board again, yet, and still discussed the idea of men in the graduate school. Judge Britt moved to recommend to the full Board of Trustees that Meredith continue "the current policy without change."[25] The vote by the committee was unanimous then and again by the full board in a called meeting on June 16. The happy ending—happy at least for the majority who had spoken—included Clara Bunn's appointment as dean of the graduate school and the program's full accreditation by the Southern Association of Colleges and Schools.

And, at least to the end of 1986, Meredith's identity as a *Baptist* college for *women* remained intact.

8

VINTAGE YEARS

AND BETTER NAMES

1986–1988

WORLDWIDE, THE MID- to late-eighties were probably similar to most years in their ratio of good news to bad, but sometimes it was difficult to sift through the bad to find the good. The nation grieved when the space shuttle Challenger exploded on January 28, 1986, killing the seven people aboard, including astronaut Michael J. Smith from North Carolina and teacher Christa McCauliffe from New Hampshire. Three months later, the world was stunned by the tragic accident at the Chernobyl nuclear facility in the Soviet Union. In April, basketball fans reeled at news of the drug-induced sudden death of the University of Maryland's star Len Bias.

In 1987, a scandal erupted when the public learned that the government had allegedly sold arms to Iran in exchange for Iran's negotiating the release of American hostages in Lebanon, the profits supposedly aiding the Contras in Nicaragua. But Americans turned their attention inward when Wall Street experienced "its three biggest one-day point losses ever."[1]

Presidential politics of 1988 produced possibly as divisive a campaign as most voters had ever witnessed; but when election day ended, Republican George Bush and his running mate, Dan Quayle, had soundly defeated their Democratic counterparts, Michael Dukakis and Lloyd Bentsen, in the race for the presidency and vice presidency, respectively.

In the same time period, the Higher Education Research Institute at UCLA published its findings from a survey of students at 550 colleges:

Today's college freshmen are more likely to drink beer, but less likely to smoke cigarettes and cling to liberal political ideas than their counterparts of 20 years ago. They also made higher grades in school than their predecessors, but need more remedial help in college. They are . . . far more interested in being well-off financially.[2]

And the turmoil in Southern Baptist life continued, although it seemed that no particular cultural phenomena were at play, other than the shift of some of the populace to the religious far right, perhaps egged on by televangelists and their guest celebrities and an obsessive hunger for power.

But one would find it difficult to categorize any year's worth of Meredith news as bad; a historian of the era would more than likely say, with Dean Burris, "It was . . . a vintage year."[3] Or, in light of Meredith's naming or renaming entities as diverse as the newspaper and the graduate school, the historian might also quote poet Thomas Moore: "Oh, call it by some better name. . . ."[4]

DURING THOSE TIMES, one of the most recognized names among Southern Baptists was former president of the United States Jimmy Carter, who accepted Meredith's invitation to deliver on September 11, 1986, the second Lillian Parker Wallace Lecture. The one-time president and the beautiful autumn evening attracted to the Elva Bryan McIver Amphitheater an audience of about 3,000 people. The words they heard were indubitably Carter:

We are the most powerful nation on earth—economically, militarily, politically—and with that power comes a great responsibility. We are so powerful we need not fear others . . . ; however, we are not all powerful. Our power and influence are limited . . . but there is no reason why we cannot live within the limits and still apply moral standards to our dealings with other nations. One of the most important ones, I think, is that search for peace. Peace is a part of *agape* love. Peace is also a part of justice. And for a nation as powerful as we, when faced with a potential dispute with another national directly, or with a region that is in dispute—like Central

The Hon. Jimmy Carter, thirty-ninth president of the United States, delivers the Lillian Parker Wallace Lecture on September 11, 1986.

America or the Middle East or the Persian Gulf Region—the whole world should know that the United States of America is a champion of peace and is working—not through military means, not through threats, not through the interjection of troops—but through diplomacy and negotiation to bring disputing parties together. To me, this is a sign of greatness.[5]

In his lecture titled "America: A Champion of Peace?" Carter also said,

I am a Christian, but I could not make a policy as a president or governor to sacrifice the well-being of the people who had elected me in order to award someone else in a foreign country. I couldn't have sacrificial love for others, so the highest standard that a nation can hope to achieve is justice.[6]

At a news conference earlier in the afternoon, he answered questions in Jones Auditorium to a full house comprising much of the Meredith community, as well as reporters and photographers from twenty-five news organizations. He spoke of peace in the Middle East, terrorism, Social Security, sanctions on South Africa, the Panama Canal Treaty, the hostages in Iran, the Soviet invasion of Afghanistan, and the grain embargo, among other topics. A newsman asked, "Since you were so instrumental in getting the treaty signed to begin with between Israel and Egypt, are you ever called upon nowadays for your expertise in these matters?" Carter answered wryly, "No. I have not been called on by the Reagan administration for my expertise in any matters."[7]

Dr. Cochran of the religion department asked, "in light of the Baptists' contribution to religious liberty and to church-state neutrality, how do you, as a Baptist, respond to the recent demands of the religious right, some of whom are Baptists. . . ."?[8] Carter was not reticent in expressing his opinion, which echoed some of Meredith's fears:

I think there is a growing danger that the fundamentalists or right wing extremists—or whatever you want to call it—are closing their grasps on the institutions of the Southern Baptist Convention —on colleges, home missions, foreign missions, building programs, and that sort of thing. And this is a great concern to me. I think the trend is very strong . . . .[9]

Continuing his response, he seemed to equate the new denominational leaders with television evangelists in general and with Independent Baptist pastor Jerry Falwell in particular:

Nothing that the Southern Baptist Convention can do—or the TV evangelists—could shake my faith in Christ or my commitment as a Christian to follow his precepts. And I don't let Jerry Falwell or anyone else define for me what is Christian. You know, there was a time when Falwell said that anybody who was for the Panama Canal Treaty is not a Christian; anybody who would support SALT 11 was not a Christian; anybody who was for the department of education is not a Christian. Now, in a very Christian way, as far as I'm concerned, he can go to hell.[10]

The hushed seconds that followed were interrupted, at first by the gasps of those who questioned their own hearing, and then by the cheers and applause of those who knew they heard correctly and liked what they heard. Renee Keever later wrote that Carter's "condemnation of the Rev. Jerry Fálwell and the religious right . . . drew national attention to the former president's visit . . . prompting network television and radio coverage, as well as reports in the *Washington Post, New York Times, Chicago Tribune,* and smaller newspapers across the country."[11] In fact, at least one newspaper in almost every state in the Union reported Carter's view of Falwell, as expressed at Meredith College in Raleigh, North Carolina. Lewis Grizzard titled his syndicated column "Carter's the guy to disconnect Falwell's hotline to heaven."[12] Some journalists took Carter to task; many sought Falwell's response (he would pray for the former president, Falwell said); but most news simply reported the facts. If "Meredith" had not been a household word before Carter's visit, it certainly carried a more familiar ring afterward.

As the "holy war" roared on, Meredith students fought their own religious skirmishes. Soon after Jones Chapel was completed in 1982, the *Twig* had campaigned for Sunday services there, publishing a flurry of letters, as well as editor Linda Sellers's opinion piece titled "But where are the people?"[13] In 1986, the paper again took up the cause, quoting the Reverend Sam Carothers on the difference between a chapel and a church: A church, Carothers said, is "made up of people committed to doing something, who then group to form a church." He added, "We actually have a chapel, " not a church. Reporter Kim Allen sought to refute Carothers's logic, citing St. Mary's Episcopal services on Sunday and North Carolina State's weekly Catholic mass."[14] Cynthia Church's editorial in the same edition alluded to Meredith's argument that students should associate themselves with local congregations: "For a small-town girl, a big city church can be intimidating—so much that the student doesn't go at all. . . ."[15] Enthusiasm for Sunday worship in the chapel soon waned, however, and more than a decade later, Meredith still held its traditional Wednesday services.

Losing the battle for Sunday worship on campus did not deter students' efforts to effect change. One of their quests in the eighties was a better name (they said) for their newspaper, the *Twig.* But the *Twig* was more than just a name; it was a sixty-five-year-old tradition. For eight years, however, members of its staff had hinted at a name change, beginning, apparently, with the edition of February 2, 1978:

What's in a Twig? Twig is used by the British as a slang term meaning to observe or understand; it is used by Americans to mean a small, fragile, often flimsy shoot of a tree.

It is a consensus of opinion among the newspaper staff and various innocent bystanders that twig . . . is not an appropriate name for a newspaper. After much deliberation and lobbying in the smoke-filled rooms of second floor Cate Center, we declare a revolution—we want a new name for our beloved, respectable newspaper!

Lest we be branded as "good-for-nothing-tradition-breakers," let us announce that we are.[16]

In response, Maggie Odell, '77, immediate past editor, dashed off a letter from graduate school:

I take issue with the adjective, "flimsy," to describe the American usage of the word "twig." After a long, long winter, the new twigs bearing fresh, bright leaves and colorful flowers may indeed be fragile, but they bear up well enough under strong Marsh winds.

Take heart, Editor: at least you are not encumbered with the embarrassment of being THE HERALD for the Angel Farm. I say along with Lewis Carroll, "With a name like yours, you might be any shape, almost."[17]

Readers, both for and against the name change, took the matter seriously; for example, trustee Marion Lark, pastor of First Baptist Church in Henderson, submitted the name *Angel Dust*. But somehow the campaign lost its fire and only flickered until 1981, when an editorial by Sonya Ammons reignited the issue: "To have a college newspaper, which should be an area of strength in any college community, represented by a name which suggests weakness and fragility seems inappropriate. . . . A twig is that part of a tree which is easily broken and tossed away. Our paper should be a more important part of our lives at Meredith than the small twig at the end of a branch."[18]

Mary Beth Smith, '82, shot back with a letter to the editor: "Think twice before changing the name. We humans are easily broken, too, but I hope not insignificant."[19]

Once again, in 1985, a different editor confronted the same issue in the same paper of the same name:

> For the last two issues, the *Twig* has run an ad concerning the fact that the editors and newspaper staff, in conjunction with the publications board* are considering changing the name of the Meredith College weekly newspaper. Included in the ad was a form asking readers to voice an opinion about whether or not this step should be made.[20]

To the prevailing objection to change—"It's been the *Twig* since its birth!"—co-editor Church responded, "Personally, this seems contradictory coming from a group of women who usually can't wait to change their traditionl name—the one they have had since birth—at marriage."[21]

In the last issue under its old name, the *Twig*'s co-editor Beth Blankenship urged readers to "Be a part of the new tradition!"[22] The student life committee approved the change on January 21, 1986, and, on that date, the Meredith College student newspaper officially became the *Meredith Herald*. The literary magazine—the *Acorn*—and the yearbook—*Oak Leaves*—stayed with the symbolism and remained true to the traditional association with the "City of Oaks."

THE NAME "GADDY-HAMRICK" soon became as recognizable on the campus as "the *Herald*" or "Wainwright" or "Weatherspoon" or "Jones." The long-awaited art center took shape in 1986 under the name that grew out of Meredith's long and warm association with the Gaddy and Hamrick families. The late Claude F. Gaddy was the first executive secretary of the Baptist State Convention's Council on Christian Higher Education. A Meredith trustee in the forties, Gaddy was affectionately known in North Carolina as "Mr. Baptist." And the late Fuller B. Hamrick, a native of Shelby and also a well-known Baptist layman, served as bursar of the College from 1929–43. Their families honored their memories and the College with a generous gift toward the art center.

Groundbreaking ceremonies took place on June 16, 1986, at a location just west of the Carlyle Campbell Library and near the Weather-

---

*The publications board was formed in 1985 as an advocate and guide for student publications.

spoon Building. In August and September, the College continued wrestling with the dilemma of needing—wanting—more building than the money on hand would finance. But after months of discussion, the trustees authorized the addition of a wing to house a gallery and an art history classroom/theater, deciding that the College should borrow the needed funds to "cover construction costs until other funds are available."[23] Obviously, the art faculty was ecstatic. Gaddy-Hamrick "will be an important first step in establishing Meredith College as a center for women in art,"[24] said department head, Craig Greene. No other four-year art program could be found in the area.

Although the art center was not quite complete as the spring semester got underway in 1987, the building opened anyway, and it was finally dedicated on March 27, 1987, after the original February date was snowed out. Mrs. Gaddy, the former Mary Lily Duncan, '42; Charles Gaddy, Jean Gaddy Scholl, '49, and Lorena Gaddy Goodwin, son and daughters of the late Mr. Gaddy; and Olive Hamrick Miller, '40, and Martha Hamrick Howerton, '47, daughters of the late Mr. Hamrick, attended the ceremony.

In April 1987, the center hosted its first student art show. The 280 works represented "every area of the Meredith art curriculum," reported the *Meredith Herald*.[25] Dr. Greene thought the work to be "of superior quality," and, he said, "I think the abundance of energy is due partly to the centralization [in] the new building."[26] In November, the focus shifted briefly from Meredith to New York City when, by invitation, the entire faculty of the Department of Art exhibited their work in Lincoln Center's Avery Fisher Hall, attesting to the mounting respect accorded the artists. The date coincided with the annual department-sponsored tour of the city's museums and galleries.

Meanwhile, the Gaddy-Hamrick Art Center stirred the hearts of local art lovers, one of whom was Mrs. Weems. A long-time advocate for the arts—and for Meredith—and president of the Raleigh Fine Arts Society in the mid-eighties, she had influenced the moving of the Annual Wake County Artists Exhibition to Johnson Hall. Again, the *Meredith Herald* told the story:

This art exhibition made its home in the Raleigh downtown library and was later moved to the UNC campus. Two years ago, the exhibit relocated to the Meredith campus. . . .

*The Frankie Weems Gallery in Gaddy-Hamrick Art Center holds its
first student art exhibit in April 1987.*

Mrs. Weems . . . said that she thought the campus would greatly
benefit by hosting the exhibition, the only kind of art show in Wake
County that accepts and displays art in all kinds of mediums.

After making changes and additions in lighting and hanging
alternatives for the art, the Raleigh Fine Arts Society moved the
show in.[27]

Along with the College, the artists and their art appeared to benefit from
the move to the new exhibit hall. It seemed only natural, then, to name
the 1,500-square-foot gallery in the Gaddy-Hamrick Art Center in honor
of Frankie G. Weems. At an appreciation dinner for her and President
Weems, trustee chairman Seby Jones announced the surprise and unveiled
a plaque for the gallery:

THE FRANKIE G. WEEMS ART GALLERY
FOR HER INTEREST IN THE ARTS
FOR HER INVOLVEMENT IN EDUCATING STUDENTS
FOR THE ARTS
FOR HER OUTSTANDING SERVICE TO MEREDITH
AND THE GREATER RALEIGH COMMUNITY
THE BOARD OF TRUSTEES OF
MEREDITH COLLEGE
DEDICATE AND NAME THIS EXHIBITION GALLERY
IN HONOR OF AND APPRECIATION FOR
FRANKIE G. WEEMS
SEPTEMBER 25, 1987

Jones also seized the opportunity to tout the building: "Stephen Litt, art critic for the *News and Observer*, wrote of the 'small handsome gallery' and predicted it could become 'one of the most important spaces to view art in the Triangle area,'" he said.[28] And *Meredith* took its turn to exult. In the Fall 1987 issue, Renee Keever wrote about "A Center for Women in Art":

> Through the long, sunny windows of the painting studio. . . , Dr. Craig Greene, head of Meredith's department of art, pointed to another art building of note. The sharp, sleek angles of the North Carolina Museum of Art rise above the treetops, but its shadow is not too long.
>
> "We like to think of the museuin as one of our laboratories," Greene said with a laugh. "It has a superb collection, and since we can get there in five minutes, we use it like another one of our classrooms."[29]

As Greene and his staff rejoiced that the long wait was over and a common roof finally sheltered all their programs, the staffs of publications, public relations, continuing education, the writing center, and information services happily made plans to spread out over art's vacated territories in Jones Auditorium and Johnson Hall. The offices of public relations and publications, formerly the office of college relations, would share new space in Johnson Hall's east wing, third floor. The department had operated in the division of institutional advancement until the election of LaRose Spooner as vice president of administrative affairs, successor to Mr. Baker, who retired in 1987. At her new post, Dr. Spooner accepted the redefined responsibilities of promoting the College "with an eye toward a unified marketing approach."[30] She would direct the staff most responsible for publications, advertising, news, and other means of reaching the public, while her predecessor would temporarily sever his ties of more than two decades and serve a two-year assignment in Germany as general secretary-treasurer of the European Baptist Convention. Spooner had joined the mathematics faculty in 1967. In 1993, she spoke freely of how "Raising the Sights of Women" had raised the sights not only of students but also of faculty members: "Many of us . . . were encouraged to go on and get our doctorates, maybe to look beyond what we were doing," she said.[31] She earned the Ed.D. in adult education, with a concentration in administration, at North Carolina State, later moving into Meredith's administration as director of financial aid and of institutional research. She had been assistant to the president since 1980 and was secretary of the corporation. Spooner held the bachelor's degree from Tift and the M.A.T. from Duke.

Jerry McGee accepted a vice presidency at Furman University, his resignation creating an opportunity for part of his staff to reorganize under Dr. Spooner's supervision before his successor, Dennis Taylor, assumed the responsibilities of vice president on July 1, 1987. A doctoral candidate at North Carolina State University, Taylor came to Meredith from there, where he had been a development officer and executive assistant to the vice chancellor. His term at Meredith was short-lived, however; he came in July and left in November. In January, 1988, Murphy M. Osborne, Jr., was introduced as the new vice president for institutional advancement. He would be responsible for "comprehensive advancement planning and staffing, current fund, capital fund, and endowment support."[32] Dr. Osborne had been executive director of the Children's Home in Winston-Salem and had held vice presidencies at High Point and Catawba Colleges. His bachelor's degree is from High Point College, his master's from the University of North Carolina at Chapel Hill, and his doctorate from the University of Tennessee. *Meredith* reported that Osborne "likes the religious dimension at Meredith and the 'high standards of excellence' he finds in the Meredith people. . . ."[33]

It was 1988 before the reorganized staff of public relations and publications settled into new third-floor offices, with Jeannie Morelock and Carolyn Robinson, respectively, heading the two sections. The space included a graphics studio with enough sunlight beaming through the huge old Johnson Hall windows to stir creative juices. The offices were next to the expanded information services department, directed by Glenn Sanderson, who was responsible for the telephone system, much of the computer management, and other technological services. The writing center had opened September 1, 1987, on the ground floor of Jones Auditorium, with Nan Miller, instructor of English, as director and with a staff of students providing "one-on-one tutoring to all levels of writers at any stage of the writing process."[34]

The continuing education staff was as elated with its handsome new suite on the lower floor of Jones Auditorium as was the art department, with its "everything under one roof" miracle. And the chain reaction continued: when continuing education moved from its cramped quarters on the northern edge of the campus, security and maintenance moved in.

Because of the increasing numbers of adult women, continuing education, in particular, needed expanded offices. For example, the sixty-three new re-entry students who, in the summer of 1987, had already preregistered for the fall term, represented a 110 percent increase over the number of registrants in 1986. And the 1986 count had been up 50 percent from 1985. Other statistics were also impressive: Four of the thirty-eight re-entry women in the Class of 1986 graduated *cum laude*; three *magna cum laude*; and one *summa cum laude*, the latter being the only member of the class to graduate with highest honors. A year later, thirty-two of the 334 undergraduate degrees were awarded to women over twenty-three. Dr. Ironside believed the College had "positioned itself geographically, historically, and in terms of its will and motivation to do wonderful things. . . . [W]ho would have dreamed that this piece of farmland would be on the edge of one of the prime areas in this whole country for business, for industry, for people needing the kinds of things that a college can give?" she asked.[35]

Some of the services the College offered through continuing education sprang from requests for classes or workshops for off-campus organizations as diverse as the IBM Corporation and the Wake County Schools—in 1985—to the Instrument Society of America—in 1987. The IBM Corporation had selected twenty-five women employees to move from "the production line to administrative work as secretaries."[36] And for a year, Meredith provided instruction in typing, office management, language arts, and business writing to the women, who not only moved up in their jobs but also earned transfer credit. The Wake County School System asked for and received a fifteen-week program to help improve the math skills of thirty-one elementary teachers as they developed teaching strategies for their young charges. Then the Instrument Society of America, a professional association of engineers, wanted an intense four-day leadership training period for its volunteers. The first year's training was so successful that the society asked continuing education to repeat the process in 1988, 1989, and 1990. While Meredith led the workshops on the east coast, Cal Tech held similar sessions in the west.

In 1988, when the editor of *Meredith* interviewed newcomer Page Potter, director of the legal assistants' program since October 1987, Duke

Law School graduate, and member of both the Illinois and North Carolina Bar Associations, she made a statement that would startle readers unfamiliar with the College's philosophy of continuing education: "A person who goes through our paralegal program" she said, " knows more about the nuts and bolts . . . of practice than someone graduating from [a major university] law school."[37]

It was no wonder the dean remarked, at the end of the 1987–88 academic year, "All in all, it was a good year, perhaps a vintage year."[38] It was also the year that Meredith was chosen as one of the two private colleges in the state to participate in the North Carolina Teaching Fellows Program, to begin in the fall of 1988. Of the thirteen colleges and universities entrusted with the state's prestigious program of attracting four hundred of the best high school students to the teaching field, Meredith and Elon were the only independent institutions. The state would award $5,000 per year per Fellow, and Meredith would coordinate grants to make up the difference in tuition and fees. Recipients would repay their college loans by teaching for four years in North Carolina following graduation. In the first class, twenty-eight Teaching Fellows enrolled; of those, "one [had] already appeared at Carnegie Hall, another at Lincoln Center."[39]

President Weems believed Meredith's selection as a Teaching Fellows participant was "a clear indication of the regard professional educators throughout the state" held for the College.[40] His words came home to education department head Gwen Clay, who, returning from a meeting sponsored by the Wake County Public School System, reported, "The comments about the Meredith [education] program by people who are working with student teachers were so incredibly positive and so abundant, I almost felt a little embarrassed."[41]

Some of the Teaching Fellows were also Honors Scholars. In 1987, when the Class of 1991 arrived as freshmen, twenty-two of them joined the twenty-four sophomores, twenty-seven juniors, and seventeen seniors to complete the first generation of honors students. The College had set a goal of $1,000,000 to endow the program, and minutes of the Board of Trustees for February 26, 1988, recorded the successful endeavor: "The College now has funds and commitments for honors scholarships totaling $1,183,000."

Of the honors program, Rhonda Zingraff, professor of sociology, said she believed it had influenced the entire campus. "I have been very pleased at the differences I can recognize because of [it]," she said. "I think that students . . . not in the honors program benefit by realizing that their thinking can be taken seriously, too—that they are here to do more than just meet the requirements."[42]

The honors students, the Teaching Fellows, and all other students benefited from vintage years. In the spring of 1987, the College developed a pilot capstone course to serve "as a culminating experience to the general education requirements, focusing on thinking processes, broad synthesis of content, and values in action."[43] Students would use the knowledge gained from both their general education courses and their major(s) in a "wholistic overview of scientific and cultural changes in society and action directed toward contemporary problems produced by these changes."[44] The first capstone course, Human Horizons, was team-taught by members of the art, chemistry, and psychology faculties. While the pilot program was "extraordinarily successful,"[45] attracting about fifty students, it would undergo another trial year before becoming a permanent part of the curriculum.

"Capstone courses" entered the academic vocabulary, which also came to include such phrases as "contract majors"; "interdisciplinary majors" or "interdisciplinary studies"; and "independent studies." Interdisciplinary studies (IDS) were offered from time to time by several departments and were "designed to encourage synoptic thinking on themes that cut across several disciplines."[46] One of the popular interdisciplinary studies appeared in the catalogue for the first time in 1988, although it had been offered a few years earlier: Women's Odyssey explored historical, minority, and cross-cultural perspectives of women. A contract major was allowed when the student requesting it won the approval of the appropriate department heads and successfully petitioned the Academic Council for a specific course of study. Dean Burris personalized the program in his annual report for 1988: "A number of contract majors were approved. Of particular note was the one in Art History for Sarah Lemmon, Professor Emeritus of History." So in 1991, Dr. Lemmon would receive the A.B. degree from Meredith, becoming a bona fide alumna after having served on the faculty or the administrative staff since 1947. But fifteen years before she earned her Meredith degree, she was the first non-alumna invited to deliver the annual Alumnae Day address.

Many new majors required no special vocabulary, though they sprang from new career opportunities for women: speech and theatre in 1987; dance; child development; clothing and fashion merchandising; foods and nutrition; and interior design in 1988. The latter four subjects had been offered as concentrations in the home economics department, but, by changing them to majors, said the Academic Council, "the students will gain greater depth in their chosen field of study and earn degrees that have greater visibility and are more consistent with Departments of Home Economics elsewhere, or with accreditation (as with the A.D.A.)."[47] Dean Burris pointed to the nutrition program's success in 1988: Five of its students won scholarships "from various outside organizations. Of particular note was the first student in North or South Carolina to receive a North Carolina Diet Center scholarship (one of ten given in the nation)."[48] As home economics redefined its concentrations, sociology and politics jointly administered a new one in criminal justice.

A peruser of the college catalogue needed only to read the course descriptions to be reminded that the eighties offered an unprecedented array of choices. But surrounded by sometimes-intimidating course descriptions, a simple, old-fashioned, one-hour course titled English 150—Spelling—appeared in the 1988–89 and subsequent catalogues. Skeptics inferred that the computer's spell checker was to the ability to spell as the hand-held calculator was to the ability to recite the multiplication tables, but experts adamantly refuted the theory. In any case, some courses never reached obsolescence; others outlived their times and were relegated to history. For example, Spelling was voted in, and Typewriting was voted out. No longer useful in the Information Age, typing suffered the same fate in 1988 as that of its business partner, shorthand, in 1986. It was the end of an era. Typewriting and shorthand had been offered since the 1899–1900 catalogue of Baptist Female University's School of Business: These courses, read the old catalogue, "are usually taken together and are offered to those who wish to prepare themselves for office and general reporting work."[49]

In the lively Department of Business and Economics, now rid of its pre-technological-era curriculum, Donald Spanton, who had served for a brief time as acting head, agreed in 1986 to wear the title permanently. A native of Rochester, New York, Dr. Spanton received the B.S. degree in managerial engineering from Rensselaer Polytechnic Institute, the M.S. in engineering from Georgia Institute of Technology, and the Ph.D. in business management from American University. His career had already taken him to service in the army, to the Lockheed Corporation, to IBM, and to the Federal Government. A few years after joining the faculty, when corporations were "downsizing," forcing faithful and experienced employees to alter their lives, he dispelled any notion that his department at Meredith would encourage its student executives-to-be to "go and do likewise." For example, "our faculty talk about hiring and firing, sexual harrassment, ethics, and family values, along with marketing and business law," he said. "The women's movement, affirmative action, equal opportunity—whatever label you want to put on it—has certainly had an impact on the materials with which we work," Spanton added. "Many of us use the *Wall Street Journal*, for example, as a supplement to textbooks, and the textbooks themselves carry articles on social science-like research, some of it quantitative, some of it qualitative, but it is there."[50] In the past decade, the department's focus had significantly broadened because of society's expectations of women—and women's expectations of themselves. Spanton gave an example of obsolescent thinking: "I get about one call a year from some irate gentleman from downtown Raleigh who wants to know when I am going to send him a decent secretary. I tell him we are not in that business anymore."[51]

But Meredith was always in the business of change. That long-time colleagues filled vacated positions had never been uncommon, as was the case when Allen Page, who had taught in the Department of Religion and Philosophy for fourteen years, succeeded the retiring Roger Crook as department head. Dr. Page had come to the College in 1973, unwittingly drawn to the alma mater of his wife, his mother, his sister, and seven of his aunts. A graduate of Mars Hill and Wake Forest, Page pursued graduate study at Southeastern Baptist Theological Seminary before completing the M.Div. at Union Theological Seminary and the Ph.D. at Duke. In the four years that he headed the department, he witnessed a decline in the number of religion majors. "I think it had to do with the role of women in the Southern Baptist Church," he said. "While, in the broader spectrum, women were being encouraged to pursue ministry, in the Baptist context, they were being discouraged . . . . I think another significant issue has had to do with the broadening roles of women generally . . . in the expansion of opportunities in business."[52] The year of Page's appointment to the administration was a vintage year for him in more ways than one: also in 1987, his book, *Life After Death*, rolled off the press and out of the bindery.

In the same year, Burgunde Winz became head of the Department of Foreign Languages, succeeding Anne Kurtz, who continued to teach. No newcomer to Meredith, Dr. Winz had been a member of the department since 1978 and had completed the Ph.D. at the University of North Carolina at Chapel Hill after joining the faculty. She arrived in the United States from Europe in the late sixties and taught on the high school level— for a time at Broughton in Raleigh. She speaks fluent English, German, and French, having grown up in Ludwigsburg, West Germany. After having earned her bachelor's and master's degrees at ADI-Germersheim, she left Germany to become an interpreter in France. "I once even interpreted for Mitterand before he became President," she told the *Meredith Herald*.[53] Winz said she wanted her department to be sensitive to students' needs. "I'm very thankful that Meredith has never dropped the language requirement in general education. . . . In a year's time you can teach [students] very little, as far as speaking goes, but I think you can teach a lot of culture and civilization."[54] The department has added two semesters abroad—one in Madrid for Spanish students and one in Angers, near Paris, for French students. Because of possible financial and other restraints, study abroad has not been a requirement; however, about 99 percent of French or Spanish majors have taken advantage of the opportunity.

The art department offered a semester in France, as well. Artist Ben Long, who had spent some time on the campus painting the portraits of Governor Hunt and President Weems, was named an adjunct professor of painting and, as such, instructed ten students in his Paris studio, beginning in the fall semester of 1987.

In contrast to long-time colleagues wearing different titles were new acquaintances wearing familiar ones. In 1987, Virginia Knight assumed leadership of the Department of Mathematical Sciences, succeeding Ed Wheeler. Dr. Knight's background included impressive experience in computer technology. At North Carolina State University, she had been a research associate in the Department of Electrical and Computer Engineering, and prior to coming south, she had served Western New England College as assistant dean in the School of Business and as chairman of the Department of Quantitative Methods and Computer Information Systems. She holds the A.B. from DePauw University and the A.M. and Ph.D. from the University of Oregon. Of women's colleges, Knight said,

I feel that women are very encouraged in women's colleges. Knowing what I know now about them, I think I would have gone to one. . . .

When I came to Meredith, the first class I walked into was an advanced calculus class. It was a course that I'd taught many times before, and it was usually a small class at other places. My first class at Meredith had thirteen students in it, which was about average for advanced calculus, and it was just so amazing to me that all these thirteen students were women. I just loved it, because I had certainly not ever taught an advanced calculus class or been at a school where thirteen women took advanced calculus. Another thing I noticed was that our department had an average of between fifteen and twenty majors each year. Let alone the male/female issue, that's more math majors than most liberal arts colleges our size have."[55]

Knight also told of finding at Meredith a mathematical sciences faculty of seven women: "I guess for my first two years there were all women faculty in this department. We never looked into it, but we wondered at the time if we were the largest all-women math department in the world. . . ."[56]

Math students continued to excel, according to Dean Burris in 1987: "Of particular note was the success of our students in the prestigious William Lowell Putman mathematics competition. They were 71st in the nation, ranking above such schools as Duke and Wake Forest."[57]

As earlier chapters of this record suggest, the people who arrive and others who leave play into the dynamics of education. Nineteen eighty-seven was unusual, however, in that so many legendary members of the faculty and staff chose to retire, either then or in late 1986. The retirees' combined length of service totaled more than 250 years: Betty Jean Yeager, '47, faculty secretary, 39 years; Roger Crook, professor of religion, 38 years; Harry Simmons, supervisor of buildings maintenance, 38 years; Virginia Scarboro, secretary to the vice president for business and finance, 26 years; Leonard White, professor of art, 23 years; Joe Baker, vice president for administrative affairs, 21 years; Kay Friedrich, instructor of home economics, 20 years; Dorothy Quick, circulation librarian, 17 years; Marie Capel, director of career services and cooperative education,

16 years, and Cleo Glover Perry, '45, director of alumnae affairs, 12 years.

In 1986, Doris Allen Litchfield, '54, succeeded Mrs. Perry as director of alumnae affairs. As an alumna, Mrs. Litchfield was no stranger to the Alumnae Association, but also, she had worked briefly with Mae Grimmer from 1957–58. Conniesue Barfield Oldham, '73, came "home" to Meredith as dean of graduate studies and as faculty development officer, a recently established position. Raleighite Gordon Folger, who had for five years directed the activities of the local Women's Center, succeeded Marie Capel in career services. And Ruth Balla was introduced to the community as the first director of academic computing.

Academic computing was a natural next step. As long ago as 1985, an IBM System 36 computer had replaced the old System 34, allowing the accounting office to use a payroll module to ease the pains and strains of pay day. Also, the registrar's office and the students eagerly awaited the fall term, which promised registration by computer. And the book store was putting in place a computerized system for ordering supplies and streamlining the inventory. By 1988, every department possessed a computer. President Weems, who warmly welcomed all advances in technology, said, "Meredith has embraced the cybernetic age with enthusiasm."[58] He displayed his own enthusiastic acceptance of the Information Age at opening convocation in August when, with the assistance of the media services staff, he presented to the community "all the multi-media opportunities which exist at Meredith College," according to the *Meredith Herald*.[59] From an audience whose reaction to convocation was often lukewarm at best, the accolades were generously bestowed. Cara Lynn Croom wrote, "This convocation broke the mold of traditional speeches . . . , creating an excitement about Meredith and future opportunities."[60]

Computer laboratories represented tangible progress, and endowed lectures brought intangible rewards. In 1988, the Department of Religion and Philosophy introduced the Mary Stowe Gullick Lectures in Christian Ethics and the Mary Frances Preston Lectures in Biblical Studies, while the Department of Business and Economics inaugurated its Business Executive Program, which also included a lecture series. Trustee Jonathan Gullick had established an endowment "to express a commitment to higher education, to perpetuate the memory of his mother, and to enhance the Christian influence on the Meredith campus."[61] Charles Barham, also a trustee, endowed the Preston Lectures. Mary Frances Preston was well-known as a Christian educator and for family ties with Meredith. Her husband, E.S. Preston, was director of public relations, 1949–50; her daughter, Jerrie Preston Oughton, graduated in the Class of 1963; and her daughter-in-law, Dorothy Knott Preston, '54, is a professor of mathematics at the College. James McClendon of the Divinity School of the Pacific gave the first Gullick lecture, and John Lewis, senior minister at Raleigh's First Baptist Church, delivered the inaugural Preston Lecture. Also, Bill Carl, co-founder of the Golden Corral Corporation initiated the program designed "to bring outstanding business professionals to the campus for lectures and interaction with students, faculty, and the public."[62]

Also in 1988, the music department inaugurated its chorus for children in the community. After a time, however, it accepted girls only—and that by audition. Eventually, two choruses emerged: the Meredith Girls' Chorus for elementary school children and the Meredith Girls' Chorale for middle school girls, both directed by Frances M. Page, assistant professor in the department. Meanwhile, the traditional Meredith Chorale performed in New Orleans Mendelssohn's *Elijah*, with the New Orleans Symphony and a choir from the Baptist seminary there.

Other students continued their travels as well. In 1987, one could choose the regular Meredith Abroad program in Zurich and London or a study group in Greece, France, Spain, Germany, or Mexico. For some students, of course, to attend Meredith was to study abroad. In 1988, thirty-eight young women—the largest number ever to enroll from other countries—boosted the international population. But that year, students learned of a rather radical departure from the usual meaning of foreign study: In addition to the choices of a semester with Ben Long in Paris or at the Catholic University in Angers, there was the possibility of study in China, sponsored by a consortium of six colleges, including Meredith and Wake Forest University. Dr. Winz of the foreign language department was probably not exaggerating when she said, "Dr. Webb [director of international studies] and we work together very well and find the students any kind of program in the world where they would like to go."[63]

At home, Cooperating Raleigh Colleges worked under a similar principal—finding a student any kind of course among the local colleges and universities she would like to take. The consortium observed its twentieth anniversary in 1988. At the time, Dr. Weems was in his second term as president of the organization, and Rosalie Gates, associate professor of history, was in her seventh year as director.

SOUTHEASTERN BAPTIST THEOLOGICAL Seminary, Meredith's neighbor twenty miles to the north, announced on October 22, 1987, that its president, Randall Lolley, and its dean, Morris Ashcraft, intended to resign. The press release stated that President Lolley and Dean Ashcraft have "made it abundantly clear that they will not implement the policies of political fundamentalism now being enacted by a narrow majority of [the] board of trustees. . . ."[64]

On October 26, Reginald Shiflett, Meredith's faculty affairs committee chair, sent notice to the faculty and administration that "Due to the recent events at Southeastern Baptist Theological Seminary, there will be a special faculty meeting at 3:00 P.M. on Friday, October 30. The attached resolution will be the only item of business." The resolution, as passed by the faculty, read,

> We, the Faculty of Meredith College, wish to exprss our distress about the actions recently taken by the Board of Trustees at Southeastern Baptist Theological Seminary.
>
> We respect the commitment to freedom and diversity exemplified by Southeastern Seminary throughout its history. We believe that recent actions by the Board of Trustees endanger academic freedom and blur crucial distinctions between education and indoctrination.
>
> We support the faculty of Southeastern Baptist Theological Seminary in their struggle to maintain academic freedom.[65]

A 1986 message from President Weems to the college community had predicted Southeastern's fate. Throughout his ten-page document titled *A Matter of Importance*, Weems alluded to a "conservative special interest group":

> Their ultimate goal is to propagate their philosophy and beliefs. To accomplish this they must have control of the institutions. . . . Even a small number of vocal trustees can have a profound effect on the policies and direction of the institution. Should these people who represent this special interest group gain a majority of seats on the board, the nature of our institution will change.

For almost ninety years Meredith has operated with freedom, integrity, and in accordance with true Baptist principles. It seems incredible that within a short period of time it is possible that our college could be controlled by a special interest group determined to use the institution for its own purposes.

While I have no assurance that these dire concerns will come to fruition, I am convinced that the wheels of change are turning inexorably in that direction. . . . It is my opinion that our faculty, staff, and trustees should make the discussion of these issues an item of high priority.[66]

The "high priority" discussions regarding affairs at home often commingled with conversations about actions and events abroad. In that era, one of the topics of frequent discussion—and moral despair—was the practice of apartheid in South Africa. On February 6, 1987, the Department of Religion and Philosophy sent a memorandum to the faculty affairs committee:

We wish to present to the faculty for deliberation and action the following resolution: In order to participae in the struggle against apartheid—internationally recognized, according to Webster's Third New International Dictionary, as "a policy of segregation and political and economic discrimination against non-European groups in the Union of South Africa"—the Meredith College faculty calls upon the Board of Trustees to join Meredith with other educational institutions and organizations in fighting this evil with the weapons not only of education but also of divestiture.

Therefore, we request the Board of Trustees of Meredith College to examine its endowment portfolio and to eliminate all investment instruments in those companies currently doing business in South Africa, and to inform the faculty of the nature of the action taken.

On February 20, 1987, the faculty passed the resolution with an amended final sentence:

Therefore, we request the Board of Trustees of Meredith College to examine its endowment portfolio and to eliminate all investment instruments in those firms with direct investments in South Africa. . . .[67]

When the full board met the following September, Charles Taylor reported to the finance committee that the administration "was prepared to instruct the College's investment managers who purchase securities directly in the name of Meredith not to buy any securities for the College's account from firms which do business in South Africa unless such firms adhere to the Sullivan Principles in the treatment of their employees in South Africa."[69] In the executive committee for November, trustee Charles Barham interpreted the Sullivan Principles as "a set of general statements in support of positive efforts to protect human rights."[69] Barham said the finance committee believed "that this should be the thrust of the College's position on its investments."[70]

For many students, the issue of the day, every day, was the future. For example, at that time in history, a college degree no longer guaranteed a job; however, students were also concerned about their communities and the world at large. *Meredith* conducted a non-scientific survey, asking for thoughts from randomly selected young women. Some of the comments follow:

Cara Lynn Croom '89, an English major from Carrboro said, "The issue that concerns me most is the problem of the homeless in Raleigh and even in the small cities of North Carolina. Far too many people are living on the streets and must rely on food gathered from the trash cans and alleys of 'the richest country in the world.' "[71]

Mary Leslie Joyner, '90, an international business and Spanish major from Farmville, said, "I am concerned about the widespread use of drugs in the nation's high schools, the spread of the AIDS virus in such an alarming manner, and the condition of the job market for college graduates."[72]

Mary Dickson, '89, a social work major from Aurora, Ohio, said, "Homelessness and poverty. As a social work major . . . my classes in this area have heightened my awareness of these increasing problems. . . . We as a society must face up to this and do something about it."[73]

Jennifer Corn explored such issues as date rape, diet pills, AIDS, and eating disorders in her *Meredith Herald* column, "A Woman's Room." But always at issue were campus living conditions. In 1986, the predicament of overcrowding prompted discussion of whether to construct another residence hall. Dean Sizemore alluded to the seriousness of the problem for residents, particularly for the fifty-one who were "housed in 'auxiliary' spaces, including converted parlors, converted study rooms, converted maids' rooms, and 22 rooms in freshman housing which were converted from rooms for two to rooms for three." She said, "The effects of overcrowding rippled throughout the campus, affecting quiet hours, study habits, roommate tension, hall unity, student attitude, school spirit, parental satisfaction, and ultimately the quality of life and education at Meredith."[74]

The overcrowding eased somewhat the following year, but other housing problems did not. The large freshman and sophomore classes of 1986 translated into the large sophomore and junior classes of 1987. Therefore, said Sizemore, "about 80 juniors had to be housed in traditionally sophomore housing, and 40 sophomores housed in traditionally freshman housing." There was "a significant surge of parental complaint," she said.[75]

In the fall of 1987, students who wished to do so could live on a fitness hall (no smoking) in junior and senior housing, or on a Spanish or French hall. In her 1988 assessment of student housing methods, Sizemore added a new twist: "Freshman roommate assignments are based on computer-selected personality/life-style similarities taken from personal data information cards submitted by the students. Results of the computer-based roommate selection have been amazingly positive."[76]

Occasionally, a student equated satisfactory living conditions with having her car on campus. In February 1986, only juniors and seniors were granted that privilege, except under unusual circumstances. The trustees, however, wanted to extend the offer to sophomores who earned a 2.5 grade average or higher. But once a car arrived, it had to be parked somewhere, and the College found it necessary to raise parking fees simply to "alleviate the current crowded conditions. . . . "[77] To the chagrin of some of the neighbors on Faircloth Street, a mammoth expansion in 1987 created 180 new spaces on the east campus, but the discreet landscaping in and around the huge lot allayed the fears of nearby homeowners. In 1988, fifty additional parking places were marked off between the Mae Grimmer Alumnae House and Cate Center. Automobile privileges were extended to sophomores in 1992–93 and to freshmen in 1995–96.

Parking spaces were at a premium and therefore precious to students, faculty, and staff alike. But they simply represented convenience, or the lack thereof. The old Bee Hive, on the other hand, elicited nostalgia with every brush stroke as it became a giant canvas for seniors' art. Kim Allen titled a 1986 *Meredith Herald* piece, " 'Bee Hive' becomes ode to senior class."[78] In the tradition of painting the exterior of the old wooden structure, members of the Class of 1986 spent $100 and part of April to create their masterpiece. They included their Cornhuskin' themes; a poem to their little sisters in the Class of 1988; poems to their Poteat Hall residence director, Frances Thorne, and their director of student activities, Rhoda Sowers; and a poem by Robert Frost in memory of their deceased classmate, Jacquelyn Edwards. It was the last class of "artists" to exhibit a mural there; at least, no subsequent class saw its art preserved for an entire year. (In the nineties, seniors exhibited their artistry by painting messages, slogans, and class numerals in the short tunnel—between the main campus and the grounds of the president's residence—supporting the I-440 overpass.) In his 1987 annual report, Vice President Taylor alluded to the demolition of "the last of the 'temporary' wood frame buildings which have served as classroom space over the years." (The Bee Hive was part of the old auditorium building, which had housed the music department from 1926–1949.)

Other of the original campus buildings received attention when, after sixty years, the College air conditioned Brewer and Faircloth Residence Halls in 1987 and Vann and Stringfield in 1989. Lest some readers of this history know only an air-conditioned world, let the record be set straight: For most of the sixty years before air conditioning in the residence halls, the fall semester started in September when nature's cooling had already begun.

IN 1987, THE College participated in the nationwide observance of the 200th anniversary of the United States Constitution, with most of the commemorative rites taking place in September. A photograph published in *Meredith* told some of the story: Dean Burris was pictured in a period costume, including a three-cornered, plumed hat, with Vice President Thomas, also in costume, marching beside him to the beat of his drum and the trills of her fife. The backdrop for the photograph was the quadrangle, where a festival kicked off the period of celebration with "a theme of life in the federal period of American history. Pageantry, costumes, food, games and music evoked the life and times of the people who wrote the Constitution by which we govern our lives today."[79] Among other programs commemorating the anniversary were special short courses and a rousing debate on the question of "What Does the Constitution Mean Today?" The debaters were an unlikely pair—George McGovern, United States Senator (D-South Dakota), 1962–80, and unsuccessful candidate for the presidency in 1972; and Phyllis Schlafly, president of the conservative Eagle Forum organization and the outspoken activist who was credited with leading the battle to defeat the Equal Rights Amendment. The status of women, as represented in the Constitution, was only one of many questions raised in the debate. A student asked, "What, if anything, should the constitution say about women in American political and social life?" Schlafly responded,

> It is a gross error that the Constitution is antagonistic towards women. This myth has been propagated by the feminist movement. . . . From the day the Constitution was written, a woman could have been president, vice president, senator, representative.
>
> There was absolutely no bar to women doing anything. . . . Now indeed there was a fact that women could not vote. But voting is not a Constitutional right. Voting was determined by the states. . . . All kinds of people . . . did not vote in 1787, of which women were only one of those types of people.[80]

While gentle, McGovern's rejoinder was, nevertheless, firm:

> No American should be discriminated against on the grounds of sex. Not until passage of the 19th amendment and the ratification of that amendment . . . were all citizens treated alike pertaining to voting.
>
> We should all rejoice over the marvelous devices of government, protections, and freedoms the Constitution gives to everyone in the United States. One of the rights is the opportunity to bring that Constitution into line with the changing circumstances . . . and insights and wisdom of our society.
>
> Unfortunately, there remains . . . a large body of federal laws, . . . thousands of statutes, . . . hundreds of state laws, regulations . . . which have the cumulative effect of setting up certain barriers to women. . . . The purpose of the ERA [was] to make it easier for women, and even men, to enjoy full political and social equality without regard to sexual discrimination or favoritism.[81]

The fall courses which focused on the Constitution were The Cultural Context, a study of the period which produced the Constitution; Current Controversies, based on the Public Broadcasting System's television series, "The Constitution: That Delicate Balance"; and Proposals for Change, a course that led students "to encounter proposals for Constitutional change as if they were delegates to a second Constitutional Convention."[82]

At the time of the federal festival, the college people were still a bit heady from the Triangle's having hosted the 1987 summertime Olympics Festival, which brought 3,000 athletes and more than 300,000 spectators to the area. While most of the Olympic games were held at the large universities nearby, three events of the modern pentathlon took place on the Meredith campus. In addition, the College was the "Olympic Village" to 300 athletes, including Greg Luganis, gold medalist in diving competition. Meredith, Peace, and St. Mary's, the three women's institutions of Cooperating Raleigh Colleges, teamed up to air radio commercials throughout the festival, and Meredith featured its champion sprint cyclist, junior Gretchen Holt.

IN 1986, THE North Carolina Democratic Party selected Meredith for its winter seminar, the *Meredith Herald* reporting that attending dignitaries included Lt. Governor Bob Jordan, Attorney General Lacy Thornburg, Wade Smith, and Liston Ramsey, among others. But the campus as a temporary site for a statewide seminar bore little resemblance to the campus as the permanent home of student traditions. In the annual hunt for the shepherd's crook, juniors went sleuthing in the wrong direction, missing the hiding place on the third floor of Heilman Residence Hall, so the victorious seniors adorned the crook with a pretentious bow of green and white, their class colors, and their president carried the staff as she led her classmates through their little sisters' daisy chain on Class Day. (The 1986 version was a far cry from the first crook hunt in 1906, when juniors found the crook, and seniors had to drape it in black.[83]) As the crook hunt ended, the senior picnic began. It seems to be a foregone conclusion that the seniors will never remember the picnic food but will never forget the reading of the last wills and testaments nor the pronouncements of class prophecies. Sports made headlines in both the spring and fall semesters. In April, for example, Coach Cynthia Bross fielded Meredith's first fast-pitch softball team.

In 1987, Stunt Night, reported the *Herald*, would no longer be "a smaller version of Cornhuskin'" in that an overall theme would be predetermined by the MRA (Meredith Recreation Association), and each class stunt would play on that theme.[84] At the suggestion of alumna Caroline Vaught McCall, '64, the College created *Meredith Writes Home*, a quarterly newsletter for parents of students; Mrs. McCall was the first editor of the publication. The North Carolina State Library selected the Carlyle Campbell Library as one of sixty test sites "for the North Carolina electronic mail/bulletin board system," giving Meredith "access to a number of electronic bulletin boards and instant written communication with the other test libraries.[85] And, for four days in October, the Moving Wall, a half-size replica of the national Vietnam Memorial in Washington, D.C., brought about 18,000 visitors to the campus. The Business and Professional Women's Club chose Meredith as the club's Employer of the Year, the College having met the criteria of involvement in and promotion of "the betterment of women in the workplace."[86] (That 59 percent of the faculty members were women doubtless helped the cause.) Alumna Christie Barbee, '83, was named Tar Heel of the Week by the *News and Observer* for directing the Raleigh Urban Ministries' soup kitchen. The feature article asserted, "Mrs. Barbee is a definite product of Meredith, a Baptist school on Hillsborough Street noted for turning out spunky, determined women."[87] An editorial comment in *Meredith*, the college magazine, read, "The 'spunky, determined' females may be significantly influenced by their college, but more than likely Meredith attracts those kinds of women in the first place."[88]

In 1988, junior Brenda Faye Anderson was vice chairman of North Carolina's College Republicans and attended the national Republican convention in New Orleans. In the tradition of the Jewish Chautauqua Society's funding a course at Meredith, Rabbi James Bleiberg taught "Resurrection in the Biblical Tradition" in the spring semester. On November 10, the College commemorated the fiftieth anniversary of *Kristallnacht*—night of shattered glass—"the first night of organized violence against Jews and the beginning of overt anti-Semitic acts by Hitler's Germany against German and Austrian Jews."[89] Also in 1988, as in every year, more Meredith people than can be reported in this volume were in the news. One newsmaker inspired Carol Brooks, a *Meredith Herald* writer:

*The John E. Weems Graduate School commencement of
August 1990 is reminiscent of the naming of the school in 1989
in honor of Meredith's sixth president.*

Catching a glimpse of what has helped someone become successful
is, for the student, like emerging from a fog of books and studies
into the light of accomplishment. Treasuring those glimpses and
learning from them becomes very important as each of us seeks success 'in our given field. One such example of success is Margaret
Person Currin, ['72] a Meredith alumna. On March 11, Currin was
sworn in as U.S. attorney for eastern North Carolina.[90]

The *U.S. News and World Report* for October 10, 1988, ranked Meredith fifteenth among the nation's 167 small comprehensive colleges. The
editors based their findings on the quality of the student body and faculty,
financial resources, and the percentage of freshmen who eventually graduate. The magazine's survey divided colleges and universities into five categories, Meredith's bracket being "small comprehensive college"—small
because its enrollment was fewer than 2,500 students; comprehensive because it "offer[ed] students the fruits of both academic worlds: The vast
array of liberal-arts and professional programs found at larger institu-

tions and personal settings traditional at schools specializing in the liberal arts."[91] In its introduction of "the best colleges," the article said, "Here are those schools . . . that have discovered a host of ways to set themselves apart from the crowd."[92] John Weems, the president of the fifteenth best small comprehensive college in the nation, credited the faculty—their "hard work and high standards"—for the recognition.[93]

A month later, the trustees, at their November 21 executive committee meeting, unanimously accepted George McCotter's recommendation to name the graduate program the "John E. Weems Graduate School of Meredith College." *Meredith*, among other news vehicles, reported the "unprecedented move," saying it marked "the first time in the 98-year history of the college that a school or program has been named for an individual." The magazine also noted, "In his 18th year as president, Dr. Weems is credited with playing a major role in the establishment in 1983 of the graduate programs in business, education, and music."[94] And President Weems said, "Nothing the trustees could have done would have pleased me more than this."[95]

THE BEGINNING PAGES of this chapter introduce the years 1986–88 in the context of national or world events, while the ending paragraphs seem to tuck the years safely away in the narrower confines of Meredith. But "vintage years and better names" can never be tucked safely away. They are out for all to see as they make the history of the College.

9

IN PURSUIT

OF EXCELLENCE

1989-1990

"THE PRESENT IS that exciting moment where past and future, the completed and the incomplete, come together," reads the January 1989 report of the President's Task Force for the Pursuit of Excellence. "We feel that we stand at such a moment in the history of Meredith College," a moment of "extraordinary opportunity for us to pursue an even more excellent way than we have observed in Meredith's past. . . . "[1] For almost two years, the task force had met, researched, discussed, dreamed, believed, and, finally, reported, at the same time acknowledging other groups that had envisioned a future of excellence for the College: The Alumnae Association's new visions committee, for example, had published in 1987 "a range of issues related to excellence and Meredith's mission for its second hundred years."[2] The faculty affairs committee had developed ideas that excited its members to the point of presenting their thoughts to some of the administration.

In January 1987, the faculty had asked President Weems to name a task force "to explore, develop and refine concepts of excellence and to find ways of implementing them."[3] He appointed four trustees; four vice presidents; six faculty members (one of whom was Allen Page, task force chair); four alumnae; and two students to handle the assignment. Their work proceeded along the lines of their own questions: What would it mean for Meredith to achieve excellence in community spirit? In student population? In the academic program? In faculty and staff development? In physical facilities? In fiscal resources?[4] The report of the task force comprised sixteen recommendations, many of which have been, are being, or will be implemented.

To arrive at its recommendations, the task force considered several assumptions put forth by the president in 1986–87. The assumptions addressed the past, the present, and the future. On them, Weems had said, the College would find its direction and plan its future. The first assumption was almost a given: that Meredith would remain "a small, liberal arts, church-related, regional college for women."

"Small" is a relative term. As Meredith grew, it saw the demise of customs intrinsic to a community in which employees knew one another and usually held each other in high regard. One such loss was the weekly lunchtime "coffee," for which individuals or groups volunteered —by signing a list on the kitchen door in Vann—to provide refreshments. For partakers, the choice between the coffee and refreshments in Vann Parlor and lunch in the cafeteria was usually a moot point. Tasty finger food notwithstanding, the beauty of the coffees was the camaraderie between faculty and staff. While the practice has been discontinued and the work force has grown too large for each employee to know everybody else, the spirit still lives. Meredith, one might say, is a rather large small college.

But the entire college community knew Frankie Weems. Her death on January 16, 1989, following a long battle against leukemia, cast a pall of sadness over the campus. Throughout her illness, which included a bone-marrow transplant, she had been optimistic and courageous; and throughout her years of good health, she had responded graciously to Meredith's affection: on Alumnae Day in 1972, for instance, when the Alumnae Association awarded her honorary membership, and on September 25, 1987, when the College named the new art gallery in her honor. In the meantime, she had effectively served the larger community, particularly through the arts. On January 18 in Raleigh, her friends and family at a packed Hayes-Barton Baptist Church paid tribute: "To remember Frankie Weems is to remember the legacy of her loyalty to relationships, particularly to her family, the energetic vitality with which she gave herself to her community, and the quiet strength with which she fought her extended illness."[5] Her immediate family comprised her husband, President John Weems; their daughter, Nancy, '83; and their sons John Mark and David. Her mother and a sister also survived her.

At commencement in May, Meredith also paid tribute to the late Eleanor Layfield Davis, '32, when, for the first time, the already-festive occasion was embellished by Mr. Davis's gift of a ceremonial mace. Egbert L. Davis of Winston-Salem chose the work of art to honor the memory of Mrs. Davis, a widely recognized impressionist painter. At Meredith, her name had always been associated with art. In fact, she was the first alumna invited to exhibit her work in a one-artist show on the campus. And an art scholarship was established in her name shortly after her death in 1985. But she was also an alumna, a trustee, and a benefactor.

A historic "symbol of authority and order in pageantry," the ceremonial mace "was used by Cambridge University as long ago as the 13th century. Traditionally, it is carried by the marshal who leads the academic procession."[6] At commencement exercises in 1989, associate professor of psychology Rosemary Hornak was the faculty marshal and Meredith's first mace bearer. Schiffman's Jewelers of Greensoro designed and produced the mace. Its natural oak staff and sterling silver acorns and oak leaves were "symbolic of Meredith's heritage and . . . century-long location in and association with Raleigh, historically known as the 'City of Oaks.'"[7] Other elements of the mace included an iris, the college flower; a replica of the presidential medallion; and an ellipse, on which the original building of Baptist Female University and the present Livingston Johnson Administration Building were engraved.

As the College remembered Mrs. Davis and Mrs. Weems, it welcomed others to new places of service: Sonya Walters succeeded Billie Jo Kennedy Cockman, '79, as director of corporate and foundation relations; Rebecca Askew, '76, just a year away from having chaired the institutional development committee of the Alumnae Association, followed Chandy Christian as director of annual giving; and Carson Brisson, former registrar and assistant to the dean at Southeastern Baptist Theological Seminary, succeeded Charles Davis as registrar. Dr. Brisson's three-year-old son explained his father's new job: "He counts people at Meredith Cottage."[8] And, until September 28, 1990, when Margaret Weatherspoon Parker, '38, was elected to the position, the College needed only two fingers to count the number of women who had chaired the Board of Trustees. Although Mrs. Parker was the first woman so elected, circumstances had called both Elizabeth James Dotterer, '30, and Sarah Elizabeth Vernon Watts, '34, into service, each woman having presided over one meeting.

Mary Johnson left her post as head of the education department to become dean of the John E. Weems Graduate School. At the time of her appointment to the deanship, Dr. Johnson chaired the North Carolina Professional Practices Commission, was a member of the International Reading Association, and was an appointee of the State Board of Education's Evaluation Committee on Teacher Education. Gwendolyn Clay succeeded Johnson as education department head. Dr. Clay had been at Meredith for only two years when she won the 1987 Pauline Davis Perry Award for Excellence in Teaching. Both her B.S. degree in mathematics education and her Ph.D. degree in secondary mathematics education came from North Carolina State University. In the interim, she earned a master's degree in secondary mathematics at the University of North Carolina at Greensboro. Of her students heading for careers in teaching, she said, "One of the hardest things we have to do is to make sure [they] understand the realities of the workplace, help them build skills and abilities to cope with that reality, and, at the same time, help them hang on to that vision and idealism that made them want to do it in the first place."[9]

Louise Todd Taylor followed Betty Webb as head of the English department, where a change at the top occurs every five years. Dr. Taylor holds the A.B. from Swarthmore, the M.A.T. from Duke, and the M.A. and Ph.D. from Florida State. She joined the faculty in 1978 after having taught at Campbell University. Teaching is not the only way a professor relates to her students, Taylor said. "We have to take our heads up out of the books and out of the library . . . and be aware that some young woman may have enormous personal problems. Today we just have more students who face health problems, family problems, problems with depression . . . and if we are so focused on the *Odyssey* that we don't see this young woman's problems, we are not serving her or her college program."[10]

IF PEOPLE AT colleges like Meredith do indeed have a sense of kinship, as the opening paragraphs of this chapter suggest, then family disagreements occasionally arise. Such was the case on February 23, 1990, according to the *Meredith Herald*'s report of a silent protest of about one-hundred students in Bryan Rotunda:

> The purpose was to show their support for their student government, for the Honor Code, and for the "fair and impartial treatment of all students" according to their banner which hung in Johnson Hall [all] day. . . .
>
> At 8:10 A.M. President John Weems joined the students on the steps and did not leave until almost 3:00 P.M. when he was called into the Board of Trustees' meeting.[11]

The demonstration followed the president's veto of the Honor Council's decision to mete out to a student that, in his judgment, was too harsh a punishment for an Honor Code violation.* In the complicated case, several factors seemed to have been at work: Dr. Weems had never before overturned an Honor Council decision; the accused student and her parents were friends of the president; and the matter was prematurely discussed throughout the campus when discretion should have prevailed.

In Bryan Rotunda, silent students sat along the walls; some faculty, staff, and other curious onlookers stood at the edges of the crowd; and President Weems sat near the bottom of the red-carpeted stairs that descended from the second level. From time to time, supporters joined him. It was an uncommon occasion—reminiscent of the sit-ins of the sixties. Also unusual was the common ground of the opposing sides. To some, including most of the students, the president's action suggested favoritism; therefore, they said, they were there "to show their support for the Honor Code."[12] Nona Short, assistant professor of photography and foreign languages, who sat with Weems for a time, was the faculty member most involved in the case and had appealed to the president to intervene because, she said, "she felt that the charges were not in line with the offense." Ms. Short added, "I am here in support of the Honor Code as it stands. I believe that the president worked within that. . . ."[13] Finally, President Weems declared that his hour-after-hour presence on the steps

---

*It was the president's right to veto the decision; however, this situation prompted an amendent to the SGA constitution, mandating that the president confer with a committee of the dean and the chairs of the faculty affairs and student life committees for community advice in "all cases recommending suspension or expulsion," according to Dr. Jackson, vice president for student development.

also was to show his support for the Honor Code. It appeared, therefore, that all participants demonstrated for the same purpose but from different perspectives. Dean Dorothy Sizemore, praised the student leaders for "their maturity and strength of leadership."[14] And Susan Gilbert, professor of English, wrote to the *Meredith Herald*:

> Enormous disagreements exist in the current case, among students and faculty, as well as between students and administrators. The disagreement . . . did not begin with the President's action. . . . It was there, apparently, from the first. Faculty closest to the students involved disagree over the nature of the offense. Truth does not falter when two women disagree. I continue to trust them both; so, I believe, do you. . . .
>
> So long as we know the integrity of truth does not mean unanimity of judgment, we can deal with each other in trust.[15]

Crowded conditions sometimes strained relationships; however, in 1990, when 1,239 students lived in residence hall space for 1,231, tension was nominal. But the statistics might have reinforced the idea of Meredith's attractiveness to prospective students or made the case that it was not so small a college, after all. Add to the enrollment figures the fact that the greatest competition for students came not from other "small" colleges for women but from the state's largest universities,* and the data become even more surprising. But the president brought to earth those of the community whose expectations, he thought, were unrealistic, again reminding them that "the number of high school graduates peaked in 1979" and would "continue to decline through 1995."[16] He also cited statistics bearing out the precipitous fall in the number of women's colleges—from 285 in 1965 to 93 in 1990, and, of those 93, half were "vastly different from Meredith," he said.[17]

But to make sure the student marketplace heard the message, the College unveiled a heretofore-untried procedure in getting the word out to prospective students. With the public relations and publications offices, the admissions staff developed a recruitment video and ways of ensuring

---

*In 1989, Meredith's primary competitors for students were, first, North Carolina State University; second, the University of North Carolina at Chapel Hill; third, East Carolina University; and fourth, the University of North Carolina at Wilmington.

its effectiveness. Director of Admissions Sue Kearney explained, "In addition to on-campus use with visitors, the video is available for viewing in over 1,350 high schools and is also distributed to students for in-home viewing. In the fall [of 1990], five hundred schools will have Meredith's video for school-to-home lendings."[18] From the video came a sixty-second television commercial that was seen by an estimated 1,000,000 viewers during intermission at the North Carolina Symphony's 1989 Labor Day pops concert on the campus. The commercial received an Award of Special Merit from District III of the Council for the Advancement and Support of Education (CASE), an organization for communications and marketing professionals in higher education. District III, which included more than six hundred colleges and universities in nine southeastern states, also gave Meredith an Award of Excellence for the design and use of its new graphics identity package.

Identity took on a whole new meaning when representatives of Walt Disney Studios looked at the campus as a possible site for a feature film. "While Meredith was not the final location selection," said Jeannie Morelock, director of public relations, the College "was honored to be considered."[19] Mrs. Morelock, nevertheless, soon had other reasons to celebrate when Southern Bell agreed to feature the College on the cover of its 500,000 Wake County telephone directories to be distributed in 1991, Meredith's charter centennial year.

IN THE ASSUMPTION that "The College will continually move to improve and develop its faculty and staff," the task force recommended that some plan be devised to "attract from the outside or cause to rise from the inside those distinguished faculty and staff who are going to make this a more excellent institution."[20] Compensation increases were high on the list of desirable ways to fulfill the recommendation, and, in 1989–90, evidence supported efforts in that direction. Salaries increased in amounts above the inflationary level and "topped the national average for higher education salaries."[21] Also, faculty and staff alike welcomed year-end bonuses for longevity. They liked, too, the possibility of tuition-free courses, even as they compensated for time missed from work; and the long-time practice of medical benefits, even if they paid for their own dependents' coverage. And, in 1990, John Saunders, assistant professor of religion, particularly liked receiving the first Sears-Roebuck prize for excellence in teaching. The Sears-Roebuck Teaching Excellence and Campus Leadership Award swelled the number of tangible accolades, such as the FAME awards in teaching, research, artistic achievement, and special service.

The College rewarded itself by establishing its first two endowed professorial chairs: the Mary Lynch Johnson Chair of English and the Irving H. Wainwright Chair of Business and Economics. In a college-wide ceremony that included the naming of alumna and professor of English Ione Kemp Knight as the Mary Lynch Johnson Professor of English, department head Betty Webb said,

> In the classroom [Dr. Knight] was awesome. . . . She would get so excited about the passage under examination that she'd leave the podium but continue to recite lines. When she would eventually come to the end of what she knew by heart, she would blink herself awake and dash back to the podium looking somewhat embarrassed. We weren't exactly sure where she'd been but we loved her for going.[22]

Lois Frazier, head of the Department of Business and Economics since 1954 and later director of the MBA program, postponed her retirement for a year to serve as the first Irving H. Wainwright Professor of Business and Economics. An "outstanding teacher and administrator, planner, thinker, doer, and friend,"[23] Dr. Frazier was active in the Raleigh Business and Professional Women's Club, had been inducted into the Y.W.C.A.'s Academy of Women, and had steered Meredith's business department into the Information Age. Her appointment came just months before Mr. Wainwright's death on August 26, 1990. The late Irving H. and Harriet Mardre Wainwright were long-time benefactors. Together they bequeathed to Meredith approximately $2 million, according to early estimates of Mr. Wainwright's estate.

In that period, an ongoing topic of conversation was that of terminal degrees as they related to promotions and tenure. A condition of the assumption on faculty development was that the College would try to employ faculty members with doctoral degrees or, otherwise, encourage teachers to return to school. But was one required to earn a doctorate if doctorates were rare in her or his field? What of the C.P.A. who taught accounting? What of the artist who taught studio art? What of the dancer? The interior designer? What of the computer expert? The uncertainty was put to rest by a proposal from the president and the dean and by a vote of the Board of Trustees:

> Teachers in the arts, interior design, accounting and computer science who hold an appropriate master's degree and/or professional certification in the absence of the doctorate, will be considered for promotion and tenure in accordance with established procedures and regulations.[24]

No uncertainty clouded the purposes of the 1990 Jesse Ball DuPont Religious, Charitable, and Educational Fund grant of $151,200 for four years of training teachers of and implementing capstone courses. That fall, Rhonda Zingraff, sociology, and Garry Walton, English, prepared to teach Living Revolutions, the spring capstone course; and in the spring, Allen Page, religion, and Gwen Clay, education, would be planning the fall 1991 offering. Rosemary Hornak, psychology, and Reginald Shiflett, chemistry, had taught Human Horizons: Past and Future for four years.

TEACHER TRAINING AND course implementation—the dual purposes of the DuPont grant—provide for the reader a natural progression from the second assumption to the third: i.e, the inference that faculty development would intrinsically lead to a stronger instructional program. One of the conditions of strengthening instruction was the internationalizing of the curriculum. In 1989, Vice President Sandra Thomas; Blue Greenberg, art; and Carolyn Grubbs, history, accompanied students on a seventeen-day study tour of Egypt and Turkey—with emphasis on study. The students could apply for independent study credit in history, art, and archeology.

While Meredith Abroad had been a mainstay of the instructional program for several years, it had focused primarily on Europe, until the College looked eastward in 1990. President Weems; Dean Burris; Betty Webb, director of international studies; and Donald Spanton, business and economics, flew to China to arrange a five-year faculty exchange program with the Dongbei University of Finance and Economics in Hei Shi Jiao, Dalian. At the same time, Bernard Cochran, religion and philosophy, taught at Yangtai University; and Vivian Kraines, mathematical sciences, conducted a computer software workshop for college professors at

Shanghai Normal University during her extensive travels in China. Ben Judkins, visiting professor of sociology, taught at Obirin University in Japan. Weems said,

> We need to truly globalize our education and make eastern studies an integral part of a student's experience. . . . Should Meredith make a serious eastern commitment, it would be positioning itself as one of the forerunners of the educational movement in the United States.[25]

IN THE TERM immediately preceding the expeditions to the Far East, the travelers and their colleagues on the campus had enjoyed two visiting Chinese scholars from Beijing. First to arrive was seventy-five-year-old Lugi Yao, an artist on her first venture outside China, whose stay was supported by a Kenan grant. She returned to Beijing one week before the infamous human rights eruption in Tiananmen Square; and the second scholar, Wang Yunkin, made his way out of China just after the uprising. Wang, a Fulbright scholar, lectured in Meredith's Department of History and Political Science as well as at North Carolina State. In Beijing, he was a researcher at the Chinese Academy of Social Sciences and secretary-general of the Chinese Political Science Association.

Dean Burris said, "International education has taken a quantum leap and challenges us to encourage permeation of the whole curriculum with international concern."[26] Students who spent the summer of 1990 studying in Europe lived in both Zurich and London. And still other groups, including faculty members, traveled in Greece, Switzerland, and Mexico. In the fall, twelve students left for Paris to study art with Ben Long.

Miles away—both literally and figuratively—the College acted on a strictly "at home" matter, deciding to discontinue the equitation program. Since 1944, when the first horse, belonging to a homesick student, had occupied the stables, equitation was offered as a course in physical education, its popularity peaking in the mid-sixties when about forty horses and two hundred students underscored the program's success. In the late eighties, however, few students and few animals attested to the obsolescence—at least for the Meredith campus—of horse, stable, and riding ring. But student equestrians who wished to continue riding classes for credit were happily welcomed at local stables.

The department that had once beckoned students to horseback riding was, in 1990, emphasizing dance. Two stories in the same edition of the *Meredith Herald* attested to the popularity of the Dance Theatre. One touted the dance company's invitation "to perform in a gala . . . to be presented by the National Dance Association" in New Orleans in April.[27] The newspaper also promoted the Dance Theatre's annual spring concert of original work by students, faculty, and guest artist, Gary Masters.* Masters, a member of the Jose Limon Dance Company, would be performing "Voices of the Spirit," a commissioned work set to Bach's *Brandenburg Concerto No. 3*. Alyson Colwell, assistant professor of dance, titled her work "Triple Play," and Annie Elliott, also an assistant professor, selected the music of Elvis Presley to say "farewell to a bygone era"[28] in her "Requiem." Student works included those of Nancy Sills and Amy Salter, two of the first dance majors.

The performing arts had made history in 1989 when Meredith and the A.J. Fletcher Foundation announced "the establishment of a series of seminars with world-renowned musicians, actors, directors, and other artists, to be offered through the Fletcher School of the Performing Arts [to be] based at the College."[29] The foundation saw the move as an educational opportunity for singers in the National Opera Company, for Meredith students, and for the community; and David Lynch, head of the Department of Music and the Performing Arts, saw it also as a way of "bringing true cultural greatness within the reach of our community" and as "an exciting dimension to the arts in the Triangle area."[30] Nico Castel, principal artist (tenor) with the Metropolitan Opera Company, was the first guest, teaching master classes and performing on the campus for four days in February.

Many memorable visitors, and perhaps some who were not so memorable, entered the campus gates each year. A few were never heard from —or of—again. Others lingered, even after they left, because of some wisdom they introduced to a mind or some epiphany to a spirit. Jane Goodall was one of those lecturers who haunted the campus after her two-day visit on April 21 and 22, 1990. The expert on primate behavior was in the United States to celebrate her thirtieth anniversary with Gombe Stream Research Center, her base of operations in Tanzania,

*Through the Kenan grant, the dance program was able annually to attract national artists.

Jane Goodall, world-renowned expert on primate behavior,
enjoys a 1990 visit with President Weems on her visit to Meredith
during a thirtieth anniversary respite from Gombe Stream Desert
Research Center in Tanzania.

where she was "still conducting what is recognized as the longest unbroken study of any animal species in the wild."[31] In an hour-long lecture in Jones Auditorium, Goodall carried her audience through exciting discoveries about—and gentle acquaintances with—the chimpanzees in Tanzania. And she added an interesting observation about women: "I don't know that an ability to study animals is genetic—inherited. It can't be. But I think what may be inherited, particularly in women, is a certain degree of patience. . . ."[32]

Goodall's visit occured two years after Lyn Aubrecht, professor of psychology, had met her at the North Carolina Museum of Natural Science. *Meredith* reported Dr. Aubrecht's having suggested, "it would be a fine thing if some day we could get you on campus because your life has in it a message for young women, regardless of what they want to be."[33] Thereafter, he corresponded with the proper people, including Goodall herself. Finally, he said, "a beautiful thing happened—she told her people [at] the Jane Goodall Institute in Tucson that the only thing she knew that she was going to do in 1990 was to come to Meredith College."[34]

Another speaker, whose work has inspired many a scientist, had few miles to travel to her September 17, 1990, engagement at Meredith: Gertrude B. Elion, recipient of the Nobel Prize for Medicine in 1988, drove only the distance from Burroughs-Wellcome in the Research Triangle Park, where she had worked since 1944; or from Duke, where she was research professor of pharmacology and medicine; or from the University of North Carolina in Chapel Hill, where she was an adjunct professor of pharmacology.

The history of the period points to further undergirding of the instructional program and to indications of existing academic strength. Acts of strengthening the curriculum included the offering of new majors; examples of existing strength were found in the 1989 establishment of Pi Epsilon Mu, national mathematics honorary society, and installation of Alpha Lambda Delta, national honor society for freshmen. A further illustration of strength came with the American Bar Association's re-approval of the Legal Assistants Program. Dr. Ironside said, "Despite the recent emergence of at least two other paralegal programs, the Legal Assistants Program at Meredith, as the only program in the state which is both post baccalaureate and ABA approved, retains its leadership role."[35]

With less fanfare—except, perhaps, for the staffs of student publications—the publications board announced the availability of academic credit through Individual Special Studies for work on the *Meredith Herald*, the *Acorn*, and *Oak Leaves*. "The Board feels that academic credit will make it easier to fill editorship positions as well as retain qualified staff members," read the *Herald*.[36]

IN CONSIDERING THE assumption "that Meredith will continue to assess the adequacy of its physical facilities," the assessors used such words as "beautification," renovation," "modernization," and "innovation." In 1989, the College beautified the entrance to the Frankie G. Weems Art Gallery, planting a garden there and dedicating it on commencement weekend, 1989, to Cleo Glover Perry, '45. The college magazine reported, "Cleo Perry has a garden named in her honor. It's fitting. She's a garden lover, and she has earned the honor. . . ."[37] Mrs. Perry was president of the Alumnae Association, 1966–68, and the fourth director of alumnae affairs, 1976–86. In the latter position, she lifted the importance of alumnae giving to a new level.

The Frankie G. Weems Memorial Garden, also on the grounds of Gaddy-Hamrick Art Center, was dedicated on May 9, 1990. A vine-covered archway is the invitation to enter the little garden nook, and a bench surrounded by and facing a profusion of blue periwinkle is the invitation to stay. The identifying plaque cites Mrs. Weems for "her love of nature."

In the spring of 1989, the Board of Trustees resolved to consider a recommendation of the task force to construct "a new building for specialized classrooms and faculty offices."[38] Only a month later, at the April executive committee meeting, President Weems announced that trustee Hubert Ledford had indicated his intention to give a significant sum toward the proposed building, which would probably house the Departments of Education, Psychology, and Foreign Languages. The trustees immediately moved to name the building for the donor, and their vote was upheld by the full Board in September 1989. A trustee and former chairman of the Board, Ledford, then retired, had been a co-chairman of the Board of Directors of Durham Life Insurance Company in Raleigh. The Ledford Building would become "the first of three academic buildings to be consructed inside the new loop road."[39]

The loop road was more than simply a way of getting from one place to another. It connected the existing campus streets in such a way that the distance from the front drive, down past the lake, to the rear of the campus, and around the loop road back to the front drive measured one mile. The route, well-lighted and secured with strategically placed emergency telephones, was soon known as the Meredith Mile by the joggers and walkers who sometimes outnumbered automobiles, and whose fitness goals were admirable. An eavesdropper heard a faculty member prophesy that if students were as obsessed with fitness of mind as of body, the word "college" would take on a whole new meaning.

On the western side of the campus, at its intersection with the front drive, the new road yielded the right-of-way to a traffic circle at a six-by-eight-foot gatehouse, which was put into operation in September 1989, two months before the road was opened. A writer for *Meredith* seemed to grasp, at least to a point, the function of the gatehouse:

Visitors who need directions to Carswell Concert Hall, who want to know where to park for Open Day, where to deliver flowers, or how to reach I-40 are making use of the new gatehouse. Opened last September and staffed by security personnel, the facility assures convenient access to the campus for visitors and guests.

Additional security for students is also a factor. Dan Shattuck, chief of security, points out that the gatehouse provides the only access to the campus after the late-night closing of the gate at Faircloth Street.[40]

The small building ceased to be controversial to students once they knew it would not detract from the almost-pastoral picture of the campus from Hillsborough Street. The structure also illustrated Meredith's smart use of technology. Dean Sizemore explained, "Students will enter the residence halls after hours by electronic release of the lock after proper identification. Entry will be monitored by a security guard in the gatehouse by use of a closed-circuit camera."[41]

In the process of constructing the road and the gatehouse, the College demolished the old farmhouse—the home economics department's haven for refinishing furniture—which had stood on the property even before Meredith claimed the vast expanse of land once known as the "Tucker Farm." News of the razing of the old house was simply included in a list of jobs completed; nevertheless, the wording was interesting: "Demolished the old farmhouse visible from the Beltline."[42] The hidden message in the statement was obviously about image, the beltline offering travelers a panoramic view of the campus to an extent not possible from any other vantage point. Perhaps the old house *was* at odds with age and place, but the parking lots that dotted the grounds were definitive signs of the times. A new paved lot at Cate Center accommodated the automobiles of sixty commuters. But long-range plans called for additional green space. After studying the grounds and layout of the buildings, a consulting architect recommended, for beauty and safety, the return to a pedestrian campus, with parking confined to the periphery. A cautious Charles Taylor, vice president for business and finance, emphasized the phrase "long-range": "What is envisioned by an architect in 1989 may not resemble the actual product in the year 2000 or beyond," he said.[43]

While the campus plan focused on the future, the need to renovate ex-

isting buildings appeared always to be in the present—or, sometimes, in the past. In 1989, two separate entries—one in the August minutes of the board, and another in the annual report—were commentaries on moving full speed into the future while running to catch up with the past: The trustees learned that Vann and Stringfield Residence Halls were finally air-conditioned, after having stood for more than sixty years without that modern touch of comfort. And readers of the annual report were hustled into the future by the news that, in the following year, the central heating system would be connected to "the energy management microprocessor."[44] After salaries and benefits, the electric bill required the largest outlay of funds. In fiscal 1989–90, the cost of electricity totaled $535,000, and, with the air-conditioning of the last of the major buildings, there was little hope for less energy usage.

AS THEY CONSIDERED assumptions, members of the the task force often saw the word "continue," as in "Meredith will *continue* to improve the total environment for learning and personal development among its students." The total environment would include, but not be limited to, spiritual life, services and support, and activities. Spiritual life has long been a component of the "education of the whole person," to which tenet the College holds tenaciously. Examples punctuate the pages of this book. But, in the prevalent atmosphere of the Baptist life in 1989, trustees wanted "a concise report . . . , demonstrating how the operation of the College during the preceding school year has been in furtherance of its stated purposes and consistent with the mandate of its charter."[45] The administration obliged and, through a sixteen-page document titled *Christian Dimensions*, made the case. The report included Wednesday worship and other services, such as the traditional Moravian Love Feast at Christmas and the annual alumnae gathering at commencement; curriculum offerings in religion; the Freeman Religion Club; Religious Emphasis Week; the Staley, Gullick, and Preston Lectures; community ministry; the CROP Walk for raising money for Church World Service; the MCA Outreach Team, which responds to churches in search of student-led programs; recruitment of Baptist students; and *Branching Out*, the MCA (Meredith Christian Association) newsletter.

Components of the philosophy of "wholeness" also included physical and emotional support. One of the services not heretofore offered by the health center was a gynecological clinic, established in the fall of 1989 and conducted by a nurse practitioner. And Meredith, like the culture at large, provided support groups, at first for students from dysfunctional families and for those with eating disorders. But in a span of five years, the young women also sought counseling in gender issues, learning disabilities, and general therapy—and some as adult children of alcoholics. Beth Meier, who succeeded Gina Roberts as counselor in 1993, reported that her attempt to start a "Wonder Women's Blues" group "didn't get off the ground. . . ."[46]

Support groups of a different ilk were undergoing change. Students who had been bound by interest in another language and culture and had lived together, either on a Spanish or a French Hall, would hereafter have a home of their own in the new "IHOM" (International House of Meredith) as Janie Mullis, international studies editor of the *Herald*, wrote. Mullis failed to explain her play on "IHOP" (International House of Pancakes), which was a mile or so down Hillsborough Street, but she enlightened her readers as to the change: "Meredith College no longer offers a foreign language hall or the Carroll Annex freshman residence hall. Instead, the College has combined the two to become our new International House."[47] She said the twenty-two occupants included ten who were Spanish-speaking, six who were French-speaking, and six who simply wanted to live there.

Brenda Faye Anderson, Ellen Belk, Carol Brooks, Paige Gunter, Mary Moore, and Krista Holloman found their own support group among college Republicans. On January 20, 1989, the six students attended the inauguration of George Herbert Walker Bush as forty-first president of the United States. President Bush's oath of office and attendant ceremonies also marked the Bicentennial Inauguration of the United States, a slogan reading "1789–1989—George to George" appearing on banners and buttons. The *Meredith Herald* reported that "All students were able to attend one of the two Young American's Balls Friday evening," at both of which the president and vice president appeared.[48] But the students' biggest thrill might have been their introduction to President and Mrs. Bush at the White House.

From support groups, attention turned to sports groups when, again, WRAL-TV telecast the 5:30 sports news live from Superbowl VII, the intramural flag football finals in 1990. Sportscaster Bob Holliday said, "We try to cover non-traditional sports, and women playing football is certainly that."[49] Before 250 fans, the seniors of second-floor Barefoot won 24–12 over the juniors from first- and second-floor Poteat. Activities like

intramural sports contributed to the environment of the college experience, as did intercollegiate sports. In NCAA Division III, student athletes
competed in basketball, softball, golf, tennis, and volleyball. "Meredith
athletics took a leap forward"[50] with the arrival of Coach Carl Hatchell,
the first full-time basketball and softball coach. Under Coach Hatchell,
1990 was a banner year for basketball, reported the *Meredith Herald*.
As of December, the team's won-lost record was 12–4, and freshman
players Jennifer Norris and Sylvia Newman contributed significantly to
that success.[51]

Regardless of athletic prowess, the sports program probably could
never vie for the passion for Cornhuskin'. The student newspaper implied
that the competition became more intense each year. But in 1990, students took one small step toward pre-Cornhuskin' civility by replacing
the courtyard toilet paper fights with can art contests, using aluminum
drink cans to create murals. After the judging, the cans were sold for recycling, and the profits went to the winners' favorite charity. Many of the
older and wiser heads, who had seen some yesterdays, surmised that
Cornhuskin' could hardly be less competitive, given the conditions that
prompted United States President George Bush to plead, in his 1987
speech accepting his party's nomination, for a "kinder, gentler nation."

Cornhuskin' notwithstanding, the fall academic term could hardly have
had a better start than to have *Money Magazine* name Meredith as nineteenth on the publication's list of the nation's best buys among private colleges. The *Money College Guide* ranked the best buys by such measure-
ments as the amount of money devoted to student instruction; the number
of students who later earned Ph.D.'s; the graduation rate, SAT scores and
class rank of incoming freshmen; the student-faculty ratio; the number of
books in the library; and the College's management of financial aid.

THAT THE COLLEGE was considered a "best buy" by a national publication undergirded the assumption that "Meredith will continue to be affordable to the constituency it has traditionally served," although much
of the burden of increased tuition and fees "will fall to families and students," predicted President Weems.[52] The worry had already begun in
March 1989 when Weems informed trustees of "a shortfall of North Carolina Legislative Tuition Grant funds for students attending private institutions."[53] By the time the executive committee of the board met in April,

Weems had written to parents of in-state students and to trustees and associates, urging contact with their representatives. Better news was on the agenda the following August, and the president thanked the trustees for their contributions to the overwhelming flood of letters to legislators: The General Assembly approved increases of $50 each for the tuition grant and the contractual program. The total grant, then, would be $1,150 per year for each full-time student from North Carolina.

In an unusual twist of circumstances, the College sometimes asked not so much whether students could afford Meredith but whether Meredith could afford some of its students. In 1990, freshman applicants in general were 11 percent fewer than in 1989; however, Teaching Fellows clamored for admission. "For some unknown but remarkable reason," said the president, "Meredith became one of the more attractive schools in North Carolina for Teaching Fellows. . . ."[54] The College's financial outlay for the first year of the highly desirable program was $30,000; one year and fifty-one Teaching Fellows later, it was $85,000. The state's obligation of $4,700 per Fellow was a fixed amount, but college expenses were not; so managing the widening financial gap perplexed decision-makers until, in September 1990, the trustees voted to retain the Teaching Fellows Program, to limit future classes to fifteen Fellows, and to raise tuition enough to close the gap.

Because freshman applications were fewer, Meredith could afford to enroll more transfers than ever before in the history of the College. The *Herald* reported that the 111 new transfer students from eleven states represented thirty-two colleges and universities. At the same time, an alarm sounded from John Hiott, director of scholarships and financial assistnce: For some time, he said, Meredith had met 100 percent of a resident student's financial need. But, he added, "1990–91 is likely to be the last time the College can say this with confidence. The increases in cost with no increases in grant resources [have] forced this office into making larger loans."[55]

"CHANGE IS UNAVOIDABLE and desirable in higher education," stated an assumption that unmistakably applied to the past, present, and future. Change indeed came to Meredith in the last decade of the twentieth century—as it had in the first and all decades between, and as it always will. Technology alone challenged higher education to advance rapidly in knowledge, use, and equipment. After several years of work, the College and Cablevision of Raleigh negotiated an agreement whereby "all residence hall rooms, classrooms, and offices [would] be wired for campuswide communication."[56] The capabilities extended beyond students' rooms, classrooms, and offices to include assembly areas, as well. For example, an overflow crowd from Jones Auditorium could assemble in Cate Center's Kresge Auditorium to watch a live performance via cablevision. Media services, the staff of which were among the primary negotiators for the service, claimed that the co-axial cable link between Jones and Cate "effectively enlarged" Jones by 25 percent.[57] Fortunately, the service was available for the Centennial celebration in 1991.

A reader of the president's annual message for 1990—particularly if she or he knew of Weems's penchant for electronics—could sense excitement in the author's words and style:

> Television is now on the air at Meredith 24 hours a day. To allow for Meredith activities to be announced and viewed simply by turning on a video receiver, three channels were reserved for the College's use. These three channels will carry live programming originated by faculty and students. The channels are also available to broadcast filmed materials into each residence hall room. . . .
>
> The library's media services can originate programming for classrooms on demand. Recitals, public performances, and plays can be delivered to each residence hall room and campus office. The use of these three channels is limited only by our imagination.[58]

The three channels, 5, 10, and 13, originating in the Carlyle Campbell Library, were in the care of MCTV (Meredith Cable Television) and Cynthia Bowling, cable administrator. Channels 10 and 13 were for educational purposes only; Channel 5 was the vehicle by which announcements reached the entire campus population; it was Meredith's "24-hour info-center" that was "fast, easy, and free!" said the *Student Handbook*.[59] Central services boasted of a FAX machine; the library boasted of capabilities to offer "more systematic and sophisticated training in videography, editing and writing for video";[60] and information services boasted of Cam-Tel, the telecommunications system.

The Information Age advanced alongside a decades-old concern for ecology, dating from the 1962 publication of Rachel Carson's landmark exposé of environmental pesticides, the best-selling *Silent Spring*. And on Meredith's campus, there arose among faculty and students alike a growing desire to protect the planet. About 1990, the College began a recycling program, at first collecting paper only. A February 1990 edition of the *Herald* reported a collection of "18,000 pounds of paper since last December."[61] Members of the faculty criticized the unavailability of recycled paper in central services, where copy machines were at full speed almost every day. While Vice President Taylor explained that moisture in recycled paper affected the machines, he promised to stock it anyway and took the opportunity to remind the faculty of the collection barrels that were strategically placed around the campus.

FOR THE MOST part, the College was a good citizen in and for its environment, and the administration anticipated no change, according to the assumption that "Meredith will continue to serve the greater Raleigh community." One of the most effective ways of serving Raleigh and Wake County was through the continuing education program, which, said Dr. Ironside, was "struggling to keep up with its own success."[62] In 1989–90, a rush to enrichment and special programs attracted 2,600 students, making it necessary to limit to sixty the number of non-credit courses taught in a semester. In the summer, the program served children, youth, and public school teachers, and one of the incentives for teachers was the awarding of teacher renewal credits in addition to continuing education units. The re-entry program grew, as well, then totaling 20 percent of the undergraduate population.

Miscellaneous archival records attest to the continuing good will of the community toward the College and vice versa. That Meredith gave the community a learning environment, a civic forum, a wedding and reception site, a sports arena, a playground, and, simply, a pretty place was more a rule than an exception. For example, in the category of civic forum, continuing education had coordinated the Great Decisions Lectures in Raleigh since 1979. In 1989, "participation surpass[ed] all previous records."[63] As a sports arena, Meredith hosted the 1989 State Games of North Carolina Amateur Sports, the Elva Bryan McIver Amphitheater's serving as the setting for opening ceremonies; the Weatherspoon Gymnasium's supplying the basketball court for girls' statewide competition; and the residence halls' furnishing beds and baths for coaches and athletes. As a playground, the campus was affirmed by the *Spectator* magazine's nominating it as Raleigh's best place to fly a kite.

THE ASSUMPTION ADDRESSING such important matters as financial security and Meredith's relationship to North Carolina Baptists stated, "Meredith will improve with the implementation of systematic planning techniques and the acceptance of constructive change." The planning process included a capital campaign to raise $10 million. The goals of the Second Century Challenge, as the effort was called, comprised the $2,200,000 Ledford Building; one-hundred First Family scholarships of $25,000 each; an increase in unrestricted giving; and an emphasis on planned giving. Out of the latter objective emerged the Heritage Society, an organization of future givers who had named Meredith in their wills. The 156 charter members already represented 56 more than the goal set for the Charter Centennial in 1991. But the major thrust of the Second Century Challenge was $6 million for scholarships.

Financial prospects were promising; however, Meredith's Baptist State Convention-related status was uncertain. In 1990, President Weems titled a portion of his annual report, "A Clear and Imminent Danger," which focused on that uncertainty: "It becomes important for those of us related to Meredith to consider all the options available and begin to position the institution for possible external attacks of a nature we have never before experienced," he warned.[64] One of the statements in that particular publication must have opened some eyes to a reality not previously discussed, at least not in the obvious archival sources: In the event of a takeover by fundamentalist trustees, Weems said, Meredith would more than likely become coeducational because "Women have not been the first priority of the conservative movement!"[65] In an executive committee meeting in November, he reported to trustees the changing status of other Baptist institutions (Furman, Stetson, Baylor) to their conventions (South Carolina, Florida, Texas) and potential changes for Meredith. While Baptist policymakers struggled, Baptist college students went to their spring BSU (Baptist Student Union) conference and elected senior Amanda Carroll president of the state organization.

IN THE FIRST assumption listed in this chapter, the president predicted that the College would always be church-related. And the last assumption also implied an "always": "Meredith will continue to stress academic excellence as fundamental to its mission." In 1989, teams from six accrediting agencies visited the College: the Southern Association of Colleges and Schools (SACS); the National Council for Accreditation of Teacher Education (NCATE); the North Carolina Department of Public Instruction (SDPI); the National Association of Schools of Music (NASM); and the North Carolina Teaching Fellows Commission. To be examined for accreditation was to spend months of committee introspection and hard work prior to an accrediting team's site visit. Committees and individuals who gave their all for the cause were ecstatic when things went well. For example, a *Meredith Herald* reader could sense the exhilaration of Susan Gilbert, English, who directed preparation for the SACS visit in November 1989: Dr. Gilbert said the visiting team was "glowing with praise" for Meredith.[66] The more subdued minutes of the executive committee of the board for November recorded, "The members of the team were very complimentary of Meredith and her programs."[67]

The National Council for Accreditation of Teacher Education created its own excitement: In its first visit ever, NCATE recommended no changes. In the many years of the organization's existence, it had scrutinized only six other schools that passed the test without warranting a single recommendation, but Meredith wore the crown as the *only* college ever to achieve the distinction the first time around; all the others were reaffirmations of the original accreditation. Mary Johnson coordinated Meredith's work in preparation for NCATE's site visit.

THE FIRST PARAGRAPHS of this chapter imply that Meredith will remain a small college. However small it is, was, and will remain, the 1990 commencement exercises testified to rapid growth in the eighteen years of the current administration. At some point during the ceremony, Dr. Weems awarded a diploma to the student who defined the point at which 50 percent of all Meredith graduates had been handed diplomas by the sixth president. Furthermore, 80 percent of the living alumnae had graduated between 1972 and 1990. All the graduates who have been, and all those who will be, stand on common ground. The Task Force for the Pursuit of Excellence said as much:

> While we are unable to predict the future with certainty, we must prepare our graduates to live in it as responsible citizens who are prepared and capable of dealing with change. We wish to educate them as leaders, as people who make a difference, in directing the future. Most critical is that learning is a life-long, integrative process.[68]

10

HERITAGE AND VISION

1991

"HOW DO YOU say 'Happy 100th Birthday' to a college like Meredith?" With an eye toward 1991 and in quest of a centennial theme, the Centennial Commission had put the question to the college family in 1989, promising the creator of the best slogan a prize of $100.00 and gifts commemorating the one-hundredth anniversary of the chartering of Baptist Female University by the Legislature of North Carolina. At a college-wide theme picnic on April 13, 1989, Gay Elliott, secretary to the campus minister, was declared the winner. One of 350 entries from students, faculty, staff, alumnae, trustees, and parents, Mrs. Elliott's slogan had been preprinted in Meredith maroon on big white pins, which soon adorned shirts, sweaters, notebooks, and backpacks all over the campus. And from that day forward, until the Centennial celebration closed in 1992, all printed materials, including the college stationery, carried the theme, "Honoring Our Heritage . . . Expanding Our Vision."

The College has indeed honored its century-long Baptist heritage, never ceasing to pay homage to those nineteenth-century visionaries who gave it life, those women and men who "planned, prayed, sacrificed [it] into existence."[1] But, amid all the honor and glory, some of its history also encompassed situations that fell somewhere between the extremes of life-giving celebration and life-threatening struggle. The college magazine alluded to Meredith's heritage:

Independence—a mark of true Baptists everywhere—assumed its relentless and rightful stance in the life and times of the North Carolina Baptist Convention from the organization's inception in 1830.

Baptist churches have cherished their autonomy; Baptist people have preached—and practiced—the priesthood of the believers; Baptist organizations have bowed to no hierarchical assembly. While Baptist colleges may have experienced a lesser degree of independence because of the convention's practice of electing the colleges' governing bodies, the institutions have . . . remain[ed] academically free, politically untainted, and—in the case of Meredith —adamantly separate.[2]

The article more specifically covered Meredith's early years: From its beginnings in the 1830s, "with the radical notion of some progressive Baptists to provide for women an education separate from but equal to that of men,"[3] Meredith has been fought for and fought against; loved and merely tolerated; poor and relatively prosperous. North Carolina Baptists have always played a part in its life and death decisions. Three years after Baptist Female University was chartered, and four years before it opened its doors to students, some Baptists would have been happier for Wake Forest to accept women than to have proceeded with BFU. And in 1923, there was a movement afoot to merge Meredith and Wake Forest. Another in 1939, according to the *Biblical Recorder*, "proposed the moving of Meredith to the Wake Forest campus as part of one great institution."[4] And, in 1942, when Wake Forest voted to allow women students, still another groundswell for merger loomed large. "To the Convention's everlasting credit," said the *Meredith* article, it pledged its continued cooperation and support of Meredith as a four-year college for women.[5] The late Gerald Johnson, a prominent writer, editorialized in 1944 that, by its tenacity toward the status quo, Meredith was a "gone gosling."[6]

President Weems tells the story of generous Baptists, who, one year during the Depression, allocated to Meredith half the total contributions to the convention in order to keep the College "open and alive."[7] He also relates,

In 1955 Meredith was offered the Reynolda Estate of 150 acres in Winston-Salem for its campus, plus $1,000,000 for campus construction. This offer was predicated on the condition that the Presbyterians would buy our campus and locate the new school they were starting, here. The Presbyterians chose to build their new school, St. Andrews, in Laurinburg.[8]

But as the College approached its Charter Centennial, it faced one of the more ominous struggles of its existence. Trustee George McCotter had sounded an alarm as early as 1980, warning the board that fundamentalists would gain control of the Southern Baptist Convention "state by state and college by college."[9] McCotter's signal possibly rescued a dark reality from its prison of denial, but he would help to brighten the future for *all* of like mind and spirit by his efforts in founding Friends of Missions, an organization of moderate Baptists. And President Weems recalls "that the Southern Baptist Alliance, a broader-based moderate constituency, 'was born in the conference room' of . . . Jones Chapel."[10]

The convention's power to elect trustees, granted in 1927, stemmed from the creation of the Cooperative Program and its subsequent annual allocation of funds to Meredith and other Baptist institutions. And, so far, neither the convention nor the College had been seriously bruised by the intermittent crusades against Meredith's separatism and independence or, on the eve of its one-hundredth anniversary, against Meredith's freedom. Rather, such encounters had often served as healing agents. But, from the early eighties to 1991, the College wondered whether future clashes would lead to divorce of the two entities. Should radically conservative Baptists dominate the board, said the then-current trustees, Meredith would lose its identity and its freedom, as had some of the seminaries. The only solution, it seemed, was to find a way for the College to elect its own trustees. In the executive commitee meeting on January 14, 1991, Margaret Parker, trustee chair, appointed a charter resolution committee comprising Leon Smith, chair; David Britt, Norman Kellum, Theo Pitt, Charles Barham, and Barbara Allen, with President Weems *ex officio*. In February, Parker added Eugene Boyce, college counsel, to the committee.

In the meantime, the convention wanted a "blue ribbon" study committee to consider *all* sides, *all* potential problems, of *all* Baptist institutions and then make its own recommendations. Gene L. Watterson, president of the Baptist State Convention, and Roy Smith, executive director-treasurer, along with some other convention leaders, thought

Meredith was moving too hastily and that the trustees should give the convention committee, only then being formed, an opportunity to function. Both Watterson and Smith wrote to the trustees on February 21, 1991, pleading that they take no action at the the next day's meeting. The following is a summary of Watterson's reasoning:

1. A fear that any unilateral move to alter the relationship might cause an emotional upheaval, which would express itself in political polarization and a catalyzing of anti-higher education elements within our convention.
2. There is no pressing or imminent danger of an influx of trustees who hold philosophies of education or theologies that are counter to the present circumstance.
3. Meredith, as well as other institutions within the Baptist family, now enjoy virtual autonomy in the selection of trustees. . . .
4. A special committee to study and recommend changes with regards to trustee selection is in the process of formation. [Among] some suggestions of . . . that committee . . . [is] the idea of allowing the institution to have complete autonomy in the selection of whatever percentage of trustees that it desires, with the understanding that the North Carolina Baptist State Convention funding to the institutions would be reduced by that percentage.[11]

But the suggestions went unheeded. Unanimous action by the trustees came on February 22, 1991, when the Board voted to amend the charter, basing the legality of its vote on the state law that requires them "to act in the best interest of the organization for which they have been elected trustees."[12] The board had concluded that "some ultimate takeover of the College by a non-sympathetic group was not in the best interest of Meredith."[13] In the resolution to amend, however, the trustees reaffirmed Meredith's Baptist heritage:

> *Resolved*, that the Board of Trustees affirms its deep and profound appreciation for the century of unselfish support and oversight given to Meredith College by the Baptist family. The Board of Trustees further affirms its intention that Meredith College remain a North Carolina Baptist College of Christian higher education, its

intention to elect trustees who are North Carolina Baptists, and its intention to further the purposes of the institution as they are stated in its charter. The amending of the charter . . . in no way indicates a new direction for the institution. Rather, it reflects the ongoing desire of the Board of Trustees to be good stewards of Meredith's Baptist heritage, to protect academic freedom, to safeguard the financial security of the institution, and to comply with the public policies of the State of North Carolina.[14]

Most constituents of the College happily received the news. The faculty had left no doubt as to its position on the matter when, on February 15, it passed its own resolution urging the trustees to "rescind the previous action of the Board . . . and to create a self-perpetuating Board of Trustees comprised of North Carolina Baptists which will ensure the preservation of academic freedom while preserving the historic mission of the college as a Baptist institution."[15]

Responding to Meredith's turn toward further independence, the convention placed in escrow the Cooperative Program's annual allocation of approximately $1 million to the College.[16] Dr. Weems said, "I've never dealt with anything of this magnitude. We're speaking of eternal consequences here."[17] The overwhelming number of letters of appreciation and support somewhat lightened the load. For example,

As an alumna, I appreciate this move being made to safeguard Meredith's future and to protect her heritage. You certainly have my strong support!
—Carolyn Carter, '73, Raleigh[18]

Congratulations. It is a great step for the College.
—William C. Friday, Chapel Hill[19]

I applaud your courage and foresight. Meredith College should not become a victim of the circumstances creating turmoil among Southern Baptists today.
—Rebecca O. House, '74, Burlington[20]

Believe me, I understand something of the dimensions of your struggle personally and professionally, along with the Meredith trustees. Count me in your corner.
—W. Randall Lolley, Greensboro[21]

On February 26, The *News and Observer* ran an editorial titled "Meredith, out of the fray," suggesting that "if the conflict escalates between conservatives and moderates in the State Baptist Convention, Meredith College will not be one of the 'spoils of war.' "[22] The editorial complimented the College, the faculty, and, finally, the trustees, who "did the only thing they could do in distancing themselves from the grasp of those in the convention who would close doors."[23]

By memorandum on March 20, 1991, President Weems gave the faculty a state-of-the-relationship report:

I have heard from more than one hundred people from outside the immediate Meredith community expressing enthusiasm for this move. . . .

I also think it is important for you to know that as of today I have not heard from a single fundamentalist criticizing our action. Further, there have been no "letters to the Editors" that I know of critical of this action. . . .

We are not without our problems, however. The officials at the Baptist State Convention headquarters are having difficulty with our recent action, and I anticipate that most of our future problems will come from those Baptists at the Convention we thought we were closest to.

After many meetings, uncertain funding, and the threat of a lawsuit, Meredith, via a trustee committee chaired by Norman Kellum, proposed to officers of the convention and its General Board that "All mention of the election of trustees be moved from the charter of the institution and placed in the by-laws."[24] And, to comply with the convention's constitution, the Meredith delegation also agreed to submit to the convention's nominating committee a list of potential trustees, from which the convention, then, would elect a slate to serve the College. Meredith's governing body would follow suit, electing the same trustees, thereby adhering to the provisions of the amended charter. With the agreements understood by all sides, eventually Campbell, Chowan, Gardner-Webb, Mars Hill, and Wingate— the other five convention-supported colleges and universities—also moved wording regarding trustees from their charters to their by-laws.*

---

*Wake Forest University had redefined its relationship with the Baptist State Convention five years earlier.

In 1991, if the question again arose as to how to say "Happy 100th Birthday" to a college like Meredith," the answer could well have been, "Keep it academically free."

IN 1988, PRESIDENT Weems had named Jean Jackson, '75, assistant professor of English, to head the Centennial Commission and had appointed seven others who, with Dr. Jackson, formed the executive committee: Anne Clark Dahle, '54, director of re-entry programs; Janet Freeman, librarian; Bluma Greenberg, instructor of art; Carolyn Barrington Grubbs, '60, associate professor of history; Brent Pitts, assistant professor of foreign languages; Carolyn Covington Robinson, '50, college editor and director of publications; and Betty Webb, '67, professor of English. Jackson continued some of her teaching duties but also opened a centennial office in Johnson Hall. With the executive committee, fifteen additional committees and innumerable subcommittees planned a year "filled with opportunities for intellectual and spiritual growth. . . ." and "[w]ith renewed commitment to honor our heritage best by expanding our vision of what is possible, right, and good for the life of the College as it enters a second century of educating women."[25]

On February 26, 1991, a coterie of Meredith people visited the Legislature of North Carolina to witness the House and Senate's passing of resolutions honoring the life and work of Thomas Meredith and his leadership in founding Baptist Female University. Senator Betsy Cochrane, '58, and Representative Judy Hunt, '71, sponsored the resolutions.

February 27, 1991, Charter Centennial Day, was one of the more memorable Founders' Days in the life of the College. It was crammed with events, people, and heritage. Ruth Schmidt, featured speaker at the morning convocation, was president of Agnes Scott College, also a college for women; her title was "Women's Sphere in the 21st Century." Dr. Schmidt admonished women's colleges to "take seriously our history as pioneers in a new social order, our resources of people—students being primary—and devote ourselves to preparing women to lead us into new ways of thinking and doing, toward a whole and just society in the sphere which is the globe."[26] Dr. Jackson, Dr. Lynch, the Meredith Chorale, President Weems, and T. Robert Mullinax, executive director of the Council on Christian Higher Education, were program participants. The traditional wreath-laying rites at the Thomas Meredith memorial site followed convocation. Arranged by the Granddaughters' Club—an organization of daughters and granddaughters of alumnae—the moving ceremony included an antiphonal naming of some of the women and men—"a cloud of witnesses"—who had influenced the school and its students through the years. And, then, to the music of flutes, strings, and singers, party-goers came and went to the mammoth birthday celebration on all three levels of Bryan Rotunda.

In the afternoon, Jones Auditorium filled with witnesses to *Parable of the Morning Star*, a centennial play by Carolyn Covington Robinson, directed by John Creagh, and performed by members of the faculty and student body, as well as the young son of a faculty member. A fictional story based on historical fact, the play introduced Jennifer Jordan, a college-age young woman of the 1890s, who, in a conversation with her father's friend O.L. Stringfield was inspired to enroll in Baptist Female University. Her struggle to enter the university and her determination to stay there were probably not unlike the efforts of many young women of her day, and later. In *Images: A Centennial Journey,* Suzanne Britt, who narrated the drama and played Jennifer as an adult, wrote of her character, "Her passion for learning and her commitment to risk and challenge are characteristic of all Meredith women who have overcome obstacles to arrive at their own commencements."[27] Elizabeth Eisele played young Jennifer; Garry Walton was O.L. Stringfield; Jean Jackson was Lily B. Pearson; Owen Zingraff was William; and Jack Huber and Christa Phillips played Will and Mamie Jordan.

A late-afternoon centennial vespers service replicated the first chapel service of Baptist Female University in 1899. The printed program showed the order of both services:

Scripture: 1899, Albert Meredith Simms, Trustee; 1991, Mary Virginia Warren Poe, '48, Trustee
Prayer: 1899, J.W. Carter, Pastor, First Baptist Church, Raleigh; 1991, R. Wayne Stacey, Pastor, First Baptist Church, Raleigh
Introductions: 1899, President James C. Blasingame by John E. White, Secretary, Baptist State Convention; 1991, Vice President and Dean Allen Burris by Roy J. Smith, Executive Director, Baptist State Convention
History of the College: 1899, Dr. Thomas E. Skinner, Chairman,

Board of Trustees; 1991, Margaret Weatherspoon Parker, '38, Chair,
Board of Trustees

Remarks, N.C. Superintendent of Public Instruction: 1899, C.H.
Mebane; 1991, Bob Etheridge

Remarks, Superintendent, Raleigh Public Schools: 1899, E.P.
Moses; 1991, Robert E. Wentz

Remarks, Representative of Shaw University: 1899, Charles F.
Meserve, President; 1991, Ernest L. Pickens, Executive Vice President

Other Denominations: 1899, represented by Joseph E. Brown, President, Citizens National Bank: 1991, representatives introduced by
the Rev. Sam Carothers, Campus Minister

Raleigh Churches: 1889, represented by Joseph D. Boushall and
Needham B. Broughton, Trustees; 1991, representatives introduced
by Mr. Carothers

Benediction Hymn: 1889 and 1991, "Praise God from Whom All
Blessings Flow"

WHEN SANDRA DAY O'Connor, Associate Justice of the United States
Supreme Court, accepted the Centennial Commission's invitation to
speak, she became the third Lillian Parker Wallace Lecturer, having been
preceded by Sir Harold Wilson, former prime minister of Great Britain,
in 1978, and Jimmy Carter, former president of the United States, in
1986. The first woman to sit on the Supreme Court, Justice O'Connor
took the oath of office on September 25, 1981, after having been confirmed on September 21 by a vote of 99–0 in the United States Senate.
Her lecture on March 11, 1991, was titled "Women and the Constitution." She said,

Happily, the last half of this century has witnessed a revolution in
women's legal and political status. My chambers window in Washington, D.C., commands a view of a small brick house, the headquarters of the National Women's Party and the home of suffragist
Alice Paul. It serves as a daily reminder to me that less than seventy-
five years ago women had yet to obtain that most basic civil right,
the right to vote. It also serves as a reminder that single-minded de-

*Sandra Day O'Connor, Associate Justice of
the United States Supreme Court, delivers the third
Lillian Parker Wallace Lecture on March 11, 1991.*

termination and effort *can* bring about fundamental changes in
even a well-entrenched system of discrimination.

O'Connor concluded her lecture with a personal word to, and about,
young people:

> I enjoy speaking to young women and reminding them of the all-
> too-recent history of women and the law. Young people tend to be-
> lieve that conditions in the world in which they find themselves
> have *always* existed. In fact, there have been dramatic changes in
> conditions for women in the United States, and those changes have
> occurred for the most part, in my lifetime. It is important to re-
> member that everyone in this room is part of the process of making

real the promise of equal justice under the law. And each one of us has a role to play in completing that task.

Anne Bryan, '71, president of the class that established the Lillian Parker Wallace Endowment, moderated an afternoon symposium on "Women, the Law, and Justice O'Connor." U.S. Attorney Margaret Person Currin, '72; legal services attorney Martha Dicus, '71; North Carolina Representative Judy Hunt, '71; and Wake Forest University law professor Suzanne Reynolds, '71, formed the panel.

FRIENDS OF THE Carlyle Campbell Library made one of its contributions to the Centennial at the annual spring dinner on April 9, when Rebecca Murray, '58, professor of education, reviewed her new publication, *This Essential Part: The First 1000 Books of the Library of Baptist Female University*. For $100, one could buy Dr. Murray's book and, with it, a brick—an identifying brass plate affixed—from old Faircloth Hall, which had recently been razed and removed from the parking lot that then occupied the site of the original campus downtown. *This Essential Part* was the first publication of the new Meredith College Press, established in the centennial year.

On April 24, the Rev. F. Sue Fitzgerald, '52, director of Christian education ministries at Mars Hill College, preached her second baccalaureate sermon to a Meredith congregation, the first having been at commencement in 1975. Her centennial year message was titled "They Hung Their Harps on the Willows."

Jean Jackson's centennial notes record commencement speaker Erma Bombeck as "Syndicated columnist, author, broadcaster, one of America's favorite humorists."[28] Jackson quoted the opening sentences of Bombeck's commencement address:

> Although we have never met, there are some things I already know about you. I know you are frightened about what the future holds. I know you are apprehensive about being on your own for the first time. I know you are asking yourselves, "What do I do now?" After a dramatic pause she added, "But I'm not here to address you parents. I'm here to talk to your children."[29]

The speaker identified herself as a "card-carrying feminist" who had worked "to bring about equality under the law for women. We have brains and we were meant to use them." But, she said, her marriage and children were more important than anything else. "My two careers don't control my life. I control my life."[30] Finally, Bombeck admonished the graduates, "Don't confuse fame with success. One is Madonna;* the other is Helen Keller."[31]

Of the 391 members of the Centennial Class, sixty-five were re-entry women and twenty-one were Honors Scholars, representing the largest number of graduates, to date, in both categories. And one was Sarah M. Lemmon, professor emeritus of history, who received her fourth degree, a Bachelor of Arts in art history. Of her previous degrees, the Bachelor of Science, the Master of Arts, and the Doctor of Philosophy, none was earned at the College, but Dr. Lemmon, who had taught there for almost her entire career, had become a bona fide Meredith alumna. At the commencement ceremonies, Flora Ann Lee Bynum, '46, and Jean Batten Cooper, '54, each received an Alumna Award for their service to Meredith and to their community. (Both recipients were from Winston-Salem.) And Christie Bishop Barbee, '83, received the Recent Graduate Award. Also recognized were winners of the FAME Awards: Deborah Smith, associate professor of biology, for teaching; Mary Thomas, associate professor of foreign languages, for research and publication; Rhonda Zingraff, professor of sociology, and Clyde Frazier, associate professor of politics, both for their contributions to the College and its programs; and the Sears-Roebuck Teaching Award: Nan Miller, instructor of English.

In the company of 700 women who returned for reunions, classes, meetings, and other types of *College* events, Alumnae College made its debut on the weekend following graduation, May 17-19, replacing Alumnae Weekend at commencement.** Mimi Holt, '67, president of the Alumnae Association, said, "One of our biggest challenges is developing programs to meet the needs of this incredibly diverse group of women."[32] And of the women, she said, "Right now we're feeling kind of schizophrenic because we're so often accused of living in the past. Well, indulge us in the centennial year. We're also very focused on the future."[33]

---

*In the event that readers of this history outlive the memories of Madonna, they should know that she was a controversial but sometimes celebrated singer and actor of the period.
**Alumnae College reverted to Alumnae Weekend in 1996 but was thenceforward held on a weekend following commencement.

IN THE FALL term, the Centennial celebration continued. Banners waved along the front drive, and an interest center of photographs and memorabilia attracted people to Bryan Rotunda. Craig Greene, head of the art department, displayed five centennial etchings, which he had produced on a press "exactly like the one Rembrandt once used to produce his own prints."[35] The etchings, including one scene from the old campus, and four from the "new," were on sale for $200–$300 each. Meanwhile, Suzanne Britt, prolific writer and instructor of English, watched the progress toward publication of *Images: A Centennial Journey*, a literary and pictorial history of the College, comprising intriguing essays by Britt and colorful photographs by Chip Henderson, Steve Wilson, and other photographers. Most academic departments created their own Centennial projects: for example, Roger H. Crook, author of several books and former head of the Department of Religion and Philosophy, wrote *Symmetry*, a history of the department, which was published in 1992. The department of home economics sponsored a program on Historic Fashion Silhouettes, with Vickie Berger, curator of the historic costume collection at the North Carolina Museum of History, as speaker.

The first major centennial event of the fall term was the Honors Convocation on August 26. It might have been helpful if every member of the audience had been an Honors Scholar as biopsychologist Jerre Levy, a professor in the department of psychology at the University of Chicago, lectured on the topic, "Getting Your Head Together: The Two Sides of the Human Brain." Dr. Levy's speech exploded a popular myth or two:

> Do some people think mainly with the left half of the brain and others with the right? Does the right perceive the sizes and forms of objects in pictures according to literal measurements in the two-dimensional plane and the left according to meaningful inferences about the three-dimensional world that the picture represents? When meaning and the inferential possibility are removed by turning pictures upside down, does this activate the right hemisphere and inhibit the left? Is the left active and the right idle and witless in some domains of human behavior and vice-versa for others? Such assertions have been repeatedly made in the popular literature, but none has even the slightest grain of truth.

After spending twenty years "trying to pull the two hemispheres [of the brain] apart," in search of the differences between the left hemisphere and the right, she said, she was now "trying to put them back together— as I think all human beings are trying to do."[35]

PHYLLIS TRIBLE, '54, Baldwin Professor of Sacred Literature at Union Theological Seminary, "came home" to Meredith on September 30, 1991, to deliver the Staley Distinguished Lecture on Women in Religion in the 21st Century. She titled her lecture "A Striving After Wind." Of the speaker, Dr. Jackson said,

> Recognizing the Bible as a patriarchal document has led some feminists to denounce it as "hopelessly misogynist." Other feminists sometimes "reprehensively use documents to support anti-Semitic sentiments." Others "read the Bible as a historical document, devoid of any continuing authority, and hence, worthy of dismissal." Still others "insist that text and interpretation provide more excellent ways." The last, she claims as "my niche." It gives her a chance to explore the "pilgrim character of the Bible. . . ."
>
> She said, "As you prepare here at Meredith College to enter the twenty-first century, I am sure you will not go empty-handed. Our complicated and complex world almost requires that you enter with a lot of baggage. . . . may I suggest you take that ancient and perdurable book, the Bible, but do not take all the partriarchal baggage that attends it.
>
> "Insist that the text and its interpreters provide more excellent ways. . . ."[36]

While Dr. Trible was on the campus from September 30–October 2, she, in her own excellent way, conducted classroom discussions and led a symposium with other women in ministry: Kelley Milstead, '86, a hospital chaplain; Maggie O'dell, '77, assistant professor of religion at Converse College; Deborah Steely, executive director of Planned Parenthood Public Affairs of North Carolina; and Anne Burke, '87, executive director of Raleigh's Urban Ministries Center.

Also at the end of September and beginning of October, a play commissioned for the Centennial premiered in the Studio Theater. Tom Cope was playwright and Nan L. Stephenson was director of *Journey Proud,* an introduction to Judith Wilde, a ninety-six-year-old woman, who "examines the high points of her life" and "reveals her personal view of the accomplishments of Southern women."[37]

IN APRIL, THE College had launched the $10,600,000 Second Century Challenge capital campaign, with Raleighites Barbara K. Allen and Philip Kirk, Jr., as co-chairs. Soon thereafter—and even before, for that matter—Vice President Murphy Osborne continually announced news of gifts and grants, to which the Winter 1992 edition of *Meredith* attested: the late Irving H. Wainwright had bequeathed $1,473,940 to the College, $800,000 of which would establish a scholarship in the donor's name; the Jessie Ball DuPont Foundation had awarded a grant of $183,600 to support ten Teaching Fellows; and the A.J. Fletcher Foundation's gift had totaled $250,000. Dr. Osborne also said that trustee William W. Lawrence and Mrs. Lawrence of Sanford and alumna Dorothy Loftin Goodwin, '47, and Mr. Goodwin of Apex had established unitrusts ranging in amounts from almost $200,000 to $300,000, the Goodwins' trust to be divided between Meredith and the Baptist Children's Homes.

Additional good news came by way of the Heritage Society, an organization of supporters who had named Meredith the beneficiary of insurance policies, wills, trusts, and other types of planned gifts. The society's goal was one hundred charter members through 1991. A year earlier, as reported in the previous chapter of this history, the goal had already been exceeded by fifty-six. At the society's October 1991 meeting, with three months still to go in the Centennial year, the number had climbed to 250 charter members. Mabel Claire Hoggard Maddrey, '28, served as president of the society. Speaker for the centennial-year meeting was C.C. Hope, who, as a Ronald Reagen appointee, had directed the Federal Deposit Insurance Corporation.

THE CENTENNIAL DANCED into the Raleigh Civic Center on November 15, as the Meredith Entertainment Association hosted the White Iris Ball for "festive Meredith students and their handsome dates"—so said the *Meredith Herald*.[38] The White Iris Ball blossomed into a tradition that night, a dance by the same name having been held every year since 1991.

Dance was on many minds at Meredith about that time of the year. Liz Lerman and the Dance Exchange, widely recognized for an unusual approach to programs of their art, were in residence from November 10–23. Lerman choreographed a centennial work, which was performed by students and alumnae. Jean Jackson, director of the Centennial Commission, was one of the dancers. In fact, she told *Meredith* that "the funniest moment" of the Centennial was "When I found myself in a rehearsal room preparing to dance in public—and people were going to pay to see me."[39] The magazine reported that the Liz Lerman dance performances "brought to startling awareness both the possibilities of intergenerational and experimental dance theatre as well as the tensions and triumphs of women."[40]

THE FINAL OFFICIAL Centennial activity of 1991 was a book tea in Bryan Rotunda, honoring Suzanne Britt, author of *Images: A Centennial Journey*, and Chip Henderson, primary photographer for the pictorial history. Britt and Henderson signed books for two hours on the afternoon of December 4, while Bill Wade, controller, and Donald Spanton, head of the Department of Business and Economics, played background music on the piano. The year of the Centennial had captured the essence of Meredith's special ambiance, as quoted from Images: "Meredith College is a world of light and meaning—not the world its women were born into by chance but, rather, a world searched for, singled out, *chosen* when the time has come for such choices."[41]

THE YEAR-LONG CELEBRATION spilled over into 1992, lasting through Founders' Day. On February 6, the cast of Alice in Wonderland gave their all to the Centennial performance, and on February 10, the executive committee of the Board of Trustees passed a resolution of appreciation for Jean Jackson's "leadership in the directing of the celebration of Meredith's centennial."[42] A framed copy of the resolution was presented to Dr. Jackson on Founders' Day.

Following a community breakfast in Belk Hall on February 24, Patricia Schroeder, member of the United States House of Representatives (D-Colorado) delivered the Founders' Day address titled "Women in Leadership." Jackson said, "From her opening remarks, Rep. Schroeder urged participation in government. She told the senior class, robed for Founders' Day, 'you look great in basic black, and I hope you're all on the way to the Supreme Court.'"[43]

She urged women to go to Washington to see Sewall House, "where women stayed during the entire campaign to get women the right to vote." Purchased with funds provided by North Carolina's Sewall family and filled with North Carolina furniture, the house provided a residence for suffragists because "proper ladies at that time could not come to Washington and stay in hotels." Citing those "proper" ladies, Schroeder marvelled at the "amazing commitment that women made at the turn of the century to get us the right to vote— the century we are living in. It had to be gutsy," she said.[44]

On February 26, the college community gathered to worship and to focus on the future of the College, and, immediately afterward, to plant a symbolic oak tree just outside of Jones Chapel. Since the Centennial's official beginning, the grounds had grown greener and shadier by the addition of seventy-five trees. A grove of oaks—one tree for the Centennial director and one for each member of the executive committee—was planted between Joyner Hall and the Mae Grimmer Alumnae House, and new crape myrtles, in honor of committee chairs and other dedicated movers and shakers, were set out in carefully chosen sites around the campus. Thus, the observance of Meredith's Charter Centennial came to a close.

Words of the editor of the *Biblical Recorder* in the late 1800s span the years:

If it required a century to complete the Baptist Female University, it would be worthy of our labors and prayers every moment of the time. Let us not bother our minds about time: God rules, and we have but to do our duty, and look to Him. No one need fear that what he shall do for this institution will be lost. It will last as long as the world shall last.[45]

II

"A CLOUD OF WITNESSES"

1991–1993

The graduation of the first class from Baptist Female University occurred on Wednesday, May 21, 1902, at eleven o'clock. The exercises began with a prayer offered by Dr. Thomas E. Skinner, pastor emeritus, First Baptist Church of Raleigh, which invoked "Heaven's blessings on the 'Immortal Ten,' that they might add the glory of true Christian lives to the honors of intellectual attainments."[1]

THE TEN YOUNG women of the first graduating class of Baptist Female University apparently left untarnished the shining epithet given them by Dr. Skinner in his prayer, although in their student days, before they became "immortal," two classmates were severely chastised for using "unbecoming language."[2] As a centennial commemoration and labor of love, education professor Rebecca Murray* delved into the past to bring to memory those first ten graduates—all from North Carolina: Mary Estelle Johnson, was honored by her daughter, Martha Salisbury Smoot, '33, and other family members and friends, by making possible the Estelle Johnson Salisbury Memorial Organ, dedicated April 10, 1983, in Mere-

---

*On June 6, 1992, Rebecca Murray, '58, professor of education and head of the department, 1977–82, died at her Raleigh home. The Class of 1993 established a scholarship in her memory.

dith's Jones Chapel. Sophie Lanneau became a "pioneer missionary" in Soochow, China, where she founded and was principal of the Wei Ling Girls' School. Elizabeth Parker continued her studies in art—primarily in New York, but also in Europe—and became a professor of art. Rosa Catherine Paschal did graduate work at both the University of Chicago and at Yale. BFU called her back as an assistant in mathematics and, later, lady principal. When the institution changed its name to "Meredith College," she requested that her title be changed to "dean of women." Mary Perry taught "all grades" and recalled "such great disparity in my classes that some were learning to read while others were translating Latin."[3] She married one of her students, and they influenced three of their five daughters to attend Meredith. Margaret Whitmore Shields's early forays into the "real world" took her to Baptist churches over the state to speak on behalf of the University. In her subsequent studies at Harvard's Radcliffe College, she attended classes with Helen Keller and Annie Sullivan. As a Meredith trustee, she was on the committee that chose the present site for the campus. Minnie Wilma Sutton was president of the class. The scant information about her leads only to the facts that she married, had a daughter, and died prematurely in Richmond, Virginia. Elizabeth Gladys Tull returned to her hometown, where she was a homemaker, a church woman, and "an astute business woman," having kept "her own set of books for the family business." Eliza Rebecca Wooten was remembered by her daughter as "a real intellectual" and by her fellow students as the Gibson Girl of her class. She was a librarian and a church school teacher. Marjorie Kesler was the "first of three students to receive the M.A." Later, she also studied at Columbia University. After teaching in Texas and living in the Midwest, she returned to her birthplace to live "amid the dearness of things long remembered and the charm of the ever new."[4] Five of the young women pursued graduate work; four graduated with honors; three reared daughters who became alumnae; two were on the payroll of Baptist Female University, and one was a Meredith trustee. Their diversity, Christian witness, intellectual rigor, and commitment to education for women contributed to the forming of Meredith's direction.

The Granddaughters' Club has also effectively honored the memory of some who have gone before. In a relatively new Founders' Day tradition at the Thomas Meredith Memorial, members of the club (students whose mothers and/or grandmothers are/were alumnae), usually read antiphonally the names of founders, trustees, alumnae, faculty, administrators, and benefactors who have joined Meredith's metaphorical "so great a cloud of witnesses," as set forth by the writer of the Book of Hebrews:

> Wherefore seeing we also are compassed about with so great a cloud of witnesses, let us lay aside every weight, and the sin which doth so easily beset *us*, and let us run with patience the race that is set before us, looking unto Jesus the author and finisher of *our* faith; for the joy that was set before him endured the cross, despising the shame, and is set down at the right hand of the throne of God.[5]

Dummelow's *One Volume Bible Commentary*, recommended to students by Ralph McLain (one of the "witnesses"), instructs that the word "witness"

> passes easily over to the further sense of 'spectator'. . . .The writer conceives these heroes as surrounding in a cloud . . . , the arena in which the present generation of God's people are running their race. Once they were themselves runners; now they are promoted to the rank of spectators. Their presence and example ought to be a stimulus to those running now.[6]

"Those running now" are not yet the "spectators" alluded to in the Book of Hebrews; nevertheless, as participants, they also witness and witness to all the ramifications of higher education for women in the latter years of the twentieth century. The longer they run, the more their longevity gives Meredith "a stability that any college in the nation would envy," wrote President Weems in 1992.[7] In 1991, for his twenty years of "leadership and contributions" to the school, the trustees rewarded the president with a trip around the world.[8] He and the five vice presidents had served a combined total of ninety years, with Dr. Spooner's tenure of twenty-five years outdistancing the others and Dean Burris's twenty-three years capturing a close second place. The full-time teaching faculty, numbering about one-hundred, averaged approximately ten years each, but Phyllis Garriss, music, claimed forty-one years, and Jay Massey, health, physical education and dance, who was retiring, had amassed thirty-five. Of the staff of almost 200 people, nineteen had served fifteen years or more, but Dru Morgan Hinsley, '52, manager of the college store, held the record at thirty-nine years.

Students—as students—have a limited longevity, but they are alumnae forever and, therefore, stay in the "race." The long list of exceptional alumnae in Meredith's history includes Mabel Claire Hoggard Maddrey, '28, in whose honor the parlor in the Mae Grimmer Alumnae House was named in 1992. It also includes Mary Howard, who, in 1991, wore her commencement robe as a mantle of determination. Of her, *Meredith*, the college magazine, reported,

> Mary Howard, '91, was 77 years old when she earned her bachelor's degree in art. . . . She could have told commencement speaker Erma Bombeck a thing or two about the "trials and fibrillations" of women who are determined to have it all.
>
> Mary's vita reads like an only slightly condensed version of a C.I.A. file. In addition to pursuing her primary interest in art, Mary has been to secretarial school, taken real estate courses, written short stories, invented a collapsible easel, and operated a restaurant. She has also won several ribbons for her art. Now she can add "college graduate" to her list of credits.[9]

TO SOME DEGREE, reorganization occurred regularly among the runners in the administration, faculty, and staff. In 1991, Allen Page left his faculty niche for the administrative post of dean of undergraduate instruction and registrar, and Bernard Cochran succeeded Dr. Page as head of the Department of Religion and Philosophy. Dr. Cochran came to Meredith in 1960. He had earned the bachelor's degree at Stetson University; both the bachelor and master of divinity degrees at Southeastern Baptist Theological Seminary; and the Ph.D. at Duke. He said he was unconcerned that fewer numbers of students sought majors in religion than those subjects leading to more lucrative careers. And he encouraged even those planning vocational careers in ministry "not to load up on all religion courses but to supplement them with literature and abnormal psychology. Goodness knows," he said, "we need a few abnormal persons in the profession." Cochran continued, "Our ideal, as I express it, is to encourage [students] in intelligent faith and—with their moves into areas of math and science and business or in liberal arts courses— facilitate for them a better understanding of religion as they sort out their own personal beliefs and an understanding of their religious experiences and traditions."[10]

Also in 1991, Donald Spanton, head of the Department of Business and Economics, occupied the Wainwright Chair of Business, succeeding the retiring Lois Frazier; Harold West, Jr., followed retiree Wortham C. (Buddy) Lyon, Jr., as director of planned giving; and Madalyn Gaito succeeded Cynthia Edwards as director of student activities, when Dr. Edwards accepted an assistant professorship in psychology.

By 1992, the offices of public relations and publications had merged into one—the office of college communications, with Jeannie Morelock the director and Steve Mosley the publications manager. And in 1993, Dr. Spooner, the vice president over that division, also took under her administrative "wing" the office of admissions and the office of scholarships and financial assistance, both of which had previously functioned in the division of student development.

At the retirement of Ellen Ironside in 1992, Mary Johnson, dean of the John E. Weems Graduate School and director of the Teaching Fellows Program, added to her responsibilties the deanship of continuing education. Dr. Johnson had headed the education department from 1985–90. And when Jay Massey retired as head of the Department of Health, Physical Education and Dance, Marie Chamblee, a fifteen-year veteran of the department, succeeded her. A graduate of East Carolina University, Dr. Chamblee earned the M.A.T. and Ph.D. at the University of North Carolina in Chapel Hill. She was hired, she said, "to teach health classes, to coach basketball, and also to teach the physical activity classes. [But] that first year I taught fitness classes, badminton, and volleyball and all kinds of different things," efficiently adapting to the varied duties because she was a generalist, "which is good at a small college where you have to do everything."[11] Since joining the faculty in 1977, Chamblee has seen Meredith become "much more competitive [in athletics] than it ever was before."[12] After all, women have become better athletes, and the College systematically recruits players, even though it offers no athletic scholarships. Of dance, Chamblee said, "When I first came here we had one dance instructor. Now we have three full-time and two or three part-time. . . . We have grown from being a general service program of three or four dance offerings a semester to where now we have twenty, as well as a major and a K–12 teaching certification program."[13]

Also in 1992, Najla Nave Carlton, '79, became only the sixth director of alumnae relations for the ninety-year-old Alumnae Association. Although the organization is as old as the first graduating class, it was not served by a full-time director until Mae Frances Grimmer, '14, accepted the post in 1928. She remained at Meredith for thirty-six years, retiring in 1964 and living nearby until her accidental death in 1983. But one year before her retirement, Miss Grimmer saw the growing Alumnae Association's financial affairs win their rightful place in the college budget, eliminating the need for alumnae dues. In 1993, at fiscal year's end, 36 percent of the alumnae had contributed $267,898.00 to the general college fund. And in 1992, three alumnae had been responsible for a grant from the Palin Foundation of $100,000 toward establishing a faculty chair in the English Department in honor of alumna and English professor Norma Rose, '36. The foundation awarded the grant at the suggestion of Margaret Bullard Pruitt, '37, and her daughters Margaret "Peggy" P. Benson, '64, and Shannon "Shan" P. Rock, '68.

On May 21, 1902, Sophie Lanneau, one of the "Immortal Ten," was elected first president of the Alumnae Association, and on May 26, 1993, Mary Jon Gerald Roach, '56, was elected forty-eighth president. Lanneau, Roach, and the forty-six women in between served terms varying in length from one to six years; however, in 1990, the term of office officially became one year, with each candidate's having gained experience through a term as president-elect. The other presidents in the period of this chapter were Mimi Holt, '67, 1990–91; Nancy Young Noel, '57, 1991–92; and Lois Edinger, '45, 1992–93. Between March 1990 and June 1991, four of the Alumnae Association's past presidents died, an unusually high number for so short a span of time: Lula Ditmore Sandlin, '12, president 1922–23; Kate Johnson Parham, '14, 1929–31; Sarah Elizabeth Vernon Watts, '34, 1956–1958; and Lois Morgan Overby, '35, 1958–1962.

In 1993, Elizabeth Vann McDuffie joined the staff as director of scholarships and financial assistance following the retirement of John Hiott, who had also served both as registrar and director of planned giving. And visiting professor Nana Khizanishvili, a native of the Republic of Georgia in the former Soviet Union, charmed the campus. She had taught English in Tblisi, Georgia's capital city, but, at Meredith, "Dr. Nana," was a part-time visiting professor of Russian studies, a first for the College. She and her Georgian family lived in the Lemmon Guest House across Faircloth Street from the campus. Her husband, Iraklie, was an established

star of Russian films, and their daughters Ticko, 13, and Ann, 8, were enrolled in local schools. Dr. Khizanishvili said to *Meredith*, "Everyone here
[in the United States] is so happy, so rejoicing . . . thinking that the Soviet
Union no longer exists. I don't want you to become relaxed and think
that everything is so well and nice. . . . You can*not* kill a monster. The
Communist system is just like a dragon in a fairy tale. You chop off one
head and another emerges. . . ."[14] Through special arrangements, including a Kenan appointment, Khizanishvili was able to remain on the faculty
for a second academic year.

The college family cheered as its student members excelled. In 1991,
the *Herald* congratulated five musicians who made headlines when, in the
seventh annual Student Concerto Auditions, they won opportunities to
perform with the Raleigh Symphony. The chosen few were vocalists
Susan Wall, '92, and Heidi Sue Williams, '91; and pianists Alice Nell Jor-
genson, '92, Michele Daughtry, '93, and Heidi Ann Williams, '93.[15] And
the community applauded the findings that, in 1991, "close to 25% of
Meredith graduates are engaged in some form of continued education
(frequently part-time) six months after graduation."[16]

"Cheering on" is a literal interpretation of support for Meredith's
1990–91 basketball team. With a won–lost record of 18–3, the players
proved that a winning team could generate a rapid heartbeat—or at least
a generous outpouring of mild enthusiasm—in even the most staid of
scholars. Dean Burris's report to the trustees on February 22, 1991, is a
case in point. The minutes read,

> Dr. Burris commented on faculty promotions and tenure appoint-
> ments made for the coming year, changes in the art major and art
> curriculum, the upgrading of the curriculum in the Interior Design
> program to meet national standards, the on-going assessment of in-
> stitutional effectiveness, capstone studies, the effect of current
> world events on international study and travel, and the winning
> Meredith basketball team.

And President Weems proudly announced that the team had "the best
[women's basketball] win–loss percentage of any college or university in
North Carolina."[17] Enthusiasm for basketball escalated as statistics improved. In 1993, point guard Lesley Cox remembered her elation at seeing an extra row of bleachers installed in the gym to accommodate the

crowds. That year, the enviable record was 23–1, Meredith having lost 64–61 to Methodist College in early February. Of women's teams in Division III of the NCAA, the Angels ranked first in field-goal percentage (51.5%); second in victory margin (83.6 to 54.8); fourth in field-goal defense (31.1%); seventh in scoring offense, and ninth in free-throw shooting (72.3%).[18] "Seniors Sylvia Newman and Jennifer Norris, with shooting percentages of 63.4 and 57.2, respectively, were listed among the top national scorers. . . . Lesley Cox also ended the season nationally ranked in assists at 6.8 per game."[19] In 1988, the first team to play under Coach Carl "Sammy" Hatchell, had recorded a 7–14 season; since then, Hatchell has recruited good student athletes—a challenging occupation when "[s]everal of the current players were offered athletic scholarships at other schools, but turned them down to come to Meredith."[20]

Also in 1993, a team of nine members of the Meredith Christian Association headed for the Florida beaches at spring break, as did thousands of other students from all directions. But this team, with their "coach"— campus minister, Sam Carothers—spent much of each day helping to build a Habitat for Humanity home in St. Petersburg. The roof and the siding were MCA members' contributions to the future home of a single mother and her three children. The popular project in St. Petersburg began for the MCA in 1989 and was still on the spring-break schedule in 1998.

While MCA students contributed time and energy to a cause, trustees, administrators, faculty and staff, alumnae, and other benefactors found cause to contribute materially to Meredith through the $10,600,000 Second Century Challenge. Early in 1992, for example, Betty Webb, English, challenged the faculty to endorse a five-year goal of $100,000 and 100 percent participation. At mid-year, Vice President Murphy Osborne reported that Meredith "has recently completed its best fundraising year in the 101-year history of the College."[21] The record-breaking 5,776 gifts to the College in 1991–92 totaled approximately $4.4 million, including $1,345 million in unrestricted funds. In March 1993, less than a year later, Osborne announced that not only had the faculty met its goal of $100,000 but also that the capital campaign had been "successfully completed with 11.8 million dollars raised."[22]

POLITICS DOMINATED THE national news in 1992, as members of both major political parties thrust their ideologies on the voters. William Jef-

ferson Clinton, the first Democrat to be elected president since Jimmy
Carter won in 1966, had challenged Republican incumbent George Bush
in a bid for the White House. Closer to home, in the most expensive campaign for governor in North Carolina's history, Republican hopeful Jim
Gardner lost to Democrat incumbent James B. Hunt. In a story titled
"Political Climate Forecast: Warm and Partly Women," the college magazine featured three politically astute elected officials, who happened to
be Meredith women: Sarah Parker, Associate Justice of the Supreme
Court of North Carolina, the only woman to be elected to a statewide office that year; Betsy Lane Cochrane, '58, State Senator and minority
whip; and Judy Hunt, '71, a member of the North Carolina House of
Representatives.

In the story of Justice Parker, the magazine read, "The imposing dom-
inance of heavy law books lining the walls of her Justice Building office is
in stark contrast to the computer parked on her desk, whose screen lights
up with the words 'Go Heels!'[23] "Following her sophomore year at
Meredith, Sarah Parker transferred to the University of North Carolina,
where she earned the A.B. as well as—in 1969—the J.D. "While she is
the third woman to sit on the State's highest court, she is the first to reach
that pinnacle initially by election."[24] She is a Democrat, the story continued, "so how come the newspapers labeled her conservative? She
laughed. . . . 'I don't think you can categorize me as liberal or conservative. I am a moderate. I don't approach cases with an agenda. It depends
on what cases I get and where the law is in the development of those
cases. . . . All cases are significant to the litigants.' "[25]

Betsy Cochrane, the first woman to preside over the State Senate, did
not aspire to a political career, she said; she was recruited. In her third
term in the Senate after having already served four in the House, she commented to the magazine, " 'Being a Republican woman in a Democratic
male domain,' is an obstacle. '[O]ur success does not come as automati-
cally as that of the majority party. I guess I've been fairly successful, but
I chose my battles.' "[26]

Democrat Judy Hunt was in her fourth term in the State House of
Representatives, despite the fact that her five-county district in the moun-
tains of North Carolina is traditionally Republican. Of her first race, she
said, "Nobody thought I had a chance to win, but my encouragement
came from those who thought it was okay to run even if I didn't. . . ."[27]

And of women in political office, she said, "We are nowhere near pro-
portionately represented, but there are men here who are more sensitive
to women's issues and women's problems than some of the women."[28]

Also featured in the article was politico Carol Lancaster Milano, '79,
who had immersed herself in the political process, even though she held
no elective office. When Ms. Lancaster was a student, she was possibly
the busiest Young Republican on the campus, and her passion for politics
then set her course for the future. *Meredith* reported, "She climbed
quickly but through many steps from the menial tasks of a campaign volunteer [for Ronald Reagan] in her hometown of Atlanta to the awesome
responsibilities as director of public liaison at the State Department,
where she was special assistant to Secretary of State James Baker."[29] She
will remember the experiences of the latter role for her lifetime, she said.
For example, she preceded the American delegates to the 1991 Middle
Eastern Peace Conference in Madrid "to work with the king's staff and
the protocol staff 'to get it all set up.' "[30] With less enthusiasm, she remembered that she and Secretary Baker—then secretary of the trea-
sury—were traveling in Europe in 1987 when the stock market crashed,
and they stopped in Stockholm "to recuperate from the blow."[31]

Same magazine, different story: Vice President Thomas wrote of the
primary role of Bridget McMinn, '78, in President Clinton's inaugural
ceremonies. McMinn and some friends discovered at dinner one night
that they could fashion a presidential inauguration to rival that of the
best of brainstormers. They created a "full-blown proposal complete
with music, themes, and inaugural activity,"[32] delivered it to the Democratic National Committee and, finally to Harry Thomason, inaugural producer. In keeping with their proposed theme, "Let Freedom
Ring," one of the suggested activities was the simultaneous ringing of
bells throughout the country, as well as from the space shuttle, "as a
participatory symbol of unity, diversity and hope for a new President
and for America."[33] While McMinn and company's theme was changed
to "An American Reunion," the bells indeed rang, but the alumna
barely had time to hear them in her frantic pace as deputy director of
the 1993 inaugural balls and dinners. " 'It was a life-changing moment,' she said. . . . "[34]

At Meredith, the History and Politics Club, the SGA, the Residence
Hall Board, College Republicans and Democrats, and the Watkins Com-

munication Club had designated a day in September 1992 as Political Awareness Day. While the state and local politicians on hand perhaps seized the day to garner votes, students took advantage of the opportunity to discuss issues and ask questions.

The *Meredith Herald* ran an interesting Point/Counterpoint feature one month before the 1992 elections. Kelly Phillips wrote on behalf of presidential hopeful Bill Clinton:

> It is not surprising that more viewers tuned in last week to watch the presidential debates than the World Series. Never before have the American people had so much at stake in an election. Unemployment is up, real incomes are down, health care costs are up, and consumer confidence is down. America is desperate for a change.[35]

Beth Lowry supported incumbent George Bush:

> Change for change's sake is not the answer. Governor Clinton says that because of the current administration, America is falling apart at the seams. We are the world's superpower. . . . If Bill Clinton has little or no faith in America, why should we have faith in him as president?[36]

In September 1992, during the heat of the campaign, Hillary Rodham Clinton, wife of the Democratic challenger, spoke at North Carolina State to college newspaper editors, as Traci Latta and Tracy Rawls reported in the *Meredith Herald*: "If she becomes first lady, Clinton wants to break away from the traditional role . . . ,"saying she pictured a time "when the role [of spouse of the president] is NOT gender-specific."[37]

IN THE TEN years since the Equal Rights Amendment had failed, "falling three states short of ratification,"[38] gender-specific roles remained problematic in American culture, as did myriad other ingrained societal habits. The all-male Senate Judiciary Committee's televised hearings on law professor Anita Hill's sexual harrassment charges against Clarence Thomas, President Bush's nominee to replace retiring Supreme Court Justice Thurgood Marshall, seemed further to divide the sexes. But whether by design or coincidence, Meredith offered programs for women *and* men that might have alleviated—or at least helped assuage, however subtly— some of the residual effects of obsolete gender-based traditions. A 1990 edition of *Angels Aware*, newsletter of the Alumnae Association, had insinuated as much in its promotion of the first annual Alumnae College: "We look to Alumnae College as a chance to reunite with friends, to refresh our minds and spirits, and to restore our perspective on what being a Meredith woman means."[39] And an unidentified alumna was overheard vowing that the weekend restored her perspective on "what being a *woman* means. Period."

Leadership institutes were popular—and some were not gender-specific. For example, in May 1993, continuing education brought Stephen Covey, a management expert and best-selling author, to the Sheraton Imperial in Morrisville for an annual "Lesson in Leadership" seminar. Covey's best-selling book, the 7 *Habits of Highly Effective People*, "embrace[d] the concept of ethics in business."[40] Limited to 1,000 participants, the seminar attracted eight to thirty managers each from IBM, SAS Institute, Capital Associates, Research Triangle Park Institute, and Kerr Drugs.[41] A month later, the John E. Weems Graduate School sponsored the Challenge of Leadership Institute—for women only. The conference, funded by the Z. Smith Reynolds Foundation, invited women managers to spend a week on the campus "exploring concepts associated with leadership."[42] The president reported that the event was "such a success that participants requested an on-going institute. . . ."[43]

In February 1993, the North Carolina chapter of the Association of Women in Mathematics sponsored Sonya Kovalesky Day at Meredith, at which time fifty selected high school juniors and seniors came to the campus to learn how women "use math and computers in their careers, see computer demonstrations, and gather information in mathematics and computer science. . . . "[44] Virginia Knight, head of the Department of Mathematics and Computer Science, talked about Sonya Kovalesky after the second annual event in 1994, at which some middle school students were also invited, more than doubling the number of participants: Dr. Knight, who was named national director of the Association of Women in Mathematics in 1993, described Kovalesky as a nineteenth-century Russian mathematician who specialized in differential equations and whose "work and research are well used now." Kovalesky was able to "bring together her career in mathematics and her life as a mother and a society woman,"[45] leading one to imagine that she was a nineteenth-century embodiment of the late twentieth-century's "super woman."

*The Founders' Day wreath ceremony at
the Thomas Meredith Memorial reminds participants of
"the great cloud of witnesses" gone before.*

IN 1992, MEREDITH was one of eight colleges in the state and one of 111 in the nation on the John Templeton Foundation Honor Roll for Character Building Colleges. The Honor Roll, explained the foundation, "is to supply students, parents and philanthropists with a valid means of discerning which educational institutions promote high principles, values and traditions."[46] Also, the College was included in the 1992 *Barron's Best Buys in College Education.* Each of the 300 schools listed, said the publication, "consistently received high marks in terms of faculty attention to students, inspiring and useful programs, and opportunities for personal and professional development."[47]

But despite its successes, Meredith saw its enrollment statistics slip slightly in 1992–93, the first such downward turn "in more than twenty years."[48] Forty-nine fewer students than predicted resulted in a budget shortfall, and the trustees recommended in November 1992 "that the President become personally involved in student recruitment to help reverse the enrollment trend and to help with the projection of more accurate numbers for budgetary planning."[49] Vice President Taylor reportedly prepared a "three-case budget: . . . "best case, worst case, and most likely case."[50] The trend was not a serious matter, thought the administration; in fact, a decline had long been predicted, but the College disallowed the employment of any new personnel and, in 1993–94, froze salaries for faculty and staff. But by the February 1993 executive committee meeting of the trustees, President Weems worried that he "had not emphasized sufficiently the value of a raise" and that an increase of just $50 over the $400 already added to students' tuition bills would "yield a raise of about $200 per faculty and staff member."[51] George McCotter made the motion, the trustees voted, and the personnel actually realized a raise of about $250 each. In other action, the College moved swiftly to invite Stamats Communications, Inc., a consulting firm with a national reputation in marketing research, "to help us more effectively and efficiently meet our recruiting and enrollment goals."[52] In assessing the state of the College, Stamats responded, "It is important to note at the outset that Meredith has a long, proud history and over the past 100 years the College has enjoyed many successes. Furthermore, the College has evidenced great foresight and stewardship in responding to the changing market. Meredith is not facing a crisis. It is, however, facing some challenges. . . ."[53] For the most part, insisted the consultants, Meredith's strategies were working well, as enrollment statistics and financial history bore out; however, they said, "the time to act is now, rather than later. Each day that slips by means that competing institutions have more of a foothold in your market and in the hearts and minds of your prospective students."[54]

New *direct* marketing strategies will be visited in Chapter 13. It is interesting to note, however, that some of the old *indirect* marketing strategies were simply programs and traditions which had been integrated into the academic and social life of the community simply because they were the right things to do at specific times in history. Meredith Study Abroad, on-campus cultural events, continuing education, the honors program, and Teaching Fellows are good examples.

Meredith Study Abroad had enjoyed almost two decades of study in foreign cultures; however, in 1991, the College elected to cancel all summer programs abroad because of the serious conflict in the Middle East. Iraq's invasion of Kuwait in 1990 reached all the way to the United States, when President Bush dispatched armed forces to defend Saudi Arabia, another wealthy neighbor in the line of march. Operation Desert

Shield affected the Meredith family in the same ways it touched other communities. The *Meredith Herald* was aware: "Daily doses of tragic headlines and confusing news stories generate a very real need for information and emotional support for the campus community," it read.[55] The division of student development as well as some academic departments tried to address in an organized fashion the needs of that student generation, which knew little of wartime. And the Meredith Christian Association sponsored a special service, fashioning a worship center of a glass bowl filled with desert-like sand, into which participants buried their written prayers and concerns.

Cultural exchanges were possible despite the unrest. In February 1991, ten visitors from Moscow State Institute of Inernational Relations swapped thoughts with Meredith students and faculty on such topics as the war in the Middle East, the Russian people's perception of life in the United States, and their own lifestyles in the USSR. Less than a year later, the world took note of the break-up of Soviet Russia.

In 1992, four representatives from Dongbei University, Meredith's "sister university"in Dalian, China, toured the campus and signed "the second stage of a formal faculty exchange agreement."[56] Li Kejian, Zuo Xiuyin, Liu Jianmin, and Zhou Yue came to Meredith, following up the 1990 visit to Dongbei by President Weems, Dean Burris, and Professors Spanton and Webb. Immediately preceding the Chinese delegation's arrival, Susan Gilbert, English, and Burgunde Winz, foreign languages, had taught for a summer at Dongbei. Also, Dongbei's Professor He had taught Chinese history and culture at Meredith in the 1991–92 term.

In addition to cultural exchanges between nations, the College had offered opportunities for cultural events throughout the years; in 1992, however, the division for student development designed a Fall Semester Area Cultural Events Subscription Series: for a season's ticket, one could enjoy a Latin American Festival and a production of *Driving Miss Daisy* in September; the *Little Foxes* and the North Carolina Symphony in October; a fall tour of Chapel Hill, Duke University, and Old Salem, as well as the Preservation Hall Jazz Band in November. Except for local flavor, the cultural benefits of the horseback riding session and the pig pickin' scheduled for November 15 remain debatable.

Meredith provided its share of culture, such as theatre—"among the Triangle's and state's highest quality educational theatre programs"[57]—

dance, music, and guest lecturers. While each Centennial speaker left her own signature, other guests of the same period also brought celebrity and substance to appreciative audiences. For example, Helen Vendler, well-known poetry critic, lectured in successive years, speaking in 1991 on Yeats and in 1992 on Gerard Manley Hopkins. Sponsored by the Mary Lynch Johnson Chair of English, Vendler was professor of English and American literature at Harvard; poetry critic and author for the *New Yorker*, and reviewer for the *New York Review of Books* and the *New Republic*.

James A. Forbes, Jr., senior minister of New York's Riverside Church, inaugurated the Jo Welch Hull Lectureship Series in March 1992, with his lecture, "A Deeply Moving Religious Experience." Announcing James Hull's establishment of the lectureship in honor of his wife, a Meredith news release reported that Jo Welch Hull, '53, had "devoted most of her adult life to the process of education."[58] Mrs. Hull was an educational consultant in Greensboro, North Carolina, and had been a classroom teacher as well as a director of Christian education in churches of several denominations. At the time of the announcement, Dr. and Mrs. Hull were coordinators of the Piedmont Interfaith Council (PIC), of which organization Mrs. Hull was a co-founder.

David Steele, curator of European art at the North Carolina Museum of Art, delivered the first Mercer-Kesler Lecture Series on Art and Religion, established in 1993. The endowment had been funded by Annie Mercer Kesler, '18, and Carolyn Mercer, '22, to honor their father, Isaac Morton Mercer, associate professor of religion, 1928–39; and John M. Kesler, their husband and brother-in-law, respectively, an architect and a former trustee. The Kesler-Mercer Endowment specified the purchase of library resources in the fields of visual arts and theology and the sponsorship of lectures in the areas of visual arts, archtecture, and religion.

Audiences reacted gratefully to educational experiences like the Hull and Mercer-Kesler Lectures and others in the several series offered by the College. While the lectureships were not under the aegis of continuing education, their benefits fell into the category of "lifelong learning." But continuing education regularly sponsored its own educational programs. And the division never forgot children. In the summer of 1993, it provided two events that attracted youngsters of differing interests: One program was a performing arts camp, in which children from five to fifteen years of age learned some of the basic skills of acting, the use of music and dance in dramatic productions, and theater technology. And they pooled their knowledge to produce a musical as the grand finale of their three weeks at Meredith. The second "special" was a computer camp for children as young as nine and as old as fourteen, whose instruction included word processing, graphics, and programming "in a learning environment that was fun, creative, and educational."[59] The only apparent disadvantage to the computer camp was that some of the youth who applied had to be left on the waiting list.

Waiting lists were not unusual. Had Meredith not been forced to limit the number of new Teaching Fellows in 1991, it possibly could have enrolled sixty freshmen in the program. But the 1990 "bumper crop" of forty-one freshmen had "forced the College to look at all aspects of the Program in terms of growth and longevity"[60] and had resulted in the Teaching Fellows committee's recommending restriction of acceptances, at least for that year. The College, therefore, enrolled only nineteen, making the total number in all classes 112. Minutes of the faculty meeting for August 13, 1991, state that "Meredith has the lowest transfer rate of all 13 participating institutions," despite the demanding academic requirements. From the beginning, the College had stipulated that the 40 percent of the young teachers-to-be who were not already honors students would be required to take fifteen hours in Honors and to write an honors thesis. Although they were necessarily limited in number, the Teaching Fellows did not "limit their talents to campus. Project HALO (Help and Learning Outreach) was initiated by one of [the Fellows] as a means of providing assistance to at-risk students in the Wake County Public School system."[61]

The program received a significant boost in 1991, when the DuPont Foundation awarded a grant of $183,600 to finance ten Teaching Fellows for four years. And, in 1992, such major corporations as ABB, Burroughs-Wellcome, First Citizens and First Union Banks, and GE Capital Mortgage Company pledged a total of $192,580 in support.

Although the Teaching Fellows program was new, it had already become a tradition worthy of bold print display in the recruiting materials of the colleges and universities that administered it. But non-academic traditions also attracted prospective students' attention. A string of winning seasons in football or basketball, for example, might reach more prospective students for a major university than the best admissions counselor ever could. At Meredith, however, the traditions categorized as "good times" and "class competition" were better known for pleasing current students than for attracting new ones. And memories of them lingered in the hearts of students and alumnae alike. For example, in November 1995, when Carolyn Carter, '73, spoke to the juniors—Class of 1997—at a dinner celebrating the wearing of their new Meredith rings, she remembered Cornhuskin':

> My husband, Lennie, and I were married on a beautiful June day five years after I graduated from Meredith. We were in the Bahamas the next day, in the water, incredibly blue water, glorious sky and sun. We were looking at each other adoringly, and Lennie said to me, "Carolyn, yesterday was the most wonderful day of my life."
>
> And I said, without thinking, "Yesterday was the most wonderful day of my life too, except for the day that my class won Cornhuskin'." And the miracle is, we're still married. . . .

As previous chapters in this Meredith story verify, Cornhuskin' was the premier tradition for class competition. In 1991, the instruction committee suggested that the Academic Council "consider ways of reducing the conflict between Cornhusking [sic] and the learning process."[62] By way of the democratic process, the council requested "that the Student Life Committee re-evaluate the time of week and semester for Cornhusking out of concern that Cornhusking succeed."[63] Almost a year later, but before the 1992 version of the big event, a decision was reached, according to the *Meredith Herald*: "After much deliberation, the . . . Academic Council voted in favor of cancelling classes after 5:30 P.M. on Cornhuskin' night."[64] But 1992 was a year of Cornhuskin' reform. The Meredith Recreation Association (MRA) sponsored the annual bonfire on Sunday night, with band music by Virtual Reality, with toasted marshmallows, and with "big sis/little sis bonding."[65] Monday night was entertainment night, when the class co-chairs "revealed their classes' themes in a skit. . . . After the skit, the traditions co-chairs, Ellen Powers and Amy Willard, announced the rules for the scavenger hunt which followed."[66]

In a *Herald* editorial following the main attraction on Thursday night, Amity Brown, editor-in-chief, wrote,

> At this time last year, everyone on campus was licking their wounds, trying to recover from a particularly vicious Cornhuskin'. I'm glad to say that this year was not the same. . . .

I will have to admit some of the attempts at being positive were a bit strained. . . . To be honest, and I think a lot of juniors and seniors will agree, some of the positive efforts were a tad insincere to begin with, but reached near-sincerity by the end of the week.[67]

And in both the "thrill of victory" and the "agony of defeat," students turned to food—breakfast food—served from 11:00 P.M. until midnight by faculty and staff volunteers.

Stunt—another long-standing tradition—had already seen reform in 1990. The *Herald* reported the 1991 contests:

For the second year in a row, Stunt was similar to a field event. Students participated in a three-legged race, egg toss, flour power, halo chase, and sponge toss to try to win points for their class. . . . Three lucky students from each class got the opportunity to throw wet sponges at President John Weems, Dr. Carson Brisson [registrar], Sam Carothers [campus minister], and Janice McClendon [director of residence life]. . . ."[68]

A lip sync contest—new in 1991—also made the grade, the 1993 *Oakleaves* having described a photograph: "Seniors Jodi McCann and Jill Barlow perform in the senior stunt lip-synch [sic] to the song ['So Long, Farewell'] from *Sound of Music*. There were quite a few teary eyes at the end of this song."[69] The same yearbook recorded a Fall Fest in September; a Halloween mixer, Parents' Weekend, and the White Iris Ball in October; and Little Friends Weekend in March.

Pasttimes were almost as standard as traditions. Janie Mullis, writing in the *Meredith Herald*, alluded to ongoing problems—real or perceived—between students and college food services, but her article showed a forgiving spirit. And well it should have:

Complaining about dining hall food is a classic college pasttime. By participating in the Interfaith Food Shuttle, ARA Food Services may have redeemed itself in the eyes of many. The shuttle is a program organized by several local volunteers who pick up leftover food from Meredith, St. Mary's, and Peace College[s] five days a week. ARA provides meal services to the three schools. The food is transported to the Salvation Army and to Agape Place.[70]

The food donated by Meredith in compliance with North Carolina's "Good Samaritan Law," amounted to "ten to twenty servings of five or six different menu items."[71]

IN 1991, FOR the first time in forty years, Meredith trustees elected their own successors. In the Board meeting of November 18, Charles Barham moved to elect to four-year terms Jane S. Byrd, Rogers H. Clark, Jean B. Cooper, George V. McCotter, Ruby C. McSwain, Ernestine Newman, J. Earl Pope, the Rev. Mack Thompson, and Claude Williams. The first class under the amended charter took office January 1, 1992.

WHILE MEREDITH WAS redefining its relationship with the Baptist State Convention of North Carolina, it was also claiming a place "out front" in the Information Age. A new computer program, first used in 1991, had simplified the process of registration as well as provided a comprehensive academic file on every student. But that program endured a low profile compared to the three television channels available to every residence hall room, classroom, office, and public area, as reported in Chapter 9. Immediately, the channels had been put to use as the faculty requested 208 of the 305 programs broadcast in the spring of 1991. And focusing on opportunities at hand, the *Meredith Herald* announced that January 10 "marked the kick-off for the new . . . Video Club" and its eight-week introduction to the equipment and its use.[72] As to the future, Weems predicted,

> The new liberal arts will be heavily seasoned [with new educational delivery systems that] will astound the intellect. . . .
> Our students will be able to go to the library, secure a disc, and visualize living history as part of their out-of-classroom assignments. Science laboratory demonstrations will be created in full color and rotated 360 degrees in any magnification that suits the teacher. . . . Renowned Shakespearean actors can come to life in the classroom.[73]

Technology came to life in the classrooms, the offices, the laboratories, the residence halls, and even the theater wing with its new computerized box office. The offices of public relations and publications disposed of their old typesetter and stashed away obsolete art boards, hot wax machines, and type galleys in favor of desktop publishing; the office of scholarships and financial assistance had already amassed five years of experience with software that managed the processing of its work; and career services was the first office to test the FAX system under development for campuswide use. Voice mail was a phenomenon of 1992, as was the addition of four new computer science courses to the nine already listed in the catalogue. Life was made easier by technology—except, of course, for those times when an electronic wonder caused a deadline racer seemingly to lose two laps for every one gained. For example, the *Herald* for September 16, 1993, ran an apology for a missed publishing date, and the staff knew where to place the blame: "To err is human, but it takes a computer to really screw things up."[74]

MEREDITH "DIPT INTO the future, far as human eye could see," as did the young speaker in Tennyson's "Locksley Hall,"[75] but, in some areas, such as architecture, the College clung to a past that had served it well. When architects F. Carter Williams and Associates designed the new Hubert Ledford Classroom Building, they "signaled a return to the more traditional modified Georgian design of the original campus buildings."[76] Whatever style the design represented, members of the psychology and education departments were eager to move out of crowded Joyner Hall into the new quarters. On February 28, 1992, at the semi-annual meeting of the Board of Trustees, Bob Bryan, development committee chair, had expressed "great pleasure" in moving that the "College proceed with the construction." But all the steps—the authorization, groundbreaking, construction, and dedication—made for a long process. Groundbreaking in April and excavation in July signaled that Ledford Hall, one of three academic buildings of the future, was underway, with Peden Construction Company as the general contractor.

In 1991–92, Meredith converted the Ellen Brewer House from a practice house for home economics students in home management to an infant and toddler lab home for child development majors practicing child care. The program would provide internships for approximately ten students per semester. But as much for the benefit of babies and their parents as for students, the new Ellen Brewer Infant and Toddler Lab Home first made available ten slots—six full-time and four part-time—for babies as young as three months and as old as three years, many of whom were children of Meredith employees. The home economics department had, since 1960, made good use of the building as it was originally intended, but times had changed, as borne out by an interesting—if not surprising—1987 report of the committee on child care for the Meredith College campus: "Information gained from recent articles on child care reported that eight million women in the labor force have children under six years of age. In addition, two-thirds of women working outside the home have school-age childen. Many of those who are responsible for the children are single parents."[77] The staff for the new lab home comprised a caregiving director, a caregiver, a faculty coordinator, and approximately ten students per semester. Renee Prillaman, assistant professor of home economics, coordinated the project. Even in its change in emphasis, the department was firm in its belief that it continued "the Brewers' commitment to provide quality field experiences for Meredith students."[78] Ellen Brewer was department head in home economics from 1922–66, and the house named for her was funded largely by her cousin Talcott Brewer.

Renovations in Belk Dining Hall in the summer of 1992 transformed the refectory, which had been fondly likened to an airplane hangar, into an attractive area with a fresh look and a quieter, more amiable ambience. Architect Mark Dickey said, "We wanted to give the interior of the dining hall more of the character of some of the other traditional buildings. . . . The new ceiling and division of the space into two separate dining rooms will help."[79] A food court separated the two dining areas. And downstairs in the same building, the old President's Dining room gave way in 1993 to the new Wainwright Conference Suite, comprising five rooms designed for meeting and dining. According to President Weems, "The decor is as uplifting as the current dining space on the upper floor,"[80] and the attractive outside entrance elicited almost as many compliments as the refurbished interior. The suite proved as beneficial to off-campus guests as to Meredith gatherings, frequently calling on ARA food service to cater meals for several groups at the time.

VARIOUS NEWS ITEMS gave witness to "the running of the race." For example, in 1992,

> Dr. Osborne described the success of the first Scholarship Appreciation Dinner where donors were paired with recipients. One-hundred seventy-five donors and students attended.[81]

And Mary Thomas

> introduced a new concept to Meredith Coursework, a program encouraging Meredith faculty to be lifelong learners. Currently, faculty are offered tuition remission for courses taken; next semester $50 per semester hour completed will be an added incentive.[82]

In 1993,

> The Student Government Association (SGA) is sponsoring Faculty Appreciation Day, Friday, according to Jennifer Hartig, SGA president.[83]

Also in 1993,

> According to a report by the city's planning department, Raleigh experienced the fastest growth since 1990 as 7,963 people became residents during the city's last fiscal year. Raleigh's population now stands at 230,418.[84]

AN ASTRONAUT PEERS through space that separates her from the planet she knows, and, through the clouds, she witnesses the earth as one entity, with no divisions by race, wealth, religion, or political ideology or by continents, countries, counties, cities, or colleges. Like the astronaut, the cloud of witnesses sees Meredith poised for the twenty-first century, and the lines of demarcation have dimmed. In the nineties, the view *from* the College was wider, more urban, and more diverse than it was in the early seventies. And the view *of* the College was also broader, in part because women had been assimilated into the culture and, therefore, were speaking in louder voices than, say, the Immortal Ten, who had contributed effectively but were rarely heard by their society. Infant-toddler day care; the comparative wealth of alumnae; cultural exchanges; highly credentialed faculty; computers; sophistication of academic offerings; attention from national magazines; state-of-the-art equipment; and insistence on academic freedom and, therefore, a clearer independence, were among the strengths of a college sending and receiving messages to and from a different world. In 1993, only eighty-five of three-hundred women's colleges had survived the previous two decades.

12

ALIS AND OTHER

WONDERLANDS

1993–1994

"THE MEREDITH COMMUNITY celebrated the arrival of ALIS last Wednesday at an official 'tea party' in Carlyle Campbell Library," wrote Jennifer Munden in the October 10, 1993, issue of the *Meredith Herald*. "Faculty actors from . . . 'Alice in Wonderland' were . . . surprise guests. . . ."

ALIS (pronounced "Alice") was an acronym for Automated Library Information System, and its installation in the library was cause for celebration. In the same jovial spirit of the Meredith family's vicarious joining of the Mad Hatter's Tea Party at the faculty's every-college-generation production of *Alice in Wonderland*, these party-goers raised their teacups to ALIS, another electronic wonder on the campus. The user had only to key in her/his needs—by title or subject or author—to start ALIS's search of the main or the music library, or even the computer catalogs of North Carolina State, the University of North Carolina at Chapel Hill, and Duke to bring up on the screen available information. In other words, said Janet Freeman, college librarian and guardian of the new system, "The year 1993–94 may well be called the 'year of bringing up ALIS.' "[1] In an article for *Meredith*, Freeman said she "envisions future 'libraries without walls.' The library, she predicted, 'will be able to provide the users with information they need whether we own it or we don't—we have the means to find it and bring a copy to the user. It's about access, not ownership."[2]

The few discouragers present that day in October were grieving at the demise of the card catalog, which, via the seekers' manual search, had been faithfully supplying information by title, author, subject, and Dewey Decimal System for decades. "You could *browse* through the catalog," one mourner was heard to say.

A reader browsing through the Fall 1993 issue of *Meredith* would see Anne Pugh's lengthy treatise on computers and the various uses of the technology in several departments. From her own office, Pugh, '82, noted that Charles Taylor "detaches the Notebook (portable computer) and carries it with him as he makes his rounds. Notes made on site can be printed out when he's back in the office and appropriate action taken."[3] The sophisticated Internet had become a valuable tool. Ruth Balla, director of academic computing, named its primary functions: "E-mail, Telnet, and FTP [File Transfer Protocol]."[4] Ted Waller, technical services librarian, frequently used e-mail. "It's just as easy to send a message to Australia as Apex," he said.[5] Waller's colleague Judy Schuster, a reference librarian, found that the Internet expanded her "access to materials here enormously."[6] And Jeannie Morelock, director of college communications, accessed ProfNet, "a free news service that allows journalists and authors to scan over 230 U.S. and international campuses for faculty experts' input."[7] But to President Weems, "one of the most significant additions to the modern office" was the FAX machine.[8] Weems noted that "today's students are outcome oriented," and that "[o]ne of the most important outcome-related skills our students need to compete in today's markets relates to computers."[9]

An information systems council, formed in 1993, saw the "big picture" of a campus-wide data base and network and coordinated those installations. Simply put, uses of technology continued to multiply. For example, the Center for Communications at the Microelectronics Center of North Carolina (MCNC) linked Meredith "with a global communications network called 'superhighways of information.'" The College was one of eight select North Carolina institutions of higher education to be able to avail itself of this "electronic pathway to the world."[10]

And beginning in the fall of 1993, a student's electronically read CamCard was her pathway to a cashless society. The CamCard was issued to each student and served as both her credit and identification card almost everywhere on campus, including the dining hall, vending and copy machines, voter registration desks, the bookstore, and the library. It would also allow her entry to locked classrooms and laboratories. Tales of lost or forgotten cards are not among public records; however, the *Meredith Herald* once published the "Top Ten Excuses For Not Having Your Cam-Card"—a parody of a regular feature on the *Late Show* with David Letterman:

10. I left it on my cafeteria tray, and it went through the garbage tray line.
9. I let a girl who looks kinda like me use it so she could eat lunch—she forgot her card, too.
8. I left it in the left pocket of my dark blue jeans, or was it the back pocket of my slim fit jeans [?]
7. It got ruined during the down pour [sic] of rain on Cornhuskin' night.
6. A bouncer took it away from me when I tried to use it to get into a bar on Tuesday night.
5. I got locked out of my suite yesterday, so I used it to break into my room. Too bad it cracked in half.
4. The cashier at Ann Taylor thought it was my credit card—she cut it in half.
3. Some how [sic] Vogue magazine got it. They liked it so much, my picture is going to the cover next month.
2. I thought it was my bank card, but when I put it in the teller machine, it ate my CamCard.
1. Look, I just don't have it O.K.? I have better things to do than keep track of my CamCard.[11]

The college magazine prophesied that, with the CamCard, "Meredith students will get a crash course in personal finance for the 21st century."[12] But for campus citizens who still had an affinity with the use of cash, Wachovia Bank installed an ATM (Automated Teller Machine) in Cate Center.

IN 1994, THE City of Raleigh became a "wonderland" in itself, when *Money* magazine rated it the best place to live in the United States. And once again, the college occupying 225 prime acres of Raleigh's western edge, was ranked by *U.S. News and World Report* in the "top tier of Southern colleges and universities," the magazine citing Meredith's awarding a "full range of bachelor's degrees, the majority in occupational and professional fields, and . . . at least 20 master's degrees yearly.' "[13] Also in 1994, and for the second consecutive year, Meredith was included in *Barron's Best Buys in College Education*, a guide for prospective students seeking "the most for their education dollars."[14]

What part Meredith played in Raleigh's No.1 ranking would be impossible to pinpoint, but, at the very least, it contributed positively to the cumulative fortune of the City of Oaks. Through the years, the College consistently enriched the intellectual climate of the region. To introduce by name all musicians, novelists, poets, theologians, humanitarians, and other scholars—and, yes, entertainers—who have appeared as guests on the campus, would be to create a tome of lists; but to include a random sample of the visitors in the time period of this chapter may well serve history: In April 1993, George McGovern, former United States senator and the Democratic Party's presidential nominee in 1972, lectured on "Achieving Peace: Recommendations for U.S.-Arab-Israeli Policy." Winner of seven Emmy Awards and a Tony, singer Ben Vereen came—not so much to sing, although he sang; not so much to dance, although he danced; not so much to act, although he acted—primarily to speak to his audience on "overcoming adversity."[15] Vereen was at Meredith on February 28, 1994, by invitation of the Association of Black Awareness and the convocation committee. Poet Dana Gioia, author of *Daily Horoscope* and *The Gods of Winter*, spoke on "What Are Poets For?" at an Honors Convocation on October 4, 1994. Joanne Greenburg, fiction writer and anthropologist, discussed a writer's life in convocation on October 24. One of Dr. Greenburg's well-known novels is *I Never Promised You a Rose Garden*.

MEREDITH WAS COMMITTED to developing the leadership potential of all its students of all ages. In 1994, the College was able to strengthen its resolve considerably when the Broyhill Family Foundation established the Broyhill Leadership Institute—"the first program of its kind in North Carolina"—with a view toward developing "a lifelong-leadership program."[16] Mary Johnson, dean of the John E. Weems Graduate School and of continuing education, would coordinate the institute's agenda. Johnson said it would incorporate existing leadership programs, such as the semester-long Emerging Leaders Seminar for freshmen and sophomores, inaugurated in 1990–91, and would comprise "a Leadership-in-Residence Program; the Broyhill Lecture Series; and Servanthood," giving students "opportunities to develop leadership in the areas of teamwork, decision making and mentoring."[17]

An article on mentoring by Alumna Del Hunt Johnson, MBA, '91, introduced readers to a three-year-old program of *"wo-mentors,"* conceived by Rebecca Oatsvall, business and economics, and by Donna Forrest, '91. Members of Tomorrow's Business Women, a national club with a chapter at Meredith, teamed up with women who could expose students to the business world through the experiences of conversation, office visits, and professional meetings. In 1994, each of twelve women, four of whom were alumnae, was mentor to a student. Gina Ledbetter Harwood, '93, a pharmaceutical sales representative, was one of the alumnae: "This seems like an extension of Meredith's big sister program. I really feel that kind of bond," she said.[18]

Perhaps recognizing Meredith's leadership in and advocacy for the public schools, the Department of Public Instruction selected the College as one of ten institutions of higher education in the state to host an annual North Carolina Teaching Academy, a new General Assembly-approved program of in-service training for public school teachers. The academy's method of "teachers training other teachers" would bring approximately one hundred teachers to the campus for each of three one-week summer sessions.

But long before such sophisticated programs for leadership development were in place, and prior to society's ready acceptance of women as leaders—except in areas known as "women's work"—Meredith, as was the case in every good college, enhanced its students' innate capacities to think, to act intelligently on those thoughts, and to lead. One need only to refer to Chapter 11 and the brief biographies of Baptist Female University's first ten graduates to recognize those qualities in alumnae of the earliest generations. And from the Class of 1927, Laura Weatherspoon Harrill emerged as one among many visionaries to commit to strong leadership on behalf of the College. As earlier chapters attest, Mrs. Harrill influenced and supported countless efforts to improve the campus and its tools for learning. Also, she was president of the Alumnae Association in 1942–44 and recipient of an Alumna Award in 1969. She had served as a trustee and had chaired the Board of Associates. After years of honoring

Meredith through her leadership, particularly in the area of philanthropy, Mrs. Harrill was on the receiving end of the honors in 1994 when the College presented to her the first Outstanding Alumna Philanthropist Award. She met the award's criteria of a "significant level of giving"; "visionary leadership"; involvement with the college; "commitment to Meredith's mission"; and encouragement of "philanthropy of others."[19] And before the award was announced, her son and daughter-in-law, James and Donna Harrill, established the $100,000 Laura Weatherspoon Harrill Scholarship Fund "to honor his mother . . . and to perpetuate her interest in providing love, friendship, and support for Meredith College."[20] In an interview with *Meredith*, the philanthropist turned philosophical, saying, "I think the right kind of education is the only thing that's going to save us. . . . Tell [alumnae] just to keep loving Meredith."[21] If their participation in the Second Century Challenge campaign measured their esteem, alumnae had already heeded Harrill's admonition. Of the 5,000 donors to the fund-raising effort, 4,000 were alumnae.[22]

In 1994, a criterion of one of FAME's Harrill Presidential Awards was "excellence in student advising," and Garry Walton, English, was the first recipient of the award under that category. In 1993, Harry Eberly, a member of the Board of Associates, and Mrs. Eberly established the Harry and Marion Eberly Faculty Development Awards "to recognize accomplishment and to encourage on-going development of faculty."[23] The very first presentations went to Larry Grimes, biology; and Carl Hatchell, health, physical education and dance.

At a special convocation on September 23, 1994, Murphy Osborne, vice president for institutional advancement, announced completion of the Second Century Challenge, the three-year effort that had raised $11.8 million, surpassing its $10.6 million goal. To an audience of celebrants wearing "Meredith Pride" pins, Governor James B. Hunt, keynote speaker, said,

> The students here are inspired by great women and men. They are empowered. They feel it and their lives show it. . . . In the next century, we need to dedicate ourselves to making North Carolina and the United States all they can and ought to be. Do it the way Meredith has done it all of these years and put a spark into everyone of the United States to fan and flame up.

Dedicated on February 25, 1994, Ledford Hall, with its "archways and Palladian window treatments" is said to be one of the handsomest buildings on the campus.

Reporting on the fundraising effort for *Meredith*, Del Hunt Johnson wrote of the "unusual twist" that allowed donors to see the tangible evidence of their contributions before the campaign ended.[24] For example, the new classroom building for education and psychology was high on the list of priorities, and, following a substantial gift from Hubert F. Ledford, in whose honor the building was named, contributions and pledges came quickly. Construction began in July 1992, and, before the campaign ended, donors witnessed the completion of Ledford Hall and its domination of the landscape to the southwest. But prior to the final stages of construction, the College found merit in expanding the use of the building by finishing the attic for the Department of Sociology and Social Work. So the three departments moved into a new home during the 1993 Christmas break, and all were ready to begin spring semester classes there.*

Ledford Hall, a 25,000 square-foot building costing $2.675 million,

---

*The three-department exodus from Joyner Hall provided space undreamed of for the Departments of English, Foreign Languages, History and Politics, and Religion and Philosophy. A major renovation of Joyner took place in the summer.

was dedicated on February 25, 1994, in the company of a crowd of Meredith advocates who expressed appreciation to Mr. Ledford and to others who had contributed financially and otherwise. With its "archways and Palladian window treatments incorporated in the three-story facility's brick and stone exterior,"[25] Ledford was considered to be one of the handsomest structures built since the original campus was completed in 1926. *News and Observer* critic Chuck Twardy, however, reviewed the architecture of the new building in a way that flouted his bias:

> In the first step of plans to expand Meredith College, tradition once again takes the day and modernism takes a hike.
>
> Hubert F. Ledford Hall, a worthy successor to the new-Colonial structures that define the campus, is neatly detailed, and the brick-faced building has a strong presence suited to its current isolation. . . .
>
> Sometimes a traditional touch is appropriate. But it is unfortunate that we've come to regard modernist buildings as hallmarks of low-rent "practicality" rather than high-end expression. It is particularly sad that modernism has come to such a pass in a town that used to be its hotbed.[26]

Twardy was also critical of the fact that the building faced away from Hillsborough Street. And, alluding to the contemplated companion structures, as yet visible only on the master plan, he added, "It is worth noting that the planned U-formation of buildings potentially turns building backs to both Hillsborough Street and the Beltline, which would be an unseemly development."[27]

Just before the designated departments occupied Ledford, trustees considered another renovation/addition. Minutes of the Board for September 24, 1993, read, "Due to the increased interest and enrollment in the areas of physical education, health, and dance, an addition to the Weatherspoon Physical Education–Dance Building was proposed." Of course, the students and faculty in the dance program would most appreciate the expanded dance studio, and all the faculty in the department would be happy with additional offices and storage space, but the new ell at the rear of Weatherspoon would perhaps serve the greatest good to the greatest number of students and faculty and staff through its proposed fitness center. F. Carter Williams Architects, designers of the original Weatherspoon Building, would also plan the addition. Citing the Weatherspoon addition, the Joyner Hall renovation, the Wainwright Conference Center (see Chapter 11), and the Ledford Building, President Weems said, "No one is happier than I to announce that all four of these major construction projects are already paid for and Meredith remains debt free."[28]

The Elva Bryan McIver Amphitheater and its island stage had paid the price of age. More than a quarter century old, the area was not problem free. For instance, the lake reproduced algae in large supply, and water-damaged pilings surrounded the island. In the amphitheater, loosened bricks caused hazardous seating areas, and sidewalks crumbled from age and erosion. In addition to repairs to the theater, the College drained the lake and filled in the moat that had separated the audience from the stage. Jean Jackson, English, quipped, "So now we have the Meredith Isthmus." But the "isthmus" created a heretofore-missing ambiance of intimacy between audience and performers and allowed easy access from one area to the other.

Some renovations in the original residence halls might have gone unnoticed as historically insignificant—replacement of windows and electrical wiring, for example—had they not included removal of the radiators from students' rooms. But perhaps nostalgia would rise only in earlier generations of students who, as a nightly ritual, had hung their hand-washed socks to dry on the hissing, clanging, moaning heat monsters of Vann, Stringfield, Faircloth, and Brewer.

Usually the refurbishing of residence halls and classroom buildings elicited positive reactions, but sometimes renovations were necessitated by fear and sorrow of the unforeseen and the unwanted. While a smoldering mattress in a Heilman Residence Hall storage room attracted much attention in the fall of 1993, little more than clean-up was required to return to normalcy. But a year later, Jeannie Morelock reported a much larger fire—this time in a classroom building—to members of the Meredith community, many of whom were on Christmas break at the time:

> Some time in the early morning hours of Saturday, January 8, a fire occurred in the Shearon Harris Classroom Building. It appears that the fire was started by a faulty appliance in the kitchen adjacent to the first floor lounge, but the exact cause is still under investigation by the fire department. . . . No one was in the building.

The kitchen was badly damaged by heat and fire. Fortunately, the heat caused an overhead copper water line to become loose. The water from the broken line extinguished the flame, preventing its spread. Unfortunately, however, large amounts of smoke spread throughout the . . . building through the air handling system. . . . [S]oot covered almost everything on both floors.[29]

Investigators found the culprit to be faulty wiring in a refrigerator. While the amount of the insurance claims soared to $400,000, perhaps the most shocking news was that all the ninety computers in Harris were rendered useless. As sometimes happens, however, the loss became an opportunity, and the College added money from the equipment budget to the insurance reimbursement, outfitting the damaged building with a later generation of computers to replace the older machines.

While the institution had little or no control over the accidental burning of buildings and equipment, it had very much to say about the use of its own land, except, of course, when it learned in 1993 that the State of North Carolina required 6,500 square feet of campus property to widen the beltline (Highway I-440). The College and the government agreed upon a settlement of $7,500.[30] But dealing with government and negotiating with private entities were different matters. As previous chapters have noted, an organization or institution occasionally broached the subject of buying or leasing some of the prime campus real estate for its own use. Minutes of the Board of Trustees for April 11, 1994, indicate that a lease agreement with Raleigh School on Ridge Road came closer to reality, apparently, than had negotiations with the Baptist State Convention in 1980 and the Life Enrichment Center in 1984, and certainly closer than a proposal from Kroger food chain in 1993. But Meredith and Raleigh Preschool were long-time neighbors and, in a sense, colleagues at work. In the first place, more than 2,000 Meredith students had participated in the "rich, 30-year history of mutually beneficial programming."[31] For example, child development, education, and psychology students had recognized the benefits of Raleigh Preschool as a laboratory, and the school, in turn, had welcomed the resourcefulness and helpfulness of students. The agreement spelled out the conditions: Meredith would lease three and one-half to five acres of land for one dollar per year; the lessee would finance, build, and operate a preschool and elementary facility approved by the College; and, after ninety-nine years, "the building and fixtures would revert to Meredith."[32] The decision not to lease came down to two issues, said Robert Lewis, chair of an ad hoc committee to study the proposal: "governance and non-Meredith entities building on the . . . campus."[33]

A different sort of land use was credited to the rising popularity of soccer. When Meredith added the game to its lineup of competitive sports, a new playing field altered the landscape a bit, and Coach Jose Cornejo joined the adjunct faculty at about the time the field took shape across the loop road and west of the Weatherspoon Building.

AS CHAPTER 6 implies, the campus was a city—in 1993–94, a bustling city within the nation's best bustling city—attempting to plan wisely for the future and to keep in good condition both the academic and the physical aspects of past achievements. The soccer field and Ledford Hall represented physical facilities of the future; repairs to the lake and Joyner Hall represented concern for keeping useful the old. Commitment to an evening program and the awarding of another accreditation represented new academic achievements. Eighty-five percent of the fulltime faculty's having earned terminal degrees and the American Bar Association's reapproval of the Legal Assistants Program represented the importance of updating the familiar. The additional accreditation was awarded by FIDER (Foundation for Interior Design Education Research); the degree statistics portrayed the highest percentage of faculty-earned terminal degrees in the College's history; and the Legal Assistants Program was initially ABA-approved in 1983 and reapproved in 1989 and 1994. Only the evening program requires elaboration: Minutes of the Academic Council for November 1, 1994, recorded a motion "that the Instruction Committee re-affirm Meredith's commitment to providing an evening schedule in which a student may complete her general requirements within five years in the evening program and charge the Director of the Re-Entry program and Registrar to work out, in conjunction with department heads, a program of study which will meet these needs." President Weems offered the rationale:

> Wake County and the Triangle area are two of the fastest growing markets in the south for college degree evening programs. North

Carolina Wesleyan College and Campbell University already have well-established satellite degree programs in Wake County. Averett College, located in Danville, Virginia, is opening a satellite campus in the Raleigh area . . . as is Warren Wilson College located in Swannanoa, North Carolina. Most satellite campuses are located in high schools, shopping centers, and classroom facilities rented from other sources. Meredith, with its excellent location and wonderful campus, is in the position to offer evening programs with full college support facilities.[34]

Only months before the Academic Council charged the registrar and the re-entry programs director to propose a course of study for Meredith After5, the evening program, Sandra Close succeeded Anne Dahle as director of re-entry. Close, a former re-entry student herself, had served as the assistant director since she graduated, *magna cum laude*, in 1986.

Also tapped to shoulder new and different responsibilities, Carolyn Barrington Grubbs, '60, assumed headship of the Department of History and Politics and Rebecca Bailey of the Department of Art. Dr. Grubbs succeeded her husband, Frank Grubbs, who continued to teach, and Dr. Bailey had completed a year as acting head of her department, replacing Craig Greene, the new deputy director of the Department of the Deaf and Hard of Hearing for the State of North Carolina. Carolyn Grubbs, '60, joined the faculty of her alma mater in 1963 after completing the M.A.T. at Duke; she later earned the Ph.D. at North Carolina State. The popular professor received an Outstanding Teacher Award in 1978 and, in 1980, a Delta Kappa Gamma scholarship toward her doctorate. The prestigious scholarship was "the only award made in North Carolina and one of nineteen given in the United States and twelve other nations by the international society of women educators."[35] Grubbs directed the honors program from 1991–94 and continued actively to lead students and faculty members in study opportunities abroad.

Dr. Bailey was a ten-year veteran of the art department, having started there as "very part-time," she said, but she kept adding courses to her schedule until she taught on a full-time basis. Answering the challenge to compare Meredith's art facilities with other schools, she said, "I think they are as good or better than facilities elsewhere, and I'm not going to say just at schools this size. I think if you compare what we're able to offer on a square-foot basis, our students are going to come out better. . . . We really try to get to know [them] and . . . help them to become the artists that they are."[36]

Garry Walton, English, inherited the honors program from Carolyn Grubbs. And Louise Taylor extended for one year her headship of the English department when Jean Jackson, '75, who had already been named successor to Taylor, was asked to join the administration as vice president for student development, following Sandra Thomas's resignation.

While Dr. Thomas was on sabbatical leave for the 1993–94 academic term, she was elected seventh president of Converse College, also a four-year institution for women, in Spartanburg, South Carolina. In her twenty-year tenure, Meredith's first female vice president had skillfully integrated the student development division into the administrative structure. Before she left, Thomas talked with alumna Lou Stephenson Liverman, '88: "[M]y work at Meredith, my work in higher education, my educational preparation and my life experience have all led me to this moment and will serve me well. . . . I don't think you say good-bye after 20 years; I think you say, 'Thank you for the journey.' "[37]

A month or so before the deadline for accepting applications for Thomas's replacement, the *Meredith Herald* reported the search committee's having received "40–50 [applications] from all over the country."[38] But as sometimes happens, the one who seemed most qualified for the position had not applied at all. Records do not pinpoint the moment of revelation to those charged with finding the right person for the job—and for the right time—but they do disclose the fact that, effective July 1, 1994, Jean Jackson became the new vice president for student development. Dr. Jackson graduated *magna cum laude* from Meredith in 1975 before earning her master's and Ph.D. degrees at the University of Illinois, where she taught in the English department from 1976–82. She returned to Meredith in 1983. In addition to her classroom teaching, she directed internships and professional communications as well as the Looking Toward College summer program for high school students. And having completed her stint as chair of the Centennial Commission, during which time *Meredith* named her "The Centennial's Essential Quintessential Woman," Jackson had been promoted to professor of English and elected to head the department when she accepted the vice presidency. "Dr. Jackson brings to this position experience, strength, warmth, creativity, and a large dose of humanity," said President Weems. "I think she will offer the kind of effective leadership our students deserve."[39] Her leadership would express itself through the campus minister's office; the personal growth and counseling center; the dean of students' office; student activities and leadership development; residence life; and career services. Soon after her appointment, Jackson told Christina Peoples of the *Meredith Herald*, "The school mattered absolutely to me as a student. . . . Meredith is the kind of place that invites investment of self."[40] In addition to academic and personal credentials, the vice president brought to her office testaments to her talents: the Pauline Perry FAME Award for excellence in teaching (1988); the Alumnae Association's recent graduate award (1988); and the Laura Harrill Presidential Award (1992). In 1996, she would receive an Alumna Award for outstanding service to Meredith and the community.

When she moved into her office on the first floor of Johnson Hall, she found on her desk student-related issues ranging from the Americans With Disabilities Act to proposals for expanded open house in the residence halls. As to the first issue, a generic reference book calls the Act "the most sweeping anti-discrimination legislation since the Civil Rights Act of 1964."[41] Meredith's responsibilities to students enrolled under the law are printed in the college catalogue, but Dr. Jackson shed light on the realities of compliance: "This semester a profoundly deaf student has enrolled as a freshman. The College is working to provide the necessary services needed for her to function well, and at the same time evaluating the financial implications that providing these services entails."[42]

Open house in the residence halls was not a new concern. In a *Meredith Herald* editorial in 1991, Jessica Cook had referred to an "impressive," "intelligent, thorough and solid" proposal which was dismissed by the trustees in 1987.[43] The first open house finally came, coinciding with Fall Fest 1993. But in their semi-annual meeting on February 23, 1994, the trustees heard a proposal for an expanded number of open houses. Alumna Jean Batten Cooper, '54, chair of the trustees' student development committee, moved acceptance of the proposal, and members of the board approved; however, one of the male trustees requested "regular feedback," a duty which was assigned to the dean of students.[44] The new policy was restated in the 1994–95 *Student Handbook*:

A maximum of three Open Houses per semester occur on designated Saturdays or Sundays during specified afternoon hours. All open houses are coordinated with other major campus activities listed in the Student Activities Calendar.

While the above events occurred before Dr. Jackson assumed the vice presidency, she was nevertheless much involved in helping the policy succeed and in overseeing the Student Govenment Association's carrying the process through to still further expansion in 1996.

The route of proposals and resolutions led ultimately to the trustees' agenda. On August 25, 1994, President Weems wrote to members of the board a letter that began, "At a special faculty meeting on April 29, 1994, two resolutions were endorsed by the faculty."[45] And the correspondence ended with his stance on the matter: "I personally do not agree with the majority . . . and therefore cannot support these resolutions. . . ."[46] The body of the letter quoted the action of the faculty:

We, the members of the faculty, believe that diversity of experience and respect for persons are desirable of an institution of higher learning, and believing that sexual orientation ([or] marital status) does not affect faculty members' ability to fulfill their professional duties successfully, to interact productively with other members of the College community, and to make a positive contribution to the life of the College, we therefore recommend and request, first that in administering employment policies, including the appointment, tenure, and promotion of faculty members, Meredith College does not discriminate on the basis of gender, race, national and ethnic origin or sexual orientation ([or] marital status) and, second that a member of the Faculty Affairs Committee be involved in revising section 3.2.16 (Discrimination) of the Faculty Handbook accordingly.

Fifty-five of the faculty had voted in favor of the sexual orientation resolution, with 32 against it; and 58 had voted in favor of the marital status issue, with 29 in opposition. Records of the February 12 meeting of the executive committee indicate that the trustees discussed the matter and resolved

that Meredith College affirms its current employment policies, and that Meredith College makes no revision in the administration of its employment policies as suggested in the two resolutions presented to the Executive Committee by the faculty of Meredith College on April 29, 1994.

In retrospect, some Meredith people theorize that the trustees' reaction to the faculty resolutions and the faculty's counter-reaction were the geneses of unaccustomed tension between the two bodies, as implied in later chapters.

THE WINDS OF relationships and rights swirled around the wonderland of society in 1993–94. The number of youth participating in violence and crime was among those "ill winds." Senior Elizabeth Rihani, copy editor of the *Meredith Herald*, was disturbed by her world:

> Ever since I worked in Washington, D.C. this past summer, I have tried to avoid television news altogether. It just got too much to hear an impassive newscaster tell me night after night who had died, which small country had been blown off the map, and what precautions I should take when I ventured out of my home. . . .
>
> I guess we could blame inattentive parents, broken homes, violence on television, or evil messages in rock music, but I don't think any of those [is] the culprit. In fact, I have no idea how society has gotten so out of hand even in the ten years or so since I was little. . . . Well, I don't have any answers, but I do wish our society wasn't so desensitized towards all the horrible, horrible things going on these days. . . . I'm just glad I'm not a newscaster—I'd be crying through the report every night.[47]

And in her magazine story, "From Classroom to Boardroom," Del Hunt Johnson hinted that young adults in general and Meredith young women in particular might prepare to shield themselves against the storms of the workplace:

> Beyond Meredith's comforting gates lies a mean world. Seniors without job prospects face the reality of living in an underemployed purgatory, or worse, at home with parents, joining the "boomerang" generation. And while good grades look nice on paper, they don't guarantee success. An "A" in quantitative statistics doesn't mean you'll pass "office politics" where career stakes are higher.

Textbooks and classroom lectures can't cover the finer points of how to lead a committee meeting, ask for a raise or confront a difficult co-worker. That only comes with experience.[48]

But many crosscurrents of the culture stirred much ado about corporate greed and politics, some about gender and racial bias, some about violence, some about abortion on demand, and some about marital status and sexual preference—and, again, much about terrorism, following the bombing of the World Trade Center in New York City that killed six people, injured hundreds, and left a jittery public to ponder the workings of international politics and religious fanaticism.

President Clinton might have overcome any semblance of gender bias by nominating Janet Reno as the first female attorney general of the United States, who, in her inaugural year, might have overcome any semblance of partisanship by appointing an independent counsel to investigate President and Mrs. Clinton's roles in a questionable real estate venture in Arkansas. In Congress, Republicans issued their Contract with America, promising, among other things, less government intervention than that initiated by the long-time controlling "tax-and-spend" Democrats. Voters liked what they saw and heard and, on election day, 1994, gave the Republican Party majorities in both the Senate and the House of Representatives for the first time in forty years.

While political tension reached a high point, so did racial unrest. Verdicts of innocence in the trials in California of the white police officers who allegedly beat Rodney King, a black motorist, and of O.J. Simpson, a black football hero charged with killing his former wife and a friend—both white—were jeered and cheered, often along racial lines.

FUTURE STUDENTS OF the cultural influences of 1993–94 might appreciate the statement printed in the 1924 program for the faculty's first presentation of *Alice in Wonderland*:

In this country of contraries you will see and hear many strange things. . . . Come to Wonderland with Alice.

13

THE MARKETPLACE

1995

IN 1904, BAPTIST Female University, "A High Grade College for Women," advertised that six men and nineteen women composed its faculty and administration. But most of the ad copy told prospective students what they needed to know about curriculum, living conditions, and costs:

> DIPLOMAS given in the Arts, Science, and Philosophy; in Music, Art, and Expression ¶ School of the Bible under graduate of Newton Theological Seminary ¶ Thorough Business Course ¶ Exceptional advantages in Music ¶ Excellent equipment for teaching Science ¶ Club system adopted by two-fifths of the boarding pupils, at a saving of $50.00 per session ¶ Students cared for by lady principal, lady physician, matron, and nurse ¶ Another dormitory in course of erection to accommodate 90 girls ¶ Board, Literary tuition, heat, light, baths (hot or cold), fees for physician, nurse and library, $107.30 per session—in clubs, $40.00 to $50.00 less.[1]

So five years after the university accepted its first students in 1899, it sought visibility in the marketplace. But Meredith College, BFU's well-established successor, learned more about marketing strategies in the last two decades of the twentieth century than it had previously needed to know. In a 1983 publication titled *Marketing Higher Education*, authors Robert Topor and M. Frederic Volkmann wrote, "Only a few years ago, it was certain political suicide in higher education to utter the words 'marketing' or 'market research' at a faculty meeting or a gathering of the president's cabinet. . . . Now, we regularly hear deans and professors talking about targeting, market share, positioning, and feedback with the same excitement that scientists talk about discovery."[2] The change came, speculated *Meredith* in 1992, as colleges vied for students because "that segment of society's population is well into its predicted decline and . . . costs of private higher education escalate more rapidly and more visibly than tuition and fees of state-supported schools."[3] The magazine also suggested that the College competed in the marketplace not only for the enrollment of students but also for the retention of those already enrolled; for donors; for the best faculty for the money; for accreditation; for a favorable image; for the legislator's ear; for the alumna's loyalty; and so on.[4]

In intervening years, hundreds of Meredith advertisements reached their targeted audiences through almost every available medium — radio, video, television, print, billboards, the Internet. The messages were largely informational but with some imaginative — if reserved — propaganda.

But in the spring of 1996, clever ads in bold print would catch the collective eye of readers of the *News and Observer* and other publications. For students of all classifications, a message teased, "We attract the brightest, most ambitious students. (Naturally, we're a women's college.)" And in another edition, the same style would attract prospective re-entry women: "You've hemmed a skirt using only office supplies, trained your own boss and argued down a mechanic's bill. Going back for your degree will seem easy." A third in the series beckoned women with M.B.A. ambitions: "Sit around discussing economic theories, corporate strategies and the latest in quantitative analysis. You know, typical girl stuff." Advertising was expensive, but, in college and university development offices across the land, the often-quoted adage of uncertain origin was "To make money, you have to spend money."

The 17th century proverb — "Money talks" — was never more proverbial than in the nineties. As the economy fared, so fared the country. Americans seemed to be obsessed with "the bottom line" — originally a euphemism for "financial outcome" — the lifeline to everything material. The profit motive helped to define the marketplace as a territory, with or without physical boundaries, where goods and services were bought and sold in agreed-upon amounts for the current medium of exchange. But perhaps the metaphorical marketplace—a gathering place where the media of exchange are ideas and opinions—was rarely considered in those days. Meredith functioned in both forums.

ALTHOUGH THE EVENING of February 9, 1995, might better have been described as a drama than as the civil discourse usually associated with the word "forum," countless ideas and opinions *were* exchanged—dramatically. The marketplace was Belk Dining Hall turned theater, and the plot was about change at Meredith. Lead players were President Weems and Claude Williams, chair of the Board of Trustees. Others in the company were trustees, faculty, staff, and a few alumnae and students. Some of the cast performed cameo roles, which were alternately applauded and scoffed at, while many held only bit parts with no dialogue, except for whispered asides. And there was no audience; the hundreds in attendance were participants swept up in the emotion of the evening, wondering how the denouement would affect their own lives. In his invitation to the event, President Weems had touted the occasion as "the most important meeting we have had at Meredith College in the twenty-four years I have been here."[5]

He had preceded his summons with correspondence to the faculty in general, and, with slightly edited wording, to department heads. In letters dated January 31, he applied to Meredith a series of "reality checks"—an expression coined in the nineties—such as a shortfall in revenue because of an enrollment drop and an unsatisfactory student retention rate; fierce competition for the traditional-aged freshman; a burgeoning adult population in colleges and universities across the nation; a buyers' market; inefficiency in cost containment; a false sense that Triangle residents knew Meredith while, in reality, the thousands of newcomers to the area had had no contact at all with the College; a five-year decrease in numbers of full-time North Carolina students at private colleges, with 118 of the 1,733 lost students having been lost by Meredith; and the fact that "[a]ny continued loss in Meredith's market share is going to be very difficult to recover."

Weems admonished that "Meredith must act and act quickly" through a "small window of opportunity to solidify our presence in the community and firmly stake our claim."[6] Again on February 3, he expounded on the theme in a six-page catalogue of necessities for change, insisting to academic department heads that "Meredith has more opportunities than any other college in North Carolina."[7] Some of the necessities Weems cited for Meredith were "fiscal vitality"; leadership at every level of the administration; innovation and creativity; a broader clientele; an effective evening program; a growing graduate program; morning, afternoon, and evening classes on a "student-friendly" campus, where offices and services are available during off-hours and on weekends; reductions in time of committee meetings and in costs of education delivery; and a "tight-knit, cohesive administrative team," adding, "From this point on, it must be my team. . . ."[8] The perceived declaration of unilateral decision-making appeared to be the recurring conflict in the drama.

The *Biblical Recorder* ran a review, which borrowed extensively from coverage of the event by the *News and Observer*:

> John Weems, president of Meredith College in Raleigh, did a roll-call of financial pressures and called for some major changes during a special meeting of administrators, faculty and trustees on February 9.
>
> Weems said the women's college is facing the possibility of financial disaster in the next 10 years unless it becomes "more consumer-oriented" by opening its doors to non-traditional students with evening and weekend classes and accelerated programs. . . .
>
> Meredith . . . faces constant competition from other educational institutions in the city which offer regular campus programs in the Raleigh area, plus satellite programs in Wake County from schools which are outside the area. . . .
>
> According to a study in the Raleigh *News and Observer*, Weems said "the problems are many and the solutions are few. In a labor-intensive business, the only way to make major cost reductions is in personnel."
>
> That statement prompted fire from faculty present in the session and from students who watched the proceedings . . . on closed-circuit television. The students "could be heard hooting and hollering in support of faculty members, who themselves gave only tepid applause to Weems' remarks," the *N&O* reported.

In contrast, faculty gave enthusiastic applause to the critical comments of Bernard H. Cochran, professor of philosophy and religion, the newspaper article stated.

Cochran charged the school was about to "sell its soul" in the interest of increasing enrollment, the [*News and Observer*] article by Thomas Hackett said.

The professor also objected to what he called the "in-your-face" memos from the president to the faculty in recent days. Cochran also said the faculty was shocked and dismayed that there had been so little collegiality to the discussion of major changes, the article added.

Trustees praised Weems, who has been president of the largest all-women's college in the Southeast since 1972, for addressing hard financial realities.[9]

Before all reviews were in—resolutions by segments of the school, including the Student Government Association; letters to the editor of the *Meredith Herald* and to Raleigh's *News and Observer*; phone calls from parents; recommendations from the Alumnae Association; some rather formal forums, such as a series of Open Conversations, for the faculty—President Weems wrote to academic department heads:

Since last Thursday, I have had the opportunity to talk with many trustees, faculty, administrators, alumnae, and students. These conversations have been very good for me. Almost to a person those I talked with were of the opinion that Meredith could evolve, make the right moves, and continue to progress without the misplaced zeal I have exhibited in the last few weeks.

After reflecting on their comments, I am convinced they are right, and I went about pressing for immediate change in the wrong way. . . . Many of you have shared with me great ideas for change that will help us solve the problems we are bound to face within a very few years.

I am now convinced that we can move through our normal channels, without emergency meetings and without trustee oversight to accomplish all we need to do to keep Meredith at the very top in women's education. We have highly intelligent faculty and staff who can face our problems and satisfy our needs without my creating the crisis atmosphere that I invoked last week. . . .[10]

On the same day, which happened to be St. Valentine's Day 1995, Weems also wrote to students:

It has come to my attention that some of you think Meredith has made a decision to become a community college or a technical institute. Nothing could be further from the truth. *Our mission and purpose is to educate women in a liberal arts tradition.* While Meredith has evolved over the last twenty-five years, it is a much stronger college today and is considered one of the premier institutions of higher education in the state. **Meredith has always maintained a strong commitment to its historical core of traditional aged students. Whatever strategies we embark upon in the future will be designed to assure that this commitment can be maintained.** Certainly a successful college such as Meredith would have no desire to lessen in any way the very heart of the institution.[11]

Among the reams of correspondence circulated during the period was a letter to the *News and Observer* from Nina I. McClellan, a member of the junior class:

I am proud to be a Meredith junior. Classes here are demanding and challenging. I attend a college that is filled with self-sufficient, creative, strong and intelligent women. A popular misconception held by many outside of this school, and apparently by some members of our board of trustees, is that Meredith exists merely to prepare its students to become better wives and mothers. Although these roles are truly noble, they do not represent the only desires of the women at Meredith College. I know that some of us, upon graduating, will be fantastic mothers and wives. At the same time, however, we will also be fantastic scientists, teachers, politicians, artists, musicians, businesswomen, and doctors.

I hope that before [President] Weems makes any changes, he reviews very carefully the things that are right at this school.[12]

Cynthia Griffith McEnery, '70, president of the Alumnae Association, wrote to the *Meredith Herald*:

During the February 9 meeting, I expressed my support for the concept of re-engineering the college. I also expressed my concern that re-engineering must be done against an agreed-upon vision. I indicated my willingness on behalf of the Alumnae Association to participate in a process to define both the vision and necessary changes for Meredith. . . .[13]

Under McEnery's leadership, the executive committee of the Alumnae Association proposed to the trustees the appointment of a task force, whose recommendations, if underwritten by the board, "would position Meredith College for the 21st century."[14] The trustees accepted the proposal and, in a called meeting of the executive committee on March 13, 1995, also approved the composition of the organization, members of which were elected by their own groups: students Kelly Formy-Duval, SGA president, June Holland, president of the executive committee of SGA, and Alyce Turner, president of Silver Shield; faculty representatives Drs. Clay, professor of education, Knight, professor of mathematics, and Webb, professor of English; administrative staff members Drs. Jackson, vice president for student development, Johnson, dean of the John E. Weems Graduate School and continuing education, and Page, dean of undergraduate instruction and registrar; and alumnae Carolyn Carter, '73, Anne Clark Dahle, '54, and task force chair, Cindy Griffith McEnery, '70. Trustees on the executive committee were adamant that the task force report only to them and that Dr. Weems "proceed with his vision for the institution."[15]

In staunch support of the president, the executive committee, on August 21, unanimously passed trustee George McCotter's motion to "offer Dr. John E. Weems a seven-year contract extending through the year 2002."[16] An experienced president would bring stability to the College in periods of rapid change, they declared—particularly in light of the questionable relationship with the Baptist State Convention. In executive session at a called meeting on September 22, the trustees resolved "that the Board . . . by and with the concurrence of President John E. Weems, commit themselves individually and as fiduciaries of the institution to continue together in the promotion, strengthening and preparation of Meredith College to fulfill its missions, purposes and journey into and beyond the Twenty-First Century."[17] In his annual message, published about the same time, Weems said,

> The trustees have a new role to play. . . . They have always been the legal policy-making body for Meredith. Without their wisdom and guidance Meredith would not have become the institution it is today. There is more to do, however. This body of men and women literally own the college. . . . The vision of greatness for Meredith must start with the trustees. . . . It will be their expectations that continually make Meredith evolve into greatness. They must have a vision that requires us to be more than we are.[18]

While the president and the trustees seemed to strengthen their bonds and, between them, redefine trustees' roles, the faculty sensed an estrangement between themselves and the governing body, as represented by faculty affairs committee co-chairs Deborah Smith, biology, and Jerod Kratzer, education. To a September 19 memorandum to the faculty, Smith and Kratzer attached a copy of the committee's report to the trustees for consideration at the board's semi-annual meeting on September 22. In part, the report read,

> During the past year, the Meredith community has struggled with issues wrought with emotion and often delineated by blurred boundaries. It seems to us that the events of the last year have widened a chasm between the faculty and Trustees, leaving us to call loudly across the void with the hope of being heard.[19]

In regular session in October, the faculty accepted the resignations from the task force of Drs. Clay, Knight, and Webb and made no effort to elect new representatives.[20] The work of the task force declined from that point. Inasmuch as records do not report its dissolution by the body that appointed it, the task force presumably died a natural death. Meanwhile, Norman Kellum, an attorney from Greensboro, who was elected to chair the Board of Trustees, effective January 1, 1996, achieved high visibility as he met with individuals and constituent groups, narrowing some of the rifts.

THE ENROLLMENT MANAGEMENT team continued into its second year. Having been appointed by the president in 1994, the team was chaired by Dr. Spooner, who, by amendment to the bylaws, had been assigned the responsibility of enrollment. Others on the team were Gordon Folger, director of career services; Melinda Henderson, assistant director of alumnae affairs; Mary Johnson, dean of the graduate school and dean of continuing education; Sue Kearney, director of admissions and enrollment management research; Elizabeth McDuffie, director of scholarships and financial assistance; Jeannie Morelock, director of college communications; Allen Page, dean of undergraduate instruction and registrar; Reginald Shiflett, chemistry department head; and Dorothy Sizemore, dean of students. From the beginning, the team's goals included a "user-friendly" campus and improvement in the retention rate.[21]

As fans were often called the twelfth member of a football team, so Meredith alumnae could have been designated the eleventh member of the enrollment management team: Forty women in fifteen states and nine delegates from alumnae chapters in North Carolina agreed to represent the College for the admissions office. Kearney cited other volunteer efforts by the 12,000-member body of alumnae: "calling accepted applicants, hosting socials for prospects, and representing the admissions office at some college day events."[22]

By the first faculty meeting of the fall semester, members of the team were ecstatic. Kearney reported, "This year's 420 anticipated freshmen* will be the largest class ever; there will be 86 transfer students, 6 re-admits, 4 international visitors."[23]

A headline on Page 1 of the July 19 *News and Observer* had already announced the good news: "Enrollment jump delights Meredith." The article reported, "A record number of high school seniors have signed up to attend Meredith this fall. . . . Total enrollment is expected to be about 2,400—50 more women than last year." *N&O* writer Debbi Sykes said, "Something seems to be working for women's colleges even as universities have to cope with some of the smaller high school graduating classes in decades."[24] Sykes had conferred with Jadwiga Sebrechts, executive director of the Women's College Coalition in Washington:

[F]or the fourth consecutive year, applications and enrollments have increased at more than three-quarters of U.S. women's colleges.

Sebrechts attributed the trend to several factors.

One, she said, is the debate over gender sparked by Anita Hill's

---

*Later statistics show that 416 freshmen actually enrolled.

allegations of sexual harassment against Clarence Thomas during his confirmation as a Supreme Court justice. Another is the 1992 Association of University Women report that said girls were getting shortchanged in the classroom.[25]

President Weems also exuded optimism: In his annual message, he wrote,

From the incoming freshman class, 34 students are expected to participate in the Honors Program— the most freshmen ever to accept our invitation. The six recipients of the Meredith College Academic Scholarships have average SAT scores of 1328 and rank in the top one to two percent of their class. The Harris Scholarships were keenly contested, and the 12 winners bring superior academic and leadership qualities. We are also expecting 32 Teaching Fellows to enroll this fall. . . .[26]

Unclear was the ratio of a record-breaking freshman class to the experiment of allowing "all resident students . . . the opportunity to park on campus."[27] In fact, freshmen would be able to drive their own cars back to Raleigh after spring break in March. Vice President Taylor said of the enrollment management team's recommendation: "We at Meredith don't hold with the philosophy that having a car means doing poorly in school. . . ."[28]

The evening program, so vigorously promoted by President Weems, would be tested in the 1995 fall semester, although a similar plan had been recorded in the minutes of Academic Council as early as March 1983: "Dean Burris reminded the group of the College's commitment to an evening program and to the idea that students could satisfy the general education requirements for degrees by attending classes in the evenings for a period of three to five years."[29] But the 1995 version offered a more comprehensive agenda. While it started rather tentatively with twelve women, it gained momentum and, by the fall of 1996, had enrolled forty-seven new students. Specifically for working women, the program provided "an academically excellent four-year degree through flexible scheduling and sensitivity to women's needs in accordance with the overall mission of the College."[30] The idea for Meredith After5 arose, in part, from statistics showing that more than half the adult female population worked full-time. While the program faced competition from similar offerings of other local and of satellite campuses, it believed in the advantages of its all-female status. Classes in the first curriculum of Meredith After 5—majors in social work; business administration management concentration; American civilization; and a communications concentration in the English department—would also be available to re-entry women and traditional-age students. Madra Britt, who had directed the enrichment program, was named to direct Meredith After 5. Raleighites —especially those frequenting the Fayetteville Street Mall Thursday evenings for Alive After Five—related to the name of the program. "Alive After Five" was a corporate- and Raleigh Convention Center-sponsored event for the commingling of bands, fast food, and droves of people—especially young adults—for music and camaraderie. Whether on purpose or accidentally, Carol Swink used a good marketing strategy in the *Meredith Herald* by subtly connecting the college program to the weekly downtown activity with her story title, "After Five Comes Alive."[31]

The academic pulse of Meredith *before* 5:00 also beat strongly and regularly as lively new treatments were prescribed. For instance, the psychology department branched out beyond its own students to reach autistic children, when it inaugurated its "in-lab and in-home behavioral training for the children . . . ."[32] The program served five pre-schoolers in developing their "play skills, receptive and expressive language, social skills, self-help skills and pre-academics," and it also served about eighteen Meredith students in training the young women to work with autistic children and their parents.[33] A man from Raleigh approached President Weems at a Christmas party in 1995, introduced himself, and said, "Let me tell you something fascinating." The man told of his grandson's having been diagnosed with autism while the boy and his parents lived in Switzerland. Dr. Weems retold the man's story:

> In consultation with their Swiss doctor [my son] and his wife tried to determine the best course to follow for treatment for their son. Their doctor contacted a specialist in Germany for advice. The German doctor then contacted a doctor in New York City. . . . The doctor in New York City contacted a doctor in California . . . . The doctor in California, a specialist in autistic children, said that Meredith College in Raleigh, N.C., had a special program for autistic children that he thought would be very appropriate for their

child. My son resigned from his job in Switzerland, and he and his family are moving back to Raleigh to enroll his child in the Meredith program.[34]

Doreen Fairbank, Ed.D., assistant professor of psychology, was named director of the program.

Other injections of vitality included a $37,500 grant from the North Carolina Biotechnology Center to Elizabeth Wolfinger, assistant professor of biology and health sciences, for her proposal, "Integrating Biotechnology into the Meredith College Science Curriculum."[35] Use of the grant would include funding of a new course on Introduction to Biotechnology, said Dr. Wolfinger. The same department also offered a new concentration—environmental science—for students pursuing a B.S. degree in biology.

The Department of Foreign Languages acquired a state-of-the-art language laboratory in its home territory of Joyner Hall, replacing the lab in Carlyle Campbell Library. *Meredith* reported that the used equipment "was donated to a Native American group . . . for their ancestral language project in North Carolina."[36] And foreign language students with a 3.0 average, who had earned "an A in at least two consecutive semesters of study in the same foreign language," were eligible for induction into Alpha Mu Gamma, Meredith's chapter of the National Foreign Language Honor Society, chartered in April.[37]

The Department of Sociology and Social Work introduced a new minor in women's studies. And when Meredith added a licensure program for theatre majors preparing to teach theatrical arts in the public schools, the College became one of only two in the state granting licensure in the four areas of art, dance, music, and theatre arts.

Beginning August 21 on the cable channel of Cooperating Raleigh Colleges, Carolyn Grubbs, history department head, and Michael Novak, associate professor, offered a telecourse on the Western Tradition. Designed for Meredith After5 students, the course would "survey western history from its origins in the Ancient Near East to the beginnings of Modern European society in about the sixteenth century," explained Dr. Novak. "In this respect," he added, "it will correspond roughly to History 101."[38] Students in the course would participate in an orientation session to cover their responsibilities of watching the lectures and reading their assignments; and their teacher–student communication by E-mail or "telephone office hours" would suffice until Saturdays, when they would come to the classroom for "review and discussion."[39] During the summer, the media services staff photographed and edited the material for fifty-two television classes.

While the new department head in English held no classes on cablevision, he earned at least a modicum of celebrity as the first male in the history of the College to head his department: W. Garrett (Garry) Walton, Jr., holds the A.B., A.M., and the Ph.D.from the University of Virginia. At the time of his appointment, he had taught at Meredith for twelve years and had directed the honors program. He was well-versed in his department's history: "While Meredith's Department of English no longer features 'the big three' (Professors Johnson, Rose and Knight)," he said, "their dedication and commitment to excellence continue to characterize the department." He cited "exciting . . . developments of the last decade— off-campus internships, the professional communications concentration, [and] new course offerings in African-American and world literature."[40]

Although the message of Dr. Walton's appointment spread far and wide, it never quite made the *New York Times*, but news of three of his colleagues did: Dr. Knight, one of the "big three" mentioned in Walton's comments; Dr. Jackson, vice president for student development and professor of English; and Lou Rosser of the adjunct English faculty were quoted extensively by *Times* writer Sara Rimer, who interviewed the Meredith scholars at a Keats conference at Harvard. Ms. Rimer wrote in her "Cambridge Journal" for September 11, "At the opening dinner . . . , the three professors from North Carolina pointed reverently to the next table, where sat Walter Jackson Bate, the Harvard professor who wrote a biography of Keats that won a Pulitzer Prize."[41] The writer added, " 'Everyone who's anyone in the Keats world is here,' . . . said Professor Knight, brushing off her own knowledge of the poet whom she has been teaching for nearly 40 years."[42] The article, titled "At Harvard, Lovers of Beauty Sing a Collective Ode to Keats," also quoted Mrs. Rosser, who said she "required her students to memorize poetry. 'The more you say it, the more you understand it,' she said. 'And if you have to get an MRI or get stuck in an elevator, how much better to recite Keats than Snoop Doggy Dogg.' "[43] The five-column, half-page feature ended with Knight's words: " 'We have eaten, we have lived, we have breathed Keats. . . . It's like eating steak and ice cream for three days.' She could not wait, she said, to go home and read Keats."[44]

Simultaneously, Professor Rebecca Oatsvall, holder of the Wainwright Chair of Business, was eating, living, and breathing "the challenges and excitement of leading the Department of Business and Economics into the 21st century."[45] At the announcement of her appointment as head of department, she said, "[We have] the honor of being involved in many new and growing programs at the College."[46] The new programs included a major in accounting, which would lead to a B.S. degree. And, with that degree in hand, the accounting major could then complete one year in the John E. Weems Graduate School for the M.B.A. On the faculty since 1984, Dr. Oatsvall holds the B.S., M.Acc., and Ph.D. degrees from the University of South Carolina.

As Dr. Oatsvall alluded to growing programs in the Department of Business and Economics, she could also have been describing the Department of Home Economics. But just as a young woman of the nineties— perhaps the daughter of baby-boomers—might think twice before choosing a college with the Victorian name of "Baptist Female University," she might also wonder at a progressive department's retaining a "home economics" identity. So, to reflect more accurately its directions in child development; clothing and fashion merchandising; foods and nutrition; interior design; and family and consumer sciences,* it changed its name to "human environmental sciences." And to head the Department of Human Environmental Sciences rose Deborah Tippett, holder of the B.S., M.S., and Ph.D. degrees from the University of North Carolina at Greensboro and a member of the Meredith faculty since 1987. Dr. Tippett said she saw the past as a challenge for the future: "I am excited about the growth of [our] five innovative majors . . . and at the same time I am challenged by the many contributions made by the last two department heads . . . , who gave close to 75 years of combined service to the College—Marilyn Stuber's 30 years and Ellen Brewer's 44 years."[47] In the year of the change and for the first time, Meredith put in place a nine-month post-baccalaureate dietetic internship beyond the B.S. degree in nutrition, leading to a student's becoming a registered dietitian. The pro-

---

*The family and consumer sciences major replaced the home economics major in 1997.

gram was administered by the John E. Weems Graduate School; directed by William Landis, assistant professor of human environmental sciences; and accredited by the American Dietetic Association.

With a nineties name, "First Year Experience" was a new course for easing freshmen through the transition from high school to college, from home to campus, by offering strategies "for academic success and campus resources" as well as discussions "on self-esteem, diversity, values, stress management and women's issues."[48] A printed flier proclaimed, "The class is designed to aid you in becoming a master student from the very beginning of your college career! . . . Just take it!" And a handout promoting MAPS (Meredith Alumnae Preparing Students) advertised Career Networking Day for students of all classes. Leaders for the "sessions in business, communications and public relations, health sciences, paralegal and MBA programs, and in those hard-to-find jobs for liberal arts degree graduates," would be alumnae from the corporate world, state government, law firms, publications, and health organizations.

With the office of career services, the networking committee of the Alumnae Association and the office of alumnae relations sponsored MAPS, one of the early events that introduced Mary Kate Keith, the new—and seventh—director of alumnae relations. A 1982 graduate of Stonehill College in North Eaton, Massachusetts, Mrs. Keith was the first non-alumna appointed to that office. Her selection from more than seventy applicants attested to her qualifications, and her experience alone was impressive: After having directed the alumae program at Georgian Court, a woman's college in New Jersey, she was named director of alumni affairs at Utica College of Syracuse University, where she served for more than four years. In a *Meredith* article titled "The New Voice of Experience," writer Del Hunt Johnson quoted the most recent occupant of the alumnae office: " 'The alumnae are the one thing that's a constant at any college,' said Keith. 'The students change, the faculty and administration change, but the alumnae are always there. Their involvement in college issues is crucial, otherwise the college will lose its character.' "[49]

Other new directors in 1995 were Sidney L. Cruze, corporate and foundation relations; Elizabeth McDuffie, who transferred from the office of scholarships and financial assistance to continuing education's enrichment program; Phillip D. Roof who replaced McDuffie in financial aid; and Juliellen Simpson-Vos, the Brewer House Infant Care Laboratory. Three months after Keith occupied the Mae Grimmer Alumnae House, Sharon Cannon, as new dean of students, moved into the milieu of Dean Dorothy Sizemore, who, in semi-retirement, became the first director of commuter life.

The leadership demonstrated by the faculty and administrative staff was a dynamic force in every facet of the institution. While the statement seems so obvious as to be unnecessary, it may find authenticity as a reminder of this chapter's earlier assertion that the marketplace is often a meeting place where the media of exchange are ideas and opinions; that, even in its growth, the College remains a closely knit family bred of civility and cooperation, but not without disagreements; and that students are taught by bona fide professionals, as compared to some mammoth institutions, where graduate students as surrogates release professors from classroom duties for other scholarly pursuits.

As the previous chapter indicated, the College was committed to leadership skills for its students and to providing training opportunities for both its immediate and extended communities. In 1994–95, the Broyhill Leadership Institute brought to Raleigh and environs such renowned leaders as Stephen Covey—again; Denis Waitley, author of *Empires of the Mind*; Tom Peters; and Pat Heim. The institute also inaugurated its "Dinner With a Winner" series with guest speaker—or guest winner— Charlie Gaddy, the regional counterpart of the nationally revered Walter Cronkite, formerly of CBS News. Recently retired at the time, Gaddy was the long-time news anchor for WRAL-TV, the city's major television station.

Another winner was Meredith's selection by the State Department of Public Instruction as one of four ideal institutions—with North Carolina Central, Fayetteville State, and Shaw Universities—to form the state's new STAR (United Star Distance Learning Consortium) program. Designed to "assist successful integration of technology into elementary and middle school curricula,"[50] STAR would have use of the two new satellite dishes on the flat roof of Carlyle Campbell Library and would attract, said President Weems, "[t]eachers from all over the Triangle . . . to participate in interactive Satellite broadcasts which we will deliver over our campus cable system."[51] Media specialist John Kincheloe boasted of Meredith's technological opportunities:

Media services is receiving signals from space—from 25 satellites to be precise. Using our two new satellite dishes, we are able to receive an incredible range of educational programming. . . . In September, our new equipment enabled the entire campus to participate, along with 600 other colleges and universities, in a nationwide teleconference. We received the satellite transmission and delivered the live program over our cable system to more than 700 possible viewing sites on campus."[52]

Words and phrases such as "satellite dishes," "optical fiber network," "gopher," "Internet," and "World Wide Web home page" entered the language, not only of technology experts but also of English majors, social workers, athletes, musicians, and all others who aspired to the virtual realities of Cyberspace. At Meredith, the optical fiber network stretched across the campus and through appropriate buildings, including residence halls, giving students access to the Internet and to E-mail capabilities. Through the gopher, "a search and research tool" that "can navigate the INTERNET worldwide, . . . [t]he resources of 60,000 main frame computers will be available to our students instantly."[53] Already on the Internet and with a web page on line, Meredith advertised its new addresses in the idiom of the Information Age: For example, via the World Wide Web, one could reach the College at http://www.meredith.edu/meredith/.

AT ITS MORE conventional address, 3800 Hillsborough Street, the college effectively marketed itself through location and appearance. In 1994, one of the previously nondescript structures had undergone a facelift. With the option to buy, the College had leased the small modular building in 1983 in a desperate move to solve the problem of crowded housing, and, because it had been placed across the street from Carroll Health Center (then Carroll Infirmary), it was known as Carroll Annex. As the shortage of living space continued, the College had exercised its option to buy, assigning the small building to "students wishing to speak a foreign language exclusively,"[54] a concept that evolved to include "both International and American students interested in cross-cultural issues.[55] Marguerite Warren Noel, '34, had given generously of her means toward the renovation of the building that ultimately became the Noel International House. And, on Meredith's nomination in 1993, Mrs. Noel received the first Philanthropist of the Year Award from the North Carolina Baptist Development Officers' Association. The organization made a wise selection: Because of the alumna's generosity, there is a Noel Hall for visually impaired students, as well as a scholarship, at Gardner-Webb University; an endowed performing arts series at Wingate University; a scholarship at Southeastern Baptist Theological Seminary; another scholarship at Wake Forest University; the Noel Home "for girls who cannot function successfully at home or in foster care" in Caldwell County; the Noel Enrichment Series at First Baptist Church, Kannapolis, North Carolina; and, in addition to the international house, a Noel First Family Scholarship Fund at Meredith.[56] Noel International House was dedicated on April 10, 1995, three months after Mrs. Noel's death on January 25.

Students saw housing as a major attraction to or distraction from academic life. In its desire to improve retention rates, Meredith re-examined its policies and expanded its options. As a result, seniors *and* juniors could elect off-campus living, and several of them did, leaving single rooms as a popular choice for those remaining in the residence halls.

By late fall, the "house" of physical education–dance increased in value in every way: Its new 5,000-square-foot dance studio and fitness center was completed. From the start, the fitness center bulged with members of a health-conscious society, the price of admission being simply the show of a CamCard. So students and faculty and staff members alike could—and did—avail themselves of the center's state-of-the-art exercise equipment—including treadmills and muscle-toning machines—and weight-training area. The center would be open to women seven days a week, said Cindy Bross, professor of health and physical education, but Dr. Bross and her department insisted upon orientation sessions for users of the equipment. In a serious, yet trendy, passion for physical fitness, four of the eight students questioned by the *Herald* regarding their New Year's Resolutions for 1994 had alluded to the issue: Sharon Duffy, '95, replied, "I made several [resolutions]. I promised to exercise, better my eating habits, and get better organized. I am going to stop drinking caffeinated drinks." Anissa Jones, '94, said, "I promised to take better care of myself." Kristen Elliott, '97, resolved "to tone up." And Betsy Powell, '95, responded, "I'm going to cut down on the number of naps I take each day."[57]

In September, the trustees made a new academic year's resolution to renovate and add to Cate Center, the funding to come from a three-year mini campaign to raise $1,200,000 in projected costs. Architects Pierce, Brinkley, Cease, and Lee would design the structure.

In the same meeting, President Weems reported that endowment and reserves totaled more than $42,000,000, and that Meredith was again ranked in *U.S. News and World Report*'s "Best College Buys" in regional colleges and universities in the South.[58] Optimism brightened the financial picture. The Teaching Fellows Commission contributed to the sunny mood by approving Meredith and Elon's joint proposal to "limit the escalating costs" of the program. Both colleges were relieved by the commission's decision to obligate the colleges to only $5,000 per Fellow, the same amount granted by the state.[59] President Weems spoke of the action as "an incredible breakthrough" that would "allow the College to commit to the Teaching Fellows program *ad infinitum*."[60]

At the same time, 184 named scholarships swelled the coffers. Scholarships, work-study programs, and loans were primary components of the financial assistance packages earmarked for worthy students. According to the *Biblical Recorder*, "[a]pproximately one-third of Meredith students receive[d] loan assistance," but the good news was that "[n]one of the 162 Meredith students whose loan repayment obligations began in 1992 defaulted on their loans."[61] In the 147 schools surveyed statewide, reported the *Recorder*, the default rate was 14 percent, the average ranging from zero to 41.6 percent.[62]

NEITHER DID THE College default on its selection of lecturers in 1995. For instance, renowned social activist Arun Gandhi, director of the Arun Gandhi Institute for the Study of Non-Violence, and grandson of India's late Mohandas K. Gandhi, spoke in Jones Auditorium on March 29 on "Non-Violence or Non-Existence: Options for the 21st Century." Dr. Gandhi founded the M.K. Gandhi Institute for the Study of Non-violence at Christian Brothers University in Memphis. He said he "was inspired by his experiences with his grandfather in India in the 1940s, and by the time he spent in South Africa subject to the government's strict policy of apartheid."[63] His adage, "Non-violence is to violence what light is to dark," was widely quoted for a time following his lecture. Also memorable were Gandhi's "seven blunders of the world," as given to him by his

*Sponsored by the Hull Lecture Series, Arun Gandhi,
grandson of India's late Mohandas K. Gandhi and director of the
Arun Gandhi Institute for the Study of Non-Violence, visits the campus
and meets with Mabel Claire Hoggard Maddrey, '28, Meredith's
quintessential alumna.*

grandfather: "wealth without work; pleasure without conscience; knowledge without character; commerce without morality; science without humanity; worship without sacrifice; and politics without principles." The eighth blunder—his own, he said—was "rights without responsibilities."[64] Gandhi's address was sponsored by the Hull Lecture Series.

A paradisiacal state of non-violence was hardly imaginable in the global society of 1995. Shortly after United Nations peacekeeping forces withdrew from Somalia, President Clinton asked for support in sending military personnel to civil war-ravaged Bosnia, where they and troops of other NATO countries were to keep the peace following a shaky agreement between the Serbs and Croats. On the other side of the world, the assassination of Israel's Prime Minister Yitzhak Rabin threatened the long-sought peace between Israel and the Palestine Liberation Organization. Rabin's death was a reminder to Meredith of former Vice President Thomas's return from a "women's interreligious study dialogue for peace" in Israel in 1976, and her comment: "The prospects for peace are not very apparent."[65] The *Twig* had reported Dr. Thomas's meeting with Israeli women at Rabin's home, where the women had expressed their belief in their "important role in peace-keeping" but also in the dim hope that Arab and Israeli women would talk to each other.[66]

In the United States, the unthinkable occurred on that infamous day in April, when a bomb planted by an American who was angered by his government killed more than 160 people—many of them children—in the Alfred P. Murrah Federal Building in Oklahoma City. In the same month, a man in California was killed by a package bomb. Because of the growing frequency of occurrences such as the latter, the campus postal service was alerted to characteristics of packages containing bombs, and Meredith's facilities services department took seriously the warnings, issuing a terse memorandum: "Due to recent package bomb incidents, any packages that are not clearly marked with a name and/or department on the outside will be returned."[67]

When turbulence shook the political arena, it was usually in the form of verbal assault, such as in the budget impasse between Clinton and the Congress that led to a six-day partial shutdown of the government. In November, and particularly after popular Gulf War hero General Colin Powell announced his intention not to seek the presidency of the United States, the myriad Republican presidential hopefuls played one-upmanship for their party's nomination in 1996, while President Clinton ran unopposed. Powell's decision not to run for president seemed to evoke reaction from almost every corner of the world. To the *Meredith Herald*'s "Question of the Week"—"What do you think of Colin Powell's decision?"—Hannah Shelp, a sophomore, responded "If he had run, he would have made a great stride in breaking the legacy of all white presidents."[68]

Former member of Raleigh's City Council and alumna Mary Watson Nooe, '69, came to the campus in September to promote her bid to become mayor of Raleigh. The *Herald* reported, "She hopes to create a strong, diverse city where citizens know there is room for all who are here. Nooe spoke about putting Raleigh back on track to being a world class city with educated people and quality services. . . ."[69] But in the political climate of 1995, voters elected her opponent, the more conservative Tom Fetzer.

For every reminder that lack of communication fostered violence, it seemed that a new Internet devotee went on line. It would remain to be seen whether the Information Age would curtail violence. Meredith took steps toward communicating with other cultures through its Meredith Abroad and diverse travel opportunities, but traveling to another country to do manual labor was a new activity. In 1995, a team "of willing and determined volunteers" set out for two weeks of hard work in Prague in the Czech Republic.[70] "The Meredith Connection," as the team came to be known, comprised April Newlin, Jessica Drew, Megan Carney, and Jan Yow, all students; David Lynch, head of the music department, and his son, Dave; Johnny Evans, a retired educator; and their leaders, Sam Carothers and Donna Fowler-Merchant, campus minister and associate campus minister, respectively. Their task was to help transform the "new" 200-year-old International Baptist Theological Seminary campus in Prague from a state of disrepair to a livable campus. The seminary had been relocated from its long-time site in Ruschlikon, Switzerland. On the return of "The Meredith Connection," Fowler-Merchant spoke for the group:

Isaiah 42 and 65 speak of God laboring to give birth to a new ceation in innovative or unfamiliar ways. All of us were midwives in that "birth" process as we gave of our time and talents to bring forth something new in Central Europe. And who would have ever guessed that the darkness would be turned to light and the rough places made smooth by a group of American women working with a group of men from the former Soviet Union? I pray that we never forget our experiences in Prague. I feel certain that we never will.[71]

If women effectively helped bring light out of darkness and smooth over rough places in the world, then alumna and trustee Jean Batten Cooper, '54, offered a practicable suggestion to the executive committee of the board, as recorded in the minutes of the November meeting:

In keeping with the developments of other all-female institutions and in conjunction with other emphases the Meredith trustees are planning for the turn of the century, Jean Cooper challenged the board to set a goal of 50 percent male and 50 percent female board members by the year 2000. Her justification for this plan was that all alumnae of the college are female, the school depends heavily on alumnae contributions and the churches from which the trustees are chosen are all more than 50 percent female. This plan was given for the consideration of the administration and the nominations committee.

The minutes of the meeting recorded no action.

Alumnae were diligent in underscoring the importance of Meredith to women and women to society. Through monetary gifts, several graduates subscribed for the College a one-year membership in the Women's College Coalition (WCC), believing that "the association with other women's colleges of similar academic standards would be beneficial. . . ."[72] The national organization's roster of seventy-four women's colleges included Salem and Bennett Colleges in North Carolina, as well as familiar schools in other states: Brenau, Converse, Randolph-Macon, Wellesley, and Radcliffe. The coalition "is a lobbying entity for single-sex education and a research-funding entity for grants related to how women learn,"[73] explained Dr. Webb at a faculty meeting. Meredith held a one-year membership in WCC in 1988–89 but retains its more recent affiliation.

Single-sex education was a topic of spirited debate in 1995. It was the year that Shannon Faulkner became the first female cadet at the Citadel, an all-male bastion since 1842. Faulkner's legal battle for admission to the military college of South Carolina had been raging for many months, following the Citadel's withdrawal of her previous acceptance on the school's becoming aware of her gender. All in their August 22, 1994, issues, three widely circulated news magazines published stories about the case. *Time* reported that a federal appeals court had decided against her;[74] *Newsweek* pondered the possibility of the cadet's shaved head, should she gain admission;[75] and *U.S. News and World Report* said her zealous efforts compared with the struggles of the first female cadets admitted to the United States Military Academy at West Point.[76] Faulkner was eventually admitted, but the victory was short-lived. She withdrew because of "psychological stress" during hell week.[77]

Unlike the Citadel, Meredith was not supported by public money when the College argued for single-sex status in the graduate school in 1986, nor in earlier years. But the case of Faulkner versus the Citadel brought reactions pro and con among Meredith students. For example, Traci Latta's editorial in the *Meredith Herald* sided with the Citadel:

> There are just some things that shouldn't be tampered with—the safety seal on aspirin, radioactive materials and traditional institutions like the Citadel—and Meredith."[78]

And Wendy Kelly took the alternative view:

> I bet all of you out there that believe [Faulkner] shouldn't have been at the Citadel in the first place are having a ball with the recent turn of events. I can even hear "I told you so" being muttered across campus. . . .
>
> But you know what? Shannon Faulkner . . . did accomplish something by setting precedent and breaking tradition.
>
> Another woman will rise to the occasion.
>
> She will attend and graduate from the Citadel. . . . Who's laughing now?[79]

WITH WORLD NEWS as available as the nearest campus access to the *News and Observer*; as the turn of a radio or television dial; or as the click of a mouse on the Internet, the *Herald* had little incentive to publish headline news except as it applied to the College. Rather, page one carried articles of local importance—the slate of candidates for student elections in the March 1 issue; the use of computer technology at the College or a recent leadership conference at North Carolina State, in the October 25 issue; and Cornhuskin' 1995 in the November 8 issue. And in the February 1 edition, a front-page headline read, "Meredith's Cat Team's cat trap is missing." The story led with "We have all seen the many cats circling around Johnson Hall. . . ."[80] The strays had multiplied for several years until Anne Pugh, administrative secretary to Vice President Taylor, and Frank Berry of the general services staff "invested a lot of time into curing Meredith of this cat problem," including setting a trap, which, declared reporter Kimberly Zucker, was harmless to the cats.[81] Her story continued:

> However, the cat trap is missing. Pugh and Berry fear that someone may have stolen the trap because they feared the cats were being

given to the Humane Society. The "Cat Team" wants to be sure the students know that each cat is given a home.

Pugh has taken several of the cats to her own home. Since she cannot fill her entire house full of cats, she takes the rest to [her vet, who] gives each cat all the necessary shots and finds the cat a home.

Berry has been nicknamed "The Catman." He often takes the cats home to tame them and then sends them to the Second Chance Adoption Agency.[82]

The cat tale ended with a plea for the return of the Have-a-Heart trap, and, according to Patricia Blackwell of facilities services, the trap was, indeed, returned; however, as late as the summer of 1998, two cat families remained—one in the boiler room and one near Johnson Hall.

ALMOST EVERY FACET of life at Meredith made a statement in and to the marketplace; however, if page one of the *Herald* made marketing statements, they were subtle ones at best. The handsome viewbook, on the other hand, was clearly a tool for targeting prospective students. Positive statements of then-current students graced almost every double-page spread. For example, Teaching Fellow and Honors Scholar Heather Blake wrote for the book's section on academic quality. Her essay said, in part,

One of the most memorable events of my freshman year was my first art class. I had originally planned to major in biology. But because of the liberal arts curriculum, I was able to study art, an interest that has now turned into a possible future occupation! When I walked into the art studio that first day, I felt so excited—a whole new world was opened to me. I learned to appreciate my talent and enjoyed the class so much that I almost decided to major in art. Even though I'm still a biology major, I have not ruled out art. Who knows . . . maybe I'll be a medical or botanical illustrator one day.

The curriculum here is not easy, and I have to study hard to do well. But I would not have it any other way, because I'm not here just to get a degree; I'm here to learn and grow. There's so much I want to do with my life, and my education at Meredith is the perfect beginning.[83]

Essayist Heather Blake graduated in the rain on May 14, with 207 other new Bachelors of Science, 197 Bachelors of Arts, 12 Bachelors of Music, 44 Masters of Business Administration, 5 Masters of Education, and 4 Masters of Music. She heard North Carolina Senator Betsy Lane Cochrane, '58, address her class on the topic of "The Circle of Spirituality and Intellectual Discovery." Senator Cochrane said, "You leave Meredith today with skills that will help you live a worthwhile story, prepared to pursue your hopes and ambitions to the farthest star."[84]

Cynthia Affronti headed the alphabetical lineup to receive her diploma on December 16 at the first mid-year commencement ceremony since 1967. She graduated with 46 other Bachelors of Arts; 1 Bachelor of Music; 46 Bachelors of Science; 26 Masters of Business Administration 1 Master of Education; and 3 Masters of Music. As larger numbers of women completed their work after the summer session or at the end of first semester, they welcomed an optional date for graduation. At the December ceremony, reported *Meredith*, "The 600-seat Jones Auditorium was full beyond capacity with spectators. . . ." And the same newsletter quoted Dean Burris: " 'Judging from the magnitude of success of this ceremony, I'd say we're on track for continuing to have a fall semester commencement.' "[85] The graduates, with the overflow crowd of families and friends, heard one of their teachers, Suzanne Britt, address their places in the "real world" through an Emily Dickinson poem: "I'm Nobody! Who Are You?" Britt said, "Despite all the optimistic chatter surrounding this important day, where you are going and what you will do when you get there will bear a striking resemblance to all other journeys. . . . Life is life, and you are in it, like it or not. What really matters is not where you are going but what you take with you."[86].

IN MEREDITH'S JOURNEY over the years, advertising styles have evolved; however, the wording of a middle-of-the-road ad from 1991—which might have reached more parents than their college-seeking daughters —then told of and still implies an ageless bond of College with student:

Meredith's students are its raison d'etre
and its most effective advertisement.

The relationship between you and your college goes on forever.
You learn, grow, reach, enjoy, lead, decide, stretch . . . you search, discover.
Your college teaches, nourishes, challenges, encourages, allows, believes
. . . it searches, discovers.
You change. It changes. You make a place in its history. It makes a
difference in your life.
At least that's the way it is at Meredith,
the largest private college for women in the southeastern United States.
It's the way it should be—an experience for a lifetime.

14

⌒⌒ ∽◠ ⌒⌒

THE VISION REVISITED

1996–1998

Women to replace embroidery hoops with text books?
To substitute the polite arts with the liberal arts?
Women to crowd thoughts of home and heart with
philosophies of great issues of their society?

FICTITIOUS QUESTIONS FROM the literature of the Visions Program, Meredith's successful capital campaign of the eighties, alluded to the very real "half century of debate and struggle" that was "prelude to Baptist Female University." The booklet cited Thomas Meredith, a progressive Baptist preacher and the founding editor of the *Biblical Recorder*, as having "linked years of progress and temporary defeats to the school's reality." But Meredith, the man, did not champion the cause of Meredith, the college, for his own glorification. (Who would have dared, given the difficulty of the task?) "Greatness of self was far from his mind or from the thoughts of [that] handful of mid-nineteenth century Baptists who advocated education for women. The greatness was in their vision."

For as long as freshman English students have recited Chaucer or Homer, the College has periodically revisited the vision of its founders, as implied throughout this document, but rarely has the scrutiny been more intense than in the last years of the twentieth century. The re-examination of purpose and process has evolved into an extended period of strategic planning for Meredith's entry into the new millennium—and beyond. The sequence, called "Initiative 2000," and its slogans, "Defining Higher Education for Women" or "Teaching Women to Excel," are integral parts of the conversations as this chapter takes form. Revised budgets, committee and departmental planning sessions, printed documents, barrages of e-mail, and even T-shirts bearing slogans attest to the renaissance *au courant*.

Mary Lynch Johnson's *A History of Meredith College* unearthed the founders' early vision— beginning with a seed of an idea for a school, planted in the early 1800's—but the first catalogue of Baptist Female University (announcements for 1899–1900) also accounted for the "whys and wherefores" of the college for young women. Throughout this final chapter of *The Vision Revisited*, quotations from the 1899–1900 catalogue's "Introductory" are printed in italics.

"The desire for this institution was for many years expressed in this form—'We ought to do in higher education for our young women what we have done in Wake Forest College for our young men.' When we say that in the Baptist Female University this desire is being literally fulfilled we tell the whole truth; though we do not mean to say that the work is identical, since this can scarcely be desired. The standard is fully as high, the culture is quite as complete, and the ideals are identical;—so that the comparison with our college for young men will convey to those who are acquainted with that institution a better idea of the work and aims of the school of our denomination for our young women than may be conveyed in any other way."

THE NORTH CAROLINA Baptists who founded Meredith also established and pointed with pride to the college for "our" young men, which had opened its doors in 1834 as Wake Forest Institute, becoming Wake Forest College in 1838.[1] Some readers might find points to ponder in that, at Baptist Female *University*'s chartering in 1891, Wake Forest was its "big brother" *college*. Was the broader *college* education more desirable for men than for women? Was a *university* of twelve schools more appropriate for women than for men? In any case, the status of each institution was reversed in the 1900s, BFU becoming Meredith *College* in 1909 and Wake Forest a *university* in 1944.

Although "*our*" young women in the first student body were mostly North Carolina Baptists, the possessive pronoun did not then nor has it ever served as mandate for exclusion as to denomination or region. Of course, in darker days, the College excluded according to society and, sometimes, because of narrow minds in the denomination. Chapter 1 includes news of the first African-American graduate. Over the ensuing years, minority students have remained in the minority to a greater extent than Meredith might have liked, although efforts toward diversity by race, age, nationality, religious affiliation, and by programs designed to meet the needs of that diversity have been ongoing. In 1997, for example, the Association for Black Awareness decided to broaden its vision, changing its name to the "Association for Cultural Awareness" and, to reflect its new name, revisiting its purpose "to promote cultural awareness and increase knowledge of diverse women, to provide a channel through which cultural concerns may be recognized, and to unify all women at Meredith College."

For a time, Meredith sought to extend its base beyond the region; however, in the late eighties and all the nineties, it found and pronounced its strength as a regional college. But while it has expended most of its resources, both human and financial, in the region, it has welcomed qualified women from all over the United States—indeed, from around the world. In 1996, "our" young women represented twenty-three states and twenty-four foreign countries, and the 627 Southern Baptists composed 35 percent of a student body comprising 26 other denominations and religions. A clue to the diversity of the faculty emerges in the 1996 listing of the professorial staff and their scholarly credentials: the 119 full-time members earned graduate degrees from 71 institutions, 61 of which were in states outside North Carolina and in foreign countries.

"In the prolonged period in which the University was being built, the advocates of the institution argued that the North Carolina Baptists believe in the higher education for women; that they believe in the power of women in the realm of the home and the church to serve God and His kingdom; that every argument for the education of young men is but the more cogent with respect to young women; and, therefore, that the obligation to offer our young women the opportunity of the very best educational advantages at the lowest possible expense, and the wisdom of es-

tablishing an institution under the control of our denomination, were commended to us on the highest of grounds."

THE *HERALD* BEGAN in 1996 to run on its banner a line borrowed from a Meredith advertisement: "We attract bright, talented, ambitious students. Naturally we're a women's college." And, in 1997, almost a century after the early founders established Meredith, the *News and Observer* published a front-page article about women's colleges and their "new degree of equality." Reporter Cynthia Barnett had discovered that the projected fall enrollment of freshmen in North Carolina's four women's colleges—Peace, Meredith, Salem, and Bennett—jumped from 795 to 1,043. (The freshman enrollment at Meredith alone increased from 377 in '96 to 416 in '97.) Barnett wrote, "The growth follows two rocky decades in which women's colleges fought the perception that they were either too elite or not up to par with co-ed schools. Many lost the battle: of 298 women's colleges in the United States in 1960, only 82 remain today. . . . In the past decade, however, women's colleges nationwide have boosted their enrollment 20 percent. . . ."[2]

The reporter quoted Julianne Still Thrift, president of Salem College in Winston-Salem, who said that "statistics debunk the idea that graduates of women's colleges aren't prepared for the real world."[3] In March 1998, when Dr. Thrift spoke at Meredith in observance of Women's History Month, she offered some of the same "real world" statistics published in the article:

> Women's college graduates are twice as likely as their coed-campus counterparts to earn a doctorate. They are three times as likely to go to graduate school in math or science. While less than four percent of college-educated women have degrees from women's colleges, 24 percent of women members of Congress and a third of women board members of Fortune 500 companies graduated from women's colleges.[4]

And an undated publication of the Women's College Coalition asserts, "Virtually all women of science from the Nineteenth and early Twentieth Centuries received their training in women's colleges."

Organizations like the Women's College Coalition and women's colleges like Meredith long ago revisited early founders' sentiments about "the power of women in the realm of the home and the church." Indeed, inferences drawn from the BFU curriculum would credit the writer(s) of the first catalogue with the understanding that women's knowledge, interests, and influence reached beyond those limitations. Largely through their own determination have women and women's colleges not only placed women in home and church but also in all other areas of society— the arts, the sciences, the workplace, civic responsibilities, finances, politics. . . . The list continues.

In its role of pioneer, as discussed in Chapter 2, Meredith's continuing education program has learned much about women's leadership potential and has taught what it learned. In 1966, the division instituted a program through which women twenty-five or older could earn in one year leadership certification under the Broyhill Leadership Institute umbrella. The 1997–98 brochure for Meredith College Women's Leadership Program enticed and enlightened: The program's mission is "to develop competent, high-profile leaders who make a positive difference in the community." The two levels of the program would move participants toward the goal by way of "new approaches to leadership in today's rapidly changing organizational environments." Leadership symposia in 1993 and 1994 encouraged the concept. Another symposium—this one in May 1996—inspired representatives from twenty-two women's colleges, including six of the largest in the nation, throughout a day of Excellence in Continuing Education for Women. Guest speakers were Jadwiga Sebrechts, executive director of the Women's College Coalition, and Sandra Thomas, president of Converse College and a former vice president at Meredith.

And for the home college population, the office of student activities and leadership development in 1997 introduced the Sophie Lanneau Leadership Program. The example of Sophie Lanneau, '02, one of the "Immortal Ten" and a lifelong leader herself, inspired the name of the program for encouraging students to be "effective leaders and active participants in their communities."

The College escalated its own image of leadership with the 1996 founding of the Meredith Center for Women in the Arts. And, on April 2, 1997, an inaugural festival at the Gaddy-Hamrick Art Center celebrated every art form offered on the campus: visual arts, music, drama, and dance.

No intention of hyperbole hides in the high-sounding purpose of the center that unites faculty and students, campus and community for learning, teaching, research, creation and performance of the arts. Long recognized for its excellence in the performing and visual arts, Meredith has renewed its commitment to significant investment in arts support and funding with the creation of the Center. . . .

With the participation and the support of faculty and students across the traditional boundaries of discipline, the Center brings together art, dance, music and theatre for planning, production, performance, proposal writing and promotion. . . .[5]

Although Meredith had worked for a decade toward establishing the Center for Women in the Arts, Initiative 2000 gave it life. Its time had come, suggested Jean Jackson, vice president for student development, who oversaw its creation. "The arts are imbedded deeply in our culture —a means of preserving and celebrating our civilization." She added, "At a time when the arts are under such scrutiny, . . . it is vital to ensure access to all the arts."[6]*

Access to the campus was an impetus for artist-in-residence Robert Mihaly, who had begun sculpting an angel—"a very large angel," declared *Meredith*—during his tenure with the National Cathedral in Washington, D.C. The cathedral grounds were not conducive to a work of that magnitude, and Mihaly welcomed the grassy open spaces near Gaddy-Hamrick Art Center as a temporary home for his twelve-ton marble "work-in-progress." His graceful angel would remain in full view— except in bad weather when a blue tarp covered it—until it was completed and claimed by the local family who commissioned it.

Angelic choruses for children added a dimension to the arts through the music program that, historically, has served the Raleigh community as well as Meredith's full-time students. The younger singers—from Wake, Durham, Johnston, and Orange Counties—were members of the Meredith Girls' Chorus and the Meredith Girls' Chorale (for eight- to sixteen-year-olds), directed by professor of music Fran M. Page. The groups' "demanding" schedules have taken them to the Capitol in Washington, D.C.;

*In the nineties, the conservative bent of elected officials led legislative bodies to decrease dramatically municipal and federal funding for the arts. The voice of United States Senator Jesse Helms from North Carolina was one of the loudest heard against the National Endowment for the Arts.

the White House; the National Cathedral; the North Carolina Museum of Art; the Governor's Mansion; the Spoleto Festival in Charleston, South Carolina; and back home again to perform in the National Opera Company's *Hansel and Gretel* and *La Boheme*. But, added Dr. Page, "These girls come out with an appreciation of music that will last the rest of their lives."[7] An announcement in a 1997 faculty meeting was also an invitation to hear the two choral groups join the singers called "Encore!" for a presentation in Jones Chapel. Encore! was first listed in the 1997–98 catalogue, although its description was the same as that for MUS 434— "Vocal Ensemble" in earlier announcements: "A group of about 12 singers who perform literature covering material from all musical periods and styles, both on campus and off. Admission by audition only."

And it was encore! for Beth Leavel, '77, who returned to inspire the theatre wing of the College. After all, according to *Meredith*, "Leavel has made it big on Broadway (see Chapter 3), performing in such hits as *Crazy for You* and *Showboat*."[8] In 1997, at the invitation of her college contemporary, assistant professor of theatre Catherine Rodgers, '76, Leavel returned to the campus to choreograph the Meredith Performs production of *Irene* and to hold workshops in musical theatre. While Leavel choreographed the Meredith play, Sherry Shapiro, associate professor of dance and "a pioneer in the field of choreography as critical pedagogy,"[9] left on sabbatical for the Givat Haviva Institute of Education in Israel "to teach and to study the relationship between dance, the arts and education for social understanding."[10]

The "odd couple" of academe—the arts and the sciences—are mutually inclusive. While Meredith commemorated the arts, it also celebrated Women in Science Day on March 24, 1997. As prelude to the observance, scientists from the Raleigh Astronomy Club set up telescopes on the campus for the viewing of a triple treat: the Hale-Bopp Comet, Mars, and a lunar eclipse. And as integral parts of the main celebration, chemistry professor Reginald Shiflett—or Merlin the Magician for a day—performed chemistry magic; Robert Reid, biology, demonstrated and discussed plant (and animal) cloning; and Janice Swab, biology, led a campus tree tour. The featured convocation speaker was Gertrude Elion, a scientist so accomplished in her field as to have been awarded in 1988 the Nobel Prize in physiology of medicine. (See Chapter 9.) In her address titled "Challenges and Rewards of Pharmaceutical Research," she explained, "We started out with . . . the idea that we could interfere with DNA."[11] Elion told her audience of her "pilgrim's progress" as a scientist. *Meredith* told her more personal story:

> No one wanted to offer young biochemist Gertrude Elion a job after her graduation *summa cum laude* from Hunter College. In the early 40s, potential employers were convinced she would just get married and leave. Their attitude was that, as a woman, Gertrude Elion would be a distracting influence in the laboratory. . . .
>
> "I wasn't sure what I was meant to do about that," she told the convocation audience . . . . But what she did was go to graduate school at NYU and get her MS in chemistry. . . .
>
> The sad thing is, it took [World War II] to make employers realize that women might be useful in the laboratory," she said. Finally, in 1944 a small pharmaceutical laboratory in the little town of Tuckahoe, just north of New York City, took a chance on Gertrude Elion. She was hired by George Hitchings,* then head of the biochemistry department at Burroughs Wellcome. . . . [12]

Because of her gender, Gertrude Elion was shortchanged in the early years of her career, and, according to studies by the American Association of University Women, students who happened to be girls were still being shortchanged—more noticeably so in math and science than in some other disciplines. Although similar findings were later questioned, AAUW's 1996 report offered "dramatic evidence" as to the validity of theirs.[13] Taking steps toward solving the problem, Meredith; local members of the national organization, Women and Mathematics; Wake County Middle Schools; and area businesses teamed up to provide mentors—"women who use mathematics in their professions"— for middle- and high-school girls "who might be interested in similar career paths.[14]

For women in the nineties, career paths sometimes led to business ownership. In 1997, the College established "the only Small Business Center for Women in the Triangle" for women of all ages. In addition to formal teaching, workshops, and seminars, the center offered myriad resources, including a quarterly newsletter for statewide circulation and

---

*Hitchings and James Black are Glaxo Wellcome scientists who, with Elion, were awarded the Nobel Prize.

mentoring and consulting opportunities. Mentoring (a nineties word) and other forms of leadership sometimes transcended the workplace, merging with civic responsibility, as in the example of those professional women's gifts of time and knowledge of mathematics to young girls who needed role models. As alluded to in earlier passages, Meredith and its students have assumed civic responsibilities in many forms. In this chapter's time period, the culture sometimes called for extra-extra-curricular activities to take stands for the good of humankind. For example, in 1996, students Katie Robinson, Mary Sharpe, and Danielle Mir founded Angels for the Environment, a club "to promote awareness in the Meredith community of environmental concerns by working on and beyond the campus in an attempt to better the environment. "Their efforts have ranged from recycling to post-Hurricane Fran cleanup, from "creating a nature trail" to "implementing Earth Day events," and their territory has ranged from the campus through the extended community.[15]

To make statements about issues, Meredith women have sometimes collaborated with students from other area colleges, as they did on Halloween night, 1997, for a Take Back the Night rally and candlelight vigil, where students from both schools protested the atrocities of rape and other acts of violence often targeted toward victims in the darkness of night.

In both June 1997 and 1998, Meredith hosted, and students, faculty, staff, and alumnae participated in the North Carolina Triangle Race for the Cure®, a national fund-raising event "to benefit breast cancer education and research efforts."[16] Both races were staged on the campus.

The women in the race showed their true colors—as people will do—by staunchly supporting a cause in which they intensely believed. Fortunately, literally thousands of family members and friends have intensely believed in the College. While alumnae have financially supported it, usually at several percentage points above the national average, the nation's economy was always a barometer for charitable giving. In the years of Baptist Female University, legends of women and their giving trends usually referred to "egg money" or "holding back some from the food budget." In the nineties, women bought eggs (or egg substitutes) at the supermarket; they followed the stock market as investors and investment brokers; and they gave to charitable institutions. One had only to turn to the 1996–97 Honor Roll of Donors for the Meredith facts: In the

James Carter Blasingame, President, 1899–1900

Thomas Meredith Society alone, membership of which comprised contributors of lifetime gifts of $100,000–$1,000,000 or more, thirty-nine of the sixty-six individual members were women.* In 1996–97, alumnae contributed $600,472 to the College, and those who contributed $5,000 or more over a successive five-year period held membership in the Iris Society, a new giving club established in 1997.

Annually, since 1994, an alumna has been named Philanthropist of the Year. Chapter 12 introduced the award, its criteria, and Laura Weatherspoon Harrill, '27, its first recipient. The 1995, 1996, 1997, and 1998 honors went to Dorothy Loftin Goodwin, '47; Margaret Weatherspoon Parker, '38; Jo Ellen Williams Ammons, '57; and Frances Tatum Council, '38, respectively.

From the generous nature of friends and family to the competitive nature of politics is not an easy transition. But in 1996, a presidential election year, politics permeated all of society. And that the nineteenth Amendment to the Constitution, allowing women finally to vote, was not

*Twenty of the women listed gave jointly with their husbands.

ratified until 1920 should have reminded women of the urgency of their seeking office, to say nothing of their voting responsibilities. Previous chapters introduced some alumnae—but not all—who chose politics as a way of life, and a few students—but not all—who actively participated in the process. In 1966, a national survey reported, "Most students (over 80%) said they intended to vote in the . . . elections."[17] But results can never be measured in intentions. The Department of History and Politics at Meredith quoted statistics that indicated "30%–40% of all 18 to 24 year old citizens . . . typically register."[18] That year, the number of registrants at Meredith came close to the percentage of students who *intended* to vote and far above the typical college-age voter registration. Clyde Frazier and Michael Novak, professors of politics and history, respectively, had challenged Meredith students "to lead the nation in voting"[19] by registering 96% of Meredith students and getting 96% of those to vote. The slogan became "96% in '96." But the final tally was 78% in '96. After the November elections, Dr. Frazier said, "Although I'm disappointed that we didn't reach 96%, I'm happy and grateful that so many people helped. . . . We ended up processing about 400 registration forms, close to 300 absentee ballot requests, and we drove almost 75 people to the polls."[20] He identified three hardships that had a significant impact on the project: the boring election, Hurricane Fran, and a fire in Heilman Residence Hall.[21] But the *very* good news was that 100% of "the eligible full-time faculty . . . registered to vote."[22]

In the fall months preceding election day, a veritable chorus of ideologies resonated at Meredith from a choir of political partisans: David Price, political science professor at Duke and Democrat running for re-election to the United States House of Representatives from North Carolina's fourth district—which includes Raleigh; Harvey Gantt, former mayor of Charlotte and Democratic candidate for the United States Senate; Kay Bailey Hutchison, Republican, the first woman to represent Texas in the Senate; Robin Dole, daughter of Robert Dole, Republican Presidential candidate; and not-so-partisan Ferrel Guillory, coordinator of polls for the *News and Observer* and the Ford Foundation's writer-in-residence. Apparently, no presidential preference polls were taken at Meredith, but the previously quoted nationwide survey of college students, who *intended* to vote, "favored Clinton over Dole by a margin of 47.7% to 33.9%. Perot was favored by 8% of the students."[23] The Clinton re-election victory notwithstanding, the favored candidate for the Club of the Year Award of the North Carolina Federation of College Republicans was Meredith's College Republicans—for the second consecutive year.

"The institution was founded by the Baptist State Convention of North Carolina; it has been built and is now owned and controlled by this body, represented by a Board of Trustees. It is one of the few institutions in the South founded, built and conducted by the Baptist denomination."

BY AUGUST 1993, Meredith and the Baptist State Convention had negotiated an agreement that superseded the Meredith trustees' vote in 1991 regarding the election of trustees. The compromise was reflected in the College's bylaws, Article III, Section 11:

> The Trustees Nominating Committee . . . shall work with the President of the College to develop a list of trustee nominees to be provided to the Nominating Committee of the Baptist State Convention. Persons from this list will be elected trustees of Meredith by the Convention. . . .

But when the trustees convened in February 1997, they voted again to amend:

> The Trustees Nominating Committee . . . shall work with the President of the College to develop a list of trustee nominees to be acted upon by the full Board. The Board of Trustees, by majority vote, shall elect trustees from the nominees submitted by the Trustees Nominating Committee. Any member of the trustees may submit a nomination to the Trustees Nominating Committee. . . .*

In an interview with President Weems, Jeannie Morelock, director of marketing and communications, asked pertinent questions, such as "Does this action alter Meredith's mission?" And the president answered,

> Absolutely not. The decision by the trustees to establish a self-perpetuating board actually strengthens our ability to fulfill our

---

*The faculty voted to ask the chairs of the Faculty Affairs Committee to write a personal letter to each member of the Board of Trustees, "expressing the appreciation of the faculty for the action taken by the board at this time." (Minutes, faculty meeting, February 21, 1997) mission by insuring our independence and identity. Meredith was founded on, and remains committed to, the principle of preparing women to lead in, and contribute to, society. This position regarding the role of women as leaders is becoming increasingly incompatible with that of some groups within the Convention.[24]

Mrs. Morelock also asked whether Meredith would continue as a Baptist institution, and the president answered emphatically that it would—"in the same way we have been for more than a century."[25] In his President's Message for 1997, Weems wrote,

When the Trustees changed our bylaws and moved to a self-perpetuating board, they made it clear to me that their highest priority was to protect the integrity of the institution. But they also were firm in their desire to maintain the strongest possible relationship with the Baptists of the state. With this in mind, the new bylaws stipulate that the majority of our trustees be from North Carolina, and the majority of our trustees be Baptist.

In its August 21, 1997, issue, the *Biblical Recorder* reported agreement between Meredith and the convention:

Meredith would establish an endowed scholarship program for Baptist students and an Office of Church Relations. Scholarship funds for North Carolina Baptist students would continue at the current level, approximately $62,000 annually.[26]

But the strain of opposing viewpoints brought emotional stress to the negotiating table:

BSC leaders felt that Meredith's action was unwarranted and that trustees acted unilaterally without proper process and discussion. Tensions have been running high, and strong protest statements have been made by Convention leaders about the manner in which Meredith handled the situation.[27]

The matter was settled once and for all when the convention, in its November 1997 annual session, voted to amend its own constitution to reflect, in the same way that Wake Forest is affiliated with the convention, the changed relationship between Meredith and North Carolina Baptists:

Richard Tilman Vann, President, 1900-1915

Article XIV.
Relationship with Meredith College
The Baptist State Convention of North Carolina and Meredith College shall have a fraternal, voluntary relationship under which Meredith College is autonomous in governance. In order to facilitate that relationship, the College will have associate, non-voting membership on the Council of Christian Higher Education, and will be represented by the same officers as schools which are members of the Council. The Board of Trustees of Meredith College shall be elected by that Board in accordance with such procedures as that Board may prescribe. Meredith College shall not share in the distrubution of Cooperative Program Funds.[28]

Although tensions eased significantly, the change in relationship had taken its toll on Meredith; however, the sacrifice might eventually have been greater had no action been taken, said supporters of the move. One of the prices the College paid was, literally, a price paid. When the convention's executive committee voted in August 1977 to approve the new affiliation, it released the $275,000 in escrowed funds that would have been due Meredith from April 1–June 30, but as of July 1, the College would receive no Cooperative Program support. After the November convention, however, "to pay tribute to its rich Baptist history and to recognize outstanding students who are North Carolina Baptists," Meredith established, from funds previously given, the Thomas Meredith Baptist Heritage Scholarship Fund.[29] Each year—and without regard to financial need—three freshmen meeting the criteria of "academic excellence, outstanding service to church and/or community, leadership ability and the recommendation of a church official" would be awarded renewable scholarships of $1,000 each. One of the goals set by Harold West, new director of church relations, would be to increase the scholarship endowment. But mainly, he said, "we want to continue to build relations with Baptist churches and the convention." West's new responsibilities were in addition to those in his role as director of planned giving, a post he had held since 1991.

"How well this estimate of the convictions of our people was taken, let the notable opening . . . in September, 1899, bear its own evidence. From one end of the State to the other the students came; the large new building was filled to overflowing, and a commodious residence, admirably adapted to the necessities of the situation, adjoining the grounds already occupied by the University, was purchased and immediately filled with students. The fact of a new institution being compelled to enlarge its provisions in the very hour of its opening, is a remarkable one in educational history anywhere, and is worthy of record as a testimony not only to the Baptist people, but for the inspiration of all who uphold education."

THE 180 STUDENTS who enrolled on opening day of Baptist Female University exceeded the fondest hopes of the administration.* And so did Meredith's record enrollment in 1995. But a cautious Sue Kearney, director of admissions, counseled, "Given the demographic trends, that rosy picture was not a foregone conclusion. The nation, the southern region, and the state of North Carolina are still in the years of the lowest numbers of high school graduates." Kearney pointed to future challenges:

*The hoped-for number was 125, but, before the first year ended, the enrollment had reached 220. (Johnson, p. 57)

The increase in the number of high school graduates will be gradual—taking until 2004 or later to reach where we were in 1979, the peak year. As the numbers increase, so will the diversity factors. A higher percentage will be from single-parent households, from minority populations, and from economically-deprived backgrounds. There will be more students [from families] who have not always attended college and who have not been drawn in large numbers to Meredith. Among other factors that present challenges is the reality that only about 20% of students attend private institutions and that less than 5% will even seriously consider a women's college.[30]

But 1996–97 statistics gave no reasons to lower expectations. The College reported a record number of students in the fall—2,574; another record number for the spring semester—2,504; and still another record number in the first session of summer school—702.[31] In the same year, 2,882 people—both genders and all ages—took part in the community programs of the continuing education division. President Weems said, "The question legitimately might be asked, 'If you have a record enrollment each year, why is it important to trumpet it so loudly?' The answer: the attention to and celebration of . . . enrollment is generally indicative of the health of the institution."[32] Dr. Spooner's prognosis for 1997–98 was continued good health: "As of May 9, we have experienced the largest number ever of freshman deposits. We are also experiencing more room deposits for returning students than we had this time last year. This number includes many students who are returning to the dormitory after exercising the off-campus option."[33] Actual enrollment for 1997–98 totaled twenty-two fewer students than the year before; however, the good news of the highest freshman SAT scores since 1989–90 gave reason to rejoice.

Aggressive recruitment practices included telemarketing—a telephone-to-telephone approach of the eighties and nineties that apparently found no household exempt, overshadowing the door-to-door or pen-to-paper communications of earlier years. In January 1997, paid student telemarketers spent 250 hours calling 2,573 prospective students and continued phoning as the focus switched from prospects to accepted applicants. Alumnae volunteers also turned to recruiting by way of their presence at high school programs, calling, writing, and entertaining prospects and applicants. On November 1, 1996, the alumnae and admissions offices joined forces to host the first Alumnae Legacy Day, to which alumnae accompanied potential students to the campus for a glimpse into their own possible futures as young Meredith women.

When prospective students visited between 1898–1926, they probably rode a trolley or a city bus—depending on the years—to the block flanked by Blount, Edenton, Person, and Jones Streets, next to the Governor's Mansion, where sat the "commodious" buildings—the early catalogue's description—of Main, Adams, and Faircloth. But when the College moved to West Raleigh in 1926, the word "commodious" took on new meaning. The rolling acres of meadowland accommodated six permanent and four temporary buildings—before the student population boom. Then, in the 1990s, strangers—and some alumnae—relied on campus maps to identify the thirty-five functional and interesting places on the 225 acres of land between the outer beltline (I-440); Hillsborough and Faircloth Streets; and Wade Avenue. For that matter, by 1998, some of the campus residents probably found themselves in the wrong hallway as they oriented themselves in new and renovated buildings.

On February 14, 1997, the Margaret Weatherspoon Parker Fitness Center, with its state-of-the-art exercise equipment, its dance studio, and its faculty offices, as described in previous chapters, was dedicated to and named for Mrs. Parker, "highly loyal" alumna, long-time trustee and the first woman elected to chair the board, and major financial contributor.[34]

That same day, the Park Center was, as *Meredith* writer Del Hunt Johnson expressed it, another "Center of Attention." From the Park Foundation in Ithaca, New York, had come a grant for $600,000; and Meredith gratefully honored the Parks—and itself—by naming and dedicating the Park Center, "especially because Dorothy [Dent] Park is a 1936 graduate," said Vice President Murphy Osborne.[35] But before the trustees named and the contractors built the building, they—and everybody else—knew it familiarly as part of the new student services center. It would abut Cate Center, they said; in fact, Park and Cate would be "under one roof and joined by hallways." Vice President Taylor said it would be more than a building; it would also be a change "in the way we serve students."[36]

A mini-campaign for $1.2 million in building funds (later increased by $170,000 when 1,000 square feet were added to the plans) had been launched in 1996 for the new 13,000 square-foot facility and the renovation of Cate Center. By way of campaign literature, President Weems led potential donors on an imaginary tour of Park Center, though "the foundation is not yet excavated nor is the first brick laid, but the building is real and is part of our commitment to women's education." On the first floor, he directed, one would find the continuing education and graduate school offices and, upstairs, some of the offices in the division of student development, including the career center. And in the entrance to Park Center, an oil and acrylic mural—gift of the Class of 1997—would "honor and celebrate" the lives of 100 outstanding alumnae.[37] Linda FitzSimons, associate professor of art, and her assistants would research the names, and art and graphic design students would create, with names, footprints, and campus scenes, the history-by-mural.

Meanwhile, the aging Cate Center earned its due:

Other than checking their mailboxes and buying textbooks and supplies there, students for many years preferred to socialize in dorm rooms and parlors, not in their new student center. . . .

Nearly 25 years later, with a flourishing commuter student population—nearly 50 percent of the College's enrollment—the path to the Cate Center is well-worn. Nearby Harris, Ledford and Gaddy-Hamrick buildings constructed since 1972 serve hundreds of day students and graduate students, so many, in fact, that a new parking lot was completed earlier this year across from Cate Center to accommodate the overflow.[38]

A new and larger bookstore, managed by Follett, a private company in the business of college bookstores; recreational facilities; and a food court—again to be called the "Bee Hive"—would "restore Cate Center to its original purpose," promised the campaign literature. The lounge renovations gave hands-on experience to interior design students and opened a world of choices to seniors in search of a project, the Class of 1996 deciding on patio furniture for "the garden-style outdoor dining space."[39]

The new student services complex offered creative funding opportunities for everybody. For example, one's name could linger in Meredith's history for $100—the cost of a brick inscribed with the name of the donor—and class year, if applicable—or of someone to be honored by the donor. The collection of inscribed bricks would then become part of the Cate Center plaza.

Adjacent to Cate Center and in honor of the 105 charter members of the Iris Society, an iris garden—one flower per charter member—grew. The iris had long been the college flower; historian Mary Lynch Johnson wrote of a Meredith Iris, especially developed and registered in 1968 by Loleta Kenan Powell, '41, renowned iris and day lily grower, who described the blossom's "standards of creamy white and falls of maroon neatly edged with white."[40] The Summer 1997 issue of *Meredith* brought the iris story up-to-date:

> The variety "Meredith Hues" iris was created specifically for the College by Loleta Kenan Powell, '41, of Princeton, N.C. Powell, an avid gardener since the age of five, was honored in a ceremony before Meredith's spring Commencement Exercises on Sunday, May 11 [1997]. At the same time the "Meredith Hues" was recognized as the official flower of Meredith College.[41]

Just yards away from the iris garden, the Norma Rose Garden reminded passers-by of the much-loved professor of English, 1937–86. The idea of a rose garden sprang from the mind of Robin Bailey Colby, '81, assistant professor of English and Dr. Rose's former student, who thought the garden a fitting expression of regard for Meredith's own "Red" Rose—as the honoree was known by her college contemporaries. Dr. Colby selected a site along the path of Dr. Rose's daily travels: between Joyner Hall—home of the English department—and the Carlyle Campbell Library. On May 23, 1998, during Alumnae Weekend, dedication ceremonies moved to a Joyner classroom while Mother Nature generously watered the garden—and all of Raleigh. In her dedicatory remarks, Jean Jackson, vice president for student development and professor of English, remembered Norma Rose:

> [M]any of us owe our ability to read with understanding and to read aloud with passion and insight to Norma Rose. The increasing ability to read closely enabled us, as we struggled through Milton's

Charles Edward Brewer, President, 1915–1939

Paradise Lost, to understand Milton's concept of Paradise, of Eden, when he wrote in Book IV about "Flowers of all hue, and without thorn the rose" (l.26). And to compare that idyllic rose with Wordsworth's description in *Ode: Intimations of Immortality from Recollections of Early Childhood*, "The Rainbow comes and goes, / And lovely is the Rose" (st.2).

I keep trying to imagine what Dr. Rose herself would say about today. I think she would be glad this area is called the Norma Rose Garden — avoiding the redundancy of the Norma Rose Rose Garden. . . .

It was a redundancy of sorts that the library had outgrown its space. The first self-contained library on the campus, the Carlyle Campbell Library was constructed in 1968 for 125,000 volumes; in 1998, it held "over 135,000 volumes plus 42,600 additional items in non-print formats. . . . In the last decade the addition of a computerized online library system and expanded media services and library instruction programs, services and staff have stretched the use of space to the fullest."[42] While no additions to the library were anticipated for the immediate future, renovations in 1998 effectively reorganized the space. In the summer of construction, workers occupied the thirty-year-old building while basic library services moved to the first floor of Stringfield Residence Hall. Ted Waller, technical services librarian, offered an opportunity for Meredith people to buy a bit of history—and nostalgia, perhaps—by way of a silent auction for the sale of the card catalog cabinets.

Another piece of history, the Fannie E.S. Heck Fountain, standing tall where walkways merge in the center of the courtyard, would be restored to its original beauty and function with financing from the Parent and Family Association.* To honor its first president, the North Carolina Baptist Woman's Missionary Union had given the fountain in 1928, when the new campus was, indeed, new.

And new by history's standards, the grounds of Jones Chapel had some dressing up to do. Because of a generous gift of $250,000, plans could get underway for the Spangler Arboretum, to be named in honor of Mr. and Mrs. Earl W. Spangler of Shelby, North Carolina.

Building and renovating, renovating and building were continual. But now and then, both the forces of nature and the errors of humankind wreaked havoc, as in the month of September 1996. Unusual for inland territories, Hurricane Fran hit the Triangle with a vengeance in the early morning of Friday, the 6th. Meredith's lost electrical power was restored that same afternoon, though many Raleigh residents were without electricity for more than a week. A month later, reported the employees' newsletter, facilities manager Clarke Suttle could not yet apply a dollar figure to campus damage "during what some are calling the 'Hurricane of the Century'":

> Most of the damage was quickly repaired, like the missing pieces of roof on Heilman residence hall and the skylights which were torn out of Stringfield and Vann residence halls. The ground floors of Ledford Hall, Poteat residence hall, and the Waiwright Suites, below Belk Dining Hall, all sustained damage from flooding. . . .

---

*Formerly the Parents' Association, this organization changed its name in 1990 to reflect the changing student constituency of the College.

What cannot be repaired or replaced are the 100–125 large trees downed around campus. . . .[43]*

Although clean-up efforts continued into the next spring and summer, "the replanting of 23 new trees and the replacement of some shrubs [had] begun the long trip back to normalcy."[44]

The second September catastrophe struck on the 17th, when students in Heilman residence hall awoke to what many thought was a 5 A.M. fire drill. "It was not. Room 201 was on fire."[45] According to a September 20 news release by the College,

> Roommates Jodi Abbate and Susan Fortunes awoke when their battery-operated smoke detector activated. According to reports, they ran from the room to the first floor and pulled the manual fire alarm, which failed to operate. . . .
>
> The Assistant Chief Earl Fowler said, "The situation with the first-floor alarm is a pure fluke—it's the first time I've ever seen something like this. . . . Apparently, this alarm has been used for many years in drills and in testing. Over the years, the activating device was worn down by the switch and it wore a groove in it." But, according to Chief Fowler, the alarm was tested in August and had been certified as operational. . . .

Various reports offered reassurance. From the *Meredith Herald* for September 18:

> At 5:01 A.M. campus security received a call from two young women who awoke to find their room in flames. When the fire department arrived on the scene by 5:07 A.M., the approximately 135 residents in Heilman had been completely evacuated, according to Chuck Taylor, Vice President for Business and Finance. . . .

From the *News and Observer*, September 18:

> Two students were treated at the scene for smoke inhalation, but there were no other injuries. The fire was contained to one room

---

*"Janice Swab, biology professor, explained that many oaks fell during Hurricane Fran because they had been damaged by Hurricane Hazel years ago" (Meredith, Summer 1997, 1).

and was put out within 15 minutes, but adjacent rooms were damaged by smoke and water. . . .

Stanford [fire department battalion chief] said an investigation found that the fire was caused by "piggy-backing," when too many plugs are inserted in one electrical outlet. . . .

The residents of the second floor of Heilman were relocated to other campus rooms that had extra beds.

A September 17 letter from President Weems to parents:

Please know that the welfare of our students is of primary concern. We will keep your daughters informed . . . , and we welcome your questions about procedures and follow-up to this frightening morning. We are very grateful that the fire was contained, that our fire training procedures served us well, and most particularly, that all of our students are safe.

And from the minutes of the Board of Trustees' meeting, September 27:

A resolution was unanimously passed by the trustees conveying to Dr. [Jean] Jackson and all members of the Meredith family the heartfelt and sincere thanks, appreciation, and commendation for the manner in which these emergencies were handled.

At the same board meeting, the trustees approved planning for the construction of a new science building and renovation of Jones Auditorium, the latter to occur in the summer of 1998.

"This year's work has been no less satisfactory. The trustees fixed their purpose to select the best faculty available. They were impressed with the conviction that they had no ordinary task and that, whatever the hazard, they were bound to establish the university's high standard. This they did—employing a numerous faculty of scholarly men and women, and providing every facility for the instruction, training and keeping of the young ladies entrusted to them. At the end of the first year they have been so justified that where many felt that entrenchment would be the order, the word is clear to go foward."

THE FIRST TEACHING faculty of Baptist Female University comprised thirteen women and five men, including President Blasingame, who also

Carlyle Campbell, President, 1939–1966

taught psychology and pedagogy. Blasingame and Delia Dixon, the resident physician and physiology teacher, held doctorates, and three of the women and one man held master's degrees. In addition to the University's professorial staff, the first catalogue listed a principal of the academy and a matron.

Twenty-five trustees composed the governing body in 1898; in 1966–67, the number had grown to twenty-eight, including lifetime member, W. Herbert Weatherspoon; and, in 1997, the board increased from thirty-six to forty members. At the November 18, 1996, executive committee meeting, Margaret Weatherspoon Parker proposed that an emeritus status be instituted, and chairman, Norman Kellum, appointed a three-member committee headed by Charles Barham to consider the matter. At a special meeting on April 21, 1997, Barham made the following motion:

> Any active or former member of the Board of Trustees who has served in such capacity a minimum of 8 years may be elected a Trustee Emeritus of the College. Such election may be made by the full Board of Trustees upon nomination of the Trustees' Nominat-

ing Committee. This election shall be for life unless revoked by the Board of Trustees and the Trustee Emeritus shall have the right to speak but shall have no vote in the proceedings of the Board. A Trustee Emeritus shall not be counted against the limitation on membership of the Board of Trustees and may not be used to establish a quorum necessary for meetings.

The motion was tabled until the semi-annual meeting on September 26, 1997, at which time it was passed.

In 1898, the trustees outnumbered the faculty. In 1997–98, when 106 full-time and 141 adjunct faculty members composed the teaching force of the College, the situation was clearly reversed. While the previous chapter alludes to a somewhat rocky path between the two bodies, this entry suggests a road to recovery. At the September 27, 1996, board meeting, faculty affairs committee representatives Susan Wessels, business and economics, and Virginia Knight, mathematics and computer science, issued a statement on behalf of the faculty:

We appreciate the more open relationship that the Board of Trustees has created with the faculty. We welcome the informal lunchroom conversations with Mr. Kellum and other Board members. The Meredith faculty is totally committed to creating a powerful future for the College. We offer our talents and energies to this endeavor. We look forward to being partners with the Board and the administration as we all work to design Meredith College for the twenty-first century.

One of the committed, Michael Novak, became head of the Department of History and Politics in 1996. He earned his B.A. from Denison University and his M.A. and Ph.D. from Harvard. Dr. Novak said his "primary intention is to follow the principle of Hippocrates: 'First, do no harm.'" The department was in the process of developing an undergraduate major in public history "that will take our graduates directly to jobs in museums, historic sites, public archives and similar activities in applied history."[46] Novak had taught at the College for nine years when he moved into his new position.

Brent Pitts came to Meredith in 1981 and accepted headship of the Department of Foreign Languages in 1997. He holds the A.B., A.M., and

Ph.D. degrees—all from Indiana University—and has done postdoctoral work at Princeton and at Ecole Superieure de Commerce de Lyon. Dr. Pitts is a firm believer in the ability to communicate "in a language other than English. . . . At Meredith College," he said, " we take great pride in producing specialists of the spoken word. Our majors know how to communicate orally in their language, and this skill alone gives them a brighter future."[47]

Also in 1997, Jerod Kratzer, an eleven-year veteran of the education department, became its head. Dr. Kratzer holds the B.S. from St. Joseph's University, the A.M. from the University of Delaware, and the Ed.D. from North Carolina State University. As he praised his department for its emphasis on "team work and collaborative decision-making,"[48] he was also highly complimentary of his predecessor, Gwendolyn Clay, and her leadership. Dr. Clay, a mathematician, was beginning a year's leave at the time of Kratzer's appointment—an absence that took her on a sabbatical journey down east into Jones County—one of North Carolina's poorest—to assist Superintendent Norma Sermon-Boyd in Teaching Math for Learning, a National Science Foundation-funded K–12 project. As Clay reported "extremely positive" results just months into the program, she also related an extremely positive story of how she came to help with it. Dr. Sermon-Boyd's initial contact with Jean Joyner of the Department of Public Instruction led to Miss Joyner's then inviting Dr. Clay and Lee Stiff of North Carolina State University to join her in hearing the dreams of the superintendent from Jones County. Among Sermon-Boyd's first words were, "I know that all of you are going to help. I've prayed about it, and the Lord has told me that you are." Dr. Stiff's ready reply was "If the Lord said so, we'd better get on with the planning."[49] And they did.

The time varied as to each Raleigh educator's presence at the Jones County project, but Dr. Clay was the only one of the three on sabbatical leave. In 1990, the number of sabbaticals awarded had increased from two to five. And, in 1997, 28 faculty members had received summer grants.

"The ideals of the University have been hinted at. Its first intention is to provide . . . instruction of the noblest and most thorough sort. . . ."

REFLECTING ON AND holding tenaciously to the vision of the early founders, the contemporary ones might construe this quotation as an unnecessary intrusion in Chapter 14. They might be right. Because this volume of Meredith's history describes in some detail the constant assessment of a curriculum taught by a highly credentialed and dedicated faculty, this chapter will not elaborate, except to report revisions, additions, and noteworthy accomplishments.

For many years, faculty members have advised students in their journeys through college; however, because of a growing adult population, an advising support center was created in 1997, but Item 9 in the 1997–98 operating budget, titled "New Initiative Proposals," did not relieve the faculty of their advising responsibilities: The center, directed by Ann Gleason, "will not be a substitute to the present system, but will allow students access to advisement when their advisors may be unavailable and will provide a resource for faculty seeking help in their role as primary advisors."

To what extent advising played a part in three accounting majors' having passed the state exam "on the first round" in 1996 is not known, but Rebecca Oatsvall, head of the Department of Business and Economics, declared the success "a very rare thing indeed."[50] In the same year, Dr. Oatsvall announced the new concentration of human resources management, available with the Bachelor of Science degree in business administration.

In 1997, several academic "firsts" made news: the mathematics and computer science department sponsored a math camp for high school freshmen and sophomores; the English department offered a summer workshop on Writing for Women; and the Mary Lynch Johnson Chair of English, heretofore held by one professor at a time, was awarded to the department's three writers: Betty Adcock, Suzanne Britt, and Suzanne Newton. The Templeton Foundation funded "Issues in Science and Religion," a program directed by Bernard H. Cochran, religion, and Janice Swab, biology. Through the program, the theologian and the scientist led Meredith in hosting a South Regional Conference workshop. The Carolinas Chapter American Society of Interior Designers (CCASID) announced the winners of the Otto Zenke student competition among Western Carolina University and Meredith and Converse Colleges, in which the competitors designed "a floor plan, elevations, samples, perspective, reflective ceiling plan, and design concept" of a fictitious hotel. First place/school: Meredith; first place/student: Pat Polumbo, Meredith; third place/ student: Laura Boone, Meredith; Honorable Mention: Amy Craig and Jenny Duncan, Meredith. Lori Brown, sociology and social work; Ann Burlein, religion and philosophy; Walda Powell, chemistry and physical sciences; and Paul Winterhoff, human environmental sciences, winners in the broader area of Capstone courses, received grants to develop new courses for 1998–99. Capstone courses, said professor of psychology Rosemary Hornak, who directed the program, "share a common goal: helping students apply their education at Meredith to society."[51] The Departments of History and Politics; of Health, Physical Education and Dance; and of Mathematics and Computer Science announced new majors: Public history would prepare a student "for employment in a variety of historical agencies, nonprofit museums and historic sites," and, as far as anyone knew, the major was "the only known program in the Nation that prepares undergraduates in public history."[52] The second new major, exercise and sports science, would offer students the option of focusing on fitness and sports management or of concentrating on teacher licensure in physical education. And, according to the 1997–98 catalogue, the major in computer information systems would give the student "facility with computer theory, abstraction, and design."

The realities of technology jump off the page in the mathematics and computer science section of the college catalogue: "Because of the velocity at which change in technology is occurring, students will learn to manage change and will acquire the ability to learn new technology, new 'languages,' and new techniques."

Writers of the first catalogue had no foreknowledge of the Information Age. Had they glimpsed the future, they might have applauded much of Meredith's use of technology. For example, in November 1996, students, faculty, and staff gathered in Ledford Hall to interact "with panelists and 10,000 students from 300 other colleges on tough diversity issues such as race, gender, class, sexual orientation, disability and religion" through a video teleconference.[53] And at the February 21, 1997, faculty meeting, Vice President Osborne alluded to a warmly welcomed grant from the Jesse Ball duPont Foundation for a "two year program of faculty and curriculum development," which, said Dean Burris, would focus on "get[ting] technology into the classroom." And dean of students, Sharon Cannon, wrote of classroom computers which would provide "tactile teaching device[s]" by transforming computer-scanned images into Braille text.[54]

Inasmuch as the culture immediately preceding the twenty-first century was so thoroughly grounded in technology, it behooved progressive colleges to provide not only understanding, skills, and equipment but also logical applications to areas outside classrooms or corporate suites. Meredith's Intranet system—accessible only through the College's own network—gave a new dimension to information-gathering. The employees' newsletter admonished, "Click onto the 21st century at Meredith College! Meredith's new Intranet is all you need to stay up-to-date with what is happening on campus" by access "to such things as a sports calendar, vaccination schedules, travel opportunities, hours for the Bee Hive and Fitness Center, speakers for chapel and classified ads."[55] The Intranet's academic section would even provide a student's assignments and departmental news.

For the dual purposes of educating and entertaining, a Meredith College Television (MCTV)-produced talk show, *Wake Up Meredith*, made its debut in January 1997. In an article for the *Herald*, student Dina DiMaio's lead sentence was "Move over Good Morning America; it's time for *Wake Up Meredith*. . . ."[56] Two weeks later, the *Meredith Herald* again publicized the show through a review by Addie Tschamler:

> When I watched on February 13, . . . the show began with professional-looking clips from Star Wars, which had been the most popular movie over the past two weeks. Host, sophomore Heidi Gruber, made mention of the movie throughout the show.
>
> Gruber began by announcing what the day's show would include: various clips of candidates for campus elections and an interview of students about the campus' latest eatery the Bee Hive. Throughout the show, there are comical interruptions by Jennifer Franklin, who plays Barbara. . . .[57]

Cynthia Bowling, cable administor, suggested the show and sophomore Courtney Duncil produced it.

Neither television nor virtual globetrotting on the Internet had yet sated the explorer's hunger for seeing and touching the world. Without travel in the eighties and nineties, *"Instruction of the noblest and most thorough sort"* would have gone lacking. Through a North Carolina Teaching Fellows Junior Enrichment Program, Maria Pellizzari, '98, went to Hawaii, Australia, and New Zealand for two weeks. Several academic departments have offered special summer studies in France, Mexico, Spain, Greece, Italy, Egypt, Turkey, Russia, New Zealand, and the United Kingdom. And the regular Meredith Abroad program moved from Switzerland in 1994 because of the relocation of its base—the Baptist Seminary—from Rushlikon to Prague, and, since that time, the agendas have included Italy, the Czech Republic, and England.

Blue Greenberg, retired member of the art faculty, had planned study trips for students for a decade before she agreed to direct travel adventures, "especially tailored to Meredith people."[58] Through the division of institutional advancement, she arranged educational tours to places as close as Williamsburg or New York and others as far away as London and Cornwall, as recreational as cruise ship excursions or golf at Sunset Beach and as educational as discovering the eastern cultures of Egypt and Turkey. An alarm signaled an abrupt change in plans for the summer of 1998: "In light of recent acts of terrorism in Egypt, the American government has strongly advised independent tour groups to rethink their plans to visit [there]."[59] In response, Meredith travelers headed for Italy instead.

The continuing education division had practiced constant assessment of curriculum in all its quarter century of service. And in 1997, it remeasured and altered accordingly its re-entry and After5 programs, the finished product becoming a well-fitting combination of the two called Undergraduate Degree Programs for Women Age 23+—or 23+, for short. The fall 1997 issue of *Continuing Education at Meredith* offered the rationale:

> With an increasing number of students working full or part-time, it was apparent that women needed more options for course scheduling and greater flexibility in the times when courses were available. By combining the programs, students can now take classes during the traditional 16 week semester during the day or night, and also enroll in accelerated evening classes that meet only 8 weeks [with] longer class periods.

Of 23+, Sandra Close, director of the new program, and Madra Britt, former director of After5 and new director of community programs, said, "In 23+, a student can set her schedule to accommodate the demands of her family, career, or other responsibilities and it can be customized every semester!"[60]

The practice of customizing was also no stranger to the John E. Weems Graduate School. "In response to the growing need in the Triangle area for teachers of English-as-a-Second-Language (ESL), Meredith College now offers ESL licensure under two . . . options: as a Master of Education with an ESL Specialty or as an add-on licensure-only program."[61] Staggering statistics underscored the acute need for the program in North Carolina: "The number of limited English proficient students requiring ESL services has grown from a reported 3,000 in 1988–89 to an estimated 25,000+ for the 1997–98 academic year. Although more than 170 different home language groups have been identified, about half of these students are native Spanish speakers. . . ."[62] Meredith's ESL licensure program was the first in the Triangle. And only one of the few schools in North Carolina to offer the Master of Health Administration, Meredith's new MHA program was launched in January 1998.

The preceding examples of academic progress reflect the early and ongoing intent of Baptist Female University in 1898 and Meredith College in 1998 to provide *"instruction of the noblest and most thorough sort"*; however, the school's first catalogue had preceded the phrase with *"not simply"* and followed it with *"but"*:

". . . but instruction made perfect in the religion of Jesus Christ. But for this desire that the higher education of our women shall be Christian, shall be surely, definitely, positively Christian, the University would never have been reared. . . ."

PREPARING FOR A planning retreat of academic administrators in 1996, Dean Allen Burris included an assumption in a January 25 memorandum to the participants: "Meredith will retain and strengthen its commitment to being a 'servant institution'—solidly grounded in the Christian tradition and related to North Carolina Baptists. Student needs will be the guiding principle for academic decision-making. The spiritual and ethical dimensions of education will be at the heart of all we do here."

And "the heart of all we do here" is also stated in the historic purpose of the College, which is found in the charter and in every issue of the college catalogue:

The purpose of this corporation is to provide for the higher education of women under Christian auspices and within a Christian context, fostering in all its activities and relationships the ideals of personal integrity, intellectual freedom, and academic excellence; and to that end, to provide operation, and development of a college at Raleigh, North Carolina, under the name of Meredith College. This institution, a liberal arts college, shall emphasize and develop its academic program in terms of scholastic standards and service, and shall maintain procedures implicit in an educational institution of high quality; and, as a Christian college, shall be primarily concerned to deepen and broaden the Christian experience of its students and to prepare them for maximum service in the Christian enterprise.

Beginning in 1997, David Heining-Boynton, psychology, chaired a faculty committee to revisit, "with extensive faculty input," the statement of purpose:"[63] The faculty recommended no changes in the purpose; instead, it developed a separate and more objective Statement of Mission, "which is faithful to the historic purpose, but interprets it in a contemporary setting."[64] The trustees approved the following Statement of Mission on September 26, 1997:

> In educating women to excel, Meredith College fosters in students integrity, independence, scholarship, and personal growth. Grounded in the liberal arts, the College values freedom and openness in the pursuit of truth and, in keeping with its Christian heritage, seeks to nurture justice and compassion. Meredith endeavors to create a supportive and diverse community in which students learn from the past, prepare for the future, and grow in their understanding of self, others, and community. To these ends, Meredith strives to develop in students the knowledge, skills, values, and global awareness necessary to pursue careers, to assume leadership roles, to enter graduate and professional studies, and to lead responsible lives of work, citizenship, leisure, learning, and service.

"Although it is the purpose of the Trustees to maintain a high standard, appreciating the conditions in North Carolina, they have arranged preparatory courses, whereby young ladies may be fitted for the higher work. . . ."

IN THE MEREDITH *Herald* for February 19, 1997, Emily Fulghum asked, "What do you get when you combine reading, writing and arithmetics [sic] here at Meredith?" And she answered, "an exciting new endeavor in collaborative learning from the same people who brought you the Writing Center in 1987."[65] When services of the writing center expanded from assistance with writing and grammar also to include tutoring in math, French, and Spanish, it became "the learning center," staffed by "superb Meredith students who have been recommended by faculty and trained to work one-on-one with their peers."[66] The center's director and assistant professor of English Nan Miller said, "Academic support for students is and always has been a priority at Meredith. . . " but insisted that the center was not strictly for remedial purposes: "While frequenters are typically students who worry about 'weak backgrounds' in English or math, others come simply for confirmation that they have understood an assignment or worked a problem correctly. . . ." She added, " 'I'm clueless,' is the complaint du jour of the bewildered student."[67]

"A subsidiary aim is that the advantages of the institution may be offered at cost. There are no profits, no dividends. The student is required to pay a sum sufficient to maintain her and obtain the services of her teachers. The cost is already decidedly less than that of institutions of lower grade."

TRUSTEES HELPED STUDENTS *"obtain the services of their teachers"* by voting in 1997 to increase, for the third consecutive year, rewards for faculty longevity. The year-end bonuses would range from $200 for a part-time faculty or staff member with 3–5 years of service to $1,200 for a full-time person with more than twenty years.

In the academic year 1996–97, only six of the thirty-seven independent colleges in North Carolina charged less than Meredith's tuition and fees of $10,990 for resident students and $7,420 for commuters.[68] For 1997–98, however, the cost spiraled upward to $12,240, an increase of $1,250.Vice President Taylor explained: "The changed relationship with North Carolina Baptists and the funding for new initiatives resulted in the largest increase in the College's history for 1997–98. In fact, the percentage of tuition increase ranked in the top ten among the nation's colleges."[69] But Taylor had already admonished, "We need to keep in mind that, even with the larger than normal tuition increase, the cost of a

Meredith education will continue to be less than any other Baptist college in North Carolina."[70] In his prediction of less drastic increases in the future, he prophesied correctly: The 4 percent increase for 1998–99 amounted to only $500.00, for a total of $12,740.

While regretting the necessity of rising costs, Meredith had no regrets about its listing in *Baron's Best Buys* for 1996 and in *U.S. News and World Report*—again for 1996 and 1997.

"In the course of time an endowment will be acquired. Already a loan fund is being accumulated. And besides, a club-plan was last year effected whereby young ladies who were desirous of helping themselves were saved considerable expense."

AS DISTANT AS the possibilities seemed in 1899, an endowment was indeed acquired. In the first twenty-five years of President Weems's administration, endowment and reserves grew from $887,000 to $45,000,000. Solid financial management, a diversified endowment investment portfolio, and increasing numbers of contributions combined to generate the positive numbers. A national economic boom did no harm. In 1995, the Dow Jones reached 4,000 for the first time; in 1997, 7,000; and, in 1998, 9,000. Meredith's good economic news in 1996 included a 26.5% growth in endowment investments; in 1997, an increase in numbers of gifts and amounts over the previous year—4,407 donors giving $2.8 million in 1996 and 5,232 giving $3,438,270 the next year; and in 1998, four one-million-dollar deferred gifts in eight months' time—"the largest demonstration of giving that Meredith has had in history," said Vice President Osborne.[71] The gifts were received as three charitable remainder trusts and a bequest. Sidney Martin, the long-time college physician, initiated the Martin Family Scholarship Fund with a gift of $1 million in honor of "the long relationship between the Martin family and Meredith College."[72] Mrs. Martin, the former Sue Jarvis, is a member of the Class of 1949, and daughters Donna and Debbie are also alumnae. And Dr. Martin's father, Leroy Martin, was a trustee. The two additional trusts were established by anonymous donors; and the $1.1 million bequest came from the estate of Ella Adams Ogburn, '30.

In 1996–97, the *"considerable expense"* of attending college was relieved somewhat by the North Carolina Tuition Grant increase from $1,250 to $1,300 and the awarding of $10,851,172 in financial aid to

1,471 students, compared to $400,000 awarded in 1972, the first full year covered in this volume. Although the later figures appeared magnanimous, they met only 80 percent of the need, as opposed to 100 percent in the recent past. The previous chapter reported the good news of a zero default rate on repayment of student loans carried by Meredith women, beginning in 1992. Though not perfect, the 1994 default rate of 1.4% was, nevertheless, excellent, considering the national average of 9%. Philip Roof, director of financial assistance said low default rates meant debts were manageable and "the job market is providing sufficient entry-level positions and salaries to permit [graduates] to repay their loans."[73] In fact news reports in May and June of 1998 assured new graduates of a flourishing job market of promising salaries—even, in the era of technology, for holders of liberal arts degreees.

"The University is admirably located. It is near by the Capitol of the State, within easy reach of the State Library. Within three blocks to the west or the southeast are the First Baptist Church and the Raleigh Baptist Tabernacle. The City of Raleigh itself is notable for its genuine culture, its quiet, orderly life and its beautiful natural environment. . . . ."

IN 1996–98, "ADMIRABLY *located"* still, Meredith remained "near by the Capitol of the State," three miles measuring a very short distance in North Carolina's bustling capital with ready transportation—so ready, in fact, that traffic snarls on Hillsborough Street might have discouraged frequent trips downtown. Students seeking a Baptist church no longer had only two choices, the 125 churches in the Raleigh Baptist Association being well within reach, as were numerous other temples of worship for a diverse student body in a cosmopolitan city.

Raleigh's *"genuine culture"* and *"beautiful natural environment"* continued as hallmarks of the region; however, a *"quiet, orderly life"* might have been questioned by the hundreds of daily commuters to the campus, to say nothing of the drivers headed for Research Triangle Park. The population more than doubling since 1970—123,793 then; 266,035 in 1997 —the city was an education in itself.

"No small part of a young lady's education is derived from the people with whom she comes in contact. Of course, proper restrictions are put

E. Bruce Heilman, President, 1966–1971

upon the student body, and contact with the general life of the City is so guarded that it may occur only under the most desirable conditions."

MEREDITH GRADUALLY LIFTED social restrictions over the years, discontinuing its *in loco parentis* position in the seventies; however, the students' struggle for the privilege of open house in the residence halls remained a major social issue of the nineties. The policy since 1993—the first year of male visitation in the dormitories—allowed, at most, three open houses per semester, always during specified hours on a designated Saturday or Sunday and scheduled to coincide with another major activity. But students fashioned a more liberal proposal for the trustees' consideration in 1996:

> The SGA proposes that the current Open House policy be extended to ten (10) hours on every Saturday and seven (7) hours every Sunday; that the extension apply only to one experimental senior residence hall; that only seniors be allowed to live in the experimental residence hall; that the number of floors designated as experimental

floors be based on the amount of senior interest; and that the current Open House policy be extended to seven (7) hours on two designated Saturdays or Sundays per month for all students not living in the experimental residence hall.[74]

With an amendment mandating that the board "be brought up-to-date on any substantive problems that develop for the administration because of this policy," the trustees adopted the proposal.[75] The students were thorough in their preliminary research and planning, the proposal having been based on an SGA referendum in 1995, in which 92% of the voting students favored the extension. And they were clever—and logical—in the wording of their rationale: "The goal of this extension is to provide a more relaxed and trusting environment for visitors and students. Benefits could include increased retention of students and more campus centered activity on weekends."[76] Jean Jackson, vice president for student development, supported their logic: "Resident students are young adults who, like other adults, like to have the choice to invite friends to their place of residence. Part of a student's developmental process is to be able to have relationships with men included, and have them on her own turf. We don't want them to always be in the position of having to go off-campus to socialize." She added, "This organized effort was an example of student government at its best. . . . To have an issue on the forefront through an entire generation of students is quite a statement in itself."[77] Paula O'Briant, director of residence life, reported 1,676 open house guests during the 1996 fall semester.

Long before open house was considered, Meredith encouraged the interaction of students with the *"general life of the city"*; i.e., local church attendance; cultural events; sports; Cooperating Raleigh Colleges; social mixers; politics; capital city learning opportunities. . . . For example, on January 10, 1997, the eve of Governor James B. Hunt's second-term inauguration, Erica Balmer, 1997–98 president of the SGA, met with Hunt and seventy other student government leaders from around the state to discuss issues in higher education and "a variety of social, political, and educational concerns."[78]

But if *"no small part of a young lady's education is derived from the people with whom she comes in contact,"* the young woman of BFU learned much about living—as well as subject matter—from the social beings around her, limited though she was by the *"proper restrictions"* imposed upon her. The same characteristics of learning have continued despite the reinterpretations through the years of "proper restrictions." In 1996, Virginia Knight (mathematics), Michael Novak (history), and the astronomy class issued a compelling invitation for students to learn something of astronomy while also seeing the informal side of their teachers. A March 28, 1996, memorandum to the college community read,

> Lord willing and the skies don't fall, this Wednesday, April 3rd, should be a big night. Beginning just before 6:30 pm, the moon will rise already in total eclipse. It will pass from totality between then and about 7:45 pm. Shortly thereafter, Comet Hyakutake should be visible, although ambient light and its position in the sky will not afford the best possible view.
>
> We plan to be stationed on the soccer field or thereabouts with some telescopes, binoculars and volunteers who will help to explain what is going on and help you to see the sights. . . .
>
> Come if you'd like, bring friends and family, hope for the best and dress for mud."

Sometimes, students taught themselves, as in the case of Collyn Evans, a freshman in 1993, who brought her own idea to fruition. Evans proposed "that Meredith . . . sponsor a student art exhibition and invite other women's colleges in the Southeast to participate."[79] Three years, much hard work, and a-decision-to-major-in-art-history later, Evans witnessed the opening of the first Annual Women's Colleges of the Southeast Art Exhibition in Bryan Rotunda Art Gallery on January 21, 1996, the show running for three weeks. The list of participating colleges was impressive: Agnes Scott, Brenau, Columbia, Converse, Hollins, Meredith, Randolph-Macon, Salem, and Sweet Briar. Speaker for the opening, Terrie Sultan, curator of contemporary art at the Corcoran Gallery in Washington, D.C., drew a standing-room-only crowd of eager listeners. Regina Reid, a studio art major, collaborated with Collyn Evans in planning and producing the exhibition. The two earned academic credit for their work under the classification of Independent Study.

Oftentimes, teachers learned from their students, as did English professor Louise Taylor. One of her American literature students asked, "Is the Hugh Meredith in Ben Franklin's *Autobiography* related to the Thomas Meredith the college is named for?" Dr. Taylor was so curious that she buried herself in researching the genealogies of both Thomas and Hugh Meredith, the latter a business partner of Benjamin Franklin. Her thorough and interesting research caught the attention of the Convocation Committee, and she was invited to translate it into the 1998 Founders' Day address. Under the title, "Searching for Hugh: The Meredith Connection," Taylor took her audience through promising discoveries that turned to false hopes before she reached the conclusion that "it appears that the Hugh Meredith mentioned in Franklin's *Autobiography* is the great-great uncle of Thomas Meredith." So the speaker learned from the student, and the audience learned from the speaker: "If you listened closely," Taylor said, "you noticed that the subtext is one of debt and repayment. And one purpose of Founders' Day is to remember our debts to those who have worked to make Meredith an institution where it is a privilege to study and a pleasure to teach."[80]

A notable visiting lecturer in early 1996 was Mark Plotkin, "one of the world's leading ethnobotanists," whose laboratory is the rain forest and who bemoans the fact that "rain forest cultures are disappearing . . . as western influence intrudes on ancient tribal knowledge of medicinal plants. . . ." Plotkin is the founder of Shaman Pharmaceuticals and author of *Tales of Shaman's Apprentice*. He told his audience, "I am a firm believer that a liberal arts education is your ticket to romance, adventure and making the world a better place."[81]

And in the fall of 1997, ethnobotanist, biologist, and anthropologist Wade Davis delivered the Honors Convocation address. His lecture, "One River: Explorations and Discoveries in the Amazon Rain Forest," was based on his book *One River*.* He lived in the rain forests to discover "the origins of many of their sacred plants."[82]

A week prior to Dr. Davis's Honors Convocation address, Doug Adams delivered the Mercer-Kesler lecture on art and religion. Professor of Christianity and the Arts at the Pacific School of Religion in Berkeley, California, Dr. Adams spoke on "Discerning Biblical Themes in Contemporary Art and Film." The *Meredith Herald* reported, "Adams examined several pieces of contemporary art by George Segal, Stephen De Staebler,

---

*Davis is also the author of the best seller *The Serpent and the Rainbow*.

Jasper Johns, and Christo, and brought the audience's attention to the [artists'] use of religious symbolism."[83]

The lessons students taught one another and, for that matter, the community, were endless. Sharing a small room with another student has stirred various emotions that the world would never see were it not for students like Tory Hoke, writer and cartoonist for the *Herald*, who introduced the cartoon characters of Meredith and Luna and their nerve-racking co-existence in a dormitory. But the College was sensitive to the problems—and joys—occurring in the period of home-to-institution adjustments, as illustrated in the title of the 1996 opening convocation: "Meredith's Little Instruction Book." Convocation committee chair, Cynthia Edwards, promoted the event in an undated memorandum to the faculty and staff, in which she solicited "short words of wisdom, advice, or lessons that would benefit anyone trying to achieve her goals at Meredith." And prior to the first annual Freshman Frolic in 1996, a banner reading "It's a freshman thing—you wouldn't understand" hung above the front entrance to Johnson Hall.

A segment of the community that everybody understood was the increasingly impressive collection of athletic teams and the coterie of student athletes that brought recognition to intercollegiate sports at Meredith. In 1996, Melinda Campbell coached the tennis team to a Division III national ranking. The coach pointed to "freshman sensation" Ann Mebane, who was named the region's rookie of the year, and who was ranked 34th. "Mebane and Dorothy Livesay received a regional ranking of ninth as a doubles team and sophomore Sarah Huffman received a regional singles ranking of eighteenth."[84] The 1997–98 team was 25th in the nation—the best ever year-end ranking, according to department head Marie Chamblee. Ann Mebane moved up to 30th. President Weems was proud of all the teams:

After just three seasons the newly formed soccer team [Jose Cornejo, coach] burst into the winning ranks this fall. The team finished the season with a 10–7 record, after just five wins during its first two seasons. The volleyball team [Kathy Mayberry, coach] finished its strongest home stand with an impressive 9–1 home record, and the basketball team [Carl Hatchell, coach] is full-steam ahead with a 7–2 start to the season."[85]

In 1997, for the first time, the tennis team competed outside the United States. At the Spring Break Sports Program in Bermuda, Meredith played the University of Rochester and Pace University, both located in New York, and Case Western Reserve in Ohio, winning over Case but losing to Rochester and Pace. In 1998, the basketball team captured a big headline in the sports section of the *News and Observer* for January 11, 1998: "Meredith has 32 assists in 90–30 victory." The article under the headline on page 16C read, "Meredith shot 53 percent from the floor and handed off 32 assists as it crushed Mary Baldwin 90–30 at home. . . ." The team accomplished its second-best record with twenty-one wins and two losses. At the North Carolina-Georgia Women's College Basketball Tournament in Greensboro in February, sophomore Beth Goodale was crowned "Tournament Most Valuable," and Aedrin Murray was named to "All Tournament." In baseball news, Andrea Carver pitched her first no-hitter in a 17–0 victory over Bennet in March.

The College welcomed individual and team accomplishments in sports, as did all of society, as exemplified in the exceptions made for a college athlete's academic requirements as well as the financial compensation paid to professional players. But Meredith unabashedly admitted that its playing field was not level with the schools whose monetary support dwindled in a losing season or whose athletes were more widely celebrated than the scholars. In 1996, one of Meredith's scholars, junior Regina Mack, was selected as one of only twenty-five students nationwide to participate in the Society of Biblical Literature's Recruitment Conference in New York City, October 11–13. Calling the selection "a rare and special opportunity" for Mack, assistant professor of religion Cheryl Kirk-Duggan identified the Society of Biblical Literature as "the major professional organization for scholars of biblical studies."[86]

Student researchers from all disciplines found their places in the sun at the first annual Meredith College Undergraduate Research Conference on April 25, 1998. Through the Creative Ideas Fund,* the College invited students to submit their research papers for possible presentation at the conference, the authors of the best three papers to win cash prizes. Guest

---

*Part of Initiative 2000, the Creative Ideas Fund awarded grants of up to $5,000 for selected projects "from all parts of the community—students, staff, faculty, administration. . . ." (Jean Jackson, memorandum to faculty, staff and student organization presidents, December 2, 1996).

John Edgar Weems, President, 1972–1999

speaker was Mary Shariff, professor of art at the University of North Carolina in Chapel Hill.

Freshman Christy Sanderson taught a valuable lesson in compassion, not only to her peers but also to viewers of local television and readers of *Meredith*, the *News and Observer*, *People* magazine, and the *Chicago Tribune*. Her widespread esteem came from the founding of her Operation Toy Box, a nonprofit agency that "collects and distributes used toys for children who are disaster victims."

Sanderson's operation evolved from her concern for children whose Virgin Islands homes were demolished by Hurricane Marilyn in 1995. Since that time, she and her helpers have provided toys for literally hundreds of children. The collaborators in her efforts included the American Red Cross, schools, churches, day-care centers, U.S. Air, Food Lion, and "volunteers who provide storage space, leadership, packing toys, and heart and soul."[87] But Sanderson's most constant helper was her mother, Carol Sanderson, associate director of financial assistance at Meredith. The compassionate student with a major in business administration on her mind evokes the choice words of Allen Burris in a 1997 interview with *Meredith*. Reflecting on earlier struggles attached to educating women and the still faint echoes of criticism toward today's curriculum designed "for work and life," Burris acknowledged the primary importance of technology to the educated woman of the nineties, at the same time articulating a necessary balance: " 'I've learned,' he says, 'that Meredith must be both high tech and high touch.' "[88]

The entire community learned a lesson in high touch from the reaction of Meredith's technology services department to the illness of a colleague. The learners included readers of Nicole Brodeur in the *News and Observer*, who told the story of department head, Ruth Balla, and staff members Doug Alm, Josh Tate, and Tim Bartlett's having shaved their heads in support of co-worker Ginny Kemp, who had lost her hair through chemotherapy treatment for Hodgkin's disease.

> "It was such a great thing to do," Kemp said. "Especially for Ruth, who had long blonde hair. I mean, that was, like, two years of her life! . . . I have always been glad I was part of this department, but especially now."
> ". . . I hope so!" said Balla.[89]

Camaraderie in any workplace rates an "A." Over an occasional lunch together, administrative assistants Sharon Woodlief and Martha Harrell, office of the president; Anne Pickard, office of the dean; Mary Ann Beam, office of student development; and Joyce Hinson, office of institutional advancement, found one another's company as pleasant away from work as in Johnson Hall—so enjoyable, in fact, that they took a cruise together. And another. The group has been on excursion by automobile, train, ship, or plane numerous times since 1996 or thereabouts, and the fact that they are still friends after all those miles is, in itself, insight as to who these women are. In the first half of 1998, they took a spring jaunt to Puerto Rico and a summer weekend trip to New York City. They call themselves the "Cruising Ladies"—a.k.a. "The Power Group."

The lure of travel brought a visitor to the campus and sent a colleague to the far-flung regions of Australia. In July 1996, Edward "Ted" Waller, technical services librarian, sent a message via the internet to librarians everywhere: "I would like to exchange jobs with someone outside the continental United States."[90] Almost a year and one-hundred e-mail responses later, Waller flew to Canberra, Australia, to work for four months at the library of Australian National University, while partner in exchange, Sherine Joacquim, signed on at the Carlyle Campbell Library. Not only did Waller and Joacquim exchange jobs but also houses, pets, and cars. Joacquim adjusted readily; however, her Meredith co-workers were a bit concerned that she commuted daily from Waller's home in Durham, driving "on the wrong side of the road."

In August, 1997, Janet Freeman, librarian since 1984, was promoted to dean of library information services. " 'There have been major changes in libraries over the past several years and this title change reflects the shift from keeper of books to provider of information,' Freeman said. 'But our basic purpose remains the same: helping the Meredith community find the information they need.' "[91] And Sue Ennis Kearney, '64, director of admissions since 1984 was promoted to dean of enrollment planning and institutional research. Kearney's new responsibilities included enrollment planning, in which she would use "work groups to address enrollment issues," explained Vice President Spooner in the employees' newsletter for September 1997. In addition, she would lead the College in defining and meeting enrollment goals. Her new role would be independent of the office of admissions, and Carol Kercheval, associate director of admissions, was promoted to fill Kearney's former position.

Sue Ridge Todd, '59, a thirty-year veteran of the registrar's office, was promoted from associate registrar to registrar. She followed Allen Page, registrar and dean of undergraduate instruction, who assumed the responsibility of academic leadership while Dean Burris took a year's sabbatical. Additional new colleagues included Alma Lane Lee, '88, director of the Teaching Fellows program; Stephanie Helms Harris, director of commuter life and special services; Anita Gunn Shirley, director of grants and program development; Robert Vetter, director for corporate and major gifts; and Mary Ann Morgan Reese, '82, manager of the bookstore. Reese's predecessor, Dru Morgan Hinsley, '52, who "piloted the Meredith supply store through four decades of cultural inventory,"[92] and her entire staff had agreed to stay on under Follett College Stores, Inc.— "the largest contract manager of college and university bookstores throughout the U.S. and Canada"[93]—when Meredith followed the business trend in 1996 of "outsourcing" (another high-tech nineties word) work; but Hinsley retired in less than a year to concentrate on treatment for lung cancer. On Friday, October 18, the entire campus celebrated Dru Hinsley Appreciation Day.

An earlier instance of relinquishing operations to an independent company occurred in 1969, when the College contracted with the Slater company as food services concessionaire. Slater later became ARA and, more recently, the ARAMARK Corporation. Accepting further responsibilities in 1996, ARAMARK added to its food service operation that of the administration of facilities services—capital improvements, maintenance, grounds, and housekeeping.

And, since 1996, the security staff has evolved into the campus police force under Chief Mike Hoke, a retired lieutenant colonel in the United States Marines and certified police officer, whose last military assignment was that of provost marshal at Camp Lejeune, North Carolina. Vice President Taylor's annual report for 1996–97 alluded to the "576 hours of state-mandated training" that the department's eight new certified officers had undergone. In January 1997, Lisa Marie Robinson, '95, was sworn in, becoming Meredith's first state-certified policewoman.

The *Meredith Herald* playfully reported an emergency call to campus police:

> Campus police officers armed with .357 magnum pistols, a cardboard box, and a gray wool blanket proved to be more than a match for an intruder in Johnson Hall last Wednesday.
>
> While concerned Johnson Hall staff members looked on nervously, officers Timmy Morris and David Richards chased a frightened possum toward the rear rotunda [door] held open by the campus police chief.
>
> The possum exited the rotunda unharmed as staff members breathed a sigh of relief and returned to their offices.
>
> "This was a highly successful S.P.A.T. (Special Possum Administration Team) operation," commented Meredith security chief Mike Hoke. "This is the type of thing we train and remain ready for. We used the least amount of force necessary, and the suspect was released on its own recognizance."[94]*

OF ALL THE title changes and the promotions in 1996–98, two were unique in that they involved the highest level of the administration and, to accommodate them, trustee action to amend the bylaws. On September 27, 1997, such action was taken, changing the title of LaRose

---

*Vice President Jackson reported that, while in Johnson Hall, the possum had dined on leftovers from a recent Johnson Hall reception.

Spooner, vice president for administrative affairs, to vice president for marketing and the name of her division from office of college communications to the office of marketing and communications. In the same meeting, the Board of Trustees created the position of executive vice president and appointed Charles Taylor to fill that position. Taylor had held the vice presidency for business and finance since 1983; his new responsibilities meant a broader administrative jurisdiction for twelve-year veteran William F. "Bill" Wade, Jr., controller. Public relations intern Jennifer Lynch, '98, wrote in the October 1997 employees' newsletter, "Taylor will be breaking new ground as he works with the Meredith community to prepare for the future. In his new role, Taylor is responsible for overseeing the College's strategic planning [Initiative 2000] and implementation of the recommendations made in the marketing audit by Stamats." President Weems said that this recommendation of Stamats Communications* was the first of 174 to be implemented.

*Stamats Communications is a consulting firm commissioned in 1996 by the Board of Trustees to conduct a study of the academic programs and administrative structure of the College.

In the fall of 1997, Weems appointed and the trustees empowered an Initiative 2000 review team of "representatives from each of the College's major constituencies" to "prepare an institutional strategic plan document which will be proposed to the Board of Trustees [in the fall of 1998]."[95] The team included Executive Vice President Taylor; Vice Presidents Jackson, Osborne, and Spooner; Deans Johnson and Page; trustee Robert Lewis; community leader Bob Brooks; faculty members Ellen Goode and Jack Huber; students Kelly Conkling and Kristy Eubanks; alumnae Del Hunt Johnson and Cleo Glover Perry; and administrative staff members Vanessa Goodman Barnes, Gordon Folger, and Jeannie Morelock.

With approval of the Board of Trustees and, said Taylor, "Armed with historic purpose, a current mission and a stated vision for the future, the College will be on solid ground to begin developing a strategy to make the vision a reality."[96]

IN THE CONTEXT of Taylor's statement, vision suggests a beginning. And in the context of this volume's final chapter, vision *revisited* more nearly suggests an ending. And an elegiac note unavoidably creeps into conclusions. Norma Rose, professor of English, 1937–86, and department head, 1986–91, died April 6, 1996, on the day before Easter. The Easter Sunday edition of the *News and Observer* took note of the "Legendary" professor at Meredith:

> Rose retired 10 years ago when she turned 70, but she kept teaching continuing education courses in Shakespeare, grammar, and other topics until two weeks ago, when she became too sick to keep going. . . .
>
> But Dr. Rose didn't just quit.
>
> She left behind individual study guides to get her students through the rest of the term.[97]

Rose's students, to whom the reporter referred, were fondly known as "Dr. Rose's disciples." Many had sat in her classroom almost every semester since she retired from full-time teaching to enjoy the more leisurely pace of continuing education enrichment courses. Her long-time "disciples" included Margaret Bullard Pruitt, Louisburg; Alice Goodman Satisky, Raleigh; and Frances Pittman Woodard, Selma—all members of the Class of 1937 and all college contemporaries of their teacher—as well as Drs. John Dotterer and trustee Elizabeth James Dotterer, '30, Sanford; and trustee Robert Lewis, Raleigh. And although Dr. Rose probably felt like it, she didn't "just quit" editing *Chapel Talks by Carlyle Campbell*, a collection of memorable messages of Meredith's fourth president, when, for his student audience, chapel was a "required course." Although publication of the talks had been a topic of conversation for some years, its reality in 1996 was credited to Mary Lily Duncan Gaddy, '42, instigator of the project and head of the alumnae committee that saw it through. By 1998, the committee had donated proceeds of more than $4,000 to Friends of the Carlyle Campbell Library. A memorial service for Dr. Rose took place in Jones Chapel on April 26. Also a veteran of the Department of English, Helen Jones, instructor, 1969–81, died June 10, 1998. Mrs. Jones's family and friends honored her memory at a June 12 memorial service in Jones Chapel.

Evelyn Pope Simmons, associate professor emerita of economics and twenty-seven year veteran—1962–1990—of the Department of Business and Economics, died July 16, 1997. And James R. Johnson, III, also professor emeritus of economics, had retired six months before his death on July 18. Dr. Johnson joined the faculty in 1979, was named by his students Outstanding Professor for 1995–96, and was remembered at a service on September 19 in the Elva Bryan McIver Amphitheatre. The James R. Johnson Meredith Economic Student Fund honors his memory.

Less than a year after Drulynn Morgan Hinsley, '52, enjoyed a day of appreciation in her honor, she died on May 11, 1997. Vice President Taylor reminded the community of her long tenure of forty-three years as bookstore manager. "She has been a friend to thousands of students and staff . . . and she will be missed," he said.[98]

Lucretia L. Peterson, a member of the housekeeping staff, died March 12, 1998. Mrs. Peterson was employed by the College for more than sixteen years, having joined the staff in 1981 and retired in 1997.

On July 4, 1997, Meredith lost Elizabeth James Dotterer, member of the Class of 1930 and a trustee for many years, beginning in 1956; and, on August 31, 1997, another trustee, 1979–82, Katherine Wyatt Hodgins, '48, died. Soon after completing her first term on the Board of Trustees, Helen Harris died on May 2, 1998. Mrs. Harris and her late husband, Shearon Harris, were benefactors of the College for many years.

The Class of 1998—indeed, the entire college family—grieved long and deeply for senior Erika Suzanne Woodlief, who died in a car accident on November 15, 1997. Ms. Woodlief was riding with her mother, Sharon Woodlief, '88, administrative assistant to President Weems and twenty-seven-year employee of the College, who was injured. Erika Woodlief was a sociology major and, said the *News and Observer*,

> [she] hoped to become certified to teach kindergarten through sixth grade. . . . Erika had been inducted into Silver Shield, an honorary leadership society, and named in "Who's Who Among American College and University Students" in the past two weeks. . . . Along with her studies and participation in numerous extracurricular activities, Erika was working this semester as an intern counselor with the Wake County juvenile court.[99]

Jeannie Morelock, director of marketing and communications, told the newspaper, "Erika basically grew up on the campus. . . . Everybody knew her since she was a baby." Her faculty adviser and professor of sociology Rhonda Zingraff said, "The youth of North Carolina have lost a devoted advocate, and we have lost one of our treasured students." And President Weems added, "Erika's death was a 'crushing loss, both for Meredith College and for me personally. [She] was one of the finest women we have ever had a Meredith, a young woman of great promise.'"[100] A Service of Remembrance and Celebration for the Life of Erika Woodlief was held November 20, 1997, in Jones Chapel. Ms. Woodlief's parents, Sharon and Eugene Woodlief, established the Erika Suzanne Woodlief Memorial Scholarship to provide financial assistance to a Meredith freshman who has interest in elementary education or sociology. . . . "[101] The office of institutional advancement announced in February 1998 that "one-third of the 192 gifts received for the . . . scholarship fund were received from Meredith faculty, staff and students."[102]

Freshman Akie Segawa collapsed on a hiking trip with friends near Sanford on February 15, 1998, and died of natural causes in a nearby hospital. Ms. Segawa was an international student from Hitachi-shi, Ibaraki-ken, Japan. Her mother, two siblings, and a family friend, who traveled to Meredith to attend a February 18 memorial service in Jones Chapel, were guests of the College in the Sarah Lemmon House. "Condolence books for the family of Akie were placed around campus. Hallmates and friends . . . made and distributed white ribbons for students, faculty and staff to wear in remembrance of her."[103]

In 1996–98, Meredith lost by death approximately 200 alumnae, as well as numerous other benefactors, including, on November 27, 1996, Vivian Dawson Massey, who, with her husband, L.M. Massey, initiated the funds for the Massey House, the president's residence. These few represent the many—a host of memorable Meredith "angels" who continue to serve as guardians of the College's vision and tradition.

EVEN WHEN A colleague retires, those "still in the race" suffer a sense of loss, although retirement is a gradual process, and ties are rarely broken permanently. One need only peruse the forty-plus names on the faculty emeriti list to recognize that retirees continue to appear at special events, the library, and any number of old haunts with any number of old friends. In 1996, the College honored the retirement of Lon Avent, maintenance supervisor; Vergean Birkin, assistant professor of geography; Carolyn Barrington Grubbs, '60, professor of history; Dru Morgan Hinsley, '52, manager of the bookstore; Geraldine Myers, secretary/receptionist, office of institutional advancement; Anne Carmack Pugh, '82, administrative secretary to the vice president for business and finance; Dan Shattuck, chief of security; and Janice Shattuck, secretary, office of security. Retiring in 1997 were Jacques Comeaux, associate professor of foreign languages; Frank Grubbs, professor of history; James R. Johnson, III, professor of business; Dorothy Knott Preston, '54, professor of mathematics; and Lois Rowland, member of the housekeeping staff. The College bade farewell to fewer retirees in 1998: Marie Mason, former dean of students, professor of psychology, and, more recently, coordinator of campus activities; and Craven Allen Burris, Vice President and Dean of the College. The service to Meredith represented by the faculty and staff who retired in the three-year period totals 401 years, with Dr. Comeaux's tenure of fourteen years the shortest period and Mrs. Hinsley's 49 years the longest.

Allen Burris announced retirement plans as early as 1996, and, at his request, the Board of Trustees granted him a year's sabbatical, beginning July 1, 1997. He and Mrs. Burris spent several months in England, and, on return, he was immediately busy preparing the annual faculty lecture and, at the request of the Class of 1998, the annual baccalaureate sermon. Burris had high hopes for his sabbatical, and many of them materialized. The *Biblical Recorder* reported, "During this year, he hopes to 'retool' himself as a historian and political scientist by reading, writing and attending some classes at one of the Triangle's universities. . . ."[104] His long-range retirement prospects—learning the guitar, folk singing, woodworking, volunteering for community work, teaching, writing a book—suggested a man of many interests.[105] For *Meredith*, Anne Pugh wrote, "An educator and a people person, Dean Burris has regularly taught classes in history and politics. Some summers he has accompanied students to Europe for the Meredith Abroad program. One year the students presented him with a sweatshirt on which was printed his newly acquired nickname: 'Uncle Dean.'"[106] Burris's "Uncle Dean" shirt prompted eye-rolling and quipping, but probably not as much as has the sign on his desk that read, "Flip Not Thine Wig." The sign was a gift from his wife, Jane Burris.

Dr. Burris reflected on the "innumerable ways" that Meredith has grown. It has "nearly tripled in size," and, academically, it "offers graduate programs, a capstone program with a national reputation, and a holistic honors program." He said he will miss "the daily community with people, perhaps even committee meetings, . . . the interaction in the classroom, telling jokes in the hall, and making hard and important decisions."[107]

In April 1997, before Burris left on sabbatical, the college community threw—as someone said—"the surprise party of the century" in his honor. To be sure the dean attended his own party, Police Chief Hoke "arrested," handcuffed, and transported him—sirens blaring—to the Weatherspoon Building. He was tried for desertion before the King of Hearts (shades of *Alice in Wonderland*) and sentenced to the party. Almost overflowing the gymnasium, the crowd enjoyed antics, toasts and roasts, videos, including an Oscar-winning documentary narrated by Burris's long-time administrative assistant, Anne Pickard; a few serious goodbyes, and the announcement of a scholarship endowed in Burris's name. One of Meredith's legends, Lon Avent, who had retired in 1996 as maintenance supervisor at the College, prepared and oversaw the serving of a barbecue feast outside the gymnasium. In an open letter to the community, Burris wrote, "Meredith people, my colleagues and friends, again gave of themselves for the benefit of students as they do every day. This time they did it in my honor. . . . You people are really a piece of work."[108]

AN ERA ENDS categorically on June 30, 1999, the last day of the Weems presidency. At the November 24, 1997, executive committee meeting of the Board of Trustees, chairman Norman Kellum announced the president's plans for retirement and Vice President Taylor's added responsibilities of administering the planning and operations of the College. Kellum also said that the president would be granted a sabbatical leave for the year beginning July 1, 1998, and, in 1999, would become president emeritus.

Accomplishments of the Weems administration are documented throughout this volume, not the least of which are the growth in endowment and reserves from $887,000 to $49,500,000 and the College's debt-free status. *Meredith* published expressions of acclaim from faculty, administrators, alumnae, trustees, students, educators, benefactors, and other friends. One of the accolades came from North Carolina's Governor James B. Hunt:

> Dr. Weems has dedicated twenty-seven years of his life to making Meredith College an enriching college experience for women in North Carolina. Under Dr. Weems's leadership, Meredith College has nearly doubled the size of both its student body and its faculty, constructed twelve new facilities and founded the John E. Weems Graduate School. He has left a legacy of strength and vitality for Meredith College and for education throughout North Carolina. Dr. Weems is a great friend of mine and I sincerely thank him for making the young people of our state a priority in his life.[109]

William Friday, executive director of the William R. Kenan Jr. Charitable Trust and former president of the University of North Carolina System, also paid tribute:

> Strong colleges require strong leaders. John Weems has provided Meredith College that quality of leadership. He is a man of uncommon dedication, intelligence, integrity, and good will. This Trust's respect for him led to a funding grant to enrich the offerings of Meredith.
>
> John Weems is a respected and longtime friend with whom I have happily joined in many endeavors to benefit Meredith and our state. His tenure is marked by growth, expansion of progress and, above

all, academic excellence while maintaining essential freedom and open exchange. He has been a very good president during a stressful interval of American history. . . .[110]

The fact that, after commencement 1998, President Weems had awarded 10,587 of the 16,060 diplomas granted since 1902[111] was a telling statistic of the growth of the College in the past twenty-seven years. But Dr. Weems's life in the period of this chapter was more than diplomas and trustee meetings and technology and academic decision-making; it was also John Edgar Weems and Ruth Ellen Taylor Weems, husband and wife. Following their marriage in Florida on Thanksgiving Day, 1996, and two weeks in Aspen, Colorado, Dr. and Mrs. Weems returned to the Massey House. From an interview with Mrs. Weems, Anne Pugh reported, "Home for Ruth Ellen Weems before coming to North Carolina was a working ranch in Venice, Florida, on which she raised cattle and mined shell road-base material. Real estate development is presently also a part of the ranch's business. The ranch is now managed by her three sons. . . ."[112] The second marriage for both, the Weemses met in Blowing Rock, where each owned a home.

At sabbatical send-offs, the college community honored President Weems at an informal gathering in Belk Dining Hall on April 23, 1998, and the trustees feted him with a dinner dance at the Carolina Country Club on June 2.

TO PUBLISH AN inclusive list of all those whom the community has gained and lost in the previous three decades would be impossible. But, like William Butler Yeats, we do our part "to murmur name upon name, / As a mother names her child."[113] All who have come are appreciated; yet none who is missing is forgotten. Each name is written in the human heart and, therefore, in the annals of this history.

EPILOGUE

IN THE FINAL years of the twentieth century, the Baby Boomers turned fifty; Israel celebrated its golden anniversary of independence; Scottish scientists cloned a sheep; the White House claimed a balanced national budget for the first time in decades; *El Niño* spawned erratic weather patterns; septuplets were born into the world and survived; and Meredith prepared to say goodbye to its sixth president and to undertake the difficult search for a seventh. On April 20, 1998, the Board of Trustees finalized the appointment of a thirteen-member committee charged with the selection by April 1999 of a new president, who will be expected to assume official duties at the start of the academic year 1999–2000. Eugene M. Langley, Jr., was elected search committee chair and Faye Arnold Broyhill, '59, vice chair. Other members included Sam Ewell, Jerry Harper, Sr., Earl Pope, Judge Gary E. Traywick, and Claude Williams for the trustees; Gwendolyn Clay and Janice Swab would represent the faculty; Virginia Gentry Parker, '83, the alumnae; Amy Smith, '99, the student body; Jeannie Morelock, '95, MBA, the administration; and Harry Eberly, the community. So this volume of Meredith's biography has come full circle—search committee to search committee and an era between.

A NEW MILLENNIUM waits just over the horizon, and history, like William Shakespeare's Antonio in *The Tempest*, teaches that "What's past is prologue."[1] As the era concludes, Meredith honors the contrasts between the beginning and the end and finds the vision inevitably revisited by its people—its leavening—working "by *contagion*, until the whole is leavened."[2]

NOTES

PROLOGUE

1. Matthew 13:33 KJV.
2. Buttrick, *Parables of Jesus*, 23.
3. M.L. Johnson, *History*, 5.
4. *The World Almanac and Book of Facts 1997*, 208.
5. Ibid., 207.
6. Weems, "Upheld by the Affections of a Great People," Inaugural Address, 21 September 1972.
7. Buttrick, *Parables*, 24.

CHAPTER I

1. M.L. Johnson, *History*, v.
2. Ibid.
3. *Alumnae Magazine*, June 1971, 4–5.
4. Leslie Syron, "Notes on a Sabbatical," *Alumnae Magazine*, December 1971, 5.
5. E. Bruce Heilman, "Paraphrasing My Own Propaganda," *Alumnae Magazine*, September 1971, 5.
6. Laura Weatherspoon Harrill, "What a President!" *Alumnae Magazine*, September 1971, 4.
7. Margaret Farmer, "Multicolored Memories," *Alumnae Magazine*, December 1971, 7.
8. Ibid.
9. Minutes, Board of Trustees, 24 September 1971.
10. Ibid.

11. *Encyclopedia of American Facts and Dates*, 6th ed., s.v. "education."
12. "Are Americans Losing Faith in Their Colleges?" Editorial Projects for Education, Inc., insert, *Alumnae Magazine*, June 1971.
13. E. Bruce Heilman, "Meredith Not in Trouble," *Alumnae Magazine*, June 1971, 31–36.
14. Minutes, faculty, 18 September 1971.
15. Ibid.
16. Susan Van Wageningen, editorial, *Twig*, 16 September 1971.
17. Van Wageningen, editorial, *Twig*, 2 September 1971.
18. Anne Wall, "Juniors Take Pumpkin[;] Sophomores Place Second," *Twig*, 4 November 1971.
19. *Twig*, 2 September 1971.
20. Janice Sams and Eleanor Hill, editorial, *Twig*, 2 November 1972.
21. Meredith McGill to editor, *Twig*, 31 October 1974.
22. Farmer, "Multicolored Memories," *Alumnae Magazine*, December 1971, 7.
23. Carlyle Campbell, "The Idea of Community," address to the student body, date unknown, Campbell papers.
24. Jan Johnson, "Carol's Cart Becomes Well Known on Campus," *Raleigh Times*, 22 October 1971.
25. J. Eugene White, "Her Spirit Soars,"

Charity and Children (Thomasville), 12
September 1971.

26. Conversation with Joe Baker, 18
January 1995.

27. Minutes, called meeting, Board of
Trustees, 14 October 1971.

28. W.L. Norton, news release, 14 October 1971.

29. Ibid.

CHAPTER 2

1. W.L. Norton, news release, 14 October 1971.

2. *Twig*, 20 January 1972.

3. M.L. Johnson, *History*, 277.

4. Judy Yates and Diane Reavis, "What
a Great Day to Be Alive!" *Twig*, 20 January 1972.

5. *Alumnae Magazine*, March 1972, 12.

6. *Report of the President 1971–72*, 49.

7. *Twig*, 30 March 1972.

8. Martha Grafton, "Women's Lib: a
Second Look," *Alumnae Magazine*, March
1972, 36.

9. Ellen Bullington, "Overtime Needed
to Pull the Meredith Basketball Team
Through," *Twig*, 30 March 1972.

10. *Report of the President 1971–72*, 7.

11. *Twig*, 11 May 1972.

12. *Alumnae Magazine*, Summer 1972, 6.

13. Eleanor Gardner Bedon to President, M.C., 12 April 1970, reprinted in
Alumnae Magazine, Summer 1972, 6.

14. Dorothy Loftin Goodwin, "The
Margaret Bright Gallery of Class Dolls,"
Alumnae Magazine, Summer 1972, 8.

15. Minutes, Board of Trustees, 23 September 1972.

16. *Alumnae Magazine*, Fall 1972, 8.

17. Conversation with Allen Burris, 20
January 1994.

18. Conversation with Anne Dahle, 28
April 1994.

19. Ibid.

20. Minutes, faculty, 6 August 1972.

21. Minutes, executive committee,
Board of Trustees, 21 August 1972.

22. *Twig*, 8 September 1972.

23. Eleanor Edwards Williams, "A
Proper Title for an Heroic Poem," *Alumnae
Magazine*, Winter 1973, 14–15.

24. Minutes, executive committee,
Board of Trustees, 20 November 1972.

25. *Twig*, 8 September 1972.

26. Ibid.

27. Katherine Inez Hall v. Wake County
Board of Elections, No. 37, Supreme Court
of North Carolina, 15 March 1972, *South
Eastern Reporter,* vol. 187, N. C. Ed.

28. Ibid.

29. Minutes, Board of Trustees, 27 February 1971.

30. *Report of the President 1971–72*, 41.

31. Janice Sams, "Students Care
Enough to Become Involved," *Twig*, 27
April 1972.

32. Minutes, executive committee,
Board of Trustees, 20 November 1972.

33. *Twig*, 8 September 1972.

34. *Report of the President 1971–72*, 42.

35. *Twig*, 8 October 1972.

36. Ibid.

37. Ibid.

38. *Twig*, 30 March 1972.

39. Minutes, Board of Trustees, 23 September 1972.

40. Minutes, faculty, 14 October 1972.

41. Ibid.

42. *Report of the President 1971–72*, 33.

43. Inauguration of John Edgar Weems,
printed program, 22 September 1972.

44. Weems, "Upheld by the Affections
of a Great People," inaugural address, 22
September 1972, reprinted in *Alumnae
Magazine*, Fall 1972, 13–15, 40.

45. Ibid.

46. Ibid.

47. Ibid.

CHAPTER 3

1. Britt, *Images*, 1.

2. "Making a Case for Women's Colleges," *Wall Street Journal* (New York), 14
November 1974.

3. Suzanne Reynolds Greenwood, "The
Challenge of the Women's Movement to
the Women's Colleges, *Alumnae Magazine*,
Winter 1973, 4–5, 36.

4. *Information Please Almanac Atlas &
Yearbook 1995*, 48th ed., 430.

5. Weems, address to the North Carolina General Assembly, February 1973.

6. Ibid.

7. Conversation with Weems, 11 January 1994.

8. Minutes, Board of Trustees, 27 September 1974.

9. Clara Bunn to John Weems, 12 May
1974.

10. Allyn Vogel, "Thomas Addresses

Group at First SGA Meeting," *Twig*, 26 September 1974.

11. Genie Rogers, "V.P. Move for Good," editorial, *Twig*, 8 November 1974.

12. Mary Owens and Barrie Walton, "Weems Talks on Women's Roles," *Twig*, 1 March 1973.

13. Minutes, Faculty, 21 August 1974.

14. Phyllis Trible to editor, *Alumnae Magazine*, Fall/Winter 1973, 1.

15. Jane Cromley Curtis to editor, *Alumnae Magazine*, Spring 1974, cover 2.

16. Elizabeth Garner McKinney to editor, *Alumnae Magazine*, Fall 1974, 1.

17. *Twig*, 31 January 1974.

18. Conversation with Weems, 5 April 1994.

19. *Twig*, 4 October 1973.

20. *Twig*, 4 May 1973.

21. Woody Dicus, Cookie Guthrie, Meg Pruette, Elaine Williams, to editor, *Twig*, 21 February 1974.

22. Rogers, "Energy Crisis Ignored; Disregard Is Shocking," editorial, *Twig*, 31 October 1974.

23. Meredith McGill, "Administration Takes Steps Toward Conserving More Energy, "*Twig*, 21 November 1974.

24. *Twig*, 13 December 1973.

25. Lynne Wogan, *Raleigh Times,* 1 December 1975.

26. Sharon Ellis, "Meredith's Twelve Sisters Live in Poteat Dorm Basement," *Twig*, 4 December 1973.

27. Minutes, Academic Council, 5 February 1975.

28. Leslie Syron to John Weems, 26 September 1973.

29. Syron to Weems, 3 May 1973.

30. Greenwood, "Working With People Has a New Name," *Alumnae Magazine*, Fall/Winter 1973, 7–9, 39.

31. *Human Services at M., an Experimental Program*, brochure, 1973.

32. Greenwood, *Alumnae Magazine*, Fall/Winter 1973.

33. *Report of the President 1973–74*, 6.

34. *Twig*, 1 May 1975.

35. Conversation with R. John Huber, 18 April 1994.

36. *Report of the President 1973–74*, 25.

37. Ibid.

38. Ibid., 6.

39. Minutes, Academic Council, 6 November 1973.

40. Eleanor Hill, "Is Meredith Becoming Merely a Diploma Mill?" *Twig*, 14 February 1974.

41. Minutes, faculty, 16 February 1974.

42. Ibid.

43. Mary Bland Josey to editor, *Twig*, 21 March 1974.

44. Frank Grubbs to editor, *Twig*, 21 March 1974.

45. Conversation with Burris, 20 January 1994.

46. *Report of the President 1973–74*, 6–7.

47. *Twig*, 8 November 1973.

48. Janice Sams, "Helms Selection Not Questioned?" editorial, *Twig*, 21 March 1973.

49. Michael Hall, "M. Tastes Black Experience," *Raleigh Times*, 10 February 1973.

50. Sams, editorial, "BVU Activities Challenging,"*Twig*, 16 February 1973.

51. Sams and Hill, editorial, "Racial Prejudice Noted by BVU," *Twig*, 19 April 1973.

52. Conversation with Burris, 8 February 1994.

53. Ibid.

54. Hill, "Input Needed for Policy Revision," editorial, *Twig*, 27 September 1973.

55. *Twig*, 20 September 1973.

56. *Student Handbook 1996–97*, 77.

57. Maggie Odell, "Cadets Mixed Well," *Twig*, 17 October 1974.

58. Minutes, Board of Trustees, 22 September 1973.

59. Bill Morrison, "Musical's Inexperienced Ensemble Deserves 'Applause,'" *News & Observer* (Raleigh), 8 November 1974.

60. *Report of the President 1973–74*, 4.

61. Minutes, executive committee, Board of Trustees, 15 April 1974.

62. *Report of the President 1973–74*, 14.

63. Ibid., 5–6.

64. Ibid.

65. *Report of the President 1971–72*, 8.

66. Conversation with Burris, 8 February 1994.

67. M.L. Johnson, "M.'s Historical Collection, a Beautiful Reality, *Alumnae Magazine*, Summer 1973, 8.

68. Oliver L. Stringfield to Weems, 1 October 1972.

69. *Twig*, 5 April 1973.

70. *Twig*, 4 May 1973.

71. Rebecca Askew, "Beth Leavel Choreographs Applause," *Twig*, 31 October 1974.

72. Bill Morrison, "Musical's Inexperienced Ensemble Deserves 'Applause,'" *News & Observer* (Raleigh), 8 November 1974.

73. Ibid.

74. A.C. Snow, "Ah, Bread for the Ducks at M.!" *Raleigh Times*, 23 February 1974.

75. Sandra Thomas, "A Challenge for Global Education," *Alumnae Magazine*, Summer 1975, 4–5.

CHAPTER 4

1. Burris, "Treasure in Earthen Vessels," *Meredith*, Fall 1976, 3.

2. Ibid.

3. James M. Wall, editorial, "Carter and the Religion Factor, *Christian Century*, 31 August–7 September 1977, 739–40.

4. Burris, "Treasure in Earthen Vessels," *Meredith*, Fall 1976, 4.

5. Frank Grubbs, "Symbol To Be Recreated," *Twig*, 17 April 1975.

6. Phyllis Burnett, "Will America Recall Ford?" *Twig*, 1 September 1976.

7. Linda Williams, "Jack Ford Applauded at Meredith," *News & Observer* (Raleigh), 9 October 1976.

8. Kim Farlow, "Lancaster Campaigns at Convention," *Twig*, 8 September 1976.

9. Vicki Jayne, "Impulse Takes Two Students to Inauguration," *Twig*, 8 September 1977.

10. Allyn Vogel, "M. Gets Grant for Consciousness Raising Program," *Twig*, 11 September 1975.

11. Sarah Lemmon, conversation with Jonathan Lindsey, archives, taped 17 March 1982.

12. Ibid.

13. Angela Herrin, "Janet Guthrie Describes Turmoil," *News and Observer* (Raleigh), 21 September 1976.

14. Maggie Odell, "RSW and Sports," editorial, *Twig*, 1 September 1976.

15. "Coeds Celebrate Victory," *News & Observer* (Raleigh), 21 September 1973.

16. Ibid.

17. "Symposium on the Future Was a Spring Feature," *Meredith*, Spring 1978, 25.

18. Ibid.

19. Lemmon, conversation with Jonathan Lindsey, archives, taped 6 May 1982.

20. Minutes, Academic Council, 11 January 1977.

21. *Undergraduate Catalogue*, 1994–95, 41–42.

22. Burris to academic administrators, 25 January 1996.

23. *Report of the President 1976–77*, 16–17.

24. Conversation with R. John Huber, 18 April 1994.

25. Ibid.

26. Ibid.

27. M.L. Johnson, *History*, 253.

28. *Report of the President 1975–76*, 17–18.

29. Ibid.

30. *Twig*, 7 September 1978.

31. *Report of the President 1976–77*, 6.

32. Royster Hedgepeth, "The Hazard of Being Who We Are," *Meredith*, Fall 1978, 2–5.

33. Minutes, Board of Trustees, 24 February 1978.

34. Hedgepeth, The Hazard of Being Who We Are, *Meredith*, Fall 1978, 2–5.

35. Minutes, executive committee, Board of Trustees, 18 August 1977.

36. Vivian Keasler, "Harriet Mardre Wainwright Remembered," *Meredith*, Spring 1977, 5–7.

37. M.L. Johnson, *History*, 38.

38. Oliver L. Stringfield to Weems, 1 October 1972.

39. *Meredith College* (newsletter), April 1978, reprinted in *Meredith*, Winter 1981.

40. *Meredith*, Fall 1978, 21.

41. Carolyn Robinson, "The Chapel, a Continuing Challenge," *Meredith*, Winter 1978, 10–11, 30.

42. Marion D. Lark, "From the Inside Out," *Meredith*, Winter 1981, 13–17.

43. Robinson, *Meredith*, Winter 1978, 10.

44. Minutes, executive committee, Board of Trustees, 8 September 1980.

45. R. Frank Poole, "Convention Epilog 1977," *Newsletter, Carolinas-Virginia Region MGA*.

46. Mary Pickett, "CIM Chooses M. as Site of Celebration," *Twig*, 28 September 1978.

47. Valerie Ray, "Area Students Work with Gifted Children," *Twig*, 16 November 1978.

48. *Report of the President 1976–77*, 3.

49. *Meredith*, Fall 1977, 25.

50. Julia C. Bryan, "M. Abroad," *Meredith*, Fall 1977, 3–7.

51. Sandra Thomas, "M. Classroom in Peru," *Meredith*, Fall 1977, 8–10.

52. Ibid.

53. "M. Group Spends Holiday in Cuba, *Meredith*, Winter 1980, 24.

54. *Undergraduate Catalogue 1994–95*, 21.

55. *Report of the President 1976–77*, 16.

56. *Twig*, 3 May 1982.

57. "Alumna to Head Legal Assistants Program," *Meredith*, Winter 1980, 22.

58. *Report of the President 1979–80*, 38–39.

59. *Student Handbook 1996–97*, 99.

60. Ann Pelham, "She Sees Self as 'Generation-Gap-Jumper,'" *News & Observer* (Raleigh), 30 May 1976.

61. Virginia Norton, "Trade In: Old Experiences for New," *Meredith*, Winter 1977, 18.

62. Ibid.

63. Ibid.

64. Minutes, Board of Trustees, 23 September 1977.

65. "Hypocrisy?" guest editorial, *Twig*, 21 September 1978.

66. Susan Felts, "Library Improvements Made," *Twig*, 30 August 1978.

67. "Hypocrisy?" *Twig*, 21 September 1978.

68. Carolyn A. Wallace, untitled address, Friends of the Carlyle Campbell Library, 5 May 1977, M. archives.

69. Julia H. Harris, "Libraries Old and New," *Alumnae Magazine*, Winter 1948, 20.

70. Kristie Beattie, editorial, "Move Cornhuskin'?" *Twig*, 16 November 1978.

71. Ibid.

72. M.L. Johnson, *History*, 170.

73. Sharon Ellis, review, *Alice in Wonderland*, *Twig*, 29 March 1976.

74. M.L. Johnson, *History*, 73.

75. *Twig*, 22 January 1976.

76. Janice Sams, "Spring of Awareness," *Alumnae Magazine*, Summer 1972, 10–11.

77. Beth Wicker, cartoon, *Twig*, 22 September 1977.

78. *1979 Annual*, Baptist State Convention of North Carolina.

79. Minutes, Board of Trustees, 27 February 1976.

80. Minutes, executive committee, Board of Trustees, 21 November 1977.

81. Minutes, executive committee, Board of Trustees, 18 November 1980.

82. Minutes, executive committee, Board of Trustees, 11 August 1980.

83. Minutes, executive committee, Board of Trustees, 18 November 1980.

84. *News & Observer* (Raleigh), 18 September 1980.

85. Faculty to Bailey C. Smith, reprinted in *Meredith*, Winter 1981, 23.

86. Minutes, executive committee, Board of Trustees, 20 January 1977.

87. *Information Please Almanac Atlas and Yearbook 1995*, 836.

88. *Report of the President 1976–77*, 68.

89. Minutes, executive committee, Board of Trustees, 19 January 1976.

90. Caroline Vaught McCall, "Angels Come and Go," *M. Writes Home*, September 1989.

91. *World Almanac 1997*, 507.

92. *Meredith*, Spring 1979, 26.

93. "Campbell's Legacy to Others," *News & Observer*, reprinted in *Twig*, 1 September 1977.

94. Minutes, executive committee, Board of Trustees, 14 April 1980.

95. Burris, "Treasure in Earthen Vessels," *Meredith*, Fall 1976, 3.

CHAPTER 5

1. Susan Gilbert, Ann Kurtz, William Ledford, Dorothy Preston, Evelyn Simmons, interview, "The India Aspect," *Meredith*, Winter 1983, 2–7.

2. Ibid.

3. Ibid.

4. "Indian Ambassador Visits the Campus," *Meredith*, Spring 1983, 25.

5. Lyn Aubrecht, "D.C. Sabbatical," *Meredith*, Winter 1983, 8-10.

6. Minutes, executive committee, Board of Trustees, 17 March 1981.

7. Minutes, faculty, 2 October 1981.

8. William Shakespeare, *Hamlet*, III, i, 142.

9. Betty Webb, tribute to Norma Rose, 26 April, 1996.

10. Lisa Sorrels, "Samson Surprised by Shower," *Twig*, 1 March 1982.

11. Allen Burris, "The Academic Side," *Meredith*, Fall 1982, 3–5.

12. *Report of the President 1983–84*, 28.

13. Minutes, executive committee Board of Trustees, 12 October 1981.

14. *Meredith*, Winter 1982, 17.

15. Kelly Efirt, "Department Given New Residence," *Twig*, 20 September 1982.

16. Linda Sellers, "Frazier Discusses Advantages of New Building," *Twig*, 13 September 1982.

17. Sellers, "St. Mary's Makes Donation," *Twig*, 18 November 1981.

18. Marion D. Lark, "From the Inside Out," *Meredith*, Winter 1981, 13–17.

19. Weems, remarks, Jones Chapel dedication, September 24, 1982.

20. Duke McCall, dedicatory address, Jones Chapel, September 24, 1982, quoted in *Meredith*, Fall 1982, 15.

21. Sellers, "New Pipe Organ Highlights Chapel," *Twig*, 28 March 1983.

22. Donald C. Samson to editor, *Twig*, 28 January 1981.

23. Samson to editor, *Twig*, 29 April 1981.

24. Joe Baker, "Acting on Change," *Meredith*, Fall 1982, 9–10.

25. Ibid.

26. Minutes, executive committee, Board of Trustees, 15 February 1982.

27. "Ellen Ironside on Pulling It All Together," *Meredith*, Spring 1988, 4–8.

28. Ibid.

29. Anne C. Dahle, "Continuing Education, a Way Out for Lillie Lawson-Jones," *Meredith*, Fall 1983, 6–7.

30. Ibid.

31. Ibid.

32. Ibid.

33. *Meredith*, Spring 1983, 1–2.

34. Ibid.

35. M.L. Johnson, *History*, 111.

36. Minutes, faculty, 19 November 1982.

37. *Meredith*, Spring 1983, 1–2.

38. Ibid.

39. Ibid.

40. Weems to Academic Council, 2 October 1982.

41. *Meredith*, Spring 1983, 1–2.

42. Ibid.

43. Minutes, Board of Trustees, 25 February 1983.

44. Burris, "The Academic Side," *Meredith*, Fall 1982, 3–5.

45. President's Message, 1983, 1–26.

46. *Report of the President 1983–84*, 113.

47. Jill Kibler, "Students Experience an Unforgettable Summer," *Twig*, 2 September 1981.

48. Melody West, "Meredith Abroad Provides Fun Summer," *Twig*, 13 September 1982.

49. Conversation with Reginald Shiflett, 18 April 1994.

50. *Meredith*, Fall 1972, 17.

51. Ibid.

52. Advertisement, North Carolina Symphony.

53. Kellie Farlow, "NCSU Not All That Bad," guest editorial, *Twig*, 22 February 1982.

54. *Report of the President 1981–82*.

55. Ann Stringfield, "Rev. R.G. Puckett Speaks on Moral Majority," *Twig*, 23 September 1981.

56. Lisa Sorrels, "Mullins to Speak on Nuclear Power," *Twig*, 22 February 1982.

57. *Meredith*, Summer 1982, 12–13.

58. *Twig*, 28 January 1981.

59. *Report of the President 1981–1982*, 10.

60. Minutes, Board of Trustees, 25 February 1983.

61. *Report of the President 1983–1984*, 36.

62. Ibid., 102.

63. Ibid., 36.

64. Minutes, executive committee, Board of Trustees, 14 February 1983.

65. Minutes, faculty, 17 August 1983.

66. Melody West, "SGA Signs Petition," *Twig*, 9 December 1981.

67. Editorial, "Library or Shrine?" *Twig*, 16 September 1981.

68. President's Message, 1983, 1–26.

69. Edward Hughes Pruden, "From a Pulpit in Washington," *Alumnae Magazine*, Spring 1974, 12–13, 39.

70. "Dangerous Dispute," *Christian Century*, 7–14 January 1981, 8.

71. A. Stringfield, "Puckett Speaks on Moral Majority," *Twig*, 23 September 1981.

72. A. Stringfield, "M. Students Greet Returning Hostages," *Twig*, 4 February 1981.

73. Emily Craig, "Success for M.Girls in WQDR Contest," *Twig*, 15 February 1982.

74. Kathleen McKeel, "A Date with Carlyle?" *Twig*, 4 November 1981.

75. *Twig*, 25 January 1982.

76. *Twig*, 26 April 1982.

77. *Twig*, 22 February 1982.

78. Britt, *Images*, 62.

CHAPTER 6

1. Boyarsky, *Ronald Reagan: His Life and Rise to the Presidency*, 195.

2. Schaller, *Reckoning with Reagan, America and Its President in the 1980s*, 36.

3. Minutes, Academic Council, 10 May 1983.

4. Minutes, Academic Council, 13 September 1983.

5. Ibid.

6. "Professor Emerita Mary Lynch Johnson Dies," *Meredith*, Spring 1984, 1.

7. "'Odyssey' Set for Spring 1985," *Meredith*, Spring 1984, 1.

8. *Report of the President 1984–1985*, 162.

9. Conversation with Mary Johnson, 8 February 1994.

10. *Twig*, 1 April 1985.

11. *Report of the President 1984–1985*, 18.

12. *M.C. Undergraduate Catalogue*, 1996–97, 47.

13. *Catalogue 1899–1900*, Baptist Female University, 45.

14. *Twig*, 7 October 1985.

15. Minutes, Board of Trustees, 28 September 1984.

16. *Graduate Program Analysis and Evaluation*, February 1985, 2.

17. Ibid., 30.

18. *Report of the President 1984–1985*, 54.

19. Minutes, Board of Trustees, 22 February 1985.

20. Jennifer Bruffey, "M.C. Democrats Coming on Strong," *Twig*, 9 September 1985.

21. *Twig*, 23 September 1985.

22. Beth Blankenship, "Is Buckling Up Better?" *Twig*, 11 October 1985.

23. Cynthia Church, "'Big Brother' System Cuts Students Off from the World," *Twig*, 2 September 1985.

24. Blankenship, "Give Me Privacy or Give Me No Phone," *Twig*, 2 September 1985.

25. *Report of the President 1984–85*, 183.

26. *Report of the President 1983–1984*, 185.

27. Ibid., 167.

28. Jenny Beavers, "Shaken by Divorce?" *Twig*, 18 March 1985.

29. Carolyn Carter, address, junior class ring dinner, 16 November 1995.

30. Annette Gregory, *Twig*, 17 November 1977.

31. *Meredith Herald*, 1 November 1995.

32. Emily Pool Aumiller to editor, *Meredith*, Winter 1985, cover 2.

33. Amos Bronson Alcott, "The Teacher," Orphic Sayings [1840].

34. Phyllis Trible, tribute to Ralph E. McLain, 30 August 1977.

35. *Meredith*, Winter 1989.

36. M.L. Johnson, *History*, 335.

37. *Declaration of Independence*, 4 July 1776.

38. *Report of the President 1984–1985*, 9.

39. *Raleigh Times*, 16 November 1984.

40. *Meredith*, Fall 1982, 18.

41. Laura W. Harrill to select alumnae, reprinted in *Meredith*, Winter 1984, 27.

42. "Dorothy Gillespie Brings Her Sculpture to M." *Meredith*, Winter 1984, 5.

43. Ibid.

44. *Report of the President 1984–1985*, 9.

45. Cathy Manning, "Problems Arise with Art Building," *Twig*, 7 October 1985.

46. Minutes, Board of Trustees, 22 February 1985.

47. Minutes, faculty affairs committee, 22 February 1985.

48. Minutes, Academic Council, 8 February 1983.

49. Linda Cheek, "Calendar to Feature State Men," *Twig*, 26 September 1983.

50. Ibid.

51. Susan Harris, "Bear Spotted on M. Campus," *Twig*, 25 November 1985.

52. Ibid.

53. Minutes, executive committee, Board of Trustees, 12 August 1985.

54. *Raleigh Times*, December 1985.

55. *Biblical Recorder*, 21 December 1985.

56. *Meredith*, Summer 1986, 32.

57. Jenny West, "On Tour! The M. Chorale," *Twig*, 11 November 1985.

58. *Report of the President 1984–1995*, 15.

59. *Report of the President 1983–1984*, 175–76.

60. Ibid.

CHAPTER 7

1. Anne Saker, "A Female Minister's 30-Year Path of Righteousness," *News & Observer* (Raleigh), 8 August 1994.

2. Ibid.
3. Ibid.
4. Ibid.
5. Randall Lolley, "Last at the Cross—First at the Tomb," convocation address, Southeastern Baptist Theological Seminary, published in *Biblical Recorder*, 15 September 1984, 3.
6. Ibid. 8.
7. Minutes, executive committee, Board of Trustees, 15 April 1985.
8. Minutes, executive committee, Board of Trustees, 18 November 1985.
9. Ibid.
10. Weems, *A Matter of Importance*, 15 September 1986, 2.
11. Ibid., 5.
12. Ibid., 9–10.
13. Minutes, Board of Trustees, 26 September 1986.
14. Ibid.
15. Weems, transcribed telephone conversation with Bernice Sandler, 31 October 1985.
16. Renee Keever, "Special Report: Trustees Vote Women Only in Graduate programs," *Meredith*, Summer 1986, 1–5.
17. Minutes, executive committee, Board of Trustees, 18 November 1986.
18. Minutes, executive committee, Board of Trustees, 28 February 1986.
19. Keever, "Special Report," *Meredith*, Summer 1986, 1–5.
20. Betsy Short, "Demonstration Expresses Student, Faculty, Alumnae Discontent," *M. Herald*, 15 March 1986.
21. Page Leist, "Grad Studies Department Heads Comment on Admittance of Males Issue," *M. Herald*, 22 March 1986.
22. Ibid.
23. Ibid.
24. Minutes, executive committee, Board of Trustees, 14 April 1986.
25. Minutes, executive committee, Board of Trustees, 12 May 1986.

CHAPTER 8
1. *New York Public Library Desk Reference*, 1989, s.v. "Important Dates in American History," 738.
2. *M. Herald*, 7 November 1986.
3. *Annual Report*, 1988, 35.
4. Thomas Moore, "Oh, Call It by Some Better Name," *Ballads and Songs*, 1.
5. Renee Keever, "Jimmy Carter Comes to M.: A Day to Remember," *Meredith*, Fall 1986, 6.
6. Ibid., 5.
7. Jimmy Carter, press conference, 11 September 1986, Casette A, 4.1.6, Carlyle Campbell Library.
8. Ibid.
9. Ibid.
10. Ibid.
11. Keever, "Jimmy Carter Comes to M.," *Meredith*, Fall 1986, 2, 4.
12. Lewis Grizzard, "Carter's the Guy to Disconnect Falwell's Hotline to Heaven," *News & Observer* (Raleigh), 28 September 1986.
13. Linda Sellers, editorial, "But Where Are the People?" *Twig*, 27 September 1982.
14. Ibid.
15. Cynthia Church, editorial, "Resources Available but Worship Services Denied," *M. Herald*, 28 February 1986.
16. *Twig*, 2 February 1978.
17. Maggie Odell to editor, *Twig*, 23 February 1978.
18. Sonya Ammons, editorial, "Newspaper Title Evaluated," *Twig*, 25 March 1981.
19. Mary Beth Smith to editor, *Twig*, 23 February 1978.
20. Church, editorial, "When the Growing Gets Tough, the Tough Get Growing," *Twig*, 25 November 1985.
21. Ibid.
22. Beth Blankenship, "Change!", editorial, *Twig*, 25 November 1985.
23. Minutes, executive committee, Board of Trustees, 17 November 1986.
24. "Gaddy-Hamrick Art Center Begins to Take Shape," *Meredith*, Summer 1986, 42.
25. Jo Hodges, "Gaddy-Hamrick Hosts First Art Show," *M. Herald*, 20 April 1987.
26. Ibid.
27. Amber Burris, "M.'s First Lady," *M. Herald*, 16 October 1987.
28. *Meredith*, Winter 1988, 14.
29. Keever, "A Center for Women in Art," *Meredith*, Fall 1987.
30. Minutes, executive committee, Board of Trustees, 10 August 1987.
31. Conversation with LaRose Spooner, 13 December 1993.
32. *Meredith*, Spring 1988, 21.
33. Ibid.
34. Minutes, faculty, 18 August 1987.
35. "Ellen Ironside on Pulling It All Together," *Meredith*, Spring 1988, 5.

36. *Annual Report 1988*, 58–59,

37. *Meredith*, Spring 1988, 14–15.

38. *Annual Report 1988*, 35.

39. Minutes, executive committee, Board of Trustees, 23 September 1988.

40. Minutes, executive committee, Board of Trustees, 14 September 1987.

41. Conversation with Gwendolyn Clay, 18 April 1994.

42. Anne Pugh, "A Social Perspective," *Meredith*, Summer 1988, 5.

43. *Undergraduate Catalogue 1993–94*, 62.

44. Ibid.

45. *Annual Report*, September 1987, 60.

46. *Undergraduate Catalogue 1994–95*, 57.

47. Minutes, Academic Council, 18 January 1988.

48. *Annual Report 1988*, 33.

49. Catalogue 1899–1900, BFU, 45.

50. Conversation with Donald Spanton, 13 April 1994.

51. Ibid.

52. Conversation with Allen Page, 24 January 1994.

53. Becky Butts, "New Foreign Languages Head Hopes to Revitalize Program, *M. Herald*, 4 December 1987.

54. Conversation with Burgunde Winz, 13 April 1994.

55. Conversation with Virginia Knight, 21 April 1994.

56. Ibid.

57. *Annual Report*, September 1987, 64.

58. President's Message 1986.

59. *M. Herald*, 13 September 1988.

60. Cara Lynn Croom, "Opening Convocation Begins New Year with a Bang," *M. Herald*, 7 September 1988.

61. *Meredith*, Winter 1988, 19.

62. *Meredith*, Winter 1989, 7.

63. Conversation with Burgunde Winz, 13 April 1994.

64. American Association of University Professors, Southeastern Baptist Theological Seminary, press release, 22 October 1987.

65. Minutes, faculty, called meeting, 30 October 1987.

66. President's Message, 15 September 1986, 8–9.

67. Minutes, faculty, 20 February 1987.

68. Minutes, finance committee, Board of Trustees, 25 September 1987.

69. Minutes, executive committee, Board of Trustees, 16 November 1987.

70. Ibid.

71. *Meredith*, Summer 1988, 7.

72. Ibid.

73. Ibid.

74. *Annual Report*, 1986, 147–48.

75. Ibid., 151.

76. *Annual Report*, 1988, 159.

77. Minutes, executive committee, Board of Trustees, 10 February 1986.

78. Kim Allen, " 'Bee Hive' Becomes Ode to Senior Class," *M. Herald*, 14 April 1986.

79. *Meredith*, Winter 1988, 16–17.

80. Ibid.

81. Ibid., 23.

82. "Fall Courses Focus on the Constitution, *Meredith*, Winter 1988, 3.

83. M.L. Johnson, *History*, 135.

84. Casey Bass, "New Image for Stunt," *M. Herald*, 23 January 1987.

85. *Annual Report*, September 1987, 85.

86. Angie Stroud, "Meredith Receives Prestigious Award," *M. Herald*, 4 December 1987.

87. "Tarheel of the Week," *News & Observer* (Raleigh), December 1987.

88. *Meredith*, Spring 1988, 8.

89. Susan Worley, "Holocaust Commemoration in Jones," *M. Herald*, 8 November 1988, 6.

90. Carol Brooks, "Margaret Person Currin: From Meredith Graduate to U.S. Attorney," *M. Herald*, 1 April 1988.

91. *U.S. News & World Report*, 10 October 1988, C20.

92. Ibid.

93. *News & Observer* (Raleigh), 30 October 1988.

94. *Meredith*, Winter 1989.

95. Ibid.

CHAPTER 9

1. *Report of the President's Task Force for the Pursuit of Excellence*, January 1989, 42.

2. Ibid. 3.

3. Ibid.

4. Ibid., 6–7.

5. *Meredith*, Winter 1989, 3.

6. "Egbert Davis Presents Gift of Ceremonial Mace," *Meredith*, Winter 1990, 18.

7. Ibid.

8. *Meredith*, Winter 1990, 18.

9. Conversation with Gwendolyn Clay, 18 April 1994.

10. Conversation with Louise Taylor, 12 April 1994.

11. Jeannine Manning, "Meredith Students Stage Sit-In in Support," *M. Herald*, 27 February 1990.

12. Ibid.

13. Ibid.

14. *Annual Report*, Student Development, 1990, 112–13.

15. Susan Gilbert to editor, *M. Herald*, 27 February 1990.

16. President's Message, August 1990, 29.

17. Ibid.

18. *Annual Report*, Student Development, August 1990, 120.

19. *Annual Report*, Administrative Affairs, 1989, 28.

20. *Report of the Task Force for the Pursuit of Excellence*, 11.

21. *Annual Report*, Business and Finance, September 1990, 65.

22. *Meredith*, Winter 1990, 15.

23. *Meredith*, Spring 1979, 24.

24. Allen Burris to personnel committee, Board of Trustees, 6 January 1989.

25. President's Message, August 1990, 3.

26. *Annual Report*, Academics, September 1990, 22.

27. *Meredith Herald*, 3 April 1990.

28. Ibid.

29. *Meredith*, Winter 1989, 7.

30. Ibid.

31. "Briefing," Jane Goodall Institute, as reprinted in *Meredith*, Fall 1990, 2.

32. Carolyn Robinson, "'Gombe 30': an Anniversary," *Meredith*, Fall 1990, 3.

33. *Meredith*, Fall 1990, 8.

34. Ibid.

35. *Annual Report*, Academics, September 1990, 38–39.

36. Carol Sessoms, "Publications Board Explains Plan for Academic Credit," *M. Herald*, 5 December 1989.

37. *Meredith*, Winter 1990, 20.

38. *Report of the President's Task Force for the Pursuit of Excellence*, 11.

39. *Annual Report*, Business and Finance, 1990, 70.

40. *Meredith*, Winter 1990, 25.

41. *Annual Report*, Student Development, 1989, 144.

42. *Annual Report*, Business and Finance, 1989, 100.

43. *Meredith*, Winter 1990, 22–23.

44. *Annual Report*, Business and Finance, 1989, 105.

45. Weems, *Christian Dimensions*, September 1989.

46. *Annual Report*, Student Development, 1994–95, 6.

47. Janie Mullis, "IHOM=International House of M., *M. Herald*, 27 August 1990.

48. Krista Holloman, "Inaugural Weekend for College Republicans," *M. Herald*, 31 January 1989.

49. Kym Spell, "A Class of Champions," *M. Herald*, 1 October 1990.

50. *Annual Report*, Academics, 1989, 40.

51. *M. Herald*, 13 February 1990.

52. *Report of the President's Task Force for the Pursuit of Excellence*, 11.

53. Minutes, executive committee, Board of Trustees, 3 March 1989.

54. *Annual Report*, 1990, 41.

55. *Annual Report*, Student Development, 1990, 132.

56. *Annual Report*, 1990, 11.

57. *Annual Report*, Academics, 1989, 49.

58. *Annual Report*, 1990, 11.

59. *Student Handbook 1996–97*, 63.

60. *Annual Report*, Academics, 1990, 32.

61. Marlea Doane, "Meredith Recycling Efforts Reported," *M. Herald*, 13 February 1990.

62. *Annual Report*, Academics, 1990, 37.

63. Ibid., 39.

64. *Annual Report*, 1990, 27–28.

65. Ibid.

66. Jayne Potter, "Accreditation Team Evaluates College," *M. Herald*, 5 December 1989.

67. Minutes, executive committee, Board of Trustees, 28 November 1989.

68. *Report of the President's Task Force for the Pursuit of Excellence*, 23.

CHAPTER 10

1. Carolyn C. Robinson, "Diary of a Decision, Meredith and North Carolina Baptists," *Meredith*, Spring 1991, 9.

2. Ibid.

3. Ibid.

4. Ibid.

5. Ibid.

6. Gerald Johnson, "Meredith: a 'Gone Gosling,'" *News & Observer* (Raleigh), October 1944.

7. Weems, Founders' Day remarks, 25 February 1996.

8. Ibid.

9. Robinson, "Diary," *Meredith*, Spring 1991, 9.

10. Ibid.

11. Eugene Watterson to John Weems, 21 February 1991.

12. Weems, Founders' Day remarks, 1996.

13. Ibid.

14. Minutes, Board of Trustee, 22 February 1991.

15. Addendum, Minutes, Board of Trustees, 22 February 1991.

16. Robinson, "Diary," *Meredith*, Spring 1991, 10.

17. Ibid., 11.

18. *Meredith*, Spring 1991, cover 2.

19. Ibid.

20. Ibid.

21. Ibid.

22. "Meredith Out of the Fray," editorial, *News & Observer* (Raleigh), 26 February 1991.

23. Ibid.

24. Weems, Founders' Day remarks, 1996.

25. Jean Jackson, Founders' Day remarks, 1992, reprinted in *Meredith*, Spring 1992, 3.

26. Ruth Schmidt, as printed in *Meredith*, Spring 1992, 9.

27. Britt, *Images,* 126.

28. Jackson, "Pilgrimage to a New Century," *Meredith*, Spring 1992, 11.

29. Ibid.

30. Ibid.

31. Ibid.

32. *Meredith*, Spring 1991, 20.

33. Ibid.

34. Britt, "The Fine Art of Print Making," *Meredith*, Winter 1991, 3.

35. Jackson, "Pilgrimage," *Meredith*, Spring 1992, 11.

36. Ibid.

37. President's Message, 1991.

38. Jessica Cook, "White Iris Considered a 'Big Time' by Students, *M. Herald*, 20 November 1991.

39. Britt, "The Centennial's Essential Quintessential Woman," *Meredith*, Spring 1982, 4.

40. Ibid.

41. Britt, *Images,*1.

42. Minutes, executive committee, Board of Trustees, 10 February 1992.

43. Jackson, "Pilgrimage," *Meredith*, Spring 1992, 13.

44. Ibid.

45. *Biblical Recorder* (Quotation from editor, 1800's).

CHAPTER 11

1. Rebecca Murray, "What Shall I Make of Myself? A Glimpse into the Lives of the Immortal Ten," manuscript, 1994, 4, M. archives..

2. Ibid. 23–27.

3. Ibid., 15–16.

4. Ibid., 28–29.

5. Hebrews 12:1–2 KJV

6. *The One Volume Bible Commentary*, J.R. Dummelow, Ed., 1028.

7. President's Message, 1992, 15–16.

8. Minutes, Board of Trustees, 27 February 1991.

9. *Meredith*, Winter 1992, 25.

10. Conversation with Bernard Cochran, 12 April 1994.

11. Conversation with Marie Chamblee, 20 April 1994.

12. Ibid.

13. Ibid.

14. Anne Pugh, "Trouble in Georgia," *Meredith*, Spring 1993, 10.

15. *M. Herald*, 25 March 1991.

16. President's Message, 1991, 68.

17. Minutes, faculty, 13 August 1991.

18. *Meredith*, Spring 1993, 9.

19. Ibid.

20. Ibid.

21. *Meredith*, Fall 1992, 11–12.

22. Minutes, faculty, 4 March 1993.

23. Robinson, "Political Climate Forecast: Warm and Partly Women," *Meredith*, Spring 1993, 17–22.

24. Ibid., 17

25. Ibid.

26. Ibid., 18.

27. Ibid., 21.

28. Ibid., 19.

29. Ibid., 20.

30. Ibid., 21.

31. Ibid, 22.

32. Sandra Thomas, "Having a Ball at the President's Inaugural," *Meredith*, Spring 1993, 23–24.

33. Ibid.

34. Ibid.

35. Kelly Phillips, Beth Lowry, "Point/Counterpoint," *M. Herald*, 21 October 1992.

36. Ibid.

37. Traci Latta and Tracy Rawls, "Hillary Clinton Stresses the College Student Vote," *M. Herald*, 30 September 1992.

38. *The New York Times 1998 Almanac*, John W. Wright, Ed., s.v. U.S. Hisory, 79.

39. *Angels Aware*, Fall 1990.

40. President's Message, 1993, 1.

41. Ibid.

42. Ibid., 21.

43. Ibid.

44. Karen Howell, "Meredith Co-Sponsors Event to Encourage Women in Math," *M. Herald*, 10 February 1993, 6.

45. Ibid.

46. *Meredith*, Fall 1992, 15–16.

47. *Meredith*, Winter 1993, 3.

48. Weems, "Endangered Species," *Meredith*, Summer 1993, 3.

49. Minutes, Board of Trustees, 25 September 1993.

50. Minutes, executive committee, Board of Trustees, 23 November 1992.

51. Minutes, executive committee, Board of Trustees, 8 February 1993.

52. Ibid.

53. Ibid.

54. Ibid.

55. Julia Haskett with Cynthia Edwards, "Gulf War Support Services," *M. Herald*, 18 February 1991.

56. Julie Smith, "Chinese Reps to Visit M.," *M. Herald*, 23 September 1992.

57. President's Message, 1991, 43.

58. "Meredith Announces New Christian Lectureship," News Release, 26 March 1992.

59. President's Message, 1991, 21.

60. Ibid., 21.

61. President's Message, 1991, 21.

62. Minutes, Academic Council, 10 December 1991.

63. Ibid.

64. Sonali Kolhatkar, "Council Makes Decision on Cornhuskin' Issue," *M. Herald*, 21 October 1992.

65. Amity Brown, "Cornhuskin' Launched by Record Attendance at Bonfire," *M. Herald*, 4 November 1992.

66. Brown, "New Dimension Added to Cornhuskin'," *M. Herald*, 4 November 1992.

67. Brown, editorial, *M. Herald*, 11 November 1992.

68. *M. Herald*, 22 April 1991.

69. *Oak Leaves 1993*, 38.

70. Janie Mullis, "ARA Services Become Good Samaritan," *M. Herald*, 8 April 1991.

71. Ibid.

72. *M. Herald*, 14 January 1991.

73. President's Message, 1991, 77.

74. *M. Herald*, 16 September 1993.

75. Alfred, Lord Tennyson, "Locksley Hall."

76. *Meredith*, Fall 1992, 12.

77. *Child Care for the Meredith College Campus: A Comprehensive Report*, April 1987.

78. President's Message, August 1991, 53–54.

79. *Meredith*, Fall 1992, 12.

80. President's Message, 1993, 16.

81. Minutes, executive committee, Board of Trustees, 13 April 1992.

82. Minutes, faculty, 2 October 1992.

83. Rawls, "SGA To Sponsor Faculty Appreciation Day," *M. Herald*, 10 February 1993.

84. *M. Herald*, 8 September 1993.

CHAPTER 12

1. Anne Pugh, "At Home With Computers," *Meredith*, Fall 1993, 16.

2. Ibid.

3. Ibid., 14–15.

4. Ibid, 15.

5. Ibid.

6. Ibid.

7. Ibid.

8. Ibid.

9. President's Message, 1993, 13.

10. *Meredith*, Winter 1993, 1.

11. *M. Herald*, 15 November 1995.

12. "M. Goes Plastic: Introducing . . . CamCard," *Meredith*, Winter 1993, 4.

13. Minutes, executive committee, Board of Trustees, 14 November 1994.

14. Ibid.

15. Traci Latta, "The Star of the Scene: Ben Vereen," *Meredith*, Spring 1994, 13.

16. *Meredith*, Spring 1994, 5.

17. Ibid., 6.

18. D.H. Johnson, "From Classroom to Boardroom," *Meredith*, Spring 1994, 12.

19. Robinson, "Laura Harrill: Philanthropist Cum Laude," *Meredith*, Fall 1994, 9.

20. Ibid.

21. Ibid.

22. D.H. Johnson, "The Winning Campaign," *Meredith*, Fall 1994, 14.

23. *Meredith*, Summer 1994, 1.

24. D.H. Johnson, "The Winning Campaign," *Meredith*, Fall 1994, 14.

25. *Meredith*, Fall 1992, 12.

26. Chuck Twardy, "The Cost of the Triumph of Tradition," *News & Observer* (Raleigh), 6 March 1994.

27. Ibid.

28. President's Message, 1994, 8.

29. Jeannie Morelock, "Special Notice to the Meredith Community," 10 January 1994.

30. Minutes, executive committee, Board of Trustees, 24 September 1993.

31. Minutes, executive committee, Board of Trustees, 11 April 1994.

32. Ibid.

33. Minutes, executive committee, Board of Trustees, 22 August 1994.

34. President's Message, 1995.

35. *Meredith*, Spring 1980, 30.

36. Conversation with Rebecca Bailey, 25 April 1994.

37. Lou S. Liverman, "M. VP Chosen to Lead Converse College, *Meredith*, Spring 1994, 17.

38. *M. Herald*, 13 April 1994.

39. *Meredith*, Fall 1994, 4.

40. Christina Peoples, "New VP for Student Development Steps Up to Bat," *M. Herald*, 25 August 1994.

41. *New York Times Almanac*, John W. Wright, Ed., 81.

42. Minutes, executive committee, Board of Trustees, 22 August 1994.

43. Jessica Cook, editorial, *M. Herald*, 11 November 1991.

44. Minutes, Board of Trustees, 23 February 1994.

45. Weems to trustees, 25 August 1994.

46. Ibid.

47. Elizabeth Rihani, "Youth Today," *M. Herald*, 3 November 1993.

48. D.H. Johnson, "From Classroom to Boardroom," *Meredith*, Spring 1994, 10–12.

CHAPTER 13

1. *Meredith*, Winter 1991, 19.

2. Topor and Volkmann, *Marketing Higher Education*, foreword.

3. Robinson, "To Market, To Market . . . " *Meredith*, Summer 1992, 2.

4. Ibid., 4.

5. Weems to faculty and staff, 7 February 1995.

6. Weems to department heads, 31 January 1995.

7. Weems to department heads, 3 February 1995.

8. Ibid.

9. *Biblical Recorder*, 18 February 1995, 1.

10. Weems to department heads, 14 February 1995.

11. Weems to students, 14 February 1995.

12. Nina I. McClellan to editor, *News & Observer* (Raleigh), February 1995.

13. Cynthia Griffith McEnery to editor, *M. Herald*, 15 February 1995.

14. Alumnae Association executive committee to Board of Trustees, 24 February 1995.

15. Minutes, called meeting, executive committee, Board of Trustees, 13 March 1995.

16. Minutes, executive committee, Board of Trustees, 21 August 1995.

17. Minutes, called meeting (executive session), executive committee, Board of Trustees, 22 September 1995.

18. President's Message, 1995, 5.

19. Jerod Kratzer and Deborah Smith to faculty, 19 September 1995.

20. Minutes, faculty, 6 October 1995.

21. LaRose F. Spooner to John E. Weems, report of enrollment management team, 1993–94.

22. Sue Kearney to the Board of Trustees, 23 February 1994.

23. Minutes, faculty, 15 August 1995.

24. Debbi Sykes, "Enrollment Jump Delights Meredith," *News & Observer* (Raleigh), 19 July 1995, 1A.

25. Ibid., 9A.

26. President's Message, 1995, 28–29.

27. *Meredith*, Spring 1995, 2–3.

28. Ibid.

29. Minutes, Academic Council, 1 March 1983.

30. Attachment to minutes, executive committee, Board of Trustees, 11 September 1995.

31. Carol Swink, "After Five Comes Alive," *M. Herald*, 25 October 1995.

32. *Meredith*, Fall 1995, 6.

33. Weems, "President's Corner," *Meredith*, Spring 1996, 3.

34. Ibid.

35. *Meredith*, Spring 1995, 3.

36. *Meredith*, Fall 1995, 5–6.

37. *M. Herald*, 26 April 1995.

38. Michael Novak to M. community, 21 August 1995.

39. Ibid.

40. *Meredith*, Fall 1995, 7.

41. Sara Rimer, "At Harvard, Lovers of Beauty Sing a Collective Ode to Keats," *New York Times*, 11 September 1995.

42. Ibid.

43. Ibid.

44. Ibid.

45. *Meredith*, Fall 1995, 7.

46. Ibid.

47. Ibid.

48. Kim Highland, "First Year Experience Is Destined To Be a Great Hit," *M. Herald*, 30 August 1995.

49. D.H. Johnson, "The New Voice of Experience," *Meredith*, Spring 1995, 5.

50. President's Message, 1995, 22.

51. Ibid.

52. John Kincheloe, "Science Fiction?" *Friends of the Carlyle Campbell Library*, Fall 1995.

53. President's Message, 1995, 22.

54. Minutes, Board of Trustees, 28 February 1992.

55. Shannon Batts, "MIA Brings Diversity to Campus," *M. Herald*, 25 October 95.

56. Anne Pugh, "A Woman of Vision," *Meredith*, Spring 1995, 6.

57. *M. Herald*, 19 January 1994.

58. Minutes, Board of Trustees, 22 September 1995.

59. President's Message, 1995, 31.

60. Ibid.

61. *Biblical Recorder*, 26 November 1994, 4.

62. Ibid.

63. *Meredith*, Summer 1995, 2.

64. Christina Peoples, "Hull Lecturer Brings Message of Peace to Meredith," *M. Herald*, 5 April 1995.

65. Debbie Doss, "Communication is Major Mid-East Problem," *Twig*, 5 February 1976.

66. Ibid.

67. Facilities services department to faculty and staff, 2 August 1995.

68. *M. Herald*, 15 November 1995.

69. Clarky Lucas, "Nooe Expresses Vision for Raleigh," *M. Herald*, 13 September 1995.

70. Donna L. Fowler-Merchant, "The M. Connection," *Meredith*, Fall 1995, 12–13.

71. Ibid., 14.

72. *Meredith*, Summer 1995, 1.

73. Minutes, faculty, 16 February 1996.

74. David Van Biema, *Time*, 22 August 1994, 61.

75. Pat Wingert, "Oh, To Be a Knob!" *Newsweek*, 28 August 1995. 22.

76. Amy Bernstein, " 'Shannon Faulkner Should Have Come Here,' " *U.S. News & World Report*, 22 August 1994, 6.

77. Marc Peyser, "Sounding Retreat," *Newsweek*, 28 August 1995, 38.

78. Traci Latta, editorial, "Women at the Citadel," *M. Herald*, 19 January 1994.

79. Wendy Kelly, editorial, "Who's Laughing Now?" *M. Herald*, 13 September 1995.

80. Kimberly Zucker, "Meredith's Cat Team's Cat Trap Is Missing," *M. Herald*, 1 February 1995.

81. Ibid.

82. Ibid.

83. Heather Blake, "Why I Chose Meredith College," *M. College Viewbook*, 1994–95, 12.

84. Betsy L. Cochrane, "The Circle of Spirituality and Intellectual Discovery," commencement address, *Meredith*, Summer 1995, 6–7.

85. "Fall Commencement Draws Overflow Crowd," *Meredith*, Spring 1996, 4.

86. Suzanne Britt, "I'm Nobody. Who Are You?" commencement address, 16 December 1995.

CHAPTER 14

1. M.L. Johnson, *History*, 7.

2. Cynthia Barnett, "A New Degree of Equality," *News & Observer* (Raleigh), 11 July 1997, 1A, 14A.

3. Ibid.

4. Ibid.

5. "Committed to the Arts," *Meredith*, Fall 1997, 8–9.

6. Ibid.

7. Ibid.

8. Ibid.

9. Ibid.

10. *Nutshell*, March 1997.

11. Anne Pugh, "Making a Difference," *Meredith*, Summer 1997, 1–2.

12. Ibid.

13. Weems, "M. Creates Award Winning Math Mentoring Program," *Initiative 2000*, February 1996.

14. Ibid.

15. Mary Sharpe, "Angels for the Environment," *M. Herald*, 4 September 1996.

16. *Meredith*, Spring 1997, 7.

17. Converse Survey Reports, *M. Herald*, 20 November 1996.

18. Clyde Frazier, "78% of Resident Students Registered," *M. Herald*, 23 October 1996.

19. Frazier, "Will M. Lead the Nation in Voting?" *M. Herald*, 4 September 1996.

20. Carey Gore, "Frazier 96 in '96 Volunteers Pleased With Voter Turnout," *M. Herald*, 20 November 1996.

21. Ibid.

22. Frazier, "M. Challenged to Lead the Nation in Elections," *M. Herald*, 18 September 1996.

23. Converse Survey Reports, *M. Herald*, 20 November 1996.

24. *In a Nutshell*, March 1997.

25. Jeannie Morelock, "An Interview With President John E. Weems Regarding Recent Actions Taken by the Meredith Board of Trustees," *Meredith*, Spring 1997, 3–4.

26. *Biblical Recorder*, 2 August 1997.

27. Ibid.

28. Weems, "New Relationship with Baptist State Convention," *Meredith*, Fall 1997, 25.

29. *Meredith*, Spring 1998, 4.

30. Sue Kearney, "Challenges to Enrollment," *Angels Aware*, Spring 1996.

31. *Annual Report*, Marketing, 1996–97.

32. Employee Newsletter, November 1996.

33. LaRose Spooner to Board of Trustees, 9 May 1997.

34. "New Fitness Center Named After Alumna," *Meredith*, Summer 1996, 6.

35. D.H. Johnson, "The Center of Attention," *Meredith*, Summer 1996, 6.

36. Ibid.

37. *Nutshell*, September 1997.

38. D.H. Johnson, "The Center of Attention," *Meredith*, Summer 1996, 6.

39. Ibid.

40. M.L. Johnson, *History*, 415.

41. *Meredith*, Summer 1997, 9.

42. *Friends of the Carlyle Campbell Library*, Spring 1998.

43. Employee Newsletter, October 1996.

44. *Annual Report*, Business and Finance, 1996–97, 12.

45. Employee Newsletter, October 1996.

46. *Meredith*, Fall 1996, 9.

47. *Meredith*, Fall 1997, 14.

48. Ibid.

49. Conversation with Gwendolyn Clay, 28 May 1998.

50. Minutes, faculty, 15 August 1996.

51. Rosemary Hornak, "Capstone Course Development Grants Awarded," *Nutshell*, February 1998.

52. Allen Page, "New Majors," *Nutshell*, April 1997.

53. *M. Herald*, 30 October 1996.

54. Sharon Cannon, "New Technology for Disabled Students," *M. Writes Home*, October 1997.

55. Courtney Lancaster, "Tour the M. Intranet—a Great Way to Communicate, Conserve Paper and Stay Informed," *Nutshell*, September 1997.

56. Dina DiMaio, "Turn to Wake Up M. on MCTV," *M. Herald*, 5 February 1997.

57. Addie Tschamler, "MCTV Entertains and Informs with 'Wake Up Meredith,'" *M. Herald*, 19 February 1997.

58. "Travel Adventures Sponsors NYC Trip," *Meredith*, Spring 1996.

59. *Nutshell*, December 1997/January 1998.

60. *Continuing Education at M.*, Fall 1997.

61. *Continuing Education at M.*, Spring 1998.

62. Ibid.

63. Charles Taylor, "Initiative 2000 Sets Sights on Long-Range Plans," *Nutshell*, June/July 1997.

64. *Annual Report*, Business and Finance, 1996–97.

65. Emily Fulghum, "After Ten Years, Writing Center Improves Options," *M. Herald*, 19 February 1997.

66. Nan Miller, "The Learning Center: One Stop Shopping for Academic Success," *M. Writes Home*, October 1997.

67. Ibid.

68. Minutes, Board of Trustees 14 February 1997.

69. *Annual Report*, Business and Finance, 1996–97.

70. Charles Taylor to John Weems, 11 February 1997.

71. *M. Herald*, 18 February 1998.

72. "M. Announces new Scholarships and Gifts," *Meredith*, Spring 1998, 4.

73. *Nutshell*, April 1997.

74. Minutes, Board of Trustees, 23 February 1996.

75. Ibid.

76. Ibid.

77. Brandi Bettis, interview with Jean Jackson and Erica Balmer, "Extension of Open House Visitation Policy: A Discussion," *M. Writes Home*, September 1996.

78. Erica Balmer, "N.C. SGA Presidents Meet with Governor," *Nutshell*, February 1997.

79. Betsy Stewart, "Good Idea Turns Into a Major Art Show," *M. Herald*, 6 December 1995.

80. Louise Taylor, "Searching for Hugh: The M. Connection," Founders' Day address, 23 February 1998.

81. D.H. Johnson, "Lost in the Rain Forest," *Meredith*, Spring 1996, 7.

82. Kat Allen, "Dr. Wade Davis Delivers Honors Convocation," *M. Herald*, 1 October 1997.

83. Beth Hall, "Visiting Lecturer Doug Adams Connects Religion and Art," *M. Herald*, 1 October 1997.

84. Wendy Kelly, "Tennis Team Receives National Ranking," *M. Herald*, 7 February 1996.

85. Weems, M. Athletic Programs Boast National Rankings," *Initiative 2000*, February 1996.

86. *M. Herald*, 30 October 1996.

87. D.H. Johnson, "Operation Toy Box," *Meredith*, Fall 1997, 1–2.

88. Pugh, "Continuity and Change," *Meredith*, Spring 1997, 5.

89. Nicole Brodeur, "Her Bald Head's No Island," *News & Observer* (Raleigh), 19 September 1997, 1D.

90. Ted Waller, "Australian Journey," *Friends of the Carlyle Campbell Library*, Fall 1997.

91. *Meredith*, Fall 1997, 10.

92. *Meredith*, Summer 1996, 6.

93. Weems, "M. Outsources Bookstore Management," *Initiative 2000*, February 1996.

94. *M. Herald*, 6 November 1996.

95. Taylor, "Initiative 2000 Review Team Appointed," *Nutshell*, April/May 1998.

96. Taylor, "Initiative 2000 Sets Sights on Long-Range Plan," *Nutshell*, June/July 1997.

97. Matthew Eisley, "Legendary Professor at Meredith Dies," *News & Observer* (Raleigh), 7 April 1996, 15.

98. Taylor, "The Loss of a Friend," *Meredith*, Summer 1997, 25.

99. Steve Swindell, "Collision South of Louisburg Kills Two," *News & Observer* (Raleigh), 17 November 1997, 1B, 5B.

100. Ibid.

101. *Nutshell*, March 1998.

102. Ibid.

103. Ibid.

104. *Biblical Recorder* (Raleigh), 19 July 1997, 6.

105. Jennifer Lynch, "Allen Burris: Making Plans to Say Good-bye," *Nutshell*, November 1996.

106. Pugh, "Continuity and Change," *Meredith*, Spring 1997, 5.

107. Lynch, "Allen Burris," *Nutshell*, November 1996.

108. Burris, "My Surprise Party," *Nutshell*, June/July 1997.

109. "The Legacy of Our President," *Meredith*, Spring 1998, 2.

110. Ibid.

111. Conversation with Sue R. Todd, 11 June 1998.

112. Pugh, "A New Face on Campus," *Meredith*, Summer 1997, 4.

113. William Butler Yeats, "Easter 1916."

EPILOGUE

1. William Shakespeare, *The Tempest*, II, i, 261.

2. Buttrick, *Parables of Jesus*, 23.

WORKS CONSULTED

ADDRESSES
Campbell, Carlyle. "The Idea of Community." Address to the Meredith College student
    body, date unknown, Campbell papers.
Carter, Carolyn. Address to Junior Class, 16 November 1995.
Carter, Jimmy. "America: A Champion of Peace?" Lillian Parker Wallace Lecture, Mered-
    ith College, 11 September 1986.
Lolly, Randall. "Last at the Cross–First at the Tomb." Convocation address, Southeastern
    Baptist Theological Seminary. Published in *Biblical Recorder*, 150, no. 32, 15 Septem-
    ber 1984: 3.
Taylor, Louise. "Searching for Hugh: the Meredith Connection." Founders' Day address,
    23 February 1998.
Wallace, Carolyn A. Untitled address. Friends of the Carlyle Campbell Library, 5 May
    1977.
Weems, John E. "Upheld by the Affections of a Great People." Inaugural Address,
    Raleigh, N.C., September 22, 1972. Published in the *Alumnae Magazine*, 26, no. 4 (Fall
    1972): 13–17, 41.
———. Address to the North Carolina General Assembly in support of Equal Rights
    Amendment.

ARCHIVAL RECORDS
Annual Reports, 1972–97.
Cooper, Jean Batten. *An Oral History of Meredith College Alumnae.* Master's thesis,
    Wake Forest University, 1989.
In-house correspondence, 1971–98.
Lemmon, Sarah. Conversations with Jonathan Lindsey. Taped in 1982.
Message of the President 1972–97.
Minutes, Academic Council, 1972–98
Minutes, Board of Trustees, 1971–98.
  Minutes, Executive Committee, Board of Trustees, 1972–98.
Minutes, Faculty Meetings, 1971–98.
Minutes, Select Faculty Committees, 1985–97.

Murray, Rebecca. *What Shall I Make of Myself? A Glimpse into the Lives of the Immortal Ten*, manuscript, 1994.
Strategic Planning Documents, 1974–97.

ARTICLES, LETTERS, PERIODICALS
Bedon, Helen. Letter to the President of Meredith College. 12 April 1970.
Biblical Recorder. Select issues, 1971–98.
"Dangerous Dispute." *The Christian Century* (Chicago) XCVIII, no. 1 (7–14 January 1981): 8.
News & Observer (Raleigh). Select issues, 1944–98.
Paper Trail. Collection of papers regarding Meredith's relationship with the Baptist State Convention of North Carolina, August 1993.
Report of the President's Task Force for the Pursuit of Excellence, 1989
Stringfield, Oliver L. Letter to John E. Weems, 1 October, 1972.
Raleigh Times (Raleigh). Select issues, 1971
Rimer, Sara. "At Harvard, Lovers of Beauty Sing a Collective Ode to Keats." *New York Times* (New York), 11 September 1995.
Wall, James M., editorial. "Carter and the Religion Factor." *Christian Century* (Chicago), (31 August–7 September 1977): 739–40.
Watterson, Eugene. Letter to John E. Weems, 21 February 1991.

BOOKS
Boyarsky, Bill. *Ronald Reagan: His Life and Rise to the Presidency*. New York: Random House, 1981.
Britt, Suzanne. *Images: A Centennial Journey*. Raleigh: Meredith College Press, 1991.
Buttrick, George A. *The Parables of Jesus*. New York: Harper and Brothers, 1928.
Johnson, Mary Lynch. *A History of Meredith College*, Second Edition. Raleigh: Edwards and Broughton, 1972.
Schaller, Michael. *Reconing with Reagan, America and Its President in the 1980s*. New York, Oxford: Oxford University Press, 1992.
Topor, Robert, and M. Frederic Volkmann, *Marketing Higher Education*. Washington: Council for the Support and Advancement of Education, 1983.

COLLEGE PUBLICATIONS
Alumnae Magazine. Vols. 23 (1968)–29 (1975).
Angels Aware (Alumnae Newsletter).
Announcements, 1899–1900. Baptist Female University.
Continuing Education at Meredith.
Friends of the Carlyle Campbell Library.
Meredith (College Magazine). Vols. 1 (1976)–22 (1998).
Meredith Writes Home (Parents' Newsletter).
In a Nutshell (Employees' Newsletter). 1996–98.
Initiative 2000.
Student Handbook, 1971–1997.
Undergraduate Catalogues. 1971–1997.
Viewbook. 1992–95.

INTERVIEWS
Academic department heads
Administrators
Select administrative staff members
Select alumnae
Select trustees

REFERENCE WORKS

Katherine Inez Hall v Wake County Board of Elections. No. 37. Supreme Court of North Carolina. 15 March 1972. *South Eastern Reporter* 187, North Carolina ed. St. Paul, Minn.: West Publishing Company, 1972.

New York Times 1998 Almanac, John W. Wright, ed. New York: The Penguin Group, 1997.

One Volume Bible Commentary, J.R. Dummelow, ed. New York: The McMillan Company, 1958.

STUDENT PUBLICATIONS

Meredith Herald, 1985–98.

Oak Leaves, 1971–97.

Twig, 1971–85.

INDEX